by John Cooney

THE
ANNENBERGS

SIMON AND SCHUSTER
NEW YORK

Copyright © 1982 by John E. Cooney
All rights reserved
including the right of reproduction
in whole or in part in any form
Published by Simon and Schuster
A Division of Gulf & Western Corporation
Simon & Schuster Building
Rockefeller Center
1230 Avenue of the Americas
New York, New York   10020

SIMON AND SCHUSTER and colophon are trademarks of Simon & Schuster
Designed by Irving Perkins Assoc.

Manufactured in the United States of America

10 9 8 7 6 5 4 3 2 1

Library of Congress Cataloging in Publication Data
Cooney, John E.
    The Annenbergs.
    Bibliography: p.
    Includes index.
    1. Annenberg, Walter H., 1908–   . 2. Annenberg, Moses Louis, 1878–
3. Journalists—United States—Biography. 4. Publishers and publishing—United
States—Biography. 5. Ambassadors—United States—Biography. I. Title.
PN4874.A56C66   070.5′092′2 [B]   81-21258
ISBN 0-671-42105-0   AACR2

All efforts have been made to trace the sources of the illustrations. Any
omissions will be rectified in later printings, upon notification.

FOR LENORE

PROLOGUE

Desert heat is displacing the cool air that nightly steals over the Coachella Valley from the jagged slag heap of the San Jacinto Mountains. Normally a placid town of 21,000 residents, Palm Springs is teeming with vacationers and conventioneers escaping colder climates.

Not surprisingly, few if any people notice the black limousines that, one after another, glide up to the massive metal gate barring entrance to an imposing, fortresslike estate to the east of town. The 208-acre compound—the largest in a region of gargantuan properties—is enclosed by 6-foot-high barbed-wire-topped Anchor fencing, a forbidding warning to intruders. Any view of the interior is skillfully obscured by rows of huge, lush oleanders reinforced by a full line of eucalyptus trees. The Cadillacs and Mercedes-Benzes are chauffeured by beefy, watchful men, all of whom follow the same procedure. The driver quietly announces his arrival into an intercom system. An electronically operated gate silently swings open. Armed with a pistol, the blue-uniformed guard steps from a glass-encased booth to check the license-plate number against a list on his clipboard. Before directing the driver up the half-mile road to the main house, he suspiciously scans the occupants of the vehicle.

The wary guard has no difficulty recognizing the visitors. Their familiar faces appear constantly in newspapers and on television screens. They are tribal chieftains of the Republican party: Nelson Rockefeller, the forceful governor of New York; Gerald Ford, the party whip in Congress; Charles Wilson, the flamboyant Congressman from California. Ronald Reagan, the governor of California, had arrived the night

7

before. The last visitor is the most heavily guarded: Richard M. Nixon, President-elect of the United States.

The politicians proceed through an emerald-green oasis that was carved out of raw desert only a few years earlier, passing beds of pink petunias, stands of bougainvillea, and a dozen spring-fed lakes, ponds and streams that provide the precious water to maintain the immaculate, undulating golf course that stretches into the horizon. At the end of the gently rising driveway stands an enormous pink masonry-and-rock house topped with an orange-tiled roof that captures the brilliance of the early-morning light. This is Sunnylands, the splendid and much-talked-about five-million-dollar winter retreat of Walter Hubert Annenberg, one of the nation's richest and most private men, who is known hereabout as the "King of the Desert."

The silver-haired Annenberg, who multiplies his millions by shrewdly spotting trends and gambling on his instincts, is something of a recluse, and an oddity in Palm Springs, where retired well-to-do manufacturers and their wives now outnumber the glamorous actors and actresses and dynamic movie moguls who, from the 1920s through the 1940s, had made the area one of the country's most seductive retreats. But Palm Springs still attracts the fabulously rich, especially those who demand such intense privacy that they can shut out the world at will. Annenberg associates with active and powerful men in the area, not the aimless retirees whom his friend Nixon refers to as "people wasting their lives in the sun and drinking themselves to death." Two of the few local superachievers ever invited to Sunnylands, Bob Hope and Frank Sinatra, emulate Annenberg's aloofness— Hope in a remote mountainside villa and Sinatra in a heavily guarded estate that is constantly monitored by closed-circuit television.

The Republican Governors Conference is being held in Palm Springs, giving the power brokers who will loom so large in Nixon's Presidency a chance to gather together. Men who need a quiet time away from the public frenzy, they are in a position to shape the destiny of their nation and of the world, and they are coming to see Walter Annenberg, the son of Moses Annenberg, a convicted felon who long ago had courted danger by defying no one less than President Franklin Delano Roosevelt.

Times had changed, and so had Walter Annenberg, in the twenty-eight years since his father was branded a criminal. Upon Moses' death, Walter had inherited Triangle Publications, a Philadelphia-based publishing kingdom with a shadowy past. At the time, the privately held company had appeared doomed. But with shrewdness, determination and luck, Annenberg had turned the debt-ridden corporation into a half-billion-dollar communications empire. To this day Triangle includes the *Daily Racing Form*, the bible of the horse-racing set that he inherited. His own initial business venture, the highly successful *Seventeen* magazine, was the nation's first fashion magazine for teen-age girls. The crown jewel of the Triangle treasure trove, *TV Guide*, the national weekly periodical that he started in 1953 against the advice of other major publishers and his closest business adviser, will come to have the largest circulation of any publication in the world—nearly twenty million copies a week—and a staggering profit of about fifty million dollars a year. He has the Midas touch.

As part of Annenberg's financial visions, or "Walter's epiphanies," as they are known within the Annenberg clan, he bought television stations when the industry was in its infancy and cable-television companies when they were a mere novelty. All told, Annenberg has amassed a greater concentration of media in one city (Philadelphia) than any American communications mogul. His considerable political influence stems from the least profitable of his many enterprises, two large daily newspapers, the *Philadelphia Inquirer* and the *Philadelphia Daily News*. The *Inquirer*, his most important inheritance, is one of the oldest papers in the United States, tracing its historical roots to 1771, and its editorial voice—the stern voice of Walter Annenberg—resounds throughout Pennsylvania, southern New Jersey and Delaware.

Before television usurped much of the glamour and influence attached to newspapers, Annenberg was the youngest publisher of any major metropolitan daily in the nation. Courted by Presidents and celebrities, he has long held the power that only major newspaper publishers possess. He is often accused of abusing that privilege. Men who want to be mayors, governors or Congressmen bitterly blame him for their failure to achieve goals or for their losing coveted offices. By the age of sixty, Annenberg has many enemies.

Some of those who hate Annenberg most deeply, however, were never wounded by his newspapers. Lewis S. Rosenstiel, the strange, neurotic chairman of the liquor giant Schenley Industries, for instance, lets it be known that he wouldn't mind seeing Annenberg in his grave. Rosenstiel still smolders from the humiliation he suffered when his second wife, Leonore, a beautiful blonde much younger than himself, ran off with Annenberg. When Annenberg and Lee, as Leonore is known, were married, Philadelphia's renowned, stodgy society professed to be scandalized, not just because of the shattered marriages they left behind, but because it was rumored—mistakenly—that Lee, in order to marry the man she loved, had to give up her two daughters. There are many rumors about Walter Annenberg, and many people—unquestioningly—believe them.

Annenberg is used to criticism, the kind directed at rich, powerful and controversial men, but he has never been comfortable with it. Easily offended, he resents his critics intensely, and he believes that they deliberately distort his motives in order to besmirch his character. When he lashes back, his detractors come away shaken by the vehemence of his counterattacks. His controversial editorial stands are the most frequent cause of people turning against him, but he personally thinks that envy prompts most of the barbs that come his way. He is so certain of his views that he doesn't believe it could be anything else.

Physically, he is a big-boned man with the barrel-chested physique of a heavyweight fighter that makes him appear larger than his five feet ten inches. He was born with a withered right ear, the cause of deafness and much stress when he was younger. As he has grown older, he has learned to dismiss the deformity as inconsequential. But age, responsibilities and tragedy in his past have combined to change Walter Annenberg in many ways. By 1968, it is impossible to equate the coolly self-confident tycoon, who gives orders as naturally as he breathes, with the shy, stuttering child he once was or the carefree young man-about-town who, in the 1920s and 1930s, loved fast cars, Hollywood starlets and café society.

The years have made Walter Annenberg an intensely private man. Here at the modern Xanadu that he calls Sunnylands, he constructs a world of great beauty and tranquillity, bending nature to his will and surrounding himself with more than fifty million dollars' worth of art treasures as diverse as Ming vases and paintings by Picasso. The estate indulges his need for isolation, and it enables Lee to exchange the damp, cold Philadelphia winters, which she finds so dismal, for the warmth of California, where she had spent her girlhood.

In harmony with the vast desert that begins where their property ends, their Palm Springs home has a distinctive Mayan influence. An emblem of a fiery orange Mayan sun god adorns the front of each white golf cart, a fleet that is used to transport the Annenbergs, their personal golf pro and guests around the well-manicured links. The motif is displayed on a white flag that flutters on this December day from a towering flag pole, but it is most noticeable as the visitors arrive at the huge circular driveway that sweeps up to the massive front doors of Sunnylands. There, in the center of the driveway, looms a 30-foot-high Mayan column, a replica of one that the Mexican government considers a national monument and stands on the patio of the National Museum of Anthropology in Mexico City. The chief difference is that Sunnylands' is bigger.

As each politician steps from his limousine, he is greeted by a liveried butler, one of fifty servants, groundskeepers and guards necessary to keep the estate in proper order. As the visitor enters, immediately visible is Rodin's simple, graceful *Eve*, 68½ inches of dark-green bronze, the artist's original casting. The statue stands in a circular pool, bathing in sunlight that streams from the 38-foot apex of the ceiling and surrounded by hundreds of floating bromeliads. The butler leads the way into one of a myriad airy, marble-floored living areas, where immense windows overlook the property and, beyond, the Chocolate Mountains, the local name for the pink-tinted range to the southeast, which is the same muted color that Lee decided to make Sunnylands. Towering interior walls are hung with such paintings as Renoir's "The Children of Catulle Mendes," Picasso's "Woman with a Mandolin" and Van Gogh's "La Berceuse."

Of the day's guests, only Nelson Rockefeller is awed by the artistic masterpieces formally displayed everywhere. He confides to Annenberg that the breathtaking collection of Impressionists surpasses even his own well-known collection. The others aren't attuned to the cultural treasures, although they listen attentively as their host—as he is wont to do—enthusiastically describes in a booming voice the background of several works and marvels once at something he himself hadn't noticed before. All the visitors are impressed by the size of Sunnylands and the obvious wealth it takes to maintain a life style reminiscent of a Renaissance Venetian doge. It is impossible not to be awed by such a display of wealth as well as by the man who can wear such an immense home with ease. Time and again, they compliment Annenberg on the perfection of his golf course, which he uses daily with almost religious devotion.

Because, out of both friendship and political belief, he so wanted Nixon's victory, Annenberg is in a jovial mood as he extends his welcome in a gruff, hearty fashion. As always, however, there is a slight air of aloofness about him. Part of it stems from his habit of pausing, as though consciously taking a deep breath, before propelling himself into social situations, even among men such as these whom he knows and likes. It is also rooted in his habit of turning his head slightly to the right, an instinctive movement done to favor his good ear, but many people who don't know why find the abrupt gesture disdainful. Moreover, there is an edge of impatience about him. Unconcerned with gossip or idle chatter about inconsequential matters, he is a highly disciplined, well-ordered man who finds time too precious to waste on trivia.

Throughout the day, there is much talk of campaign debts to be paid, offices to be filled and promises to be kept. There are moments of levity as well. Gerald Ford, the Republican House leader, asks the already worn joke "Spiro Who?" But it is significant that Spiro Agnew, the former governor of Maryland who quickly became a national joke after he somehow wound up as Nixon's Vice-Presidential running mate, is not present in the flesh, merely as the butt of jokes. Agnew's opening remarks at the Governors Conference, during which he inadvertently said how glad he was to be in "Palm Beach," are recalled, and they bring smirks as well. The gaffe is considered that much funnier because of Agnew's pompous airs and perhaps also because of his self-righteous attacks on the "executioner press," which he held was best used "to cover the bottom of bird cages." Such remarks generate easy laughter at Sunnylands. None of the men present has much use for the liberal press, and they are well aware that Annenberg's newspapers are a far cry from the *Washington Post* and the *New York Times,* which lead the pack that the Vice-President-elect is baiting. Annenberg is no Kay Graham, publisher of the *Washington Post,* one of the papers Nixon so detests. Nixon is drawn to his friend Walter Annenberg because, among other things, he "is not the pusillanimous weak-kneed type that most publishers and editors are."

Annenberg takes his role of newspaper editor seriously, scorning publishers who let their editors print whatever they wish and look only at their profit-and-loss statements. "He has no patience with publishers always looking after the money," Nixon says admiringly. "He's willing to take a position even when it's going to cost him a few bucks. That's very unusual. Unfortunately, most of the publishers and many editors are unwilling to take risks except when they are tilting to the Left. They have no guts, but Annenberg has guts."

In private, Nixon and Annenberg have many conversations that mirror Agnew's comments. They are disgusted by the *Times'* and *Post*'s coverage of the Vietnam War; they feel that the two newspapers' anti-Administration reporting only helps America's enemies. The publisher agrees with Nixon that those two papers have conducted a vendetta against the President-elect during the campaign, even though the *Post* gave him its editorial endorsement. There was never any doubt as to where Annenberg stood. On October 13, an entire page of his *Philadelphia Inquirer* was almost blanketed with an all-embracing editorial, "America's Outraged Cry for Change," which condemned student uprisings, rioting welfare recipients, "the feebleness of government," and "sickness in our society." The editorial ended by urging "the election of Richard M. Nixon as our next President."

Although Annenberg is often classified as a political conservative, Nixon knows that that is a cloak which he puts on and takes off at will. Annenberg prides himself on his independence as a publisher, the ability to be his own man, not being a slave to any party or doctrine. But what motivates him politically on a national level is pragmatism; this is the finely tuned reponse of a man who wants to assure himself that he doesn't unduly offend anyone who possesses great political power. Though it aroused the resentment of more doctrinaire political conservatives, Annenberg worked smoothly with liberal Democrats, such as John F. Kennedy and Lyndon B. Johnson, and with such liberal Republicans as Dwight D. Eisenhower. This doesn't bother the equally pragmatic Nixon. He knows his friend has good reason to be wary of what a President can do to even the incredibly rich.

Like Annenberg, Nixon is in an expansive mood. Since his victory, he is showing a side of himself that few people ever see. He isn't guarded or morose or offering petty criticism of others, which many people who know him find to be his nature in recent years. Now he is talking warmly with these men, who go back with him a long way; he is speaking with a generosity of spirit that, to the onlookers, fits him well. Although he doesn't come out and say it, they sense that he truly wants to be a great President. He wants to end the Vietnam War; he wants to help poor people; he isn't, he insists, insensitive when it comes to minorities or the poor. Richard Nixon envisions himself as a President of All the People.

It is no accident that Annenberg's home is the setting for such a gathering. Nixon and the publisher have known each other since the days of the Eisenhower Administration, when they became fast friends. Like Nixon, Annenberg sees the Soviet Union as the gravest threat to world peace, and they both are firm law-and-order advocates.

Nixon immediately recognized a powerful ally in the publisher who shared so many of his views; he was always swift to cultivate someone who could further his ambitions. Annenberg willingly responded; he enjoyed being made much of by people of power and prominence as though it were a measure of his own success, and a Vice-President was certainly one yardstick to use.

Even though Annenberg is immensely wealthy, Nixon doesn't feel uncomfortable around him as he does with rich men of old wealth. The publisher, Nixon says warmly, "wasn't part of the so-called 'social elite,' " the blue-blooded aristocracy whose ease of manners and well-modulated voices made Nixon himself uneasy. There is an earthy edge about Annenberg. The publisher is a very proper man, but his drive for propriety is tempered by a rough vitality, a saving grace as far as Nixon is concerned, and a sign that Annenberg's family money goes back only one generation. Neither man, for all he has gained in life, feels himself firmly rooted as part of the American Establishment, yet each believes himself to be among the staunchest of American patriots. In the final analysis, what Nixon admires about Annenberg is a quality that he likes to think he himself possesses. "What impresses me most is his strong character," Nixon says. "His balls—his *cojones*, as the Latins put it."

Their relationship is always easy, mainly because Nixon feels he can fully relax with Annenberg. The Philadelphia tycoon is one of the few people who *never* asks anything of Nixon—even now, when his friend is in a position to grant just about anyone's wishes. Nixon's world often seems populated by beggars with hands constantly outstretched—for jobs, political support, patronage. In contrast, Annenberg for years has thrown the editorial weight of his newspapers behind Nixon and his causes without the politician ever having to ask. Quite deliberately, the publisher maintains a personal policy of independence by not making major political contributions, but he makes up for it with his editorial might. Moreover, Annenberg's hospitality is always readily available to friends. Such largesse has helped Nixon through times of intense tension and depression. After a harrowing Vice-Presidential trip to South America in 1958, when angry mobs stoned him and actually threatened his life, Nixon first stopped on his return home at Inwood, Annenberg's baronial estate on Philadelphia's exclusive Main Line, to recover from the ordeal. Again, when he was distraught after losing the California gubernatorial election in

1962, Nixon found Annenberg's door open to him, while many others snubbed him or wrote him off as a political has-been.

Of all the men Nixon knows, Annenberg always treated him with the same respect that he gave him as Vice-President, and Nixon appreciates that. Now he is in a position to perform for Walter Annenberg a grand gesture that might ease the pain of his friend's much troubled past. As he sits on a patio talking with Walter and Lee, Nixon surveys the beauty of their vast estate and believes there must be something that a man who seems to have everything wants. As Nixon considers opportunities that he might offer, one position—the ambassadorship to Great Britain—comes into sharp focus. It is a job that must go only to an intelligent and, because of the high level of entertaining, a very wealthy man, especially one whose wife is known for her taste and beauty.

But Nixon's musings about matching Annenberg with the post are more complex than simply wanting to return innumerable favors to a friend. Such a move would solve a political problem. He is being badgered by big campaign contributors who want to be ambassadors and virtually all of them want as their prize the Court of St. James. Pressure is coming from emissaries representing such rich Republicans as Clement Stone, the insurance magnate, and William S. Paley, the founder of the major television network Columbia Broadcasting System; each not only wants, but edges close to demanding the prestigious London embassy. By choosing Annenberg, Nixon sees a graceful solution. Annenberg wasn't a contributor, and Nixon can soothe the ruffled feelings of the wealthy, egotistical men who are hounding him by telling them he felt obliged to make it appear that the plum assignment wasn't for sale. Moreover, this is a key appointment that Nixon himself wants to make, and he doesn't feel that he should be pressured into giving it to the highest bidder. To date, he has left the selection of other ambassadors in the able hands of William P. Rogers, his intended Secretary of State. But Nixon wants to snap the chain of tradition. He is sick of seeing prestigious offices going to men whose qualifications seem to him little more than family pedigree and exclusive schools.

"I wanted somebody who wasn't all washed out," he says. "You know, the extreme Establishment. Annenberg is wealthy enough to buy and sell almost any of them. He has character and guts and is really American."

The more he thinks about Annenberg in the role, the more Nixon likes the idea. He wants someone who will speak up for America and not just be an Anglophile, not that he and Annenberg aren't something of Anglophiles themselves. Nixon knows that Annenberg, a blunt man, could get across the President's views to the British government; the President's will would be Annenberg's unquestioning duty. Moreover, he wants someone who lives graciously. Nixon despises the casualness of style that entered the government after John F. Kennedy became President eight years earlier. "I am not one of those who thinks that an American ambassador makes points traveling around in a Volkswagen and sleeping in a pad," he says. "I am not one who is big on state dinners and all that, but it makes a great deal of difference to others. London is supreme in that respect, and I knew Annenberg could do it. I just knew he was the right man for the job."

Instead of offering the post immediately, Nixon waits several hours rather than add to the already complex business being discussed. Finally, shortly before 6 P.M., he is ready and approaches his host. "Walter," he says, "can I have a word with you privately?"

"Of course, Mr. President," Annenberg replies, his curiosity piqued.

Leading Nixon down a corridor, he takes him into what will become known as the "Room of Memories." Today, the large chamber contains pictures of friends and incidents that are the highlights of Annenberg's stormy career. Photographs of his parents and grandparents, of Lee, and of his daughter, Wallis, line the walls. There is also a color sketch of Roger Annenberg, Walter's only son. Photos that were presented to Annenberg by political giants fill the shelves and range from Winston Churchill to Lyndon B. Johnson, the only Democrat the *Philadelphia Inquirer* had ever supported for President. With his knack for just the right touch of flattery, Johnson had signed his picture: "To Walter Annenberg, the fairest of men." This is a room few people other than Walter and Lee ever enter, a sanctuary where a man, who, though not often contemplative, at times sits quietly and tries to make peace with himself.

Nixon comes right to the point. He makes his offer, one that can place the name of Annenberg in the ranks of such men as John Adams and Winthrop Aldrich. Nixon is well aware of how much the honor of the name Annenberg means to his friend; he knows about the past that Annenberg fears has tarnished his name for all time. "Walter," he says, "I want you to be my ambassador to Great Britain."

Annenberg is stunned. The position thrusts whoever receives it into a sphere of international influence and prestige that is never erased even long after the ambassador leaves the job itself. For a businessman—for anyone—it means becoming one of the anointed. For a moment, he doesn't show any reaction. Finally, he exhales. When he speaks, it is in a slow, measured tone. "No, I can't accept," he replies. "Mr. President, this may cause you a great deal of difficulty. I earnestly believe that you are better off selecting somebody who will create fewer problems for you."

Nixon hasn't expected a refusal. He begins to argue, and when he argues, Nixon is always persuasive. The rejection simply reinforces his belief that his friend is right for the job; it takes great inner strength to banish out of hand one of the greatest honors in the world. Nixon tells the others about the offer. Ronald Reagan, who has been a friend of Annenberg's for thirty years, urges the publisher to accept. Ford, Rockefeller and Congressman Wilson press him to take it as well. But Annenberg remains adamant.

"I don't want drawing-room liberals or other enemies of the President to try and get him through me," he tells them firmly.

In truth, Annenberg would love to accept, but old worries and anxieties are welling up within him. For the most part, he has learned to control the haunting memories so they now are only a dull buzz always in the back of his mind. Walter Annenberg has spent a lifetime trying to live down the shame that once nearly destroyed him. If he accepts Nixon's generous offer, it means dredging up a terrible, turbulent period of his life, a period that was scarred by courts and police, malicious stories in the press and the chilling deathbed words spoken to him by his father, Moses Louis Annenberg. Though he doesn't realize it yet, there will be more humiliation in the months to come.

CHICAGO, MONDAY AFTERNOON. JULY 1, 1940.

It is a hot, humid day, hotter than usual. The federal District Court is so jammed with curiosity seekers that it seems there isn't enough air for everyone. Court etiquette dictates that coats and ties be worn, and most of the spectators are rumpled and wilted before the session even begins. Finally, into the building strides the man they have come to see, Moses Annenberg, who is surrounded by lawyers and hangers-on. Police officers have cleared a path for him through the crowded sidewalk from his car and open a path for him through the mobbed courthouse hallway. Walter Annenberg, Moses' thirty-two-year-old son, hurries along, a pace or two behind his father. There is the brilliant flash of bulbs as news photographers, who seem to be everywhere, snap pictures. Newspaper reporters dog their footsteps, shouting a barrage of irreverent questions, while the Annenbergs and their clique ignore them.

"Hey Moe," one reporter yells, just as they wheel into the courtroom. "Do you think you'll like prison?"

A slightly stooped, lean six-foot-one-inch figure, taller than just about everyone present, Moses takes a seat behind his chief lawyer, Weymouth Kirkland, the leader of a stable of about fifty attorneys who have worked for Moses throughout the long months of proceedings. Kirkland has managed to get this day of sentencing delayed time and again, but he has finally run out of excuses. For the occasion, Moses looks cool in his conservatively cut blue suit, blue tie and pale-blue shirt with his monogram embroidered on the left-hand pocket. The hand-tailored expensive suit holds its press better than those worn by others in the room, with the exception of the conservative gray suit worn by his impeccably tailored son, who sits to his right.

A peculiarly American success, Moses is one of the endless line of immigrants who came to the United States, started at the bottom and turned society upside down. He now rules a publishing kingdom, including one of the nation's major newspapers, the *Philadelphia Inquirer*, as well as the *Daily Racing Form*, the *Morning Telegraph*, and a wide variety of periodicals ranging from *True Detective* to movie fan magazines. Of far greater importance to the government is that until just a few months ago, he was the kingpin of the nation's gambling industry through his control of the innocuous-sounding Nationwide News Service, known in the underworld as "The Trust," which has grown through organizational genius and brutal intimidation to monopolize the business of providing horse-racing information by telephone and telegraph wire. Though the company had operated within a gray area of the law, the vast majority of its customers hadn't. Nationwide, as law-enforcement agents everywhere in the nation knew, provided bookies in thirty-nine states, as well as Canada, Mexico and Cuba, with the results of horse races from racetracks around the country. Gambling tsars, powerful men who gave grudging respect to few others, spoke with awe of Moses and his incredible wire.

If federal officials are to be believed, Moses has the highest earned income of any person in the United States: some six million dollars a year. Now he is about to be sentenced for income-tax evasion. Throughout the 1930s, the 1913 Federal Income Tax Act has been used selectively against men like Annenberg, men the government can find no other means of stopping.

Moses maintains his aplomb as he leans forward occasionally to confer with his lawyer, and smiles at his seventy-two-year-old brother, Jacob, and friends who are gathered in the high-vaulted courtroom. He even nods amiably in the direction of some of his prosecutors, whom he continues to treat with almost courtly deference. The apparent nonchalance is purely an act of will. Beneath the surface self-assurance, Moses is a frightened man, racked by a fear that people who know him well think he is incapable of. He is ill, and he has cause to believe that he may be dying. He believes there is a good chance that he will be sent to prison, and the last place he wants to die in is the stark surroundings of a prison cell.

Courtroom spectators who haven't seen him for a while are shocked by the change in his appearance. The sixty-two-year-old M.L., as he is known among friends and business associates, has always been a powerful personality. He is a hard, tough man, who, though soft-spoken, commands attention when he speaks. A scornful look from his shrewd brown eyes has made many men tremble. In court, Moses is a different man. He has aged considerably since the tax business began. His angular face, with cheekbones as high as an Indian's, is gaunt and pallid. His frame had always radiated the tensile strength peculiar to lanky, sinewy men; now he looks frail. Most disturbing are his eyes. They used to have a fixed, piercing quality, but they now waver ever so slightly. Moses, who has outsmarted publishers, politicians and underworld *padrones*, looks beaten.

He had first begun taking the Internal Revenue Service seriously only when, sixteen months earlier, a grand jury was convened to investigate. Even then, he had tried to dismiss the matter as a minor nuisance. It was all a misunderstanding, a matter of poor bookkeeping. Moses, one of the financial wizards of the twentieth century, who reputedly could squeeze a dime until eleven pennies dropped out, shrugged and said such matters as taxes baffled him. He wasn't the first rich man to use such an excuse. For the years 1930, 1931 and 1932, for instance, neither Otto Kahn nor J.P. Morgan had paid any income tax. Kahn, for one, claimed that he was "abysmally ignorant" of income-tax returns.

Moses hadn't wanted a trial, of course, and he had agreed to settle out of court. It was only money, and if it had to be paid, it had to be paid. He simply berated himself for having been caught on such a piddling charge. He would have to be more careful. Not that he hadn't been alerted about what was in the wind. Friends had telephoned warnings to his third-floor office in the gleaming white *Inquirer* tower just a few blocks north of Philadelphia's City Hall. The calls came from Chicago, Washington, New York, Miami and elsewhere. The message was always the same. I.R.S. agents across the country were poring over the finances of bookmakers trying to figure out how much they paid the Annenberg wire service. This was no routine case, he was told. It had been instigated by none other than the President of the United States, Franklin D. Roosevelt.

When a reporter from United Press called him for a comment following the indictment, Moses, with characteristic irony, replied with gallows humor: "From the efforts and demands of the government agents, it appears that I may well paraphrase the words of Nathan Hale: My only regret is that I haven't enough remaining years to give my country."

Sitting in the courtroom, Moses looks as if his quip is coming back to haunt him. Early attempts to buy his way out of the mess have failed, and he has many powerful enemies who have the President's ear. More than cash is being demanded as retribution for his having crossed swords with them, having bested them. These enemies are a varied crew and include J. David Stern, the feisty publisher of the *Philadelphia Record;* U. S. Senator Joseph Guffey from Pennsylvania; and James Cox, the former governor of Ohio. Like the President, they are Democrats, and they are all demanding his head.

Now Moses wonders whether the tactic he is following is the right one. On the advice of Kirkland, he pleaded guilty. He always trusted the lawyer, finding Weymouth's advice on a host of issues to be sound. For years, he kept the Chicago law firm Kirkland, Green, Martin and Ellis on a retainer, and he called upon Kirkland, himself, for business as wildly diverse as closing real-estate deals to locating and bringing home one of Moses' seven daughters; she eloped at the tender age of seventeen with a man who was old enough to know better. That was one mission when Kirkland had disappointed him, and Moses remained furious with his daughter for years afterward. When the idea of pleading guilty was broached, Moses at first brushed it aside. He would rather fight back than be pushed around by anyone, including the President. But due to circumstances he hadn't expected,

Moses felt that he had little choice but to accept the unappetizing path. The government threatened to pull his son, Walter, into the mess, and Moses wouldn't stand for that. Kirkland tried to ease his mind about the guilty plea. "M.L.," he said, "the government is interested in getting your money and putting you through a humiliating ordeal, but it doesn't want to put somebody your age in prison." Subsequent conversations with government officials, however, indicated that the lawyer might be dead wrong. A lot of Roosevelt's men seemed to be itching to put him behind bars.

What increased Moses' nervousness was the judge. Hand-picked for the case, James H. Wilkerson, in a similar income-tax-evasion case, had sentenced Al Capone to prison, as Moses knew only too well. The amount of Capone's back taxes was minimal compared to the kind of money the government was trying to pry out of him. But Kirkland continually assured him that he was in good legal shape, and there were few parallels between the two cases. Capone was sent to jail, Kirkland says, because he was Public Enemy No. 1. Also, Capone was a much younger man. Kirkland made much of the fact that the government has nothing to gain by imprisoning a major publisher in his sixties.

When Wilkerson enters his court to pronounce sentence, the stoicism Moses had earlier displayed begins cracking. He hasn't been sleeping well for months. He has been suffering from terrible headaches that sear his brain with blinding pain. As he stands with everyone else, he begins trembling, though he is steadied by his son, who firmly grips his arm. Together they face the judge. Beads of perspiration break out on Moses' forehead and, as the judge begins reading a ten-page opinion, the defendant's shoulders sag under the strain. His hands are shaking so noticeably that he clasps them together, but the trembling continues.

After what is only minutes but to Moses is an eternity, the judge gives an indication of what is to come: ". . . if the defendant had entered a plea of not guilty, the facts and circumstances represented by the government are sufficient to require that the issue of guilt or innocence be submitted to a jury and are sufficient to maintain a verdict of guilty if one has been returned."

A hush falls over the courtroom. The judge rapidly reviews "matters in mitigation" that the defense has presented. There is the defendant's age, the fact that he is pleading guilty and, saving the government a lengthy, costly trial. Suddenly, Judge Wilkerson, an aging man not in the best of health himself, whose tousled gray hair gives him the look of a smart small-town lawyer or perhaps the dean of a Midwestern university, raises his eyes and meets Moses'. Without glancing further at the papers in front of him, he says in the same low tone in which he has been reading, "It is the sentence of this court that the defendant, Moses L. Annenberg, serve three years in prison."

The amount of taxes coupled with penalties and interest to be paid has already been set at $9.5 million. Moses has just received the unwanted distinction of becoming the biggest and most harshly dealt-with tax evader in the history of the United States.

As the sentence is announced, Walter Annenberg unconsciously places his arm on his father's shoulder, a gesture that is as protective as it is supportive. None of M.L.'s friends notice the significance of the act. They are too distressed by the sentence. If they had, they would have dismissed it as an aberration in much the same way they dismiss Walter as an immature son who has always been dominated by a strong father. Even E.Z. Dimitman, the *Philadelphia Inquirer*'s executive editor, who is covering the case for the Annenberg-owned paper, fails to note the strength young Walter exhibits during the proceedings. Dimitman, a shrewd editor and normally an astute observer of human behavior, is a friend of the elder Annenberg's and figures he knows the father and son better than most people. But he too doesn't appreciate how much recent events have transformed Walter. It is an oversight that he, as well as many others, will come to rue.

Some reporters immediately rush from the room to call the story in to their papers. Others gather around the defendant and try to jar loose some additional bit of information that will give them an even better story, although it is hard to top what they already have. When a reporter asks Moses where the rest of his family is, he explains that he hasn't wanted them present. His wife, Sadie, and his seven daughters are anxiously waiting to hear what has happened. If the verdict was to turn out unfavorably, he hasn't wanted them suffering public humiliation, and the sight of them hearing the bad news from the lips of a judge might undo him as well. He has ordered them to wait in a nearby hotel, and they have obeyed, of course. His word is always law with the tightly-knit family. Turning to the reporter, Moses explains the absence of Annenberg women: "I don't want to give them any more of a burden," he says hollowly. "After all, I'm a convict now."

With great precision, a phalanx of bodies again forms around Moses and his son. Reporters are fended off, and the party makes its way out of the courtroom.

For his part, Walter is desolate and inconsolable. His father is the strongest person he has ever known, but during the past year he has witnessed much of that strength erode. He has seen his father behave irrationally at times and lapse into uncharacteristic dejection. There are also the headaches that send Moses into such despair that he locks himself in his office for hours until they pass, not responding to his son's pleadings and knocking on the door. All this has terrified young Annenberg. He feels that he has been cast adrift in a world suddenly without anchor.

Although he is in his early thirties, Walter, a very proper young man, has never had any real responsibility in his life. He is a vice-president in his father's company, but he plays no key role in the company's operations, and many people view his title as an excuse to receive a hefty paycheck. He has never shown an overwhelming interest in the business, and there has always been too much money in his pocket to worry about where it is coming from. There are times when Moses worries about his son. He isn't tough enough. He lacks drive and direction. He doesn't take life seriously enough. He is interested in being seen with the "upper crust," as Moses calls society people. Sometimes he even jokes about it with his son. "Walter, I don't think you'll grow up until you're sixty-five years old," he says, throwing his arms in the air in mock dismay. His son laughs sheepishly.

Occasionally, Moses confides his frustrations about Walter to editor Dimitman or a few other men with whom he feels comfortable talking about matters close to his heart. He should have done more to make the boy tougher, stronger, he repeats. Other times, he takes out his vexation on his son. For example, almost every time Walter, a person of naturally exquisite taste, makes suggestions for a magazine layout for the Sunday paper, Moses dismisses his ideas with the subtle cruelty that only a father can show to a son. Sometimes it is just a glare or a single-word rebuke. Other times, he bawls him out in front of subordinates. After such incidents, E.Z. Dimitman, who has no children of his own, thinks that if he ever does, he will never treat them the way his boss treats his boy.

What few people outside the Annenberg family realize is that Moses loves his son more than anyone else in the world. For Moses, who means to create a dynasty, Walter, his only son, is destined to carry on his name and rule the business empire he has built. Like many fathers, Moses doesn't know how to mold his son into the kind of man he wants him to be, and he falls back on an Old World belief that he must treat Walter sternly at times because his son has lived such a pampered life. Walter is well aware of his father's ambitions for him, and he is acutely conscious that he doesn't meet his father's standards. But he knows that his father's biblical harshness masks a deep love. When he hears his father time and again linked to criminal activities, Walter is humiliated to a degree that few people will ever realize. He will never believe that his father is guilty of all the dark rumors spread about him and the disheartening charges against Moses that were made by the government. The past year, Walter says, has been like "being lashed by a whip."

Young Annenberg feels enormous guilt about what has happened. When Moses entered his guilty plea, he said he had done it in order to keep Walter from being dragged through the courts. More than a few people are amazed at Moses declaring that he is sacrificing himself for the sake of his son; they know what a burden such a statement would be on any son, let alone one who stays always so close to his father's shadow. But then, Moses simply isn't himself of late, some say. Others think he might be gambling one last time on turning his son to tempered steel by using himself as the fire to do it. This act, they said, is Moses' last big gamble. That isn't beyond him. The Moses Annenberg people know is an amazingly intelligent man who has emerged from nothing and molded himself into one of the most powerful figures on the American landscape. Like the fictional Jay Gatsby, he has created himself in a slightly out-of-focus version of an American gentleman. The way he has done it is impressive, if not always admirable. It is hard to believe he will be unable to find a way to avoid going to prison.

THE
ANNENBERGS

ONE

MOSES LOUIS ANNENBERG was born on February 11, 1878, in Kalwichen, a desolate, wind-swept hamlet of fewer than twenty-five families
tucked into the northwest corner of East Prussia, close to the Russian
border. The impoverished village consisted of timber-and-stone
houses scattered near a small lake where men and boys fished when
they weren't farming the harsh land their ancestors had settled in the
fifteenth and sixteenth centuries.

His father was Tobias, the son of Israel, and his mother's name was
Sarah. There were five daughters, and Moses was the third son, after
Jacob, ten, and Max, three. The fact that Moses had a surname was a
recent innovation in this rustic outpost and showed that even sleepy
Kalwichen was part of a rapidly changing world. For centuries, the
villagers had identified themselves simply by stating who their
fathers were. But a few years before Moses' birth, census takers representing the new and ever-expanding German Empire had visited
the hamlet and in a ledger recorded names, ages, and occupations.
To avoid confusion, the government officials gave each family a last
name, one that didn't endow the recipients with much, a somewhat
wooden-sounding appendage that bound kinfolk for generations to
come. In Tobias's case, the name was the prosaic *annenberg*, meaning "of the hill"—he and his wife and eight children lived on a small
hillside.

The census was a sign of troubled times. The newly formed German state, intent upon conquering new lands, needed the sons and
taxes of its citizens and an orderly way in which to determine where
best to find both. Since disciplined Prussian armies had defeated Na-

poleon in 1871, there was nothing that could keep the victors in check. The trudge of marching armies and the clang of arms seemed to be everywhere, making many Germans as uneasy as Germany's neighbors. War, however, was only one preoccupation of the Jews of Kalwichen like the Annenbergs. A strapping man with a patriarchal beard, Tobias ran a general store and farmed a small plot of land in order to feed his large family. Occasionally, he picked up supplies in the nearest town, Insterberg, which was to the north and inland from the Baltic Sea, and on his return, he brought back news as well as goods, passing both along to his neighbors. By the time of Moses' birth, the news was usually depressing. Insterberg's markets and shops were filled with distraught, shabby men and women who were fleeing their homes in Russia. Insterberg (which in the next century would become part of the Soviet Union and be rechristened Chernyakovsk) bordered on the immense Russian Jewish ghetto known as the Pale of Settlement. If Kalwichen was poor, the Pale was a land of wretched poverty, and its misery worsened when it became the focal point in the 1870s and 1880s for a brutal persecution that was designed to rid Russia of its Jews.

First came the so-called May Laws, which banned Jews from owning or even living on lands outside urban areas. The screws were tightened in 1881, the year in which Alexander III, an uneducated military man, succeeded to the Russian throne when his father was killed by an assassin's bomb. The new tsar began a Russification movement that demanded the annihilation of the Jews. His plan was simple: Jews could emigrate, starve to death or accept baptism. The anti-Semitic campaign received gruesome support in Prussia on Christmas night in 1881, when in the city of Warsaw hundreds of Jews were beaten to death by murderous Christian mobs seeking revenge on "Christ killers."

Tobias was a man of action who would rather emigrate than await a future in the hands of violent mobs or irrational kaisers and tsars. Taking his small savings, he joined the thousands of East Europeans who were going to America. Like many of them, he went ahead alone, planning on sending for his family once he became established. That was the pattern, and when others from the region who had adopted that path wrote home to friends and loved ones, they said they never regretted leaving. They wrote of a land of wonderful opportunities, and they failed to note the dreary tenements and harsh working conditions they found, because it was useless to point out such things. The opportunities open to them were greater than most of them had ever known.

In 1882, Tobias settled in Chicago, a booming city with a population of more than a half million and such a hodgepodge of central and eastern Europeans that the city's lingua franca in many sections was German, not English. The most vital city in America, Chicago was a good place for an immigrant to find work. With its sprawling, noisy railroad and stockyards, the city radiated a raw energy that often overwhelmed the steady stream of provincial newcomers, many of whom had never been in a city. One could get lost there or, just as easily it seemed, make a fortune. Most often, immigrants just got by.

In the tradition of so many "greenhorns," Tobias began his new life as a peddler. He bought boxes of merchandise—scarves, mirrors, combs—and carried them through the streets, trying to outyell the legions of peddlers who thronged every street. Eventually, he learned the good corners to work and how to cajole customers into buying. There were times when he was afraid he would fail, that he would become one of the desolate men who had been there ten, fifteen or twenty years and spoke with shame because they had never been able to save enough to send for their families. During the next three years, Tobias tried his hand at many enterprises until he finally managed to set himself up in a small grocery business. As a sign of his comparative prosperity, he rented a store-front building on State Street, with an apartment above it. His achievement, while modest, was a major step up from huckstering goods on the street from a pushcart and renting a cot or a sofa to sleep on in the apartment of some poor immigrant family, as so many others had to do. Moreover, he now had the money to send for his wife and children. In 1885, the year before the Statue of Liberty was erected on Bedloe's Island in New York Harbor, the Annenbergs were reunited.

Sarah and the children found their new homeland a harsher, more dangerous country than the image they had created from letters and daydreams. Winter that year was exceptionally severe in Chicago, and the economy had suddenly soured. The hard times did little to halt the flow of new arrivals, who continued pouring into the city, and soon so many hungry, jobless men wandered the streets that the mayor was forced to open soup kitchens. The following spring, Chicago was still hostile, but for different reasons. Labor troubles had erupted at one of the region's biggest employers, McCormick Harvesting Machine Company. There was a pitched battle between the plant workers and scab laborers, and when the police broke up the melee, several people were killed. At a protest rally a few days later, a bomb exploded, and frightened, ill-trained police, who were there to maintain order, fired on the crowd and were shot at in return. As a result, seven policemen died and another sixty-seven were wounded; the workers suffered many, many casualties. News of such incidents raced through immigrant quarters, since many leaders of the burgeoning labor movement were foreigners. Yet, even if the new arrivals were fearful about being swept up in such violence, few left the city. They didn't know where else to go.

Tobias's store was located in a tough, predominantly Irish neighborhood known as "The Patch," where streets were noisy and dirty and always filled with commotion, and boys gained respect with their fists and played cards and dice on the sidewalks with the same intensity as older men. In such a world, Moe, the youngest Annenberg boy, picked up a love of gambling that would remain with him throughout his life. The friendships he developed were with men and boys for whom life was always a violent battle and fair play was a sign of weakness. If there was any lesson that smart youngsters learned early, it was that men who got ahead took what they wanted and that police would look the other way—for a price. Chicago already had the unenviable reputation as the "wickedest city in the nation." Brothels and gambling dens operated flagrantly with the aid of politicians and police, who openly solicited bribes. Professional gamblers who had been forced out of Mississippi River towns like Vicksburg and Natchez drifted to Chicago, where they were welcomed as long as they played by the rules of the underworld.

The prevalence of such vice was upsetting to Tobias and Sarah, who fought a losing battle to raise their children as Orthodox Jews and make them revere the traditional values they tried to nurture in their new, rootless homeland. Tobias was president of his *shul,* or local synagogue, and Sarah wore a wig over her shaved head in accordance with the dictates of her religion. Their sons, however, were more aggressive and worldly, and came to associate religion with poverty, which they determined they would escape. Moe in particular came to despise all religions as traps to keep poor people docile.

Like his brothers, Moe dropped out of school when he was twelve years old, in order to help support his family. His first job was as a messenger for Western Union, but he was ambitious and restless, and during the next ten years he changed jobs whenever an opportunity arose. He worked in a livery stable, hawked newspapers and tended bar for a brother-in-law, but none of the jobs measured up to either his keen intelligence or his ambitions. When he wasn't working, he spent much of his free time fishing in Lake Michigan and the rivers and streams around the city, a pastime that always remained his passion.

At the turn of the century, an event occurred that left a lasting imprint on both Moses and Chicago. William Randolph Hearst, the young millionaire who had rapidly become one of the best-known—if not the best-liked—publishers in America, launched a new newspaper in town. By 1900, Chicago was a frenzied city, bursting with nearly 1.7 million citizens, having a population increase of 600,000 in just a decade, which strained municipal services to the limit, gave rise to new opportunity for corruption among politicians, and provided more victims for criminals. But Hearst also saw an opportunity for more newspaper readers. There were already eight newspapers in town, including the *Tribune*, the *Record*, the *News* and the *Inter-Ocean*, and the competition was intense. Only the *Tribune* and the *News* were profitable, but that didn't bother Hearst, who was arrogantly triumphant after the already legendary battle between his *New York Journal* and Joseph Pulitzer's *World*. He was convinced that his brand of sensational journalism would prove as effective in Chicago as it had shown itself to be in New York and San Francisco even earlier. His formula was simple: Hire the best men for top pay, charge less per copy than competitors, and give the readers stories about local political scandals as well as hyped-up tales of terror, intrigue, sex, violence and pathos. Titillation came before information, and huge early financial losses could be made up from the inevitable profits once the paper was successful.

At the time, Hearst had other motives for establishing a newspaper in Chicago, motives that had much to do with his own lofty political aspirations. Already in 1900, he had managed to get elected to the powerful post of president of the National Association of Democratic Clubs, and Senator James K. Jones, chairman of the Democratic National Committee, had made it clear that he wanted the publisher to start a strong party newspaper in Chicago, a tool that was considered essential to electing a Democratic President. The demand coincided with Hearst's own publishing plans as well as his ambitions to become President himself one day. As always, he acted quickly, setting a brief six-week deadline for getting a Chicago paper on the streets. Crews of Hearst men occupied an old building at 216 West Madison Street, which soon became known as "The Madhouse on Madison Street," as frantic workers contracted for printing presses, paper and ink, and hired printers, circulation men, editors, reporters and advertising salesmen.

When Hearst's *Evening American* was launched on July 2, meeting his deadline, the Windy City became a circulation battlefield. Newspapers had always gone to great lengths to establish critical newsstand locations, and now they found that they had to fight to keep them. The circulation business in America was traditionally tough, but in Chicago, more than any other city, circulation men became their publishers' shock troops. The *News*, for instance, maintained crews of men who acted as field officers and controlled their newsboys with military authority as they dominated desirable corners. To make headway in such a town, Hearst needed men who were capable, smart and not afraid of a fight. The publisher installed Andrew "Long Green Andy" Lawrence as head of circulation and editorial. Lawrence, a veteran of past circulation battles for his boss, promised a premium salary to good circulation men who were working for other Chicago papers. One of the first to take him up on the offer was Max Annenberg, who had been working at the *Tribune*.

The circulation business obviously wasn't for the squeamish, and the burly Max Annenberg was built for the work. A natural leader with a quick intelligence and a rough charm, Max let his employers know that he could get any job done and that he had few scruples about how he did his work. Within hours after Marshall Field's, the city's genteel department store, canceled an ad from the Hearst paper, for instance, Max led a band of sixty delivery drivers and newsboys to the store. They surrounded the emporium and as terrified shoppers and store employees looked on, took up the hoarse chant: "Marshall Field's Closed! Marshall Field's Closed!" The store quickly reordered the ad.

In order to force Hearst's papers onto the streets, Max, who soon became a circulation power, needed men he could count on and trust, and one of the first he turned to was his tough younger brother Moe. The Annenberg brothers differed in temperament as well as physique. Whereas Max was bursting with animal vitality, the tall, lean and dark Moe was more controlled, less of a glad-hander, had a soft-spoken, almost deferential manner that covered a rapier-sharp intelligence. Max gained unquestioned respect through a good-natured gruffness, or, if the occasion called for it, a solidly thrown punch. Moe had a way of excitedly confiding in men about his circulation plans that made them feel special, but when he was displeased, he glared in a way that made men feel physically ill. Not infrequently, his hair-trigger temper exploded, leaving the victim of the outburst feeling humiliated. Minutes later, Moe forgot the incident and asked the man if he would like a cup of coffee. He constantly kept people off balance.

Moe was glad to take Max up on the job offer, because he was working as a bartender, position without a future. Moreover, he had just married. His bride was Sadie Cecelia Friedman, the daughter of a retail shoe salesman, who had moved to Chicago from New York when she was still a little girl. Sadie, an attractive redhead, was a year younger than the twenty-two-year-old Moe, and their match bore out the old maxim that opposites attract. The lanky, intense Moe was a brash young man who looked upon religion as a waste of time, whereas the small, round and fair-complexioned Sadie attended synagogue faithfully, and she was always eager to please, finding time for everyone.

The ambitious Moe started working for his brother as a solicitor, or what was known in the circulation business as a "40-mile-road man." Every day, he and others were dropped off in outlying districts where subscriptions, rather than newsstand sales, were the mainstay of circulation. This was where newspapers had to grow, if they were to grow at all. From early morning through late evening, he knocked on doors, talking people into subscriptions to the *American*. Like others in the job, he had to make sure that papers were being delivered once customers had ordered them; rival newspaper circulation men thought nothing of stealing bundles of a competitor's papers and tossing them in the river. Moe was prepared to do the same thing, just as he was ready to jump into the thick of fist fights that erupted when circulation street-corner confrontations became violent.

For the first time in his life, Moe found a business that was meant for him. He already knew and liked many of the men who were attracted to newspapering, like Jim Ragen and Mickey McBride, both smart, tough men who, like Moe, had eagerly entered the circulation business to escape The Patch, where they had all grown up together. To a greater degree than most such men, Moe got printer's ink in his blood. He relished the sounds and smells, the rush of papers from printing presses, the sense of excitement at deadlines. Most of all, he loved being part of a product that people read. Reading was sacred to him, and since his education was scant, he read omnivorously, especially newspapers, to improve himself. Though he knew by heart the mechanics of creating a newspaper, he never ceased to be enchanted by the process whereby words and ideas were within hours transformed into print for hundreds of thousands of people to read. He vowed that one day he would own a newspaper and that the respect accorded publishers such as Hearst would be his.

Moe did his job well and was quickly promoted, becoming head of solicitors and then an assistant circulation manager. When Hearst launched the *Examiner*, a morning newspaper, in 1904, Moe was made its circulation chief, a post his brother now held on the *American*. In both cases, the rise of the Annenbergs was marked by the growth of their reputations for ruthlessness. Their excuse, if they ever had been pressed for one, was that they adopted the tactics that not only worked, but let them succeed. Like all circulation men, they knew that publishers had little sympathy for failure. In Chicago, publishers dealing with circulation men had only one creed—"Sell 'em or eat 'em."

As Hearst now pressed to get two newspapers on the newsstands, the circulation climate got rougher and rougher. The occasional fist fights and destruction of rivals' papers, which had been the worst that happened, now became the mildest tactics in what was turning into a full-scale circulation war. Suddenly, mercenaries appeared on the scene. Hard men, many of them professional criminals, roamed the streets, assaulting newsboys and delivery drivers, overturning delivery trucks, dousing newsstands with kerosene and setting them afire, and intimidating tobacco-shop owners who sold newspapers. Moe claimed that Victor Lawson, publisher of the *Chicago News*, was responsible for the rising level of violence, while Lawson charged that it was Hearst. In any case, the gloves came off, and who started the violence mattered little, because all the newspapers hired circulation gangs and everyone felt threatened. As a precaution, Moe, in the basement of the *American*, learned how to use a pistol, and his foresight paid off one night when he saved Max's life by jamming a revolver in the ribs of a gunman who was about to kill his brother over an argument. These were times for men who were contemptuous of conventional restraints. The job had to be done and that was all that mattered.

Hearst remained aloof from the brutality, involving himself in politics, making and breaking political careers. He didn't meet with subordinates like the Annenbergs, and he was rarely in Chicago. Nonetheless, his competitive spirit not only was strongly felt, but drove everyone. The men who worked for Hearst admired him, even if they had never met him. He was tough. He had style. And he was smart enough to be above the seamier side of the business.

As Moe's fortunes increased, so did the size of his family. A daughter, Diana, who was to die at the age of five, was born within a year after his and Sadie's marriage. Then came Esther, Polly, Jeanette and Enid. By 1907, he had four daughters, and with his mounting responsibilities, he had to work "like a lean hungry wolf," he said. What was missing from his life, he lamented, was a son, and after the birth of each girl, he had a feeling of being cheated. While he had rejected his parents' religion, he had accepted their Old World view of what a family should be, and that meant having a son to carry on his name. Girls were eventually given in marriage so that another man could have children, but a son was the most important person in the world, a bridge to the future and a guarantee that the father would never be forgotten. He felt that he simply *must* have a son.

While his dreams centered on a son, they were grand in terms of his personal success. Moe was eager for his next opportunity. There was money to be made—big money—and he knew enough about himself to realize that he didn't like working for other people. The poverty of his childhood gave him an insatiable desire to accumulate wealth and power, but he had to find his niche. On a part-time basis, he had tried running a small newspaper distribution business in Aurora, Illinois, where his oldest brother, Jacob, was prospering in his own scrap-iron business. With the skills he developed, it was logical to try to become a distributor, some of whom made $20,000 a year compared with the relatively paltry salary of about $3,000 he received from Hearst. But his duties in Chicago had prevented him from devoting the time and energies the Aurora operation needed to succeed, and he had abandoned it. By 1907, he again decided to gamble on getting into the business, but it would mean his having to quit Hearst and take on the job full time.

Moe had several reasons for wanting to enter a new line of work. The circulation business in Chicago was ever heating up, and he decided that it was time to get out, being sure that one day the city had to explode in violent confrontations and he would be a prime target. In addition, there was a strained relationship with his brother Max. Both Moe and Max were highly competitive men. Not only were they in the same business, but they were working for the same organization, and it was inevitable that they would clash. In Moe's eyes, the situation was compounded by the innuendoes that he had gotten as far as he had only because he was Max's brother. It was true that Moe, as the younger brother, did look up to Max and sought his approval, but he found it intolerable that anyone else should confuse his hard work, circulation skills and abilities with nepotism. One day, he spilled out his problems to George d'Utassy, a Hearst circulation man he liked and used as a Dutch uncle on occasion. The conversation merely reinforced what he himself felt he should do. "I told him that Max was a better talker than he was, and that everyone thought he had a job because he was Max's brother," d'Utassy recalled in a letter. "That the thing for him to do was to get another job; to go to Milwaukee and handle the Chicago papers—to get in business for himself."

Thus it was that in 1907 Moe pawned $700 worth of jewelry he had given Sadie and borrowed another $1,500 to establish a news agency in Milwaukee. Before he left Chicago, he struck agreements with all of the city's papers to act as their distributor in his new town. As it was, the costs of shipping the newspapers the eighty-nine miles to Milwaukee meant that Chicago publishers were lucky to break even. Moe offered them a simple way to make a profit, since he would be the central distributor. Moe knew he could do the job—he had earned the credentials on the streets of Chicago.

Several years later, Moe's feeling of foreboding about the escalation of the Chicago newspaper war was borne out. Circulation gangs were armed with guns and knives, not just brass knuckles. Hoodlums, like Mossy Enright, Vincent Altman, Gus and Dutch Gentelman and Nick O'Donnell, many of whom would become prominent in Prohibition crime wars, held duels in the streets. Some of them also moonlighted during a gamblers' war that simultaneously rocked the city while a man named Monte Tennes—who would have an ominous influence on Moe's life in another twenty years—was trying to become the city's gambling tsar.

Murder became an accepted price for increasing newspaper sales, and gangland-style killings came into vogue. A *Tribune* thug, for example, chanced upon the Hearst gunman Dutch Gentelman, who was sipping a drink in a saloon, and shot him on the spot. Another Hearst tough was slain at the Briggs House, a favorite bar for *American* circulation men. Even the city's citizens were not safe from the lawlessness. While riding a streetcar, a Hearst gunman became enraged because other passengers were reading a competing paper. He whipped out a pistol and fired it repeatedly into the ceiling, warning the terrified riders to start buying his newspaper. The newspapers themselves never reported such incidents, and since publishers exerted strong influence in Chicago police departments, the violence went relatively unchecked.

To everyone in the business, it was no secret that more than anyone else Max Annenberg was responsible for having raised the level of bloodletting. Max had gone back to Colonel Robert McCormick's *Tribune*, even though Hearst, who was all too aware of Max's effectiveness, had unsuccessfully tried to block his defection with a court injunction. But Max had a lucrative incentive both to switch employers and to operate in a no-holds-barred manner. McCormick gave him a contract that called for increasing the *Tribune*'s circulation and cutting the *Examiner*'s—the kind of inducement Max relished. Circulation was his life, no matter what the costs. Max's name was mentioned time and again in connection with the rise in the mortality rate among newspaper distributors. Once, he was even indicted for shooting a man in the chest, but McCormick's law firm successfully pleaded self-defense on his behalf.

But McCormick knew as well as anyone that the circulation manager didn't rely simply on a casual attitude toward violence. Max knew how to build circulation the way Hearst himself liked it done—whet the public's appetite with exciting stories and eye-catching headlines. Max's favorite headline, one that he claimed was always a surefire circulation boost, was "Double Murder and Suicide." Max won his bonus. McCormick now had by his side a man whom he described as "the best circulation manager in the business."

In 1913, a truce was finally declared. Twenty-seven newsdealers had been killed and numerous others injured. Body counts of street soldiers were never tallied. By then the name Annenberg was attached to all circulation violence and had become synonymous with lawlessness. At the time, everyone knew that it was Max, not Moe, who was orchestrating the brutality, but Moe—mistakenly—would be accused in later years of being as guilty as his brother, an accusation that would haunt and rankle him for the rest of his life. Whenever his name was linked to the Chicago violence, Moe took pains to explain that he had been in Milwaukee during the worst years of the circulation wars. His gamble had paid off, and he was becoming a prosperous businessman.

Within months after entering Milwaukee, he was earning $150 a week from the Milwaukee News Agency; but, as usual, that wasn't enough. A quick study, Moe had picked up the tricks of the circulation trade from the slick Hearst men he had known, and he set about using such knowledge as well as drawing upon the Annenberg reputation for ruthlessness to build a chain of news agencies in surrounding states. If they didn't deal with Moe Annenberg, he apparently told newsboys and small shopkeepers who sold papers, they wouldn't deal with anyone. While he had begrudged being linked to his brother's notorious acts in Chicago, Moe knew how to make the best of a situation. Intimidation, however, was just one tactic of the circulation trade that Moses depended upon. He was also creative and soon had newsdealers selling magazines and candy, which they had never done before. As his own business grew, Moe observed what men who were highly successful in other businesses did. One man he watched closely was Frank L. Mulkern, known as the "millionaire newsboy" because he had started out hawking newspapers. Mulkern was an entrepreneur who borrowed to the hilt in order to invest in real estate and local businesses. He put his money to work, never investing in the safe, sure thing or letting his money sleep in the bank. He took chances.

Moe put his capital to work too, and he realized that using borrowed money shrewdly was better than spending one's own. Besides opening more news agencies, he entered such businesses as liquor stores, dry cleaners and bowling alleys. He worked hard and developed among the newsboys who bought papers from him some of the best "hustlers," as such youths were known, in America. Men named Rottman, Budner, Rosch, Reba and Ottenstein were destined to become highly successful wholesalers as a result of the opportunities Moe gave them. As he opened his news agencies, he counted on the tough, street-smart newsboys he knew and liked to run them, youths who knew how to deal with bullying circulation men and who knew the angles of the circulation trade as well as Moe himself.

Moses never condescended to such youths. Many of them became devoted to him and loved it when business was slow and he told them anecdotes about his own hard boyhood and his bartending days as well as his early newspaper-circulation scraps. He talked to them about life in a manner they well understood because they all shared the view that one had to be tough to survive. "I learned many lessons from him: the good and bad about love, beauty, politics, sex, religion, the hard facts about life, the sweet and the bitter," recalled Joe Ottenstein in a letter. As a thirteen-year-old newsboy, he first met the then thirty-one-year-old Moses, and as they grew older, Ottenstein considered Moses his mentor and "my dearest friend." As he prospered, Moe saw to it that his friends, like Ottenstein, did too, and there was no doubt among the newsboys that Moses had an amazing ability to make money. Eventually, Moe became a big enough man to go into partnership in a taxicab business with one of Milwaukee's most prominent citizens, Millionaire Newsboy Mulkern.

CHAPTER

Two

ON MARCH 13, 1908, at one-thirty in the afternoon, Moses' world took on a long-anticipated dimension. Finally, after giving birth to five daughters, Sadie bore her husband a son. The child was named Walter Hubert, after Walter Hubert Inman, an old newspaper friend of Moses who lived in Cleveland; it was natural for Moses to honor a man who was in the business that he loved more than just about anything else. The father's joy at the boy's birth, however, was tempered slightly by the fact that Walter was born with a defect. The baby's right ear was withered, making him totally deaf on that side. The blemish was minor, but Moses found it troublesome; he had wanted a perfect son, of course.

In a house full of girls, the presence of a brother was an unexpected novelty. Instead of calling him by his name, his sisters simply referred to him as "Boy," which they found both funny and fitting. It was a nickname that suited Walter, since there was something irrepressibly boyish about him, even long after his adolescence was over. In his twenties, for instance, he raised a baby antelope, feeding it from a bottle with a nipple. His mother and sisters always called him by his nickname. To Moses, he was always Walter.

The Annenberg rambling white frame house, set in a comfortable but unpretentious neighborhood of houses with large yards and neatly trimmed hedges, was an unusually hectic place. Children were everywhere, playing games, staging plays and racing through rooms after one another. When their father was home—which during the week wasn't often, because he worked long hours—the atmosphere was much more subdued. Moses admired the attitude toward children that upper-class Americans had borrowed from the English aristocracy. Children were to be seen, not heard. They should be polite and mannerly, never rude or noisy. They should be reprimanded if they broke the rules. Moses, in fact, borrowed several aristocratic affectations. According to one of them, his children called him "Governor" or "Gov." Moses was bent on acquiring a fortune, and he had started assuming some of the social trappings that often accompanied great wealth, even before he had it. But then he was always supremely confident that he would achieve what he set out to do.

Family was all-important to Moses. It was his refuge from a hard world and his relentless search to find ways to enhance his fortune. His daughters, he liked to say, were as close to him as the fingers of his hands; his son was like his right arm. He indulged and protected his children, but he engaged at times in bizarre methods to get the children to understand the world at large. After the birth of his last daughter, for instance, he decided to allow the children to pick a name for her, which would serve as a lesson in democracy. The children, however, weren't overjoyed at the baby's arrival. Two more girls, Lita and Evelyn, had been born after Walter; this last was simply one baby too many, they thought. On one of the few occasions that they defied their father, the children told him that they didn't want to name the baby and didn't even want her. Moe became angry. "This is a democracy," he declared. "Now vote." The baby became Harriet.

Moses didn't want his children to be soft, a quality that he despised. Once, he even bought the girls a gymnasium that included boxing gloves and a punching bag. His children, all of them, should be able to meet life the way he had done, and this attitude went doubly for his son. Walter was of his flesh and blood, yet when Moe looked at his boy, he didn't find too much of himself reflected in the child. Like the rest of the extremely well-mannered Annenberg brood, Walter was exceptionally pleasant and respectful. He was neat and tidy and anxious to please adults, especially his father. The rough, raw world of the Chicago streets that Moe had experienced in his childhood would have destroyed Walter—as Moses knew only too well. Whereas Moses had the coordination of a natural athlete, Walter was poor at sports, and unlike Moses, who just a few years earlier had had to use his fists on the job, the only fight Walter ever had in his life was when another youth made a reference to his "tin ear." He was a gentle boy, who carried pet white hamsters around inside his shirt. When he summered at Camp Yukon in Winthrop, Maine, Walter didn't receive any of the awards given to youngsters who competed in swimming, canoeing or wrestling contests; he was given a little cup for being the "most improved" camper and a small hatchet for being "the neatest."

Walter was a shy boy, a major reason being a terrible stutter. Simple words and phrases took him forever to say. As a result, his mother and sisters spoiled Boy terribly, to the dismay of Moses. But he loved his son deeply, and he doted on him shamelessly. For example, he frequently took him to the news agency, opened the cash register and told his son to take as much money as he wanted. As Moe stood by laughing, little Walter greedily dipped into the till, grabbing coins until his bulging hands couldn't hold any more. Naturally, Walter came to believe he could have just about anything, and if he felt thwarted, he burst into angry fits of righteous indignation. Fortunately for his mother and sisters, who tried to appease little Walter when he was in such a vile mood, such outbursts were rare. He usually got what he wanted.

A man who disliked seeing children hurt, Moses rarely ever physically punished his children, and he resorted to such a stern measure only when he believed their actions had hurt someone else. Moe whipped Walter only once. His son and a friend, Kippy Stevens, had turned Kippy's dog, Wrinkles, loose in the Annenberg house. The overexcited dog raced about while the boys laughed themselves sick, yelling "Here Rink! Here Rink!" At one point, the dog chased Lita, who fell and broke her arm. Walter was blamed.

As Boy grew older, Moses took him everywhere, even to places normally reserved for adults. When Colonel McCormick threw a lavish party for his *Tribune* men and the paper's distributors, Moe brought his son, who, as the youngest person there, sat next to Colonel McCormick throughout the dinner. Moses also spent much of his free time playing with Walter. As soon as his son was big enough, for instance, Moe stuck a cue in the boy's hands and taught him to play billiards, a game he himself loved. Sometimes, after coming home late, Moses took Walter to the basement billiards room and they played through the night. Boy quickly became proficient at the game. He had to. At Moe's insistence, they bet on each game. Moses believed something was worth doing only if it entailed winning or losing.

An extravagant, gregarious man who enjoyed being surrounded by friends, Moe frequently rounded up cronies and employees and their sons for overnight hunting and fishing trips. Besides his newspaper friends, Moe had pals who were tough, cynical city detectives as well as other businessmen. They were rough-and-ready-type men, the kind he liked most; he wanted Walter exposed to men who weren't smoothed out by generations of money. He might be the Gov at home, but he was most comfortable with men who worked hard, knew what they wanted, and had come from the same street-savvy background that he himself had. To Moe's disappointment, Walter didn't share his passion for the manly sports of fishing or hunting. Whereas Moses could, with an air of contentment, stand with a fishing pole in his hands for twelve hours, Walter was soon jittery and bored and would rather be off playing games with the sons of his father's friends. And Boy wasn't overly enthusiastic about hunting either; he gave it up for good when he was in his early twenties—he had wounded a buck and tracked the creature for hours, listening to its plaintive and strangled cries. "The poor thing sounded human and I could never shoot anything again," Walter said.

Ever conscious of his son's deformity, Moses took him to several surgeons while he was still a boy in hopes that something could be done. The doctors told him to wait until Walter was physically mature before subjecting him to an operation. When Walter was old enough for the procedure, he decided against undergoing the painful ordeal of surgery for what could be uncertain results. In the interim, Moses routinely asked surgeons if some new procedure had been developed, but it never was. He would have paid anything or gone anywhere to find a doctor who could help.

Although he spent much of his free time playing with his favorite child, Moses didn't neglect the rest of the Annenberg brood. Sunday was the day he devoted to the entire family, the time he relaxed away from work. Often he gathered the children together and outlined his business operations in a way that they could understand. To Moses, the ways of making money were the most fascinating stories in the world, and by now he had a wealth of experience to draw upon for his tales. There was the string of newspaper and magazine distributorships in surrounding states, and there were the interests in real estate, liquor stores, laundries, bowling alleys and drugstores. One of the odd games he had the children play was making lists of his holdings. The lists got longer and longer. The girls and Walter believed such an activity was perfectly normal, that all fathers told their children business as well as fairy tales. Since Moses' fertile imagination seized new ideas and put them into action, he always had something exciting to tell them. He built apartments, for instance, atop a shopping center with the idea that it would be convenient for people to live with stores so near, and he installed in the apartments the new Murphy beds that folded into the wall in order to save space. The children found his stories enchanting.

Sunday mornings he often gathered the children on his and Sadie's huge bed and spun wonderful fantasies for them that had nothing to do with money or the way it is made. Moses would open the magazine supplement of the *Milwaukee Journal* and rapidly finger the pages until he found something exotic, such as a two-page picture of a dirigible and then he took them on an imaginary adventure on an airship to Egypt. He described the white organdy dresses the girls wore and how they stayed in Cairo's fanciest hotel. Whereas other children might think they were listening to fairy tales, the Annenberg brood half-believed that what they heard would become reality. Whatever the Gov said seemed to come true.

Another part of the Sunday ritual was his reading aloud the editorials from Hearst newspapers. His favorite columns were written by Arthur Brisbane, who appealed to millions of readers by prescribing a dose of wisdom for the common man. Raptly reading Brisbane's words, he told the children to pay heed to such a sage. Moses also showed them the graceful drawings of Winsor McCay, who illustrated Brisbane's columns. Later in the day, he entertained his family by playing the violin while his son and daughters sprawled around his feet. He had taught himself to play by listening to his collection of classical records, and his bizarre style of playing made the children laugh since he clamped the violin between his legs like a cello. Playing was a pastime he reserved for his wife and children; they were the only ones who knew of his talent. The children felt that no matter whatever happened or whatever they did, Moses' strength and easy self-confidence would protect them. Boy and his sisters idolized him. Years later, after most of Moses' daughters had married time and again, Enid offered what to her seemed like a simple explanation for the many marital failures of the Annenberg women. "Our father ruined us for other men," she said. "He was the strongest man we would ever know, the only one we could look up to. No other man could approach him."

Indeed, the entire family would get caught up in the excitement of his schemes and fantastic dreams. In 1913, for instance, he was trying to think of a promotional effort that could be used by newspapers to boost circulation. He often sat about the house on his time off, his mind spinning out ideas that he hoped would make him a fortune; he would, as always, be looking for what was both practical and obvious. He knew that the simplest idea could also be the best, and he thought that too many smart men never made money because they dismissed the apparent. Turning to Sadie on this occasion, he used her nickname when he asked, "Little Woman, what do women run out of most often?"

His wife thought for a moment and unhesitatingly answered, "Teaspoons."

Moses intuitively believed that she was right. "That's it," he said. Turning to the children, he excitedly told them, "Little Woman has just made us a fortune." His enthusiasm was infectious, as always. The children believed.

Moses' idea was to have newspapers sell silver teaspoons as a promotional tool to build circulation. The spoons, imprinted with the official seal of each state, could be redeemed by subscribers submitting a coupon from a paper plus fifteen cents. A different spoon could be offered each week, and the promotional campaign could run most of the year. Moe established a new company, a habit he had for each new venture he entered, and called it the International Souvenir Spoon Company. He contacted W.M. Rogers and Sons, a manufacturer, to make up some samples, which he showed to newspaper circulation men. As he had hoped, the idea caught on, and soon papers across the nation were licensing his idea. Sales outpaced even Moses' expectations, with the *New York Sunday World* alone selling 150,000 spoons one week. W.M. Rogers placed the largest order for silver that the company ever had and, in all, more than a billion spoons were sold. At age thirty-six, Moe, who was clever enough to keep a small percentage of the sale of each spoon, became a millionaire. With each new success, Moe's vision expanded and he was about to take the promotional idea to European newspapers when his plans were dashed by the outbreak of the First World War.

Flushed with the exciting success of the teaspoons, Moe embarked on a vastly different venture—he constructed the largest parking garage in Milwaukee. The garage was again one of the needs that he saw. The growth of auto traffic was phenomenal just within the brief span of years he had lived in the city, and parking space couldn't keep pace with demand. When the structure was completed, Moe was as enthusiastic about the building as he had been about his spoons, and as a way of boasting of his achievement, he filled an entire advertising supplement of the *Milwaukee Journal* with promotion of it. In his euphoria, Moses even sent a copy of the ad to his brother Max in Chicago. Several days later, however, he was crushed when the supplement came back in the mail with a note scrawled across it in Max's handwriting: "Stop building garages with Chicago Tribune money." Moe was so distraught that he began crying. It wasn't just that his brother had turned his boasting to ashes; Moses was angry with himself for having shown weakness in hoping that his brother would acknowledge being impressed.

It was in such a state that his little son, Walter, found him. Walter, who was about nine years old at the time, became alarmed. This was the first time he had ever seen his father cry. The sight made him feel terrible and lost, and Max's words burned themselves into the boy's memory so that he would be able to recall them verbatim for the rest of his life, the recollection always rekindling the shame and embarrassment he felt at his father's humiliation.

The note dashed any hope of reconciliation between the brothers. Soon Moe was sneering at Max's comparatively modest income when stacked up against his own. When Max was named head of the circulation department for the Tribune Company's *Daily News* in New York at a salary of $150,000 a year, Moe dismissed him as "my brother who isn't doing well." And in memory of Max's nasty act, Moe ten years later sent his brother a funeral wreath for his fiftieth birthday.

While it was characteristic of Moses to have sentimentally hoped that blood would have obliterated the earlier differences he had had with his brother, it was equally characteristic of him to deal harshly with a rabbi who called upon him one day. Moses had always given generously to the man's Temple because his wife wanted it, not because he himself had any use for either the man or the house of worship. The rabbi, who was seeking further donations, went through the usual amenities while Moses listened with an air of polite boredom and then wrote out a check for one thousand dollars. When the rabbi examined the sum, he acted insulted and launched into a tirade against the paltriness of the check from someone of Moses' obvious wealth. "I do you the honor of coming to your office and you have the effrontery to offer only this?" he demanded. Moe listened as his own wrath mounted. "Get out," he said quietly. "Get out, or I'll throw you out!" The words brought the rabbi to an abrupt halt. Moses wasn't in the

least intimidated by his histrionics, which apparently had shamed
other rich men into bigger donations. The rabbi ran from the office,
convinced that the man he had just insulted was as completely capable
of carrying out his threat as he was of signing a check.

That evening an angry Moe came home and told Sadie that the children weren't going back to the Hebrew School they attended on weekends. Though tears came to her eyes, Sadie knew it was useless arguing with her stubborn husband once he had made up his mind on such
a matter. Boy and his sisters were delighted. "We never wanted to go
anyway," Walter said. "Though it hurt my mother, we couldn't believe our good fortune."

In 1917, Moe's career took another strange twist, one that brought
him back into the heart of the newspaper business, not just the distribution end. Arthur Brisbane, the Hearst columnist he admired so
much, had bought three Milwaukee daily newspapers—the *Evening
Wisconsin*, the *Free Press* and the *Daily News*—and merged them into
a single newspaper that he called the *Wisconsin News*. Casting about
for a circulation chief, Brisbane asked an acquaintance, Joseph Uilien,
the head of Schlitz Brewing Company, to recommend someone for the
job. He wanted a take-charge person, a dynamo who would see to it
that the newspaper grew fast. Uilien, who along with others in the
local power structure had been impressed by Moses' energy and his
knowledge of the newspaper business, immediately suggested him.
When Brisbane met with the thirty-nine-year-old Moses, he found
that Uilien's recommendation was on the mark. Moe's sharp intelligence, toughness and ready access to newsstands were just what he
was looking for. Instead of asking him to become head of circulation,
he asked Moe to take on the job of publisher.

There was much that Moses and the handsome, bookish-looking
Brisbane had in common. Both were bright, exceedingly ambitious
men, who would stand for little getting in the way of what they
wanted. And both wanted vast fortunes. Brisbane, an extraordinarily
facile journalist, made no bones about working only for money, not for
intangibles such as love of words or news or even power. Early on he
had struck a deal with Hearst that he write his column and act as an
editor for papers and that his salary be tied to circulation growth. Before long, Hearst had been forced to pay him an exorbitant salary. One
of Brisbane's favorite ploys when introducing himself, and one which
other newspapermen found obnoxious, was his saying: "I'm Arthur

Brisbane and I make a salary of $260,000 a year." He was the highest-paid journalist in America, this son of a socialist never tired of telling anyone who would listen.

Brisbane produced an estimated 500,000 words a year, much of it nonsense that contradicted positions he had adopted only weeks earlier. His success was a reflection of the lack of education abroad in the land where even his helter-skelter knowledge and half-truths were viewed by so many people as erudition. But the column he rattled into a dictating machine also had the ring of simple truth about it; people loved it, and more than two hundred newspapers carried it. In his personal life, however, Brisbane was an enigma. At times, he was an optimist and most affable; other times he was cruel. He was also unscrupulous, blatantly using his column to tout stocks and real-estate deals in which he had an interest. Moses cynically accepted those characteristics, probably being relieved that the sage whose ideas he had so often read to his children was just a man like so many other men he knew. But Moses also thought of Brisbane as a person of sophistication and learning, since the writer could talk about history and philosophy; as their friendship grew he had Moses reading the likes of the philosopher Spinoza. Moreover, he set Moe laughing with his personal philosophy: "Always remember that it is impossible to exaggerate the stupidity of the public."

When he assumed control of Brisbane's paper, Moses was charged with excitement. He had always wanted to run a newspaper and he had a host of ideas for promotion that he wanted to test. But, according to a story that was circulated, the new publisher didn't get off to a smooth start. On his first day on the job, the editorial office of the *Wisconsin News* wasn't exactly full of diligent workers. The newsmen were shooting craps on a circular copy desk, which Moe took as a challenge to his new role as publisher. "Hey, you guys, that is not allowed," Moe shouted. "You should know better."

The game went on, nobody paying attention to the new boss. Finally, an exasperated Moses rushed up, grabbed the dice and tossed them out the window. He turned to the grumpy men and lectured them about gambling in the newsroom. When he walked in the next day, he met the same scenario. This time, Moe, who didn't want to alienate his new employees, was ready with a new tack. Pushing into the center of the circle, he threw down twenty dollars, thinking such a big bet would break up the game. "Now, you mugs, fade that," he challenged. The newsmen looked at one another. The previous limit

on betting had been two dollars, and there was a moment of uncertainty. But one after another, they began putting up money, until
Moses' twenty-dollar bet was met. With the roll of the dice, Moses
lost. Not just once, but again and again. The wager grew higher with
each toss. Finally, Moe had had enough of meeting employees on their
own terms. "To hell with this," he groaned. He threw the dice out the
window.

Despite such an inauspicious beginning, Moe quickly showed his
employees that he knew the business. Under his direction, the paper's
circulation moved up to 80,000 from the 25,000 it had been when he
walked in the door. He was also bent upon improving himself now that
he held such a prominent position. Editors passing his office saw him
with his feet on his desk dictating letters to a stenographer and trying
out newly acquired vocabulary. Each time he rolled out a new polysyl-
labic word, he cast a cautious glance at his secretary to see her reaction.
If she winced, Moe changed the word or altered the sentence.

Soon it was obvious to everyone at the *News* that Moe loved the
work and that he had a fatherly attitude toward his employees. Striding through the editorial and composing rooms or passing the loading
platform, he called workers by their first names and asked them how
their families were. Occasionally, as a reward for a good story or a job
well done, he took some of the newsmen fishing, and in the summer, he
held picnics for the entire staff. When a photographer at one such picnic arranged the employees for a group photo, the line was so long that
his camera didn't have a wide enough lens to take one picture; two
were to be spliced together. After the photographer took the first shot,
Moe ran down and joined the crowd in the second shot. When the pictures appeared as one, the boss showed up in two places at the same
time. It seemed as if the ever-in-motion Moses had finally accomplished what he had always verged on doing.

The following year, Brisbane, who was always seeking to turn a
quick profit, sold the *Wisconsin News* to Hearst for a great deal more
than the paper had cost him. Such an arrangement made Brisbane
money, which he loved, and it enabled Hearst to expand his publishing empire painlessly. Already, many publishers were reluctant to sell
their newspapers to Hearst, because of his volatile politics or reputation for publishing scandalous papers, or both. At Brisbane's urging,
Moses remained as the *News*'s publisher. Fortunately, Moe liked the
idea of working for Hearst if he were to work for anyone. Having
never met the famous publisher, Moses stood in awe of him, consider-

ing him a publishing genius. He admired Hearst's mass-merchandising techniques, his "give 'em what they want" brand of journalism. Moreover, Moses was impressed by a rich man who worked hard instead of idling his time away and he admired Hearst's standing up for the workingman, a position that coincided with Moe's most cherished principles.

Brisbane was sure that Hearst would be as impressed by Moses as Moses was by Hearst; so, shortly after he sold the *News*, he brought the two men together. When Moses finally met Hearst, he was taken with the fact that "W.R.," as Hearst was known, loved newspapers as much as he did. As a sign of his infatuation with the Hearstian world, he dropped the name "Moe" and became "M.L." For his part, Hearst liked this hard-driving man from Milwaukee, and he began inviting him to New York for periodic visits to his headquarters. Besides giving him a view of the inner workings of a powerful corporation, Hearst exposed Moses to a much more sophisticated world than he had ever known. Hearst himself lived in a palatial triplex apartment on Manhattan's Riverside Drive and he had an enormous home at Sands Point, Long Island. The publisher wined and dined like an Oriental potentate, and he took Moses to elegant restaurants and ordered delicacies that weren't attainable in Chicago, let alone Milwaukee. Moses watched carefully and learned what it was like to live in great style.

Upon returning from such forays, Moses had in tow baskets of oysters, mussels and clams that were carefully packed in ice for the journey from New York. When he tried to get his children to experiment with the new foods, however, they shied away with barely concealed horror. This was hardly the reception their father had hoped for, but, unknown to Moses, Sadie had warned the children that they would die if they ate such things. She believed it was bad enough for her husband not to observe Jewish dietary laws, but Sadie tried as best she could to see that her children did—even if it meant telling them shellfish would poison them. With heavy hearts, the Annenberg children waited for their father to keel over after devouring his terrible feasts.

On one trip to New York, Moses showed Hearst a particularly clever promotion plan for merchandising a magazine. Hearst was both pleased and impressed, and he made one of his snap decisions: "I want you to come to New York and take charge of the magazines," he drawled.

Upon reflection, Hearst expanded the offer to include being responsible for the circulation of all the newspapers as well as the magazines. The salary was $50,000 a year, which was hardly a lure to a man like Moses who was already earning $350,000 a year from his own enterprises and owned in excess of $2 million in Milwaukee real estate. Nevertheless, Moses, as Hearst well knew, was seduced by the power and prestige of Hearst's publishing kingdom; he accepted the job, knowing he would be the most powerful circulation tsar in the nation. Moreover, Hearst struck an agreement with him, one that he had offered only to Brisbane and a few others that he invited into his inner circle—he told M.L. that he could continue his outside business operations. Moses felt that he had outgrown Milwaukee.

The move to New York was accomplished with whirlwind speed. The children were taken out of the German-English Academy they attended. Movers packed their belongings. Goodbyes were hurriedly said. Within three days after their father announced they were moving, the Annenberg children were on a train speeding to New York and a very different life from the one they knew. In exchange for their comfortable house in a prosperous but unprepossessing neighborhood, the Annenbergs were thrust into the fantasy world of the very rich, whose homes were institutions that were maintained by the toil of maids, cooks and butlers. Children's games gave way to horseback-riding lessons. Their former school, which had been close to home, was replaced by boarding and finishing schools. Home was now a gracious Manhattan apartment as well as the palatial estate on King's Point, Long Island, that Moses bought from George M. Cohan, the American showman who created such Broadway hits as *Hello, Broadway* and *Broadway Jones.* Another of Moses' dreams had become a reality. To the children, it was like one of their father's Sunday-morning stories.

Moses' responsibilities with the Hearst organization were awesome. He had to oversee the economic well-being of nineteen newspapers published from Boston to Oakland, California, as well as a half dozen magazines, including *Cosmopolitan* and *Harper's Bazaar.* One of the advantages he gained in hiring Annenberg, however, as Hearst well knew, was Moses' own network of news agencies, which now stretched across the country. Through M. L.'s possession of such a network as well as his reputation for allowing nothing to stand in his way when it came to circulation, Hearst knew his circulation manager wouldn't fail him. Thus, it was with complete confidence that Hearst asked Moses to take on the additional responsibility of publisher of his newest paper, the *New York Daily Mirror*, a duty that Annenberg accepted with relish.

One reason M.L. found the *Daily Mirror* assignment appealing was that the paper was in direct competition with the *New York Daily News*, whose circulation department was now headed by his brother Max. Max had become a very powerful figure within the Tribune organization, having befriended Joseph Patterson, who had left the *Tribune*, where he had been copublisher with his cousin Colonel McCormick, to become publisher of the *Daily News*. Like his brother Moe, Max had developed a penchant for living the life of the well-born. He could be seen in riding habit trotting a horse through Central Park, which was across the street from his elegant apartment in the Essex House on Central Park South. But behind his façade of gentility, Max was still a very tough man, as a hoodlum who once threatened him in his office found out. Despite the thug's being armed, Max grabbed him and beat him senseless. He might have killed the man if he hadn't been dragged off him by *News* employees.

Knowing his brother, Moses took no chances when launching the *Mirror*. He turned to Lucky Luciano, the young New York underworld boss and partner of Meyer Lansky, for help in getting the new newspaper onto the streets. The circulation business still depended as much on muscle and intimidation when starting a paper as it did in Chicago nearly twenty-five years earlier. Luciano, whose primary businesses were numbers and loan-sharking, soon had goon squads spread out over the city so they could seize and hold prime corners for the *Mirror*. Max had his own gangs, and the circulation business heated up as the Annenberg brothers squared off against each other. Delivery trucks rumbled through Manhattan streets carrying "peacemakers," strong-arm men who rode along to see that nothing happened to the papers or drivers. Once the *Mirror* was on the street, legitimate slick sales-promotion efforts took over. For his part, Luciano got caught up in the work that was asked of him, and he admired Moe's tough, nononsense directives as to how to go about the job. "I used to think of the *Mirror* as my paper," Luciano later said. "I always thought of Annenberg as my kind of guy."

Moses was pleased with the way things were going. Near the entrance to his office, he hung a framed letter from Brisbane that stroked his large ego: "When I persuaded you to come to New York and presented you to Mr. Hearst, I told him I was doing him a much greater favor than if I had given him one million dollars in cash." Brisbane could have thought of no greater compliment, and Moses would have wanted none.

Since their first meeting in Milwaukee, Moses and Brisbane had become very close. They entered a number of business deals together, investing in New York real estate and buying the *Elizabeth* (New Jersey) *Journal* among other ventures. They knew one another well enough to keep a wary eye out whenever they entered such deals. Indeed, they had such a mutual distrust that when they passed the time playing cards together on the long train trips to Hearst's California estate, San Simeon, each asked a third party to keep an eye on his hand whenever he had to leave his seat. While he was a quick man to take advantage of any situation, Hearst was no match for Brisbane, and he came to expect little of the deals he himself entered into with his editor. "It always comes out 90 percent for Brisbane and 10 percent for Hearst," he noted wryly.

While thinking up new ways of selling papers, Moses and Brisbane often acted as talent scouts for the Hearst organization. When men got a call from the well-paying publishing empire, they usually jumped at the huge salaries they were offered. Some, however, refused. One such man was Oscar Ameringer, who because of his politics and writing ability was sometimes called "the Mark Twain of the labor movement." Moses had invited Ameringer to New York for an interview after recalling how many people in Milwaukee—including his wife, Sadie—had bought a rival paper just to read Ameringer's column. When he and Brisbane took the newsman to lunch, they ate hurriedly, and revealing their still rough edges and love of gambling, they sat playing dice while making their pitch. The tempting salary they offered was $12,000 a year with limitless possibilities. "Look at Arthur here," Moses said of his friend Brisbane. "He gets $260,000, and in my opinion, you write a damn sight better column than he does." Whether it was the dice playing or something else, Ameringer refused to join them, which wouldn't have bothered either Moses or Brisbane. If a man was, in their estimation, *fool* enough not to improve greatly his financial status, he wasn't worth hiring.

While Moses' blunt style may have put some people off, there were many men who found it an attractive way of doing business. One day, while walking along Fifth Avenue near 42nd Street, for instance, Moses ran into George d'Utassy, the old Hearst circulation man who had urged him to move to Milwaukee years ago. When Moses heard that his old friend was out of work, he took him to the offices that he kept for his own enterprises, shoved d'Utassy into a chair and said, "That's your desk and you're on the payroll."

"That's wonderful," the flustered d'Utassy replied. "But what do you want me to do?"

"I don't know," Moses said. "You sit there and you'll find something to do."

Though he was busy looking after Hearst's interests, Moses still found time to watch for new publishing ventures that would help him as well. In 1922, for example, Brisbane showed him a copy of a special-interest publication that was a potential gold mine. It was the *Daily Racing Form*, a newspaper devoted to horse racing. The paper printed the names of horses that were to appear in races that day along with details of their previous performances. The *Racing Form* had been started in 1894 by a former sports editor of the *Chicago Tribune*, Frank Bruenell, who had eventually moved the sheet to New York. The publication had a small circulation, but it gave the unambitious Bruenell and his wife, who worked with him, a nice income.

The paper's owner, however, didn't realize what a potentially big money-maker he had on his hands. Gambling fever was sweeping the nation in the early 1920s. Horse racing was on the rise, recovering from a wartime slump so there were now twenty-nine racetracks in the United States, though only a handful operated at any one time. Millions of people were eager to bet, and Moses believed that with the aid of promotional razzle-dazzle he could beef up the *Racing Form*'s circulation or launch a rival publication. When he told Bruenell that he wanted to buy his publication, the editor cannily recognized that his buyer wasn't a man who wanted to haggle. He placed a price tag of $400,000 on the *Racing Form*, and he told Moses that he wanted the money in cash. Moses immediately contacted Peter Brady, head of the Federation Bank and Trust Company in New York, who was known in his off hours as the banker who escorted the well-known columnist Louella Parsons about town. Moses explained the deal, adding that he wanted the money wrapped in old newspaper so he could deliver it to Bruenell. When Brady, who had dealt with Moses for years, heard that the circulation tsar intended to walk the streets with $400,000 wrapped like fish under his arms, he howled with laughter. Nonetheless, he did as he was asked.

At the same time he was nailing down the financial end of the agreement, Moses lined up two Hearst men to run his new venture. They were Joe Bannon and Hugh Murray, who became Moses' partners in what quickly became a highly profitable operation. Under Moe's direction, the *Form* became seven papers, not one. Without the aid of electrotypes or matrices circulated from a central source, the paper was duplicated in Toronto as well as six American cities: New York, Chicago, Miami, Houston, Los Angeles and Seattle. The price was a steep twenty-five cents near the printing locations and as much as double that in outlying areas. The new *Form* was so accurate and contained so much information that it swiftly became recognized as the leading authority in the racing business. From the paper's charts, bettors knew how horses ran at every stage of previous races, positions that were noted at the track by crack observers. The head of the *Form*'s crew at each racetrack used field glasses to "call" each phase of the race. Once the starting gate was sprung, he called to a clerk, who wrote down which horses got away first, second, third, et cetera. He repeatedly called out information at various stages of the race, including the fractional-mile posts that the horses passed.

Moses was intent upon expanding his new paper across the country. The *Racing Form*, he knew, had national potential, but there were similar racing sheets published elsewhere. Though they weren't as good as what he had turned the *Form* into, they were still competition. But he had learned from Hearst how to deal with that inconvenience.

THREE

SEVERAL MONTHS AFTER buying the *Racing Form*, M.L. Annenberg packed his son off to a boarding school. He wanted Walter to have the best of everything, and that included an education. More, he wanted his boy raised as a gentleman, so he sought a school with a touch of class.

He knew little about such matters, but he was well aware that men he occasionally did business with who were affiliated with the nation's elite schools, such as Groton and Exeter, would never recommend the son of a Jew for admission to their alma maters, let alone Moe Annenberg's boy. Through a friend among the Hearst executives, he learned about Peddie School, an undistinguished private academy in Hightstown, N.J. The school was run by Roger W. Swetland, a man of high energy, powerful physique and an air of unquestioned authority, whom Moses thought a stuffed shirt after meeting him. The man was a strict disciplinarian, who flogged students he found wanting, a practice Moses despised. Nevertheless, the school was close to New York and it didn't have a "Jewish quota" or policy of rejecting Jewish students that so many academies had, and Moses might have thought that Swetland, whom he took to calling a "windbag," might even toughen up his son.

Besides, M.L. liked the idea that Peddie was both a private school and yet a fairly democratic place that could continue his own work of keeping Walter from becoming a little snob. Peddie, for instance, was egalitarian enough to see that poor boys didn't suffer unduly in the midst of richer ones; Swetland insisted that no matter how wealthy a boy's family, the youth should receive no more than two dollars a week allowance. The idea appealed to Moses more in principle than in practice; he always gave Walter a great deal of money, often handing him hundreds and even thousands of dollars he won at poker.

The school was named after Thomas B. Peddie, a Scottish immigrant, who had made a fortune manufacturing luggage and who had once been mayor of Newark. In 1867, the egotistical Peddie had taken up the financially shaky Baptist School on an offer that anyone who donated $25,000 would have the privilege of renaming the institution. By the time Walter arrived, the twelve-year school had a population of 350 boys, who were mostly the sons of self-made men. The offspring of several foreign diplomats as well as the two sons of the President of Panama gave Peddie whatever social cachet it had. A generous sprinkling of bright but poor scholarship boys worked off their tuitions and raised the academic standing of the enrollment.

Walter, a courteous, quiet boy, quickly learned that his father's money stood for little at Peddie. More important was a boy's ability on the playing field. Sports were vital, because it was the one area where Peddie could compete with other private schools. When youths from more prestigious rival academies, such as nearby Lawrenceville, visited, they sneered at Peddie's handful of red-brick buildings scattered over a rather bleak 25-acre campus, but they couldn't denigrate the competitiveness of Peddie's athletes. No one, however, could mistake young Annenberg for an athlete. At age fourteen, he was of average height and weight, but he wasn't agile or aggressive. Yet, because sports were in such vogue, he determined to participate. He doggedly played third-string football and basketball, and he was on the school track team for three years, even though he never excelled enough to win a varsity letter. Nevertheless, "Annie," as he came to be known, was always in the stands cheering for school teams, and it never seemed to bother him that he wasn't gaining personal glory on the football field or baseball diamond.

Away from school, Walter was the sort of very privileged boy that only the son of an extremely wealthy and well-connected man can be. For example, whereas other boys only knew Arthur Brisbane and Damon Runyon as romantic figures and newspaper bylines, Walter knew them personally. Brisbane, for instance, took him to the training camp of the boxer Luis Angel Firpo, the "Wild Bull of the Pampas," who was preparing to face heavyweight champion Jack Dempsey at the Polo Grounds in New York in the second "Million Dollar Fight" staged by the slick promoter Tex Rickard. When the fight was held in

September 1923, Annie Annenberg sat in the front-row press seats next to the famed Damon Runyon. During the first round, Dempsey was belted from the ring and the fifteen-year-old boy and Runyon helped push him back in. Dempsey went on to knock out the Argentinian while the enthralled private-school boy drank it all in.

As part of his education, Walter was occasionally taken along when his father went to see Hearst. Moses knew how long it had taken him to feel at ease with the rich and powerful, and he wanted his son to gain such poise early. He realized that the more his boy was around such men, the more Walter would take for granted the control money can bring. One of the lessons to be learned by the kind of astute businessman he wanted Walter to be was an understanding of the sort of men who shaped the world. During such encounters, Walter was obviously impressed by Hearst, especially by his regal life style and the kindly way the towering man with the falsetto voice dealt with the son of his circulation tsar. On one such visit, Hearst enthusiastically announced that he had just received a shipment of antiques from Spain, including a chair for which he had paid $100,000. Antique collecting was one of Hearst's passions, but it didn't prevent him from pointing at the valuable chair and motioning the boy to sit on it. "Walter," he said solemnly, "you be the first." What impressed young Annenberg far more than anything else about Hearst was the respect he elicited from Moses. Walter knew there were few men his brash, cynical father admired, and Hearst was one of them. The boy's image of Hearst as a great man would continue for years, until he himself one day faced the publisher's renowned toughness in business.

What Moses never revealed to Walter were the tough methods he used as well. At the time, for instance, he was shrewdly using his position as the Hearst Corporation circulation manager to promote his own major new interest, the *Racing Form*. In addition to depending upon his own news agencies to sell the publication, Moses was forcing retailers to take the racing paper under the threat that he would cut them off from the Hearst magazines and newspapers, which provided a substantial part of their income. If he knew what his circulation tsar was up to, Hearst didn't do anything to put a halt to the practice. He probably didn't care in any event. Under Moses' strong hand, the Hearst publications were flourishing, so the publisher had no reason to criticize his circulation chief or his productive tactics. But it was common knowledge that Moses was becoming such a dominant force in the race-sheet business that even Hearst probably was unable to stop him. Moses was rapidly expanding his publication empire by buying racing papers from coast to coast. In New Orleans, for example, he paid $50,000 for the Bulletin Printing Company, and in San Francisco, he bought the Peerless Overnight Handicap and Run Down Sheets for $4,000. When money didn't work, his own tough circulation men, who relished their task of helping small publishers change their minds, took over. Finally, Moses left Hearst in 1926, his business having become too pressing.

Like Hearst in his circulation battles, Moses now wanted to put some distance between himself and the unseemliness of methods used for his papers' growth. He cared little for the details of violence, but considered them necessary ways of doing business. All he wanted was the most efficient way of getting on with the job, and he accepted no excuse for failure. Sometimes, however, he had no choice but to know exactly what was happening, because the strong-arm tactics resulted in lawsuits against his companies. In 1927, for example, Sol King, who published a racing sheet known as the *Daily Payoff*, sued him for having a racing-newspaper monopoly. King, a well-known Broadway character, had started a racing paper that had cut deeply into Moses' New York paper. In his suit, King charged that tires of his delivery trucks had been slashed and his plants sabotaged. In court, however, King couldn't prove either that Moses had a monopoly or that he was responsible for the violence. Few of Moses' rivals had the nerve to step forward and accuse him of driving them out of business, and most of them sold out rather than fight the consequences. As far as Moses was concerned, the only result of a suit such as King's was that he was embarrassed by having his name publicly linked to what he considered an unfortunate side of the business.

As Moses' grip on the racing-publication business tightened, his reputation as a brutal circulation mogul who would stop at nothing was enhanced. His world became more dangerous, and even death threats had to be taken seriously. Never, however, did he believe for a moment that his business methods were wrong. Nonetheless, Moses' goal in life became to see that his son was fortunate enough to take his place in the kind of life where muscle wasn't required for maintaining empires. He wanted Walter to be lucky, because Moses believed that aside from hard work, initiative and intelligence, luck played a critical part in everyone's life.

Poor people, such as his own parents had been, Moses thought, were unlucky more than anything else. Thus, he took great pains to impress upon his son the idea that life was a deck stacked against most people and the vast wealth that had been bestowed upon him placed him under an obligation to help the less fortunate. No one knew better than Moses what it was like to grow up in deprivation. The man who coolly accepted vandalism of a rival's printing plant or a brutal beating of a newspaper distributor or publisher felt great compassion for the poor, and he never believed there was a contradiction in his attitudes. One was simply business. Thus, Moses, with more than a trace of superstition, passed out money to poor Negro men, bums and the handicapped, as he walked along the street. He gave generously to poor families he read about in the newspapers and he quietly supported families who had lost their fathers through tragedy. When handing out money as he walked along with his son, he repeatedly told his boy, "There but for the grace of God go you and I." And he meant it.

Moses, however, also let his son know that there was an elite in society, a group of quicker, more intelligent men who seized opportunities that were offered and gambled in order to succeed. While juggling the lessons his father taught him, Walter became in effect an "elitist-populist." He felt strongly about the poor, but he wanted to become part of the strong, gambling elite, men like his father. Moreover, Walter also knew that he was a "rich man's son," a phrase Moses used with a mixture of contempt and pride. Yet Moses continued to indulge his son. He had missed most of his childhood and youth, because he had had to work, and he never begrudged lavishing money on Walter; he knew that money can often breed in a young man a self-assurance that he might otherwise never acquire.

To further his son's education as a man of the world, for example, Moses saw to it that Walter spent his summers away from Peddie, in Europe. After World War One, America's new millionaires sent their sons and, on occasion, their daughters on the Grand Tour, as though their offspring were emissaries to show the Old World they had left that they had struck it rich. The Continent was the mecca of art and culture, and it was the duty of many such young men to see as much and spend as much as possible. Beginning in 1925, Walter spent his vacations avidly pursuing Europe's pleasures. His favorite city was Paris, where he was exposed to such establishments as 32 Rue Blondel, which was renowned for pretty waitresses who, clad only in shoes, served drinks to ogling men and schoolboys, and he received a titillating tour of the exotic brothel, the House of All Nations, which was frequented by European royalty. It was in Paris that Walter developed a passion for dancing. More often than not, he passed evenings doing the tango at Les Ambassadeurs, a well-known club. Otherwise, he and wealthy young friends toured nightclubs on the Left Bank. He was quite the young man about town, indulging himself with abandon. For example, Walter and a few cronies were reprimanded by the police and made to pay damages in connection with one of their escapades. While tipsy on champagne, they amused themselves by pulling plants from vases on the balcony at Montmartre's Place Pigalle and tossing them at startled pedestrians.

In his later years at Peddie, Walter developed a reputation as a young man who knew how to enjoy himself as well as one of the school's smartest dressers. Once he became conscious of clothes, Walter always prided himself on the quiet elegance of his appearance. Whereas his father had closets full of suits, but wore the same few gray ones most of the time, Walter liked to dress exquisitely. Young Annenberg also kept a Ford roadster hidden off campus, a practice that Peddie forbade, a prohibition that the wealthier boys tended to disregard.

As a sign of his popularity, Walter's room was decorated with items the other boys pilfered from the Waldorf-Astoria Hotel when they visited New York. Several years of snitching towels, blankets, sheets, teapots, glasses and more bearing the monogram "WA" left his room looking like a Waldorf-Astoria gift shop until his mother visited one day and greeted the sight with dismay. Sadie made her son call the hotel and tell Oscar Tschirky, the Waldorf's world-famous host, that he would return the booty. Walter reluctantly obeyed and gave Oscar a date and time when he would arrive in his mother's big black limousine. It took two bellboys three separate trips with a hand truck to unload the car. In recognition of his honesty and to curry favor with a wealthy family, Oscar invited him to his office and gave Walter a steak for lunch.

In his senior year at Peddie, Walter exhibited signs that he had more than a little of his father's canniness about him. He headed the school's prom committee, and, for the first time in memory, the event showed a profit. His secret was badgering a number of local merchants into advertising in the prom program. He impressed his classmates further by indulging in a highly rewarding hobby. His father had formed a stock-brokerage house, Annenberg, Stein & Company, which had a seat on the New York Stock Exchange. Starting with $10,000 in poker winnings his father gave him, Walter began investing in the stock market—and making money at it. In short order, other boys were seeking his advice as the school's financial wizard and even some masters weren't above asking for a tip or two. The recognition was almost as good as the fame basked in by the school's superb athletes. It was the kind of achievement he could brag about to his father. In light of such success, it was hardly surprising that Annie Annenberg, who in his junior year was voted "The Noisiest" in his class, received the most votes in his senior year for being the "Best Businessman" as well as the "Most Likely to Succeed."

Soon Walter was putting much more effort into watching his stocks than into his schoolwork. His heart had never been in his studies; he was always more interested in having a good time. Years later, however, he wrote to one of his teachers, Carl Geiger, that he was the person who had inspired him to do his best. Geiger, a kindly man with a wry sense of humor, found himself a little nonplused by the way Walter remembered his school days. "He never worked his hardest while he was here," Geiger recalled. "He enjoyed life too much for that."

For all his emphasis on fun, Walter remained a very proper young man. Before he graduated, for example, his father sat him down one day and as Walter listened attentively, Moses bluntly talked about sex. "You're old enough now to have a woman," Moe said, adding that he would help his son find a sexual partner if Walter felt so inclined. The boy mulled over the proposition seriously for several minutes and responded with characteristic pragmatism. "No, I'm not ready," he said deliberately. But he hastened to add, "I should be in about six months!"

The same pragmatic sense showed up on graduation day. During his years at Peddie, Walter was rankled by the school's reputation for being second-rate. He had a keen sense of pride that made him want the best, whether it was traveling first class or buying a suit. During commencement activities in 1927, it was announced that young Annenberg, who never flaunted his wealth while a student, had donated $17,000 to the school for a new track. This was the first of numerous gifts amounting to millions of dollars that he would bestow on Peddie in an effort to make it one of the nation's superior schools, one that wasn't looked down on.

In the midst of the excitement of his son's graduation—a milestone that Moses appreciated in light of his own scant education—Moses was ever restlessly seeking new challenges, and he was examining a business that he knew could be the most lucrative he had ever touched. It could also be the most dangerous. M.L.'s particular knack was taking small businesses and turning them into major enterprises. Generally, once an operation was in motion, he left the supervision of it to others. He encouraged his managers to think of ways of maximizing profits, but ideas for entering new fields or repackaging what he already owned into different salable forms were his alone. His formula had made wealthy men of some of his friends, including Joe Ottenstein, the newsboy who had since become a power in the newspaper distributing business in Washington, D.C. Moe's businesses grew so quickly that he himself didn't know what all of them were doing at any one time. His managers reported to him mainly by mail and telephone, and as long as profits seemed reasonable that was all he cared about. Instead of paying himself a salary or dividends, he wrote a check for every-thing—whether to cover a gambling debt or to buy Sadie a new coat. He cared little for details, keeping his mind focused on ways of making big money.

The dangerous company in which he was considering investing was the General News Bureau, a Chicago operation that used telephone lines to relay horse-racing information to customers. The drawback, as he well knew, was that while a few of the customers were newspapers, the vast majority were bookies. If he entered the business, he would have to walk a razor edge between the law and the underworld. Whereas the newspaper circulation and distribution business often used illegal tactics, the racing wire openly dealt with men whose very business was a crime. The bookmakers' sinister world made the old Chicago circulation wars look like child's play. Even the muscling-in on racing papers seemed no more than a supermarket's driving small grocers out of business when compared to what he now contemplated.

Nevertheless, Moses found the wire intriguing because of its enor-mous untapped potential. It could well become a national and even international service if the demand for the *Racing Form* in Canada was an indicator. When he multiplied what was already paid for the service by the estimated 30,000 bookies across the country, the potential profits were staggering. Moreover, now was the time to buy. Monte Tennes, the once all-powerful Chicago gambling tsar who owned the wire, was losing his grip. He was fighting another gambler war similar to the one that had brought him to power twenty years earlier, but he was losing. Chicago was rocked with violence as younger hoodlums assaulted the Tennes operations. Even the corrupt, high-level city officials who had protected him for years had withdrawn their support after their homes were bombed. He had already lost control over the city's gambling dens that once had to pay him a large percentage of their house take. Worse, Monte Tennes, who had ridden in a horse-drawn carriage like royalty and who was once so untouchable that the idea of arresting him made even police laugh, was indicted on a minor gambling charge.

Originally, the racing wire was the brainstorm of John Payne, a former telegraph operator who lived in Cincinnati. In the early 1900s, he put his training to use by providing the results of horse races through a foolproof system. Someone was stationed at a racetrack, where he flashed results by a mirror code to a telegrapher in a nearby building. The telegrapher, in turn, relayed the information to bookies almost instantaneously. In 1907, Tennes paid Payne three hundred dollars a day for the exclusive use of the service in Illinois. Soon Tennes had pushed Payne out of the operation. But the mostly malleable, provincial underworld bosses Tennes liked to deal with, the old "mustache Petes," were dying off and being replaced by younger, smarter, greedier men. The generation difference was most striking when he compared John Torrio with Torrio's protégé, Al Capone. Torrio, known as "Little John" because he was so tiny, was a calm, rational gang leader who resorted to violence, even murder, when he felt it was needed, but who took no pleasure in it. He believed there was enough to go around for everyone. But Capone was brutal and demanded everything. He was too much like Tennes himself.

When Walter learned that his father was about to buy the race wire, he begged him not to. The wire's reputation was as much an open secret among wealthy young men who liked to place bets as it was among the bookies who used the service. Walter believed the business meant nothing but trouble. They already had so much property, were involved in so many businesses—the *Racing Form* was a bonanza, real-estate interests were growing, the brokerage house was going well, his father had even started a movie fan magazine. Walter didn't see why they needed it. He didn't understand his father's obsession with expanding his corporate kingdom, Moses' constant challenging himself to take on more than he had, to prove as much to himself as to others that he was capable of almost anything.

To Moses, however, the wire was more than a moneymaker. While explaining his reasons for wanting it to Walter, he turned aside the arguments that the wire was a menace to society because it dealt with bookies; he said it was actually a force for social good. He told his son people who led humdrum lives of poverty or held grinding jobs that had them working five and a half or six days a week needed something to look forward to, a chance, no matter how slight, that good fortune could come their way. A small wager could reap a large return and there were people who won, he insisted. "It isn't right to deprive the little people of a chance to be lucky," he told Walter. "If people can wager at a racetrack why should they be deprived of the right to do so away from a track? How many people can take time off from their jobs to go to a racetrack?"

Walter believed his father because he wanted to. He also knew he could never change Moses' mind, but this new venture made him feel terribly vulnerable. Years later, he justified the business by looking at Off Track Betting operations that numerous states created to raise revenues. The states were doing much the same thing his father did, he said. His loyalty to his father remained unshaken.

Ownership of the General News Bureau was divided into one hundred shares. Moses bought forty-eight, and Jack Lynch, a tough, beefy Chicago gambler, bought forty. The remainder were purchased by nephews of Tennes, Lionel and Edward Lenz. Moses didn't mind going into business with Lynch; he had been used to controlling such men all his life. Without missing a step, he quickly set about polishing his new rough diamond, having no illusions about likely problems. It was widely rumored, for instance, that Capone wanted the wire for himself. To run the operation, Moses selected an old childhood friend, James M. Ragen, who had worked for him off and on since the Chicago circulation struggles and who could always be counted on. Ragen had the right blend of high intellect, street savvy and natural leadership that Moses believed the wire needed. When the old Chicago newspaper wars had heated up and Victor Lawson, publisher of the *News*, collected a boardinghouse full of thugs to attack Hearst circulation men, Moses had turned to Ragen and his brother Frank, head of a combination political machine, sports club and street gang known as the Ragen Athletic Club. Frank was one of the toughest men in town, and Jim was no slouch either. In 1906, Jim had killed a man during a brutal fight, escaping prison by pleading self-defense.

Moses also asked his nephew, Ivan—Max's boy—to work for him. Ivan was five years older than his cousin Walter, and he had always gotten along well with his Uncle Moe despite the differences his father had with him. Moses never considered bringing his son into the business, of course. Walter, he believed, should be aloof from some of the ways he had of making his fortune. But Ivan was different. A towering bull of a young man, he played football during his year at the University of Michigan, and unlike Walter, he wasn't shielded by his father from the tough side of the newspaper circulation business. He had worked on loading platforms and delivery trucks, and, eventually, he replaced his father as the *New York Daily News* circulation chief. Moses always had a strong streak of sentimentality when it came to family, finding jobs for many of his daughters' husbands, and he wanted Ivan in the fold. But the two had a falling-out before the young man ever started working for him. Neither said what the reason was, but it was probably once again strong Annenberg personalities clashing just as Moses and Max had clashed years earlier.

While his father was seeking tough, ambitious men for the wire, Walter entered the University of Pennsylvania's Wharton School of Finance, which he chose because it was a business school. He never deviated from his desire to please his father and become a businessman. Fortunately, Penn, like Columbia University, was an Ivy League school that accepted unrestricted numbers of Jews. Unfortunately, the university, despite its admissions policy, was very much an enclave of the local Protestant Establishment, members of which ruled the city of Philadelphia from gracious estates on the posh suburban Main Line. The school was Philadelphia society's favorite, and socialites commiserated with one another if their sons insisted on attending Harvard or Princeton. As such, Penn was a prejudiced place, which Walter learned when he went to join a fraternity. Though he had no interest in religion, he wound up pledging the Jewish Zeta Beta Tau, because it was what was open to him. In the face of a slippery, condescending form of prejudice that made many non-WASP students feel insecure and somehow inferior, the Jewish students, including Walter, tried harder than their gentile peers to make sure they behaved as gentlemen. They always appeared wearing coats and ties, and they were always punctual when attending classes. They believed they had to act properly and never give anyone cause for comment. It didn't occur to them to rebel. "I never thought of myself as a boy from a Hebrew background, but I had to recognize it as other people saw it," Walter recalled. "I had to regard myself as a missionary in terms of the way I conducted myself. You're given a label and you have to shape up." It was a sentiment echoed by many men of his generation.

The most interesting aspect of Walter's life, however, had nothing to do with the university. He continued playing the stock market, avidly placing more and more buy-and-sell orders with his father's brokerage firm and becoming increasingly bored at school. The courses were stuffy and dull in comparison with the heady roller-coaster ride that he got in the market. His portfolio was now in excess of one million dollars, and he was, not surprisingly, restless and wanted to escape the schoolboy pressures of term papers and tests in subjects that didn't have much relevance to him.

After a year, he told his father he wanted to drop out of Penn. The decision was an easy enough one to make, but he knew it would hurt his father, who obviously valued a university degree much more than his son did. As Walter expected, a dismayed Moses tried to change his mind. To Moses, a university education was one of those achievements that he had dreamed of for his boy, and now he saw Walter nonchalantly tossing away the kind of status that he himself had never had within his own reach. Moses bitterly warned him that he would regret it later in life. Walter carefully weighed what his father said; he was always a respectful son. Nevertheless, he felt this decision had to be his alone, and he left school in 1928, realizing it was impossible to explain fully to his father that a university degree clearly wasn't as wonderful an achievement as Moses believed it to be. Many of his wealthy friends had left after a year or two, and despite his father's objections, Walter never felt that he had made the wrong decision. But he keenly felt his father's disappointment.

For Walter, the next year was a fast-paced one of buying and selling stocks. He was mesmerized by the ease with which money could be made. Talk about the market was constant at dinner parties and on commuter trains, and brokerage houses opened offices adjacent to college campuses and railroad stations to catch people racing to and from work. Stories about big strikes abounded, and Walter relished every minute of it. Like many others reaping mad money, he felt quite shrewd, as if he had demonstrated a special talent. Whenever his father cautioned him to be careful, Walter paid little heed; he was at last, he thought, proving himself as smart as his father. The orgy of speculation ended even more dramatically than it had begun—with the stock market crash of 1929. An estimated 600,000 Americans were caught gambling with paper profits by buying stock on margin, and Walter was one of them. One day he had a portfolio valued in excess of $2 million; the next day he was in debt for $400,000.

Moses had watched his son's enchantment with the market with a wry impatience. He himself had been so worried by what seemed like outrageous speculation that he had liquidated his own holdings in September 1929, only weeks before the collapse. Now his son had not only lost everything by gambling recklessly, but also had plunged into terrible debt. The elder Annenberg ruefully paid off his son's creditors, but he wasn't about to let Walter forget what a fool he had been. "Let this serve as a lesson to you," he lectured his son. "Never, never trade on margin."

The words were like a slap in the young man's face. Whereas only a few days earlier, Walter had considered himself a very clever fellow who was winning in the financial arena that his own father had fought in and abandoned, now he was a quite chastened son. He felt as if he had lost his father's respect, and that hurt more than anything else. Still, he followed his father's advice for the rest of his life, and he never again bought another stock on margin.

In light of what he perceived to be his son's irresponsibility, Moses decided that it was time to bring Walter into the company. His son was twenty-one years old, nine years older than Moses was when he first held a full-time job. Yet Moses was concerned because his boy didn't appear to want to do anything or, for that matter, want anything very much out of life other than having a good time. Walter wasn't amounting to much. He had dropped out of college. He had played the stock market foolishly and he had no discernible skills or overwhelming interests. The talents young Annenberg possessed had only taken him so far—he dressed exquisitely and he could order superb meals and wines in restaurants. Moses Annenberg, who had always wanted so much and was willing to work relentlessly and bend the rules to get what he desired, appeared to have spawned a decidedly unambitious boy. He had raised a gentleman.

Moses may have been exasperated with his son, but he could easily afford to pay Walter's debts. The racing wire was as lucrative an operation as he had known it would be. When he bought the General News Bureau, there were scattered around the country dozens of small businesses and a few larger ones also engaged in disseminating racing information. They ranged from a tiny service that operated from the back of Stan's Sandwich Inn in Dubuque to the Empire News Company, a sizable operation headquartered in New York. As in the case of his racing papers, Moses wanted no opposition in his path. After hiring toughs, such as Patrick "Chew Tobacco Pat" Burns and John Gordon, Ragen helped Moses map out an ambitious plan that called for the General News Bureau becoming not just the dominant race wire in the nation, but the only one. The rivals quickly found themselves locked in a war for survival. The methods were strong-arm tactics and bribes.

Because there were so many layers of corporations and subsidiaries between Moses and the sea of violence beneath him, police officers and many victims never knew who was behind the onslaught. Nevertheless, Moses moved to protect himself, as many men living nimbly outside the shadows of the law did. He began contributing heavily to political campaigns, especially those of the Democratic political machine that ran Chicago. Moses believed that money politically well spent was a good investment. Capone, as he well knew, ruled Chicago because he controlled politicians. Politicians in Chicago—or anywhere—could be bought. The General News Bureau set up a slush fund —jokingly referred to as the "widows and orphans fund"—for bribes for police and politicians. The fund distributed at least $150,000 a year.

Because of the interweaving of his many ventures, Moses' men worked for all his enterprises, not just his papers or the wire or the news agencies. The hoods on his payroll might intimidate a racing publication owner one day, a man with wires to bookies the next. To enlarge his wire, Moses had his newspaper distributors in Milwaukee, Baltimore, Washington and elsewhere set up offices linked to the Chicago-based wire and sell the service to bookies. The scheme not only was practical, but also allowed him to see his business grow by depending upon the news wholesalers he had put in business years ago. They were always loyal.

Otherwise, the service mushroomed by having Ragen buy many of the small wires outright, and, if the owners balked, they were made to see the futility of their actions. In Covington, Kentucky, for instance, a small operator named Blanie Shields heard from an Annenberg representative shortly after Moses took over. Shields, who was servicing about thirty bookies at the time, found his operation quite lucrative, and he refused the General News Bureau's buy-out proposal. But he did sell out after he received a series of threatening phone calls, his offices were sabotaged, and a General News enforcer named Lester Loughlin told him on the streets of Covington that he would be "bumped off"—as Shields later related to the F.B.I. In New Orleans, a young man named Waddie Snelling likewise found out that it was foolish to try to compete with the Annenberg operation. Joe Poretti, another General News gangster, reportedly saw to it that Snelling's offices were demolished. Moses gained a fearsome reputation.

In Philadelphia, Alfred P. Kelly, who ran another little wire business, was summoned to the offices of Pat Burns, the General News's Eastern manager, who told him that Michael J. Cusick, alias Mickey Duffy, who was the city's notorious crime boss, would bomb him unless he linked up with the bigger wire. "Duffy and his gang will throw pineapples all over your office," Burns threatened him. When summoned, Kelly had asked a city detective, Clarence Ferguson, to accompany him but to wait outside. Though Ferguson wasn't given a reason why he was asked along, he had his suspicions. Kelly was an untrustworthy little character who had his hand in a lot of shady deals. After his talk with Burns, Kelly agreed to join the General News Bureau and later did everything asked of him, including bribing police in Trenton, New Jersey. For his part, Ferguson began snooping around the wire until Burns asked Dominick "Jack" Lynch, who wasn't related to Moses' wire-service partner, to bribe the detective in order to get him out of his hair. Lynch, a handsome nightclub owner and the smooth bookie for the city's social set, made the overture, but Ferguson rejected it. His probe resulted in a raid on the General News a short while later.

Following a meeting in Atlantic City of the biggest gangsters in the nation, where a New York hoodlum named Frank Erickson proposed the idea of a national wire service, Capone discussed the idea with Moses, who flatly rejected sharing his business. The wire was thriving without the aid of Capone and that was the way Moses wanted it. Thus, within a few years, the Annenberg wire stretched across the United States, Canada, Mexico and Cuba, a vast international money machine that even the other gangland leaders hadn't considered possible when they met. And even Capone dared not challenge him.

But when Moses brought Walter into the business, he kept his promise to himself that the boy would be shielded from the dark side of the Cecelia Company, the name he derived for his holding company from Sadie's middle name. This wasn't as difficult to do as it appeared on the surface. To most people, Moses was a successful publisher, and he had his hand in a great many businesses that actually were legitimate. He was a friend of men like Brisbane and Hearst, and it was a well-known fact that he had been one of Hearst's top executives.

Moreover, his corporations were piled on one another in such a confusing way that at times it was impossible to trace him as the owner of many of them. At various times, for example, Ragen or one of his sons-in-law was listed as president of the General News Bureau. Moses never took an openly active role within any of his unsavory operations. Thus, he was well buffered from the unpleasanter ways of his making money, and he had no intention of establishing Walter in Chicago, where even a son who had an implicit, naïve trust in his father would have to stumble over the true nature of the General News Bureau and its methods of operating.

Instead, Moses placed Walter in the Cecelia Company headquarters, which at the time were at 60 Beaver Street in the heart of New York's respectable financial district. Giving him an office near his own, Moses found a job of sorts for Walter—countersigning checks. The young man did as he was told, and the job exposed him to some aspects of the business; some weeks there were four hundred or more checks going to a dizzying number of companies and subsidiaries. But Walter's job struck many other employees as pointless, and there was no illusion that the position was one of real authority; Moses kept that for himself. The father may have lacked confidence in his son, but it's just as likely that he never shared power with him because he feared he would also have to share the knowledge of how certain businesses flourished. Though he engaged some of his sons-in-law in the more sinister sides of the operations, Walter was excluded. He was always reserved for the wholesomeness that Moses wanted to achieve. Walter's newfound employment was nontaxing, the kind of pastime that a young gentleman of leisure adapted to without great difficulty. He had been signing checks all of his life.

Moreover, the job didn't interfere with his life style. There were still trips to Europe. There was New York's café society. There was California, which he found a delightful playground. Walter had visited California in his youth, but as a young man it was a whole new world. His father had started yet another publication, a fan magazine named *Screen Guide*, that was based in Hollywood. Though he privately thought the periodical somewhat embarrassing with its cheesecake photos of starlets and gushing stories about their private lives, Walter found checking up on the magazine was just the excuse he needed to visit the West Coast whenever he felt like it. Before he traveled, however, he had to swear to his father that he would take a train rather than fly. Moses was very protective of his son, and it was typical of him that he feared Walter might die in a plane crash; he was always fretting over his son.

The Hollywood Walter encountered in the late 1920s and early 1930s was a magnet for young millionaires like himself. A mecca for the beautiful and famous, the movie capital was a place where a young man with money could do just about anything. Broadway actors and actresses abandoned the stage for the fame and riches of movies. The stock-market crash and the battered economy weren't reflected in the pictures being made, such as comedies like *It Happened One Night* and adventures like *Mutiny on the Bounty*. The purpose of the films, and Hollywood itself, was to provide an uncomplicated fantasy world that was full of fast-paced entertainment. Walter found himself in a special position in this world. Because of his father's magazine, he was sought out by publicity-hungry movie moguls and stars who knew that promotion was their life's blood, and anyone who could keep them and their films before the public was treated like royalty. Through Louis B. Mayer, the head of Metro-Goldwyn-Mayer studios, Walter met legions of actors and actresses, and he loved the glitter and excitement.

Gossip columnists soon noticed the young man escorting stunning starlets about Los Angeles as well as New York and Miami. For a while, Walter was constantly seen with Lillian Vernon, a statuesque Ziegfeld Follies beauty. Later, he was routinely in the company of a young woman who was a fast rising star in the entertainment world. Her name was Ethel Merman, which she had shortened from Zimmerman, and she was the daughter of an accountant for a Wall Street brokerage firm. Then he was linked romantically with June Travis, a ravishing Warner Brothers actress. When William Randolph Hearst threw a costume party at San Simeon, the castle he shared with Marion Davies, gossip columnists determined that anyone who wasn't invited to the lavish affair was a social outcast, while those who were on the guest list were anointed. The biggest stars in Hollywood, such as Greta Garbo, Dorothy Lamour and Cary Grant, turned out in force as did top producers, directors and the playboys who were usually to be seen wherever there was a galaxy of beautiful people. In the middle of it all was young Annenberg, who was dressed as a gaucho and paraded a beautiful girl on his arm.

Then there were trips to Palm Springs, only a few hours' drive south of Los Angeles, and a favorite retreat of the movie crowd. Parties in Palm Springs were famous, as were the illegal gambling casinos on the outskirts of town. Nightly, crowds of newly rich film people threw away fortunes at the gaming tables, forcing them to go back and make or appear in yet another film. Some even needed the pressure of feeling financially strapped to buckle down to the grueling business of making movies. For young men like Walter, however, it was merely another way of having a good time. Once, he and friends who had been carousing all evening showed up at the casinos wearing pajamas and robes and gambled the rest of the night away. As dawn came up, they made their bleary-eyed way back to the El Rancho Hotel, where they were living in a cottage. To people who knew him, Walter Annenberg didn't seem to have a care in the world, and he appeared intent on keeping things that way.

Besides showing a passion for beautiful women, partying and gambling, Walter was enamored of sleek automobiles. There were the custom-made Cadillacs and the special-body Packard that he had his father buy for him. His favorite car, though, was a coffee-colored Lincoln convertible with wire wheels and a windshield between the front and back seats. It too was custom made, of course. Moses never begrudged his son such indulgences. If anything, they sparked a certain pride in the father, who also liked to live well. After all, how many men could keep their sons on the magnificent level he did. Like many fathers who had had a youth of poverty, he wanted his son to have everything he had always coveted.

Walter needed no encouragement in pursuing the pleasurable. In New York, he frequently called on Peggy Hopkins Joyce, a great Follies beauty and well-known courtesan who was courted by millionaires of all ages. Miss Joyce, who made a habit of collecting and discarding wealthy husbands, was a violet-eyed blonde who had been discovered by W.C. Fields. Alternately a show girl, screen star and clothes horse, she was an acknowledged authority on love. Newspapers relentlessly followed her exploits, and readers were titillated in the 1930s to learn about her $24,000 Rolls Royce, $80,000 swimming pool, $700,000 jewelry bills and multimillion-dollar divorce settlements. For a public that wanted to forget the dreary problems of the Depression, reading of her escapades was as good as going to a movie.

Young Annenberg was fascinated by her. He and friends visited her at the Dorset Apartments in the heart of Manhattan, where she had been ensconced by Walter P. Chrysler, the auto tycoon. She laughed and joked about the elderly mogul, while Walter and his pals smoked Chrysler's cigars, charged lunches and dinners to him, and fanned themselves with the $10,000 certified checks that the car manufacturer left for her. "The old boy can afford it," Peggy told them with a smile.

Walter later ran into her in Paris, where she was quarreling with her latest lover, an English earl. As young Annenberg watched in amazement, the earl ended the argument dramatically by tearing a strand of pearls from Miss Joyce's neck and flinging it across the hallway before storming off. Ever the gentleman, Walter helped his friend pick up the beads that had scattered everywhere.

While Walter was playing, the General News Bureau was growing and raking in a tremendous amount of money. In Chicago, the wire was aided in its expansion by a well-known character named Alfred "Jake" Lingle, an ace crime reporter for the *Chicago Tribune*. With unimpeachable sources in both the police department and the underworld, Lingle knew exactly what was happening in the criminal world, and crime was Chicago's hottest story in the 1920s. Lingle and Police Commissioner William P. Russell were so close that Lingle was known as the city's "unofficial police chief." But he was also a friend of Al Capone. The contact was the kind that newspapers long took for granted between reporters and their sources. The fact that Lingle even sported one of the jeweled belt buckles that Capone gave only to very special friends didn't bother *Tribune* editors. What puzzled some of his colleagues was Lingle's life style. He was the only sixty-five-dollar-a-week reporter in town who owned a summer home, took his family on vacations to Florida and Cuba, and had his own chauffeur-driven Lincoln. The reporter explained his affluence with a story that he had inherited fifty thousand dollars when a relative died. Moreover, he was a big gambler, frequently betting as much as one thousand dollars on a horse race. When he won, he won big.

Moses, like many others, knew Lingle as a "fixer," who sold influence with police and politicians to gamblers and bootleggers. It was natural, therefore, that he worked for "The Trust," as the General News Bureau was called in the underworld. Lingle was believed to be instrumental, for instance, in convincing two recalcitrant rival wires they would be better off as part of the Annenberg organization. One of the wires found itself being raided so often by Chicago police that the owners went to court charging police harassment. Then bookies, who used one of the competitors, found themselves unexpectedly raided as well. By 1930, the companies had submitted to acquisition by the General News Bureau.

On June 9, 1930, however, Jake Lingle's usefulness to the Annenberg wire and to everyone else came to an end. While walking through the suburban station of the Illinois Central Railroad to take a train to Washington Park racetrack, he was so engrossed in reading a copy of the *Racing Form* that he failed to notice a young man come up behind him, place a revolver next to his head and fire. The reporter pitched forward, still clutching his copy of the *Racing Form*. His was Chicago's eleventh gang-related murder in ten days. At first, Lingle was viewed as a journalistic martyr, but as his corruption was revealed, he became the shame of his profession. One reason offered for his assassination was that he hadn't secured an interest for the Capone organization in the General News Bureau.

Because of the kind of business the wire was and the type of men who used it, Moses on more than one occasion found himself matching wits with other underworld figures. Soon his only serious rival was the Greater New York News Service, which was controlled by Irving Wexler, better known in gangster circles as Waxey Gordon. Gordon had made a fortune as a bootlegger, pyramiding his East Coast operation into the nation's largest. He owned a fleet of ocean-going rum ships, gambling casinos and distilleries, as well as his wire service, which he founded despite pressure from Moses' wire. To outmaneuver Gordon, Ragen cut prices wherever the two wires were in head-to-head competition. In Trenton, New Jersey, for example, the General News Bureau began charging bookies sixty dollars a week compared with Gordon's seventy-five. In retaliation, a gang of gun-brandishing hoodlums terrorized employees and vandalized Annenberg offices in New York. Worse, Gordon began stealing information from the General News wire by tapping its lines. Moses, who never backed away from a fight, came up with an ingenious scheme to strike back. One day, he selectively deadened the portion of the wire that Gordon's men tapped by sending racing results directly to Chicago instead of broadcasting them over the entire General News Bureau system. Annenberg offices in the target area were linked to the Chicago headquarters by a special telephone connection in order to get the day's results. The final step in the clandestine plan was to ruin Gordon's wire. Annenberg men were posted at telephones near bookie outlets using Gordon's service. When results of races came over the Annenberg wire, there was a delay before they were broadcast over the portion Gordon had tapped.

In the interim, the results were phoned to the waiting men, who placed hefty bets with Gordon's customers on horses they already knew to be winners.

The clever ploy was in operation only one day. By dusk, bookmakers using Gordon's service were reeling under staggering losses. Little shops that might suffer a one-hundred- or two-hundred-dollar loss on bad days found themselves several thousand dollars in the hole. After giving them time to digest their misfortune, Annenberg men visited each bookmaker to explain what had happened. They also refunded the day's losses, saving the small-time bookies from a mad scramble for loans. In each case, the bookies were told "they were saps to take secondhand information." The ruse, similar to that later used in *The Sting*, the motion picture about gambling con men, gained Moses the deep respect of gamblers who were awed by his outsmarting the ruthless Gordon.

Moses wasn't just outwitting competitors. By 1932, he was considering shucking his *Racing Form* partners, Murray and Bannon. Though the paper's success was largely a result of his ingenuity and foresight, Moses was tired of the partners claiming that a big share of the paper's prosperity was due to them. The breaking point came when the two reacted badly to what Moses considered an insignificant matter. Without telling them, he had used the *Racing Form* presses in Baltimore to print a lurid little sex-crime magazine, which resulted in all of them being charged with sending obscene literature through the mail. The case was dropped against Murray and Bannon after they swore they had never even seen a copy of *Baltimore Brevities*, as the offending publication was titled. But the case was pressed against Moses and Walter, as well as against two of Moses' old newsboys who had remained with his organization: E.M. Budner, who headed his Baltimore news agency, and Joe Ottenstein, who held the same job in Washington. The matter was resolved when Ottenstein, Budner and two other men stepped forward and entered guilty pleas. They were fined and placed on probation.

The case had far broader implications, however, than the minor nuisance it seemed to be on the surface. Unknown to Moses, the suit was a direct result of a letter having been sent to J. Edgar Hoover, alerting the egotistical head of the F.B.I. to an article in the magazine that was critical of his agency. If there was anything Hoover couldn't stand, it was criticism, and he had ordered a full-scale investigation.

The probe was so thorough that Moses' other activities came to the G-men's attention and soon a massive file against M.L. Annenberg began building.

After Bannon and Murray's behavior over the magazine, Moses made up his mind to rid himself of his insolent colleagues. His campaign began when he beefed up the racing information in the *Telegraph*, which he had acquired on his own three years earlier, in 1929. He cut the price of the *Telegraph* to a dime from the twenty-five cents that it, like the *Racing Form*, charged, and before Murray and Bannon knew what was happening, Moses was competing directly against the *Racing Form*. With the aid of his network of newspaper distributors, strong-arm men, and tough delivery-truck drivers who could see to it that a rival's papers never made it to the newsstands, the *Telegraph* became prominently displayed by newsdealers, who received the *Racing Form* either late or not at all. While the *Telegraph*'s circulation mushroomed, the *Racing Form*'s deteriorated until Murray and Bannon saw the handwriting on the wall and decided to sell. Moses gave them a generous settlement of $2.25 million for a property that eleven years earlier had sold for $400,000. The price, however, was insignificant compared with the hefty profits reaped from the racing-paper business, which the Annenberg empire now controlled.

Meanwhile, Moses' General News Bureau partners had reasons to be distressed as well. The company was a major supplier of wall sheets and hard cards that were critical to the gambling business. Wall sheets, which listed races, horses, jockeys, morning odds and additional information that bettors juggled when deciding where to place their money, were posted on walls of horse parlors for the benefit of both customers and clerks. Hard cards were smaller versions of the same thing, which bettors carried in their pockets. What upset Jack Lynch and the Lenz brothers was Moses' establishing a rival firm, the Universal Publishing Company, that began printing the same information. With a now familiar ploy, he had undercut the prices charged by the General News Bureau for the sheets and cards and quickly became the major supplier. To guarantee that customers buying his printed matter also used his wire service, Moses had the wall-sheet and hard-card information printed in the same codes used by the wire service. Only bookies who bought both services were given the key.

The men who carried out Moses' Byzantine plots to become the sole lord of the racing-information business worked out of his Chicago headquarters at 431 Dearborn Street. Most of his companies were jammed into cluttered little offices on Plymouth Court, a tiny street that was behind the Dearborn address and was known locally as "Annenberg's Alley." The largest office was that of the General News Bureau, an anteroom which was guarded by tough, obviously armed men, who questioned any unfamiliar individual entering or loitering in the hallway. A partition with a grilled window separated the anteroom from the inner offices. The door leading into the messy, paper-strewn offices contained a large X-ray mirror to determine whether those entering were armed. Other offices were filled with harried clerks, executives and editors, and when Moses visited, the normally heated pace became frantic. Aside from devising ways of squeezing out his partners, Moses was ever eyeing related businesses on which he could bring his formidable resources to bear. Another racing business he moved into was Teleflash, a cheap national service that aired horse races as well as music and news over a broadcast system. With the aid of heavy promotion in his racing publications, Teleflash was soon in restaurants, cafés, saloons, men's clubs, offices and even people's homes, and it was yet another business where Annenberg didn't have to worry about partners.

Moses was so driven to have everything to himself that after stripping his General News partners of publishing profits, he began an earnest campaign to force them out of the race wire as well. On August 27, 1934, he formed a new wire service, which, not surprisingly, was also headquartered in Chicago. It was called the Nationwide News Service. The new concern was forged to compete head-to-head with the General News Bureau. The wire was created so quickly that General News men around the country began calling Ragen, telling him that they heard a new wire was going to compete with them. Ragen calmed them down and explained that he now worked for Nationwide and told them that if they were smart they would too. Understanding immediately what was happening, most of them switched their allegiances. The Lenzes and Lynch, who lacked Moses' quickness as well as his grasp of the intricacies of the business, soon found themselves holding onto a losing proposition. At the end of 1935, the success of Moses' strategy was only too apparent. A year earlier, the General News Bureau had a profit of more than $1.4 million, while Nationwide showed a deficit of $3,788. By 1935, the financial picture had flip-flopped. The General News Bureau lost $45,634 while Nationwide had a $1.1 million profit.

The enraged Lynch, who knew he had been made a fool of, sued Moses. The intricacies of Annenberg's devious schemes, the price cutting, deadened wires and a host of other tactics that had been used to make Nationwide dominant, were spelled out in court, and Moses didn't deny any of it. Indeed, his attorney, Weymouth Kirkland, presented a straightforward and ingenious defense: "The General News Bureau is aiding and abetting an illegal enterprise. They (Lynch and the other partners) came in here and asked the court to lend a hand to a division of profits in an illegal and unconscionable transaction." To illustrate the General News Bureau's position, Kirkland told the court the story of an English judge who in 1725 had established a precedent by refusing to aid a highwayman who tried to force another robber into dividing stolen loot. "There they wanted a division of spoils by robbers," Kirkland told the judge with a straight face. "Here they want a division of the spoils by gamblers."

Lynch had also named in the suit Charles W. Bidwell, a prominent Chicago sports figure who was president of one of Moses' enterprises, Bentley-Murray Printing Company, which had bled away Lynch's profits. Bidwell, a close friend of Moses, was a majority owner of the Hawthorne Race Track, former manager of the Chicago Stadium, and owner of the city's professional football team, the Cardinals. Bidwell's response to Lynch's charges was as audacious as Moses': "A court of equity will not entertain an application for accounting between alleged coadventurers in an alleged criminal enterprise nor aid the participant therein to recover his alleged share of the loot."

After hearing the convoluted arguments, the court decided that Kirkland was indeed correct. The business was so far beyond the law that a court couldn't possibly settle such a dispute. The case was appealed, but the Supreme Court of Illinois upheld the decision.

Though he lost in the courtroom, Lynch was determined to settle the matter in his favor once and for all. He took his case to the streets, where he was more confident of victory. Knowing that the Capone gang had long wanted the wire for itself, Lynch turned to Dan Serritella, the Illinois state senator and friend of Capone, with a proposition to force Moses out of business. Since Serritella was also a friend and business partner of Moses, Lynch knew he needed a powerful inducement to get the politician to turn on a powerful ally. But control of the Trust was the prize, and that was more than enough. On December 21, 1934, Hearst's *Chicago American* set a likely scenario for what was shaping up: "Chicago's biggest gambling war—a colossal struggle for millions of dollars—will be fought with guns unless a compromise is quickly made. Gangsters and gang weapons will decide the struggle between John J. (Jack) Lynch, a veteran Chicago gambling boss, and Moe L. Annenberg, national racing-paper owner, for control of the vast system that disseminates racing news to the thousands of Chicago handbooks."

The newspaper account merely alerted the general public to what was already well known in underworld circles. In the ever-shifting underworld alliances, Ralph O'Hara, the quick-triggered organizer of the Chicago Motion Picture Operators Union, was supporting Moses' interests, but the Capone mob was backing Lynch. Moses was marked for elimination. Frank Nitti, Capone's "enforcer," tried unsuccessfully to undercut Moses by tempting Jim Ragen to turn on his boss, guaranteeing him that he wouldn't have to worry about Moses' vengeance if he threw in with the mob. "If you come along with us, we will kill him in twenty-four hours," Nitti assured Ragen.

Moses was well aware of his precarious position, and he hired bodyguards for protection from the Capone hit men who were following him round the clock. After analyzing his situation, Moses decided that retreat was the most sensible course of action, and Miami, which was under the control of his friend Meyer Lansky, was his safest haven. The Annenberg family had often spent winter vacations in the Florida city. Though Miami was sleepier than Moses liked, he found it had a certain charm. It was a pleasant place where he could rest for a while and even indulge in publishing his own newspaper.

Years later, Ragen prepared affidavits naming those involved in the assassination plot against his boss. He let it be known that the documents were to be released on his own death. They were his insurance policy and would keep him alive for a while, but they didn't prevent the mob from gunning him down one day long after he and Moses had parted ways.

FOUR

THE BEACON LIGHTS atop the new, low-slung *Miami Tribune* building threw powerful silver beams into the dark Caribbean sky. Inside, the brightly lighted newsroom of the *Tribune*, the largest-circulation daily newspaper in Florida, was charged with excitement. Moses, the newspaper's owner, was hunched over a chattering United Press news wire, chain-smoking Pall Mall cigarettes as he relentlessly scanned each news item worthy of the wire's attention this day, April 3, 1936. An open telephone line was by his side.

Paul Jeans, the small, round-shouldered managing editor, sat at his desk, rereading several copies of the paper. With a studied nonchalance that nonetheless radiated tension, newsmen stood in knots talking with one another while Jeanne Bellamy, a young reporter capable of writing colorful copy on a moment's notice, and Dave Yeoman, a burly reporter who could wheedle a graft exposé out of a ward heeler, were checking out stories. Everyone kept an eye on Moses; the acrid aroma of his cigarettes reminded Miss Bellamy of pungent Turkish tobacco as the smoke wreathed through the air.

Suddenly, Moses ripped a story from the UP machine, grabbed the phone and yelled, "Go with the execution!"

Moments earlier, Richard Bruno Hauptmann, the convicted killer of the infant son of Charles and Anne Morrow Lindbergh, had been put to death by the State of New Jersey. The Hauptmann case had captured the imagination of the nation. The German immigrant carpenter had been discovered on September 19, 1934, with money in his possession that appeared to be part of the $50,000 ransom the Lindberghs had paid. When he was tried, his guilt or innocence was debated in the

81

press as well as in taverns, classrooms and beauty parlors, and until the end there was doubt as to whether he would be executed. Now, moments after Moses gave his order, dozens of *Tribune* newsboys were racing through downtown Miami hawking a special edition. The bold, black headline screamed: HAUPTMANN EXECUTED. The *Tribune* had just beaten its local competition, the *Miami Herald* and the *Miami News*, as well as probably every other newspaper in the United States to the street with the story.

The remarkable scoop was as simple to explain as it was ingenious. Several days earlier, Moses, who was always looking for ways to call attention to his paper and to outsmart his rivals, had Jeans make up three versions of the front page for a special edition on Hauptmann's fate. One carried the execution story. The other two bore headlines HAUPTMANN REPRIEVED and HAUPTMANN PARDONED. Thousands of copies of each front page were run off the presses and sent to the downtown distribution office, where the circulation manager rushed out the right one once his boss told him which to go with. After his coup, Moses rubbed his hands together with delight. "Never a dull moment with Annenberg around, is there?" he said to no one in particular. It wasn't really a question, it was a statement of fact.

The enterprise that marked the *Tribune*'s coverage of the Hauptmann story was typical of the way Moses ran his newspaper. Though his son, Walter, was listed on the masthead as publisher, everyone in town knew that it was Moe's paper. Like a father who gives his son an electric train for Christmas and then can't keep his own hands off it, Moses had immediately begun running the show. His taking charge was something he couldn't help, especially when it came to anything that his son had a hand in. That didn't particularly bother Walter in the case of the *Tribune*, since he was frankly somewhat embarrassed by the newspaper. A racy tabloid wasn't Walter's idea of what a newspaper should be. Nonetheless, he occasionally covered a story as a reporter and he had his own column, "Boy About Town," which ran whenever he was in the mood to write it, which wasn't terribly often. The rest of the eager *Tribune* employees found Walter's disinterest disconcerting and they believed that his nickname, Boy, was appropriate. He was a spoiled rich boy, who seemed content to remain one.

But they found his father exciting. Moses' promotional brainstorms and Jeans's nose for sniffing out scandalous news made the *Tribune* the most controversial newspaper in town. There were people who loved it and those who hated it, but just about everyone read it. The

Tribune had come to life on November 15, 1934, under the gutsy slogan "All the News Without Fear or Favor," which sounded a lot more high-minded than the publication actually was. Nonetheless, in little more than a year, the *Tribune*'s circulation had surpassed those of the *Miami News* and the *Miami Herald,* and Moses' rival publishers were furious. They referred to the *Tribune* as "yellow journalism," and they denounced Moses as a "muckraker." Frank B. Shutts, the *Herald*'s publisher, so detested the *Tribune* that he issued an order forbidding the newspaper to enter the *Herald*'s doors, forcing his editors to read copies on the sly.

For his part, Moses cared little what his angry rivals thought of either himself or his newspaper. His past circulation battles had prepared him to expect an hot reception from the competition. What he did care about was how well his newspaper served his purposes, and this it did quite ably. The *Tribune* not only enabled Moses to keep his hand in the newspaper business while he was in exile, but, more important, gave him a loud political voice and an effective tool with which to lobby for his racing interests.

The Florida where the Annenbergs had settled was wide open. The land boom that saw Miami's population soar from 45,000 in 1922 to 177,000 in 1925 had long since soured, forcing politicians to rely on the city's tourism as its economic base. This factor probably more than any other encouraged them to take a relaxed attitude toward some of the vices their more Sybaritic visitors liked to pursue. Miami was a refuge for wealthy, often bored, people who were temporarily escaping cold Northern winters, and one of the ways the visitors liked to spend their idle time was gambling. Every luxury hotel along the five-mile Miami Beach strip, including those that prominently displayed "No Jews" signs on their registration desks, as well as the Jewish hotels clustered around the sound end of the Beach, were equipped with Moses' Teleflash. It blared race results so loudly that they could be heard in the street, and bets were placed just as easily at poolside as they were in poolrooms.

The man who was getting a piece of all the action was Moses' longtime friend, Meyer Lansky, who also possessed great organizational genius. Ever since he began running bootleg liquor into Miami from the Caribbean islands, Lansky had planned to make the vacation spot a hub of gambling casinos. He had undercut Little Augie Corfano, the Miami gangland boss in the 1920s, by surreptitiously buying hotels and nightclubs in Dade and Broward counties. Before Corfano knew what had happened, Lansky controlled the biggest racket in the area and his power was almost unchallengeable. A few years later, Lansky helped Moses bring his National News Service into the area's racetracks. At one point, Joseph E. Widener balked at letting the racing wire into his Hialeah racetrack, fearing the service would act as competition to keep customers away. For a while, Moses' men were forced to call races from a helium balloon that was lofted over Hialeah, but Widener dropped his opposition, apparently after discussing with Lansky how unwise such a policy was.

Gambling was so wide open in Miami not just because politicians wanted to lure tourists, but because the city's leaders were corrupt. They were also petty. For instance, according to one story, when Lansky sent one of his lieutenants to bribe a city commissioner so slot machines could be set up around town, the hood asked how much it would cost. "Would $50 be too much?" the official asked. The deal almost didn't go through while the cautious Lansky tried to figure out the man's angle; finally, he realized there wasn't any.

Making the best of his situation, Moses determined to ease into the life of a gentleman of leisure. Several months before the *Chicago Tribune* took note of the impending gang war, Moses purchased a beautiful home at 3815 Collins Avenue, Miami Beach. Built by Albert R. Erskine, founder of the Studebaker car company, the mansion was a replica of an Italian villa and contained a swimming pool, a boathouse and dock, and all the luxuries that the Annenbergs had come to take for granted. The property was in a posh neighborhood and was flanked by the estates of C.A. McCulloch, the Chicago utility tycoon, and Gar Wood, the speedboat king. Down the road was the winter home of W.K. Vanderbilt, and only a short drive away was the regal estate of Moses' friend, Arthur Brisbane. Moses' son lived with him, and he kept bedrooms always available for visits by each of his daughters. When he invited Enid, Moses' letter wryly stated, "You can bring your husband too." This was a great concession, since he had never forgiven Norman Bensinger, who at age thirty-nine had eloped with the seventeen-year-old Enid in 1924. But Moses always wanted his children around him. Their love was the greatest security he had ever known.

During the 1920s, Miami had had four daily newspapers, but after the 1929 stock-market collapse only two remained—the *Herald*, which was owned by Shutts, an Indiana lawyer who had come to town as a federal receiver for a bankrupt Miami bank and had stayed to head one of the city's most influential law firms and become a leading power in what was still much a raw, frontier town. The other paper, the *News*, was owned by James M. Cox, the former governor of Ohio, who had proved that anyone can run for President. A short, egocentric man who, because of his cocky attitude, was known as "the Bantam," Cox had lost to fellow Ohioan Warren G. Harding. The man who actually ran the *News* was his son-in-law Dan Mahoney, who was a powerful boss in local politics.

When Moses moved to Miami, the *Herald* supported the political machine that controlled the city's politics while the *News* supported a faction that ran Miami Beach. Gambling was the major political hot potato of the day. There were rumblings in Tallahassee, the state capital, that legislation might be drafted to outlaw services that catered to the gambling industry. The pressure was coming from the state's strong antigambling Baptists, and it worried Moses, who began considering owning a newspaper as a weapon with which to defend himself. An opportunity to acquire the *Herald* had unexpectedly presented itself when a newspaper broker told Moses the paper was for sale for $1.5 million—Shutts, who was ill, needed the money to pay off debts on the property. A few days later, the price was raised by $300,000, but when Moses asked to see an earnings statement and circulation figures, the data wasn't made available to him. "I'm not interested in buying a cat in a bag," Moses told the broker, and when the man approached him later about the *Herald*, which then had an asking price of $2.5 million, Moses dismissed him. He never wasted his time and he didn't want anyone else wasting it either.

A more straightforward opportunity came his way during the winter of 1933–34, when Moses became one of a small group of investors who started a seasonal paper in Miami Beach. At the end of the winter, Moses' partners dropped out of the venture, and the paper suspended operations. When the corporation's assets, which were chiefly just the newspaper's name and a contract with United Press, were auctioned off, Moses was the sole bidder. He had plans to revive the paper on his own, and over the summer he discussed his plans with Paul Jeans, a *Racing Form* editor and the man he picked to edit the new *Tribune*. Moses always promoted loyal, smart men when he could, and he liked the energetic Jeans, who was brimming over with ideas. The two rounded up a staff and obtained several widely read columns, including Walter Winchell's and Westbrook Pegler's. Armed with Moses' blessing and a commitment that he didn't care what kinds of losses the paper sustained, Jeans jumped into the thick of Miami's political wars.

Moses couldn't have chosen a better man for the kind of paper he envisioned. Jeans knew how to publish a paper that caused a stir, caught people's attention. Rough and rowdy, the *Tribune* shot from the hip and offered something for everyone. There were imaginative circulation contests, centerfolds of pretty girls, fires or train wrecks, and stories that probed the abominable living conditions in Negro neighborhoods—a subject ignored by the other papers. The *Tribune* also gorged itself on tales of crime and corruption, particularly the latter. Smoking through a long cigarette holder in the manner of President Roosevelt and sitting with his feet on his desk, Jeans beckoned to a reporter. "Go down to the courthouse and investigate this guy," he said, giving the newsman a name of a magistrate or bail bondsman. "I think he's a crook." After days—sometimes only hours—of poking around, the reporter came back with a hot story. Jeans was usually right—but, then, just about everybody holding office in Miami was doing something he shouldn't be doing. "We're going to clean up this town, and we're going to use our big guns to do it," the little editor told his staff, and they loved it.

To keep the none-too-honest Miami police force from delving into his race wire affairs, Moses bought its cooperation by cleverly—and legally—getting policemen to take bribes. Moses announced that he was giving prizes to certain police officers whom he would select for some nebulous meritorious service. The prizes were $10 daily, $100 weekly, and $500 monthly. Thus Moses established a unique system of protection for his enterprises and he also received confidential information from police who were eager for their prizes.

While Jeans ignored the nefarious activities of his publisher, he sought out sensational stories where he was on surer grounds. The *Tribune*'s first big chance came when a political foe of Moses, Judge E.C. Collins of Miami Criminal Court, was indicted by a grand jury for accepting a bribe. A poor illiterate farmer had paid the judge five hundred dollars to get his son out of prison, where he was serving time for stealing a car. Court records showed that the young man, who had pleaded guilty before the judge, was imprisoned for two years, but a *Tribune* reporter found the sentence had been sloppily altered to a shorter period. The revelation was amazing to local citizens, because the judge had a reputation for dealing harshly with poor defendants unlucky enough to confront him and because the jurist was a bastion of Miami society and even taught Bible school in the city's First Baptist Church. But, whereas editors at the other papers revered the judge, Jeans thought he was an old fraud. While the *Herald* carried the Collins story with a one-column headline, the *Tribune* splashed his indictment across page one, and Jeans vowed, "We're going to nail the son of a bitch." The rival papers continued to make light of the incident, but the *Tribune* embarrassed the judge at every turn. The paper exposed other questionable activities of Collins, including his son's receiving a hefty mortgage for a worthless piece of real estate from a local hoodlum who, though he appeared before the judge for crimes including assault and murder, was convicted only once and that was for illegal possession of liquor. The *Tribune* disclosures were as embarrassing to the *Herald* as they were alarming to Miamians, who had never before been exposed to their politicians' seamier side. Collins was a major figure in the political machine that the *Herald* supported, and the paper even went so far as to join the judge in asking the public to suspend its judgment of his less-than-upright activities.

The *Tribune* wasn't just taking advantage of its rivals, who were looking the other way when the local establishment was erring; the paper sometimes just reacted better to stories. The *Herald,* for example, carried a short account one day of five people killed in Oklawaha, a northern-Florida town. The *Tribune* bannered the event across the front page. The incident was a shootout between agents of the Federal Bureau of Investigation and none other than Fred Barker and his mother, Kate "Ma" Barker, who had been making headlines coast to coast as they robbed and shot their way across the country. The *Tribune* pulled out all stops in graphic descriptions of the tense drama. To Jeans, it was a story made in heaven.

On occasion, the little editor showed that he could also cover a serious story better than his competitors. On Labor Day, 1935, for example, Miami Beach was whipped by horrendous winds and slammed by monstrous waves. The U.S. Weather Bureau said a hurricane was on its way, but the Bureau calmed residents of the Keys by saying the storm would pass harmlessly between Key West and Cuba. By Monday, however, Jeans knew that something was amiss. The Florida East Coast Railway had sent a train to the Keys to evacuate anyone who wanted to come to the mainland as a precaution, but by evening the train hadn't returned and no one had heard from the Upper Keys. The ever curious Jeans dispatched William Freeze, a reporter, and Harold "Red" Willoughby, a photographer, to the scene. When the pair reached Snake Creek in the Keys, both the railroad trestle and highway U.S. 1 were washed out; the Lower Keys were lashed by 100-mile-per-hour winds and mountainous waves. The death toll was obviously terrible. The enterprising Freeze inched out along the trestle as far as he dared and yelled to people on the other side: "How many people have been killed?" A straggler yelled back that five hundred were dead and he was among the few survivors. Tuesday evening, the *Tribune* brought out an edition with a headline citing the somber death toll over a story by Freeze accompanied by Willoughby's dramatic pictures. To the dismay of the newsmen at the *Herald* and the *News,* the *Tribune*'s effort was their first knowledge of the disaster. *Tribune* reporters, feature writers and photographers continued to blanket the story, and, for a week, the newspaper produced superb coverage of what turned out to be the worst hurricane ever to have struck the region. The *Tribune* carried painful pictures of Boy Scouts standing guard over coffins and stories critical of the Weather Bureau's inaccurate reports. There was even an exposé of greedy undertakers who tried to exploit the tragedy. The paper's coverage was far more thorough than any other's, and Miamians responded. Circulation soared by 10,000 copies a day.

Far more often, however, the *Tribune* was used to fend off forces threatening to pull the plug on the racing wire. Miami Mayor E. G. Sewell began a campaign to shut down the city's bookies once a grand jury indicted a group of gamblers. Religious leaders everywhere were demanding a crackdown, and Sewell, who disliked his treatment at the hands of the *Tribune,* launched his holy war by raiding the local offices of the Nationwide News Service. Quick to see the justice of the act, the *Herald* and the *News,* along with a host of politicians who were sick of the hard-nosed *Tribune,* pledged their support. But they should have known better. Miami officials acting virtuously were like drunks attempting to walk a straight line. Waiting in the wings was Moses with his belligerent editor, whose paper could make a Lion's Club meeting sound like an orgy when he put his mind to it, let alone a bunch of heavy-handed politicians who, even the mayor later admitted, were beholden to Al Capone. Soon, the *Tribune* was running stories about the city clerk who perjured himself, the bribe-taking bail bondsman, and the police chief Sam McCreary and Parker Henderson, Jr., the son of a former mayor, who had a bail-bond racket. Henderson, a crony of Capone, had arranged for the gangster to buy a home on Palm Island, a man-made slip of land in Biscayne Bay between the mainland and the beach. Jeans even contended that the machine guns used in the St. Valentine's Day Massacre could be traced to Henderson.

Despite its big circulation, the *Tribune* was such a volatile paper and offended so many important people that it never gained much advertising. But Moses didn't mind. He enjoyed the excitement, and he never lost his passion for being around editorial offices or printing plants. Almost daily, he huddled with Jeans as they determined whom to skewer in the paper's pages. Moreover, the *Tribune* gave him a great deal of political clout, which Moses liked for its own sake and because it made good business sense to have it. Jeans's job as editor, for example, made him an effective lobbyist in Tallahassee, where he vigorously opposed legislation that had any bearing on the racing papers or the wire. Another *Tribune* editor, Howard Hartley, was a lobbyist in addition to what Moses referred to as his "personal, confidential political man in Florida," whose job included keeping politicians happy. Moses had long observed how Hearst had used his newsmen and his newspapers to protect his businesses and to fight his political battles. Moses was grossing about four thousand dollars a week from Miami bookies alone, as well as what he reaped from others elsewhere in Florida, and he didn't want to lose such a healthy income by failing to take precautionary political steps.

To block legislation that might be detrimental to his interests and to press for bills that would help them, Moses tried to find politicians who were willing to do his bidding. From his earliest days in Chicago, he had viewed most office holders as mercenaries who were willing to adopt the cause of the highest bidder. He knew only too well that such greedy men were necessary to the success of an operation like the racing wire, which was so vulnerable to the scrutiny of law-enforcement officials. Therefore, Moses often sat with Jeans and Hartley discussing malleable politicians who would do his bidding. One day the name of an ambitious state senator, Peter Tomasello, was mentioned and Moses expressed a keen interest in the man. Both Jeans and Hartley warned Moses to shy away from him, because he had a reputation for passing bad checks, but to Moses that seemed like a minor vice compared with the crimes Chicago politicians, in particular, were willing to engage in for a price. "That makes no difference to me," Moses replied. "We can make up the checks."

Several days later, Moses gave Hartley an envelope containing $2,-500 and told him to fly to Jacksonville and give the money to Tomasello as an "initial contribution." When he eventually got to meet Moses, the grateful politician enthusiastically began outlining his boring political platform until he was halted by Moses with characteristic brusqueness.

"I don't care about your platform," Moses interrupted. "All I want is for you to obey orders."

"O.K. I know how to take orders," the chastened politician replied.

Satisfied that he had the right man, Moses elaborated on what he believed to be both his own unlimited power and Tomasello's good fortune in having met such a benefactor as himself. "Young man, you can go far in politics," he said. "First, I'll put you over for governor, and then I'll put you in the United States Senate."

Never one to mince words, Moses told his new protégé that in return for his patronage the state senator would have to promote gambling interests. Moses' lawyers had drafted two pieces of legislation that Annenberg wanted pushed through Tallahassee. One would legalize bookmaking and the other would legalize gambling. Tomasello, who believed the race-wire king was his ticket to the national political stage, willingly agreed to promote the bills. As his reward, Moses contributed more than $10,000 to the Tomasello campaign, and the *Tribune* quickly portrayed him to the public as Florida's shining white knight. The state senator, however, wasn't very shrewd, and he stretched Moses' patience. After refusing advice from Moses and his editors, he ran an inept campaign and it rapidly floundered. In exasperation, Moses withdrew all support from Tomasello, who lost the gubernatorial race to Fred P. Cone, a man with whom Moses had no ties at all.

With the dismal results of the gubernatorial contest behind him, Moses still wanted to keep his hand in politics, so he next ran his own candidates for political office in Miami. Mayor Sewell and McCreary, the police chief, were irksome problems that Moses hoped to solve at the ballot box. To lay the groundwork for getting rid of the two, Moses started a campaign against them, using the front page as an editorial page. When the *Tribune* was launched, Moses' intent was to have no editorial page, since the paper was only sixteen to twenty pages long, and editorials would eat into valuable news and advertising space. Now, editorials began turning up regularly, asking pointed, embarrassing questions, which deserved answers no matter what the *Tribune*'s motives in asking them were. McCreary became a special target of such attacks as: "Is the City Commission afraid that, if it throws

Crooked Sam overboard, the so-called Director of Public Safety will tell all he knows? Is there no honor among thieves in these degenerate days?"

The incensed Mayor Sewell, who was beside himself as a result of the *Tribune*'s attacks on his administration, decided to strike back. He dusted off an old ordinance forbidding the sale of publications printing racing entries, results and information, and he ordered the police to enforce it. Not only the *Racing Form* was affected, but Sewell's nemesis, the *Tribune*, was too, since it carried racing information. Not surprisingly, the *Herald* and the *News*, which likewise published racing material, were exempt from the mayor's order. The campaign, however, never got off the ground because the still sitting grand jury dropped another bombshell that blew up the legitimacy of just about anything the mayor wanted to do. The jury stated:

> We have obtained increasing and conclusive evidence that organized crime has almost reached the point of a monopoly, for which two primary factors are, in our opinion, responsible. One of these factors has to do with the conduct, officially and otherwise, of men who constitute part of our governmental machinery entrusted with the duties of fostering and maintaining orderly government and protecting communities against crime and vice, and vested with the powers of enforcement . . .

Moses and Jeans had a field day with the report, and the *Tribune*'s scalding stories bore fruit. Local church women, for instance, were so angered by what they read in the paper that the group appeared before the city commission and demanded McCreary's removal from office. The besieged Sewell defended both himself and his police chief and denounced the *Tribune* as a "scandal sheet . . . 'that ought to be stopped." During a hearing connected with a libel suit he brought against Jeans, Sewell, his voice quivering with rage, attacked both Moses and his paper—"There is a flood of foreign, I would say, gambling promoters coming into this city, and, when they are closed up by the police, they proceed to publish everything in the world in this newspaper. . . . They will blackmail anybody . . . and we are informed from Philadelphia and New York and Baltimore that they are nothing but a bunch of gambling gangsters who are worse than Al Capone. . . . If we ever have gangsters here, it's them. They are worse than Al Capone ten to one."

In rapid succession, Sewell and other political leaders filed criminal suits against Jeans and Walter Annenberg, as the paper's publisher. Bringing the younger Annenberg into the fray was a way of getting at his father, since no one believed that Walter had a hand in the political warfare. Indeed, Walter's only reputation around Miami was that of a wealthy playboy. He was in New York or Los Angeles as often as he seemed to be in Miami and when he was in town, he was rarely at the paper.

What drew him to the *Tribune* more often than not was Dorothy Day, the glamorous gossip columnist who brought a touch of sophistication to the street-wise *Tribune* as she swept to her desk in a mink coat, preparing to write about the city's wealthy and beautiful people. Otherwise, Walter squandered his days tooling around in one of his exotic convertibles, frequenting such expensive night spots as the Royal Palm, the Palm Island or the 9–2—clubs where there was dancing, gambling and illegal whiskey; even though the Volstead Act was repealed in 1933, selling liquor was still against the law in that part of the nation. Typical of the attitude of *Tribune* staffers toward Walter was that of reporter Jeanne Bellamy, who thought of him as just a kid who trailed after his father. She was amazed when she found out that he was in his late twenties, or four years older than she. "He sure as hell didn't act it," she said.

The suit against Jeans and Walter didn't bother Moses, because it obviously had little merit. He was outraged, however, by a letter-writing campaign praising local politicians and condemning him, which appeared in both the *News* and the *Herald.* His anger increased when a handbill accusing him of being a racketeer was widely circulated around town. There was no doubt as to who was responsible for such attacks, and Moses filed a civil suit against Mayor Sewell, Police Chief McCreary, City Solicitor Fred Pine, state representative S.P. Robineau and others. As always, Moses believed the best defense was a strong defense. He sought a half million dollars in damages and charged the defendants with a conspiracy against his paper.

A more serious problem than the suit against Walter and Jeans was a Robineau-sponsored bill that would make it illegal for newspapers to carry horse-racing information. The *Herald* and the *News* were curiously exempt under the terms of the proposed legislation since it was carefully designed only to affect newspapers younger than three years old. The political forces Moses was able to muster prevailed, and the bill died in committee, but it was a reminder to him of how susceptible his operations were to political power and how he needed his own strong hand in politics.

In another attempt to improve his political position, Moses decided to run his own candidates for three seats on the city commission as election time neared. His unlikely candidates were a trio of scrawny, elderly Miami businessmen, R.C. Gardner, J. J. Bridges and Mark Chartrand, whom the *Herald* attempted to ridicule by dubbing them "The Three Musketeers." Not to be outdone, Jeans seized the expression and used it as a slogan to popularize his boss's candidates. The *Tribune*'s aggressive support of the Musketeers soon turned the unknowns into recognizable politicians, much to the dismay of the anti-*Tribune* factions. The success of the paper's efforts was measurable when all three men made it into the runoffs.

Dismayed that Moses' candidates were being taken seriously, the machine politicians moved quickly to see that the Musketeers didn't actually get elected to office. William P. Mooty, the state roads commissioner, began by offering $500 toward a fund that was earmarked to buy votes and "run this racketeering newspaper out of town." Other politicians eagerly contributed and the slush fund rapidly reached $100,000. Such financing overwhelmed Moses' contributions, and his candidates went down in defeat in a vote that Jeans proclaimed the crookedest ever held in Miami. But no one, including the usually strident voice of the *Tribune*, cried foul. "It would merely have given us a reputation for being bad losers without serving a useful purpose," Jeans later stated—a little too sanctimoniously in light of what might have been dredged up about the role he and Moses had played in the election.

Nevertheless, Moses did come out ahead in the election, if only because Mayor Sewell's political grip was weakened. When the votes were tallied, only one new commissioner was indebted to the mayor for his job, and the newly constituted board moved swiftly to take positions independent of him. The commission's most important change was stripping McCreary of his job as Director of Public Safety. Though the *Tribune* applauded the action, the paper continued an editorial blitz to have him removed as police chief as well. In its flamboyant fashion, the paper started printing a series of articles about police brutality, referring to Miami cops as "Cossacks" and McCreary as the "Cossack Chief." The stories naturally didn't ingratiate *Tribune* newsmen with the beleaguered police, who retaliated like wounded bulls. Detective Chief L. O. Scarboro, for instance, smashed photographer Weston Hayne's camera, and Detective Eddie Melchen punched reporter Charles Davis in the mouth and had him locked up in the drunk tank until the *Tribune* lawyer could obtain his release.

Unknown to the *Tribune* staff, however, the feud with the police had actually been trumped up by Moses and Jeans. The pair had wanted to get rid of McCreary, of course, because he was aligned with Moses' political enemies, but they didn't want the ill-will of the police department itself. Through his police reward system, Moses had learned that McCreary and the City Commissioners intended to keep *Tribune* reporters from having access to the police department's reports on criminal investigations. Such knowledge was essential to the wire service's operations; it allowed Moses' men to keep tabs on their rivals and to head off any actions that affected them. Since such information was normally kept by the police chief, even Moses' network of police informants would become valueless in such matters. Thus Annenberg and Jeans entered into an agreement with Detective Chief Scarboro to have him destroy Hayne's camera. That action enabled Moses through the *Tribune* to obtain an injunction against the City Commissioners, the director of public safety, the city manager and the Miami police chief, thus preventing them from interfering with the efforts of the paper to obtain news. A judge permitted the injunction to be made permanent, and Moses' network of collections from gambling joints continued to operate secure in the knowledge that their source of information was impeccable.

In yet another effort to stop the *Tribune*, State Representative Robineau introduced a bill that would make a newspaper criminally liable if it even questioned the honesty, integrity or fitness of public officeholders, including "Cossack Chief" McCreary. The bill called for a stiff penalty of five years in prison and a ten-thousand-dollar fine. Robineau wasn't simply motivated out of dismay at the names hurled at his friends by the *Tribune*. He himself was constantly referred to in the paper's news columns as well as editorials as "Forty-Two Percent Pete," a reference to a loan law that he had sponsored and which fixed an interest rate that worked out to 42 percent a year. Robineau's libel bill picked up the support of other politicians who had been maddened by Jeans's penchant for calling them by less than flattering nicknames. In the *Tribune*, for example, the governor was routinely referred to as "Kingfish," while other state representatives were alluded to as "Gambler Lewis" and the "Mountebank of Marianna." Nonetheless, the bill's obvious result would be to trample on the First Amendment, and more restrained political heads prevailed. The bill was defeated.

Moses had other victories to celebrate. McCreary, who was entangled in an ever-more-complicated web of payoffs, kickbacks and brutality charges, was forced to resign as police chief, and suddenly Mayor Sewell himself was vulnerable as never before. The still-convened grand jury voted to indict a host of city officials, including the mayor, charging them with conspiring to defraud the city of tax certificates totaling $97,000. All of the *Tribune*'s predictions about the "City Hall Gang" were coming true, and to twit the *Miami Herald*, Jeans maliciously borrowed a headline "We Have With Us Today," from a regular *Herald* feature about local notables, and ran it over a doctored picture of Sewell with little woodpeckers pecking at his head and a tag around his neck proclaiming "indictment." The embarrassed *Herald* temporarily discontinued the feature.

McCreary's successor, Andrew J. Kavanaugh, was greeted with a burst of unrestrained editorial enthusiasm by the *Tribune*, but the paper's warmth cooled rapidly when the new man began cracking down on bookies who were using the race wire. Moreover, Kavanaugh began examining Moses' personal involvement in the Miami gambling operations, until he became convinced that Moses was behind the entire city's bookmaking racket. The new police chief himself traced gambling payoffs almost to Moses' front door. He learned, for instance, that Frank Hyde, who operated the Seminole Lodge, the clubhouse at Hialeah, and who was head of the wire in Miami, turned over an envelope each week containing the week's net income to a messenger boy. The youth carried the money to a vacant room in a building that housed an office of the *Tribune*, where it was turned over to another man. The final courier left the packet on a desk in the empty room and walked out. As he left, he heard a signal from another doorway that all was well; he never saw who picked up the money.

Unfortunately for Moses, Kavanaugh numbered among his friends J. Edgar Hoover, to whom he wrote about the crime network he found in Miami. "So, posing under a cloak of respectability, Annenberg, with his large publishing business, really is conducting possibly the most widespread racket in this country," he informed Hoover in a letter.

The *Tribune* was soon sticking pins in the new lawman. One of the major recommendations that the new police chief had brought to the job, for example, came from a top "G-Man," according to the political leaders who had put him in office. The *Tribune* learned that the endorsement, or at least one of them, actually came from a former Miami police chief who was then a U.S. Marshal, or a "G-Man," as a *Tribune* editorial sarcastically pointed out. Even more than Kavanaugh's moving against bookies, Moses was dismayed that the new police chief presented damning testimony about Moses himself during a Federal Communications Commission investigation of the relationship between the Nationwide News Service and the American Telephone & Telegraph Company, which transmitted the wire information. There was F.C.C. concern about the wire both because of the clientele using it and the strong-arm methods employed in maintaining the service's supremacy.

When he was called upon to testify, Kavanaugh told the Commission that an estimated two hundred Miami bookies relied on Moses' wire, and he believed the *Tribune*'s owner was receiving an income of about six million dollars a year nationally from the operation. Just how Kavanaugh arrived at that precise figure wasn't revealed, but newspapers printed it as though it were fact. The *Miami Herald* and the *Miami News* in particular delighted in reporting on the hearings, which, of course, were page-one stories for them.

Moses was embarrassed by the disclosures that he was the man who ruled the racing wire, because of the doubt it cast upon the respectability that he was trying to achieve. He liked to think of the racing wire as simply another business. When he felt called upon to reply to the police chief's charges as well as others that were raised during the hearings, he used the *Tribune* as his forum. Brazenly, he adopted the role of a bewildered, retired businessman, who just happened to have invested in a wide variety of holdings, one of which happened to be the wire about which he really had very little understanding. Moses, he himself didn't mind editorializing, was a much misunderstood man—

> I retired from active business several years ago. Before that time, most of my business was devoted to the publishing business. During my newspaper career, I was active in all the principal cities of the country. I was president and publisher of the Wisconsin News, at Milwaukee, Wisconsin, and later president of the New York Daily Mirror.
>
> Half of my business was devoted to interests in Milwaukee, where I lived—a city which is known all over the world as "the crimeless city." That is the chief reason why I find it difficult to acclimate myself to the goings on in Miami and the State of Florida. I love its sunshine and all the advantages which it has to offer.

I felt that I could hasten the manifest destiny of Miami by helping to establish an independent newspaper, the Miami Tribune, and assist in making the city realize more rapidly the great future to which its climate and strategic location entitle it.

The success of the Tribune was beyond my most sanguine expectations, thanks to our readers. In every short term, public support of the Tribune was such that it became the first newspaper in South Florida, exceeding its morning contemporary in circulation by many, many thousands. This, of course, earned the enmity of our competitor, which has from time to time resorted to unscrupulous efforts to besmirch my character.

They finally found something which they thought would support their attacks.

A corporation in which I am interested owns stock in approximately sixty other corporations, many of which are listed on the New York Stock Exchange. One of the unlisted stocks is that of a corporation engaged in the business of gathering sporting and racing news. This organization, as I understand, serves hundreds of subscribers and newspapers with racing news and racing results. The business of this organization has thus far been legal in every respect. It is said, however, that some of the subscribers have misused the racing news for gambling purposes. The same might be said of every newspaper in the country which devotes generous space daily to racing charts, selections, entries, results and tips of every kind and character, and of radio stations that broadcast racing results . . .

I, myself, have never in my life had an interest in any gambling device or business; I have never owned a share of stock, directly or indirectly, in a horse track or a dog track. I do not own any race horses.

If Mr. Kavanaugh's statement to the effect that my income is $6 million a year were true, I might have been able, with such an income, to own all the race horses in the United States and Canada, as well as the race tracks. However, with that advance publicity, I might be able to acquire a title in England where horse racing is an honorable sport, fit only for kings.

Moses didn't let his self-righteous defense prevent him from acting. The *Tribune* attacks on Kavanaugh were stepped up, and the police chief found himself subjected to intense scrutiny by the paper, so that even his role in a "suspicious" purchase of parking meters by the city was questioned. After much deliberation, Moses, Jeans, and several other men in the Annenberg camp decided that attacks in the *Tribune* were meaningless unless political action was taken as well. "Finally, we decided the only way to get rid of Kavanaugh was to abolish his job," Hartley, the editor-lobbyist, later testified. The decision, of course, meant once again getting involved in running candidates for local office, men who could dispose of the police chief if they came to power. Opportunely, elections were again drawing near for the City Commission, and Moses drafted a slate of *Tribune*-supported candidates. Thanks to lavish campaign spending by Moses and the lively backing of the *Tribune*, the Annenberg politicians won offices and, as a gesture to their benefactor, one of their first acts was to remove Kavanaugh from his job.

Besides the seemingly endless local political brush fires that Moses had to deal with, he was confronted by political issues at the state level that could prove devastating if they were allowed to get out of hand. Moses had drafted more bills that were designed to help his racing businesses, and they needed constant protection against the powerful Baptist moral outrage that sprang up at the slightest hint of anything favoring gambling. During the 1937 state legislative session, Hartley was in Tallahassee working night and day to ensure the bills' approval, but he met so much opposition that he asked Moses for additional help. "It looked like we would have to buy some people to get them through," Hartley said later. Because the legislation was so vital to him, Moses sent Jeans and *Tribune* attorney M. Victor Miller to the capital to help rally the cause. The two made the rounds of legislators' offices, but neither Moses nor Hartley nor anyone else would ever know how successful the two had been. While driving back to Miami, their car was speeding and apparently swerved to avoid hitting something in the road, skidded across the median strip and crashed head on into another car. Jeans, Miller and the driver of the other auto were killed instantly.

The little editor's death was a terrible blow to everyone at the *Tribune*, especially Moses. Jeans's ideas and bursts of righteous indignation were what had sparked the tabloid, and his death left a vacuum that couldn't be filled. Almost immediately, the paper lost much of its flash and rambunctious style, although a new editor tried to maintain Jeans's madhouse tradition. With Jeans gone, Moses lost interest in the paper. In any event, he was no longer excited by the Miami and Florida political wars in which he had once taken such a fierce interest, and he was in Florida less and less. The summer before, he had turned his attention toward a bigger, more respectable newspaper that he had acquired. He had struck an agreement to end the Lynch warfare, apparently pledging to pay Capone's Syndicate one million dollars a year in protection money so that he was free to pursue new ventures elsewhere.

Moses had bought the *Philadelphia Inquirer*, which had the prestige and class the muckraking little *Tribune* lacked. The *Inquirer* was the kind of respectable, traditional paper that he wanted as a legacy for his son. Moreover, the Philadelphia paper was the kind of major publication he had always imagined himself running one day. Moses was nearly sixty years old, and he increasingly thought about the way he wanted to be remembered. He now wanted the respectability that the *Tribune* could never give him. If he were ever pressed, he would have agreed with his son's attitude that the tabloid wasn't a proper paper for a gentleman, but he knew its usefulness, whereas his son never did. The *Inquirer* was a proper paper for his proper son. Thus, when John S. Knight, the young publisher of the *Akron Beacon Journal* who had just bought the *Miami Herald* for $2.25 million, proposed to buy the *Tribune*, Moses was receptive to the offer. The deal was straightforward, the way Moses liked to do business.

"How much do you want for it?" Knight asked.

"One million dollars," Moses answered.

Knight, who didn't like wasting time any more than Moses did, immediately replied that he was strapped for funds, because he had just bought the *Herald*. However, he made a counter offer that he hoped would interest Moses. "I have a little paper in Massillon, Ohio," Knight said, adding that he wanted to throw the paper into the transaction as part of the purchase price.

"Where the hell's that?" Moses asked.

Knight located the little town on a map, showing it was between Canton and Wooster, and south of Akron, and he took the liberty of producing a detailed financial statement that he had taken care to bring with him. Moses rapidly scanned the data, and, after a moment's reflection, agreed to sell the *Tribune* for the *Massillon Independent* and $600,000, which Knight said he could raise.

On December 1, 1937, the *Tribune*'s doors closed permanently. Knight stripped the paper of its columnists for use in the *Herald*, and he added the better reporters and photographers to his staff. Under its new ownership, the *Herald* became a stronger, more ethical paper and gained a reputation for fair, accurate reporting of local and state politics. One of the local scandals the paper covered shortly after Moses sold his paper was that two of the three commissioners he helped elect to office were indicted for trying to extort bribes from the Florida Power and Light Company.

Knight, who used the *Herald* as the flagship for a newspaper empire he would create, was destined to have future dealings with Moses' son, Walter. The deal he would strike with Walter wouldn't be nearly as much to his liking as the *Tribune*, and it would leave a bitter feeling in both men.

CHAPTER

FIVE

MOSES WAS FISHING at his Ranch A in the Black Hills of Wyoming
when he received word that the *Philadelphia Inquirer* was for sale.
The ranch was a peaceful refuge from the multitude of friends, relatives, business associates and ringing telephones that were always
competing for his attention. In the trout stream with a fly rod in his
hands, he didn't think about magazines, newspapers or the racing wire.
The serenity and the fish, which were harder to outsmart than people,
eased the tensions that built up when he was doing business.

He had stumbled upon the ranch by accident four years earlier in
1932. He and friends were fishing near Belle Fourche, South Dakota,
one of the nation's greatest cattle-shipping points. When they stopped
for lunch at a small restaurant, Moses found the trout on the menu so
delicious that he asked the waitress where they had been caught. She
told him about a small stream meandering out of the Black Hills just
on the other side of the state line, near Beulah, Wyoming. Within
weeks, he had bought 2,000 acres along the creek, erected a high
metal-wire fence around the entire property, posted "No Trespassing"
signs and stationed a guard at the gate. Soon local residents complained that he not only had shut them out of the best fishing spot
around, but also had ruined it further down the creek when he had
cleared the stream bed to keep his lines from snagging.

When at the ranch, Moses adhered to a routine he found relaxing.
He was up by six-thirty, when he had breakfast prepared by Baba
Rose, his cook, whom he flew in with him to the huge $300,000
log lodge that he had built. By seven o'clock, he was clad in baggy
knickers, a cotton shirt and a battered hat, and was heading past the

stables for fifteen horses and the duck ponds on his way to the stream. It was one such day that a newspaper broker disturbed his rhythm with news that the *Inquirer* was on the market.

Since the *Inquirer* was the kind of established, respected paper that he had always wanted for himself and his son, Moses discussed the possibility of buying it with his son-in-law J. Stanley Kahn, a bright personable man who had married his daughter Jeanette. Moses had a deep trust in Kahn and involved him heavily in many of his business dealings, a situation that created resentment in Walter, who believed his father was placing too much confidence in a man who was simply using him, much more confidence than he ever placed in his son. In any event, Moses dispatched Kahn to Paris to bargain with the owner, a former Philadelphia socialite, Mme. Eleanor Louise Patenotre, the widow of a former French ambassador to the United States. The imperious little woman lived with her son, Raymond, and they dabbled in politics and published a small-circulation newspaper, *Le Petit Journal*, which had about as much influence as its name suggested. When he returned, Kahn had arranged an option for Moses to buy the *Inquirer*, which he did.

When Philadelphia's stuffy Old Guard learned that Moses had purchased the paper, its members went into a state of shock. The Establishment knew little about the new publisher. What they did know, they didn't like. He was a crony of the infamous William Randolph Hearst. He had made a fortune in the shady business of providing information to the nation's billion-dollar-a-year racetrack gambling industry. Now, he had bought their paper, the *Philadelphia Inquirer*, the paper of the Republican party, and they found that most upsetting. There was little outcry, however, since the city father had worked for generations at avoiding problems. Their lack of courage was traceable at least as far back as 1859, when the city's leaders had refused to allow John Brown's body to be buried there for fear of riots.

Moses' new publishing venture, however, met a much louder complaint nationally. No less prestigious a publication than *The Nation* commented that the takeover was a "matter of first-class journalistic interest" to the country as a whole. "In the past, Annenberg has often acted as the 'dummy' for Hearst in the acquisition of newspapers where Hearst influence was to be kept surreptitious," the magazine warned.

The *Inquirer* was 107 years old, and over the years it had absorbed five other newspapers. The paper had supported Andrew Jackson's

Democratic administration, but had broken with him in the 1830s, when he fought with the Bank of the United States, which he found too powerful. Since then the newspaper cast about aimlessly for an editorial position. The *Inquirer* supported the liberal Whigs, for instance, and when Abraham Lincoln ran for the Presidency it gave him its halfhearted backing. The *Inquirer*'s history of firm adherence to Republicanism had begun only when the guns at Fort Sumter opened the Civil War. By the 1930s, the newspaper had a national reputation as the "Bible of the Republican Party."

What everyone overlooked about the *Inquirer*, which had taken on the characteristic of a family heirloom as far as the Establishment was concerned, was that it took a great deal of money to buy a newspaper, and, in the *Inquirer*'s case, it took someone who was willing to gamble. The paper's recent history was less than spectacular, being marked by steadily eroding circulation, advertising and quality. Beyond its respectability, the *Inquirer* didn't have too much to offer.

The sorry state of affairs, however, was relatively recent. Until 1929, the *Inquirer* had prospered under the hand of Colonel James Elverson, Jr., who had inherited it from his father, who in the nineteenth century had made a fortune publishing thrillers. The colonel himself derived his rank from membership in the First City Troop, a Philadelphia institution that was served from generation to generation by the city's best families. Referred to locally as "The Troop," the garrison dated back to 1774 and was older than any regiment in the United States Army.

A rogue of sorts, the colonel liked fine whiskey and pretty women, and he rounded out his life by being a patron of the arts as well as an enthusiastic yachtsman. He maintained two yachts on the Delaware River, one for himself and one for his wife. They lived in a sumptuous apartment in the gleaming white Elverson Building, the soaring tower that had housed the *Inquirer* since 1925. Promptly at seven o'clock each evening the colonel had the first edition of the *Inquirer* sent up to his twelfth-floor apartment, a suite of rooms that was crowded with a mishmash art collection, including five Corots, one of which, "Les Baigneuses des Iles Borromes," had cost him $50,000. He also collected scores of clocks that chimed on the quarter hour and drove everyone else to distraction. When he died on January 21, 1929, at exactly seven-thirty in the morning, his clocks unanimously and melodiously marked the occasion.

Several weeks after the colonel's death, his sixty-six-year-old sister,

Mme. Patenotre arrived in Philadelphia with the forty-year-old Raymond. A great beauty in her debutante days, she had been a belle in New York and Washington as well as in her own city. In Washington, she had met Jules Patenotre, the charming French ambassador. After a proper courtship, they were married at the Elverson home on March 27, 1894. She was twenty-four, and he was forty-nine. Patenotre later was ambassador in Madrid, after which he and his wife retired to France. Their children, Raymond, a journalist, and Constance Yvonne, who became the wife of Count Boni de Castellane, a noted *bon vivant*, were raised as members of one of France's oldest and most distinguished families.

Mme. Patenotre hadn't been back to Philadelphia for ages, and apparently she had forgotten what the city was like. At first she and her son claimed to be delighted with the idea of running a big and powerful newspaper in what they liked to describe as a "quaint" city. But soon, the *Inquirer* became less of a novelty and more of a large, complex and grinding business that had to be tended constantly. They also discovered that Philadelphia wasn't Paris, and before long it was no longer quaint, but "unpleasant." The widow began complaining. She found Philadelphia provincial and lacking in style, and, to her dismay, it was filthy. Her flustered managers and editors didn't know how to appease her, but they tried. A reporter was assigned to write regularly about how the city should be clean. Finally, the Patenotres made reservations aboard a steamer for France, but first they ordered a multitude of cost-cutting measures at the *Inquirer*, including trimming back everything from pencils to employees, especially the latter. They arranged to have a check for $25,000 mailed to them each week out of the newspaper's profits. The check was sent regularly, but the cost was greater than money. The paper's quality began slipping and many people stopped buying it. Once that happened, advertising linage tumbled.

There was another problem. The *Inquirer*'s top-echelon editors, who themselves were men of means, were out of touch with what was happening both in the nation and on their doorstep. The 1920s had been measured for newspapers in a series of sensational stories, such as Charles Lindbergh's solo flight across the Atlantic and the myriad effects of Prohibition on society. Such stories were obvious and easy to cover. But after the stock-market crash of 1929, troubled readers wanted to know about the Depression, which was putting so many people out of work and posing so many monumental problems. The

Inquirer's editors chose to ignore the day's bleak economic news. The paper made no mention of unemployment statistics. The genteel editors didn't even allow the word *depression* mentioned in print. If a Philadelphia firm went bankrupt, the fact wasn't published—such news might be upsetting. The editors formulated their blind policy as they lunched together every day at the Union League, a bastion of Philadelphia conservatism. Over their roast beef, they continually reassured themselves that it was best to keep bad tidings out of the paper. Besides, they couldn't quite understand what was happening. When the city's banks began failing, however, they finally were forced to break their silence. The news was printed in the back pages, along with stock-market quotations.

About a year after fleeing Philadelphia, the Patenotres sold the *Inquirer* for ten million dollars to the Curtis-Martin Corporation, which owned two other local papers, the *Public Ledger* and the *Evening Ledger*. The acquiring company derived its name from its two principals: Cyrus M. K. Curtis, who owned the *Saturday Evening. Post* and the *Ladies Home Journal,* and his son-in-law, John C. Martin, a former ink salesman who managed the Curtis newspaper business. Shortly after the transaction was completed, however, Martin began having financial problems, and the paper reverted again to the Patenotres. The paper's gradual decline that began when the widow and her son took over not only continued, but worsened.

Moses knew the *Inquirer*'s recent history of misfortunes—which were common gossip in the industry—but he knew that such problems could be solved with money and imagination, and he had more than enough of both. The figure widely quoted as the purchase price was fifteen million dollars, which newspapers elsewhere reported he had nonchalantly paid in cash at the height of the Depression much the way other men paid two cents for their morning papers. The actual price was far less, about nine million dollars, only four million of which was cash, while the rest was notes. But Moses was never one to disabuse the myth that he was far wealthier than he was.

If most Philadelphians' knowledge of Moses was sketchy at best, there was one man who knew enough about him to fear for the future. He was J. David Stern, the tough little editor of the *Philadelphia Record,* which was a rival of the *Inquirer.* Stern was trying to build his own publishing empire, having acquired the *New York Post* in 1933 from the Curtis estate for two and a half million dollars in notes, and he had the *Morning Post,* a newspaper published across the Delaware River in Camden, New Jersey. Unfortunately for Stern, Moses couldn't have come along at a worse time. Stern was beginning to get the *New York Post* on its feet financially, and the Camden paper's losses had been trimmed to $25,000 a month from that much a week. The prospect of competing with someone with as much money and ability as Moses Annenberg was disheartening. Yet when Bernard F. Gimbel, a friend of Stern and member of the department-store family, alerted him to Moses' move before it became public, Stern tried to sound confident. "Bernie, the bigger they are, the harder they fall," he said.

Nevertheless, the news made him frantic. He contacted the mayor and told him a wild story about Moses coming into town with a hundred gangsters toting machine guns and they were simply going to take over. The alarmed mayor sent the information along to the local office of the F.B.I. pleading for protection, which the agent in charge sensibly ignored. Nonetheless, there is little doubt that Stern was terrified about what was likely to become of his businesses, so he tried to prepare himself for a long siege. On August 1, 1936, he welcomed Moses to town with a blistering attack, the first salvo in what would become the most hard-fought newspaper war in the nation. The battle would enmesh both men stupidly in a political and publishing power struggle from which there could emerge no real victor. The *Record* raked over the new publisher's past, including the strong-arm tactics as far back as turn-of-the-century Chicago, as well as the ruthless rise of Moses' news agencies, racing papers and the race wire.

Stern's assault wasn't confined to his news columns. He took Moses to court shortly after he arrived in town. Stern had learned that a newspaper distributor in nearby Wilmington had been threatened by one of Annenberg's men. Unless the agency was turned over to a man from Chicago, the distributor was told, he would no longer be able to sell the *Inquirer*, a paper that accounted for a high percentage of his sales, especially on Sunday. The distributor told Stern that he had been accused of favoring the *Record*. The *Record*'s publisher believed he had to act quickly before the isolated incident became a pattern whereby distributors everywhere would be afraid to carry his paper, and he would be forced to set up his own extremely expensive distribution network. When the case came to trial, Stern was represented by Daniel J. Lowenthal, an aggressive, red-haired young lawyer, but all the drama was exuded by Moses' attorney, a hot-headed, handsome lawyer named Richardson Dilworth. Though a prominent socialite,

Dilworth was a decorated Marine during World War I and a tough man in the courtroom. He stormed through the proceeding, interrupting both Lowenthal and the judge so often that he was cited for contempt and fined a hundred dollars. Though Dilworth lost, Moses liked his spirit and he retained him as general counsel for his paper at a fee of fifty thousand dollars a year.

Despite his victory in the courtroom, Stern turned to other resources to help him beat back the threat posed by his new competitor. He called his friend Franklin Roosevelt at the White House and asked again for F.B.I. agents to help him, because he had reports that hoodlums from Chicago were in the city to see that more than the usual number of *Inquirers* were sold. Stern had hired a Chicago detective agency to identify any of that city's strong-arm men who came to Philadelphia and who were known to be part of Annenberg's organization. For safety's sake, he also had the Democratic governor send a squad of state troopers to look after the new circulation men, but there wasn't any trouble.

Stern wasn't the only man in town fretting about what Moses' hand on the *Inquirer*'s helm would mean. Another was Eli Zachary Dimitman, the *Inquirer*'s city editor, who was seriously thinking about quitting the paper and moving either to Chicago or New York where there were the kinds of exciting papers that he believed were the heart and soul of the news business. Under the Patenotres, he bitterly brooded, the *Inquirer* wasn't worth the newsprint it was printed on, and after he had learned that Moe Annenberg, the race-wire king, had bought the paper, he figured the situation had only worsened. The once mighty *Inquirer*, which had had such complete coverage of the Civil War that battlefield officers on either side read it to keep track of enemy movements and whose thoughtful editorials had been widely respected, was just about dead now, Dimitman believed.

Yet, Dimitman was ever willing to give any publisher a chance. A tall, thin man with a sandy-colored mustache, Dimitman had a reputation in Philadelphia for being able to publish any kind of paper any kind of publisher desired. If sex and crime were on the agenda, Dimitman splashed it excitingly across page one, or he could just as easily whip out a classy paper that had serious stories and a stolid look. He had spent more than twenty years bouncing around Philadelphia's newspapers, and his insular travels had given him a newsman's cynicism taken to the extreme. "If the *Daily Worker* paid me more than I'm getting, I'd work for the Reds," he told friends. They believed him; they also thought he would make the *Worker* a hell of a paper if he ever did. Dimitman had done it all, or so he thought.

Dimitman's first encounter with the new publisher came after he was suddenly recalled from a vacation when the news broke that Moses had bought the paper. When he got back into town, "E.Z.," or "Dimmy," as he was also known, was summoned immediately to the new publisher's office. Moses and Dimitman eyed each other for a moment. They had the same stringy build and were about the same height. Both radiated the same cynicism that each couldn't help noticing in the other.

"Sit down," Moses said, without introducing himself or making small talk. "How many editors and reporters does the paper have?"

"About fifty," Dimitman replied.

"Do you need more?"

Dimitman hesitated before answering. Cannily, he doubled the number he hoped he might get because he assumed the publisher would cut the figure in half. "Six or eight," he finally replied.

"Hire twenty," Moses said, dismissing him with the same brusqueness with which he began questioning him.

Dimitman didn't see Moses again for two weeks, because the publisher had gone to Chicago to attend to other business, but as soon as Annenberg returned he summoned Dimitman again. "How many men did you hire?" he asked.

The editor, who had been used to the dispiriting business of firing people whenever new cost-cutting measures came from the Patenotres, had been reluctant to hire too many people, thinking the new publisher would change his mind when he realized how much they were costing. He quickly realized his mistake.

"I got five men," he said.

Moses looked at him sharply and exploded: "When I give you an order, God damn it, I want it carried out. If you don't, I'll find someone who will. You aren't paid to second-guess me, but to do what I want. Now you son of a bitch, get those men!"

Dimitman was shaken, but he was also elated. Annenberg meant what he said, and the *Inquirer* was to be a newspaper again. The city editor got on the telephone and began calling friends around town. "We've got a publisher who wants to put out the hottest paper in town," he told them. "Come over and work for me while you still can." He got his men.

Under Moses, as usual, the pace quickened. Several weeks after settling in, he called all his editors together and laid out the principles that he said would guide the paper. Always a sentimental man who identified with the poor and downtrodden, Moses looked upon the *Inquirer* almost as his redemption. He wanted the paper to be a reflection of him in one of the roles he envisioned for himself, the protector of the community. "A paper is not living up to its real power in the community unless it does something," he told the editors. "I want the *Inquirer* to be the eyes and the voice and, if need be, the good hard fists of the citizens of Philadelphia and Pennsylvania." The words conveyed his quest for power and respect. Like Hearst, he was certain of his vision of the world and he cared little about the means that it took to impose that vision.

To alert the citizenry to his aims, he placed a signed editorial on the front page:

THE INQUIRER'S PLATFORM

To print the news accurately and fearlessly but never to be content with merely printing the news; to strive always to uphold the principles of our American democracy, to war relentlessly against alien "isms," to fight intolerance, to be the friend and defender of those who are persecuted and oppressed; to demand equal justice for employer and employed; to work for the advancement of industry in the Delaware Valley and Pennsylvania; to oppose political hypocrisy and corruption; to fight and never cease fighting to maintain the sanctity of personal liberty and the inviolability of human rights.

Once again, Moses believed every word that he had written. He had always instilled within his son that the United States was the greatest nation in the world and he also believed in a strong press that fought for the little fellow. As always, however, his vision was askew. The America of his dreams had little to do with the pragmatic, brutal ways in which he had made his money, but he never perceived this to be the case.

One fact was certain, however. Under Moses' strong hand, the *Inquirer* was humming as never before. He increased the space devoted to news coverage by four pages. Columnists and comics were added. Promotions, contests and give-aways, such as free clocks to subscribers, began boosting circulation. He pumped $25,000 a week into promotion, and he even thought of cutting the price of the paper from two cents to one cent, on the Hearstian theory that people will buy a cheaper paper. And his promotional stunts were marvelously creative. For instance, a young reporter was sent up in a plane to drop coupons that were redeemable at Philadelphia stores when matched with a coupon in the *Inquirer*. The plane buzzed schoolyards, ball fields and the city's neighborhoods while the reporter and pilot laughed themselves sick as they filled the sky with the little coupon-bearing parachutes.

Everyone soon realized that Moses wasn't going to allow his paper to be second-best to any in the city, and one reason was that he wanted to show up J. David Stern. The respectability that he hoped to achieve was constantly being called into question by Stern, who never missed an opportunity to blacken him with the tar of his old Chicago days or underworld ties. Moses vowed revenge upon Stern and anyone who supported him.

While traveling to New York one day, he spotted on the train Albert Greenfield, a tough little millionaire who had his hand in a dozen businesses around Philadelphia. He was also a major contributor to the Democratic party and a backer of Stern. When he noticed Greenfield, Moses put down his newspaper, approached and shook his hand while introducing himself. "You're a son of a bitch, Greenfield, but you're my kind of son of a bitch and I wish you were with me and not with Stern," he said, before abruptly returning to his seat, leaving the bewildered Greenfield wondering whether to be pleased or mad. Several days later, Moses made a point of asking Greenfield to lunch. The meal was quite pleasant, and the two men found a lot to talk about, unexpectedly—at least on Greenfield's part—finding that they enjoyed each other's company. When the meal ended, Moses stood up and shook the little tycoon's hand for the last time. "I like you, Al, but you're financing Dave Stern," he said coolly. "I've got to destroy you to destroy Stern."

Greenfield shortly found out what such a threat meant. The *Inquirer* began a series of articles that examined his Banker's Trust Company with the kind of intensity the little, potbellied entrepreneur could hardly withstand. In 1930, for instance, his bank had closed its doors, leaving 135,000 depositors' accounts wiped out; Greenfield had had to post an armed guard at his children's Christmas party that year. While Greenfield's financial resources weren't harmed by the notoriety he received in the *Inquirer*, Stern was in a very different and much more precarious position. The competition was forcing him to spend money he could ill afford. The anxiety he suffered, needless to say, was part of Moses' game plan. "I can lose five dollars to Stern's one dollar," he said, again drawing upon his lessons learned from Hearst.

Moses, however, took a much more active interest in all phases of his newspaper than Hearst ever did. Whereas Hearst mainly pored over the editorial content of his publications, Moses looked after everything, especially circulation, which he knew to be the key to success. He visited newsstands in different locations each evening, buying a paper at each stop and not telling the newsboy which paper he wanted. If he was handed an *Inquirer*, the boy received five dollars and was told to keep the change. Word spread quickly. Soon, whenever anyone asked for a paper without specifying which one he wanted, the chances were that he received an *Inquirer*. He also rode delivery trucks to see how the system might be improved, and sometimes deliverymen found him waiting on street corners along with newsboys so that he could see for himself that the papers were delivered on time. There was no way he would be beaten.

To give circulation a major but artificial jump, Moses told Dimitman that he wanted to publish an *Inquirer* "predate," a Hearst term for a newspaper dated Sunday but actually printed much earlier in the week. It was sent to cities and remote towns across the country so that it could be dated Sunday and give the appearance of being a circulation marvel because it had somehow arrived on Sunday. Besides being a prestige item that displayed a paper everywhere across the country, the predate helped advertising, because rates were pegged to the circulation. Dimitman was given the assignment of creating the special edition on a Wednesday, and he assumed he had time in which to think about what was needed. On Friday night, just two days later, Moses asked him, "Do you have my proofs?"

"What proofs?" Dimitman asked.

"Of the predate," Moses said. "We go to press Monday night."

The city editor rushed out, grabbed three of the paper's most facile writers, moved a desk into a corner and went to work outlining stories and laying out the paper. Annenberg found the proofs on his desk Monday morning. "Never a dull moment with Annenberg around, is there?" the publisher said as he strode through the city room.

When the predate appeared, several editors thought the new edition should have an in-house name to separate it from the other editions. After a few seconds, Annenberg suggested the title. "Jack Rabbit," he said with a sly grin. Until the newsprint shortages that developed during the Second World War, the edition, with the aid of Moses' network of news agencies, was sold in every state as well as in Canada and Alaska. Its total circulation reached 300,000. The *Inquirer*'s Sunday circulation topped a hefty one million.

Moses' ideas for boosting sales weren't simply tied to how to get more papers onto the street more quickly. Routinely, he attended editorial conferences and gave editors ideas for stories. Most often, his stories centered upon the injustices little people suffered. "We've got to do something about this!" he would exclaim.

One day he approached Dimitman. "Do you know how much pawnbrokers charge those poor unfortunates who have to patronize them around town?" he asked in outrage.

The editor was at a loss.

"Well, I do know," Annenberg said. "It's at least 60 percent a year."

As other editors gathered around, Moses painted a vivid and depressing verbal portrait of incredibly poor families pawning their last possessions, even their clothes, in order to pay their rent or buy food. The story had been done a hundred times by the Hearst papers, but Moses had his Philadelphia editors near tears as they listened for the first time to the heart-rending tale. When he ended his spiel, Moses called pawnbrokers a "bunch of sons of bitches who would sell their mothers." He demanded something done about the situation in Pennsylvania, where laws were so weighted in favor of the pawnbrokers that some were selling items pawned to them for nearly 300 percent more than what they had paid the owners. Never at a loss about how to make a good story even better, Moses suggested the kind of photograph to illustrate the situation. He wanted to depict an aged, worn woman wearing a dated, long black dress, much like those his immigrant mother wore when he was a child. The woman was to clutch a black shawl about her as she furtively emerged from a pawnshop. Three gold balls hanging over the doorway would be a dead giveaway as to the kind of shop she was leaving, but the word *Pawnbroker* would appear in the photo for less-than-sharp-witted readers.

The following day, the photographer somehow returned with exactly the scene Moses had described. A campaign about the evils of the pawnbroker trade was launched, and the Democratic administration of Governor George H. Earle and the Democratic legislature in Harrisburg were attacked for allowing such an appalling situation to exist. Through his Harrisburg news bureau, Moses introduced a bill that would limit the interest rates for pawnbrokers, who, in turn, established their own vociferous lobby. Stories about floor fights in the

State House and editorial cartoons depicting evil-looking pawnbrokers were placed on the front page. The *Inquirer* turmoil so embarrassed legislators who had originally supported the pawnbrokers that they expediently changed their allegiance. Eventually, the bill passed both houses. Unanimously. The *Inquirer*'s success, however, was far greater than merely ramrodding a bill through the legislature. Moses was getting steeply involved with the Republican party, and he was demonstrating the might of his newspaper's political muscle.

Soon, the *Inquirer* was sponsoring other legislation, which both benefited the people of the Commonwealth and enhanced the paper's reputation for being politically active. Moses, for instance, was disgusted when he found that Pennsylvania's restrictive Blue Laws, which forbade a host of activities on Sunday, such as selling alcoholic beverages or keeping taverns open, included not allowing people to pursue his passionate pastime, fishing. The idea that people who worked all week couldn't indulge in this pleasure outraged him. Besides, he had just paid $100,000 for a 5,000-acre estate on Big Log Tavern Lake, one of the best fishing areas in the Pocono Mountains, and it could easily be reached from Philadelphia. He called the retreat Sunnylands. The *Inquirer* moved quickly to amend the Blue Laws. Stories about poor, fishing-loving workers not being able to enjoy themselves appeared regularly in the paper as well as photographs of unhappy men staring longingly at lakes and streams. Editorials pitifully decrying the situation supplemented the theme. Again faced with the prospect of being branded inhuman by the *Inquirer* unless they agreed with the paper, the legislators amended the laws.

Though at first he seemed tough and forbidding to his employees, Moses quickly came to be regarded as a good-natured, easygoing boss as long as no one did anything to trigger his volatile temper. The fearsome reputation that had preceded him seemed out of character for a man who quickly got to know his employees by name whether they were truck drivers or top executives. Some of his quirks, such as his naturally suspicious nature, even came to be regarded as sources of amusement. Once, for instance, he told an editor, Richard Thornberg, "You had better watch your assistant."

"Why?" asked the editor.

"I called and he said you weren't here," Moses replied.

"But I wasn't," Thornberg protested.

"Yeah, but he shouldn't have told *me* that," Moses said.

Within a short time, Moses had a loyal following among his employees. He had hired a number of former Hearst men, such as Stud Norton, an editor, and John Fitzpatrick, who became his managing editor, but the old *Inquirer* hands enjoyed the paternalistic yet hard-driving atmosphere he created. If men were forced to work overtime, Moses gave them meal money or chits to use in the cafeteria, and just as often, he slipped them a bottle of liquor as a bonus. If a man had a new baby, he sentimentally talked with him about the importance of family and handed him a hundred dollars or more, telling him to "buy something for the most wonderful person in your life." His paternalistic concern was genuine, and he felt his employees to be an extension of his own family. For example, when a young woman named Tessye Flannigan was very ill, he visited her in the hospital, taking her flowers. He was dismayed when he noticed there wasn't a radio in her room to help pass the time. When she said the hospital didn't supply one, Moses left, telling her he would be right back. Though it was Sunday and the Blue Laws closed stores, Moses walked along South Street near the hospital peering in windows until he spotted a storekeeper taking inventory. He banged on the window, explained his mission and Miss Flannigan soon had a radio.

In addition, he developed close ties with a group of his top editors and executives. When the weather was nice, for example, Moses approached John Cummings, rubbed his hands together and asked if the political columnist felt like fishing and the pair would disappear for a day or two to Sunnylands. Of all the men Moses took to, however, his closest friend was E.Z. Dimitman. The two tall, lean, slightly stooped figures strode through the newsroom together discussing the paper, looking like a pair of strange bookends. Recalling that Herbert Bayard Swope had been named executive editor of the *New York World*, the first person in journalism to hold such an office, Moses looked at Dimitman through his gold, wire-frame glasses and matter-of-factly told him, "You're the second." From that day on, Dimitman was executive editor.

After work, the two would visit night spots, such as Benny the Bum or the Walton Roof, frequently taking a couple of the prettier girls from the classified advertising section with them, since the two shared a taste for good-looking women. On such occasions, Moses gave the bandleader ten dollars to play "She's Only a Bird in a Gilded Cage," a sentimental song that brought tears to his eyes. Once in a while, Walter accompanied them, but the elegantly attired young Annenberg was retiring on such occasions, as though visiting the establishments was a duty and he was trying to please his father. To Dimitman and most of the *Inquirer*'s newsmen, Walter was out of place in the rough-mannered world of newspapers. The excitement that flowed from his father was missing.

Walter lived in an elegant apartment in the Rittenhouse Plaza, a preserve of the city's old wealth. His bachelor suite, decorated by Terrence Robsjohn-Gibbings, who catered to society people, was done in tasteful shades of beige and pink. Unlike his father, who often said he "wouldn't give a dollar for all the Old Masters in New York's Metropolitan Museum," Walter had several fine paintings and, unlike his father, Walter was well known in café society. But while Walter's life moved along pleasantly enough in a social sense, and he had as much money and material comforts as he wanted, his work situation left much to be desired. There was a hesitancy about him when he was around his father, the look of a man who wasn't living up to expectations. Though Moses included his son in business meetings, he never gave him any real authority. When they moved to Philadelphia, Walter was nearly thirty years old, but most of the *Inquirer*'s employees thought he had just graduated from college, because he seemed so immature. Such an impression was only reinforced by the way Moses offhandedly treated suggestions his son made. The most common response from the father was a casual dismissal, while at other times, when something Walter said provoked him, Moses glared and told him, "Oh, shut up!"

Moses was sometimes irked, perhaps, because Walter's ideas seemed to criticize what he himself had always stood for. His son was as concerned about quality as he was about quantity, and Moses' years of experience had, in his own mind, convinced him that he knew what would sell. Thus, whenever Walter was brimming over with ideas, there was no one who listened to him, least of all his father. He tried out his own ideas from time to time, however, and often as not he met with failure. Moses, for instance, decided to redesign the *Inquirer*'s Sunday magazine, *Picture Parade*, so that it could compete with Hearst's *American Weekly*, which was bought as a Sunday supplement by hundreds of newspapers. In the process of revamping the publication, Walter tried to give it tone by calling for a photographic series on the world's greatest waterfalls, a picture of the Taj Mahal, and a collection of bird prints by the naturalist painter John J. Audubon. When Moses looked at the layout, he was scornful. "Audubon! What the hell did he ever do for the circulation?" he demanded.

In place of the layout, Moses ordered a series of photos on the butchering of a cow by a rabbi, which graphically traced the ritual from the first incision. With great reluctance, he dropped his notion that the spread should be in color.

On occasion, Moses yelled at his son while editors and reporters averted their eyes so they wouldn't have to witness the scene. Moses, dismayed at what he considered Walter's too-refined taste, seemed to think that if he yelled at his boy loudly enough, he could clear his head of nonsense. Other times, he simply delighted in taking him down a peg, a trait he didn't restrict to his son. One night, for example, Walter, who was dressed in evening clothes for a night on the town, stopped by his father's office before leaving. Moses looked at his smart attire and said, "Don't ever forget. When I was a newsboy, I used to get whores for swells like you for a five-dollar tip."

Walter stared at his father for a moment and then broke into laughter, which Moses joined. Beneath the surface annoyance, Walter knew that his father always had his best interests at heart. As always, Walter was in awe of his father; he was amazed at the ease by which his dad dealt with men of every stripe and deftly handled businesses of every kind. He wished he could be more like him. He knew he had his father's love; he wished he could gain his respect.

Away from the office, however, Walter was different from the indecisive young executive he was during the day. He was in command of social situations and he generated his own high-voltage energy that was focused primarily on enjoying life. For instance, he delighted in showing wealthy Philadelphia friends, such as Hope and Edgar Scott, a socially prominent couple, a side of life they had never been exposed to. When Ethel Merman was appearing in town, Walter took the Scotts to see her and they were charmed to meet a show-business personality, and it was obvious that the entertainer was crazy about Walter.

Shortly after he came to Philadelphia, however, Walter knew that his gay bachelor days were over. One evening at a New York nightclub, he saw an acquaintance, Sonny Werblin, the head of the Music Corporation of America, sitting with a beautiful, honey-haired young woman. Walter danced by Werblin's table at least twenty times pointedly saying, "Hello, Sonny," in an unsuccessful effort to meet Werblin's date. Werblin, however, was serious about the girl, and the last thing he wanted was competition from a young, good-looking millionaire. However, the next day, Walter continued his campaign to meet the girl. He bet Rhea Levy, a friend, one hundred dollars that she couldn't learn the identity of Werblin's date. Within hours, she was back for the money. The girl was a Toronto debutante, Veronica "Ronny" Dunkelman, the daughter of one of the most successful merchants in the British Empire. Walter gladly paid off. As he had explained to his sister Jan, who had been with him the night before, "that's the girl I'm going to marry."

The same week, Walter arranged to meet Ronny Dunkelman through friends. When he managed to be alone with her, he presumptuously said, "You are going to be calling me a lot." For her part, Ronny believed he was quite mad. She had never called a man in her life. When he asked her out for the following Friday, she coolly turned him down, explaining that she was spending the weekend at Princeton. For the next several days, however, Walter remained on her mind. Though she was never sure why, she canceled her weekend and sent him a telegram telling him she was free. The only conclusion she could come to was that there was an excitement about young Annenberg that she didn't find in other men. But she was appalled when they ran into mutual friends on their first date and she heard Walter telling them in a stage whisper, "This is the girl I'm going to marry in June."

Their courtship happened so quickly, Ronny hardly had time to think. Before she realized it, they were planning to be married in June. Walter immediately struck it off with her family, especially her father, who had ingeniously made a fortune by selling men's suits at one price—$14—under the label Tip Top Tailors, the first company in Canada to sell ready-made suits. Both Sadie and Moses liked Ronny as well. The girl was immediately attracted to Walter's gentle mother, but she was in awe of his father. On their first encounter, Moses looked at her long and thoughtfully. "You know," he said, "I like you. What can I buy you?"

Moses was always giving extravagant gifts to his wife and children as a measure of his love. He showered Sadie with furs and jewelry, and sometimes he did it just to quiet her down. Once, after losing $150,000 while gambling, Moses found little peace from Sadie, who told him what a wastrel he was. Finally, her complaints subsided after he bought her $150,000 worth of jewelry.

A man who lived for the moment, Moses was as willing to spend a fortune testing a new idea as he was to throw money away on gambling or presents. One day while striding through the building he stopped each executive or editor he saw. "Boy have I got an idea," he said. Swearing each to secrecy, he whispered something. Finally, he grabbed Dimitman, exacting the same oath of silence from him. The idea he excitedly outlined was for a photography magazine.

At the time, there were more than a dozen picture magazines on newsstands. At least three of them, *Pic*, *Focus*, and *See*, each had a circulation of a half million and were sensational publications depending upon sex and crime as their mainstay. Two others, *Life* and *Look*, had circulations of more than 1.5 million each and catered to broader tastes. Moses thought it wouldn't cost too much to compete. He intended to cannibalize *Picture Parade*, the *Inquirer*'s Sunday magazine, and put its best pictures from four weekly issues into a monthly magazine. The new product would be distributed nationally and he already had a title for it, *Click*. As always, he wanted to catch the public's attention.

The first issue of *Click* appeared in February 1938, and it set the tone for a periodical that dealt with Peeping Toms, white slavery, and such oddities as a sexy woman lion tamer. Early covers were pictures of beautiful actresses, including Norma Shearer and Hedy Lamarr. Soon, *Click* had an enormous audience, nearly 1.5 million, and was only slightly behind *Life* and *Look* in circulation. The magazine, however, quickly ran into problems. With a nonchalant attitude toward divorce, drinking and sex, *Click* outraged moralists. A typical cartoon showed a newly divorced woman in Reno saying, "Boy, do I feel like a new man." Another showed a lady telling a bartender, "Make that a double martini—I'm starved." Daring articles such as "A Bellboy Learns About Life, But His Classes Are Never Dull," which showed a bellboy helping a woman bathe, didn't sit well with such institutions as the Catholic Church, which condemned it, or the Canadian government, which banned the sale of it.

Worried that Democrats in the state might try to discredit him with *Click*, Moses decided to revise the magazine. Walter wanted to kill it. Disregarding his son, Moses told Emile Gauvreau, the editor of the *Inquirer* Sunday magazine, to tone it down. One of the editor's first acts was to try to reproduce a photographic essay on the art collection of Philadelphia millionaire Joseph E. Widener, whose collection of Rembrandts, Titians, Gainsboroughs and other masterpieces hadn't been seen by the public. Moses killed the Widener spread. Unknown to Gauvreau, he was the same Widener who years earlier had forced Moses to float a balloon over Hialeah racetrack for information for the race wire. Nonetheless, Gauvreau, an old pro, turned the magazine into something few could object to. He gave it a staunch patriotic look, featuring articles on Nazi Bund camps, the evils of the Communist movement in the United States, and hyped-up articles on Fifth Column brigades. After delicate negotiations, the Catholic Church dropped its objections to *Click* and the Canadian government did likewise. But the publication never thereafter effectively challenged *Life* or *Look* for leadership in the field.

Meanwhile, Moses' promotional efforts at the *Inquirer* were working. By the fourth quarter of 1937, daily circulation stood at 367,763 compared with 288,000 when Moses had taken on the paper fifteen months earlier. The *Record*'s circulation had dropped to 274,815 from 314,544 during the same period. The Sunday circulation in the quarter topped one million, or a 400,000 gain, while the *Record*'s slipped to 384,000 from 404,000. Moses, despite the increases, didn't relax the competition. More and more promotional contests were used. More news columns were added, and the *Inquirer* came to have the largest selection of comics of any newspaper in the city. Soon the *Inquirer* carried one hundred comic strips in the Sunday paper; to alert readers to the fact, a large number "100" was placed in a circle on the front of the comic section.

For his part, Stern was agonizing over what was happening, and his plight was anxiously watched by top Democrats not just at city and state levels but in Washington as well. His press was among the earliest of Roosevelt supporters and it was squarely behind the New Deal at a time when most newspapers were not. Because of his unique position as a powerful Democratic publisher, Stern was one of the few men in the nation who could simply get an audience with Roosevelt whenever he wished. Thus, while trying to find some solution to the problems he was having with Moses, Stern turned to the White House for help. He was confident of getting a sympathetic ear if only because Moses had kept the *Inquirer* staunchly Republican and was using it to attack the New Deal. At Stern's urging, the Federal Trade Commission was soon investigating the *Inquirer*'s advertising rates to see whether they were truly competitive. But to Moses, such interference seemed petty meddling and he took it in stride. He no longer considered Stern tough competition in any event. By then he realized how precarious the *Record*'s financial position was, and he dismissed Stern entirely as a threat to his newspaper, even if he didn't count him out as a political threat.

Moses' attitude about the *Record*'s being insignificant became obvious when both the *Record* and the *Evening Ledger* were about to raise their prices from two cents to three cents. The other two standard-size papers in town, the *Inquirer* and the *Bulletin,* didn't depend as heavily on circulation revenue for survival, but Moses said he would go along with the other two papers and raise the *Inquirer*'s price. His executives were amazed, saying that here was the opportunity to knock Stern completely out of the running. If the *Inquirer* stayed at two cents, no one would buy the rival. The *Inquirer*'s publisher, however, arrogantly brushed aside such arguments.

"Stern is a whipped puppy," he said. "He can't do any harm now. We can knock him out any time we wish. He might go broke if he doesn't get this added revenue, then we might get a real competitor, one with more money than Stern has. . . . Let him have the extra revenue and piddle along."

CHAPTER

Six

THE GHOSTLY WHITE *Inquirer* building was bathed in the fluttering red glow of flares that exploded in the darkness. Cannons mounted on the sixth-floor terraces of the fifteen-story structure fired every few minutes, the booms rattling windows for blocks around. Blue-uniformed, mounted policemen directed traffic at the busy *Inquirer* corner as a procession of limousines fitfully stopped along Broad Street, discharging formally attired passengers who hurriedly entered the newspaper's front doors. Callowhill Street, the narrow lane along the south side of the building, was clogged with cars as well as the usual delivery trucks, most of which were parked helter-skelter on sidewalks.

The paper was hosting a victory celebration on this evening, May 29, 1938, in honor of Arthur H. James, a Superior Court judge and the newly minted Republican candidate for governor. According to prevailing wisdom, James was sure to win the fall election and the Republican party would once again be in power. There was no more fitting place to celebrate than at the *Philadelphia Inquirer*. The fifth-floor auditorium was jammed with well-wishers. Dance bands were loaned by local nightclub owners, such as Frankie Palumbo and Jack Lynch, a friend of Moses who years earlier had tried to bribe a city detective on behalf of the wire service. But that was a distant memory as laughter flowed as easily as the river of liquor that was provided for the occasion by the owners of night spots, including the Arcadia, the Embassy and the 1523 Club, as well as one of Moses' favorite after-work haunts, Benny the Bum. Top-level *Inquirer* men rubbed shoulders with City Hall politicians, bail bondsmen, tavern

121

owners and the very wealthy, including Pews, Cookes and Wana-
makers.

Two *Inquirer* newsmen took turns manning the microphones at the
head table. Offering an endless litany of testimonials and toasts to the
candidate, they were more flattering to James as the evening revelry
wore on. Entertainment consisted of singers, dancers and comedians,
who were all introduced by the toastmasters, John M. Cummings, the
Inquirer's chief political columnist, and Joseph H. Miller, a dogged,
heavy-set reporter from the Harrisburg bureau. As Moses walked
through the crowd, he was congratulated on all sides. No one doubted
that "Old Button Shoes," as James was derisively known because of
his old-fashioned footwear, could have been nominated without the
support of the rich, powerful publisher.

To accomplish this task, Moses had given three key members of the
newspaper a free hand in helping James, a fainthearted man who
hadn't known where to begin his quest for power. The staffers were
columnist Cummings, whose skillful use of the innuendo was unparalleled in the city, and Joe Miller, whose news stories were often accused
of being two thirds Republican propaganda and one third rumor. The
third man Moses chose was executive editor Dimitman, who kept his
colleagues in check. Dimitman could be counted on to do the job right,
because, unlike the other two, he wasn't emotionally committed to the
task. The trio told James how to act, wrote speeches for him, and told
him what issues to champion. Whenever he spoke, the candidate's remarks were on the *Inquirer*'s front page, even though he was a terrible
orator who never had anything to say. His Democratic opponent,
Pittsburgh Judge Charles Alvin Jones, rarely found his name mentioned in the Philadelphia paper and, on the occasions he did, he
wished he hadn't, because the context was derogatory. To Moses,
throwing the support of his paper and big campaign donations behind
James was bound to have rewards. "The hand that rocks the cradle
will rule the ballot box," he told Dimitman.

Within the less than two years that he had been in Philadelphia,
Moses had found it incredibly easy to assume a position of power and
leadership within the Republican party. Over the years, Philadelphia—once called the "Athens of the New World" because of its vitality and wealth—had grown characterless, trapped as it was between
New York and Washington. Nowhere was its enervation more noticeable than in the power structure, which had no tradition of families

with a sense of public duty, such as the Lodges of Boston, the Roosevelts of New York or the Tafts of Cincinnati. To form a political base, Moses contributed hundreds of thousands of dollars to the G.O.P., and he joined hands with strong-willed Republicans who were determined to gain power. They included Joseph N. Pew, the Sun Oil Company millionaire; Ernest T. Weir, the powerful steel magnate; and Jay Cooke, who had inherited the fortune his father had amassed by floating bonds for the government during the Civil War and raising $100 million to build the Northern Pacific Railroad.

The last man who was part of the inner circle was Joseph N. Grundy, an old tariff lobbyist who headed the Pennsylvania Manufacturers Association, which controlled much of the Republican party outside Philadelphia and Pittsburgh. Yet another wealthy man who threw his lot in with them was Colonel Carl Lewis Estes, a strange, former New Dealer who had a list of aliases and an impressive financial portfolio. He took to traveling with James's campaign under the alias Colonel English, and donned a wig and fake beard in order to infiltrate Democratic party meetings, stealthily returning with strategy reports.

With such help, James toured the state, inveighing against the "wicked socialism" practiced in Washington, especially citing a new institution he found ominous—the U.S. Post Office. As if that weren't enough, he threatened a "drumhead court-martial of the Little New Deal," as the Democratic administration in Harrisburg was known, and he promised to "burn three thousand pages of laws" enacted under Governor George H. Earle.

Knowing that he didn't have much to work with, Moses nonetheless struggled to keep the red-faced judge before the public. One idea, for instance, was a three-page picture spread of James's life for the *Inquirer* Sunday magazine. The judge, who spent as much time getting counsel from Moses as he did campaigning, had worked as a boy in coal mines in Western Pennsylvania. It dawned on Moses that there was a ready parallel between James's hard-working, deprived youth and that of Abraham Lincoln's, and he wanted to illustrate the similarities. The task obviously was a tough one. Finally, someone found an aged photograph of boys picking coal from long chutes and, though the lads had their backs to the camera, the judge's publicity manager picked out one who, he assured everyone, was little Arthur James, aged twelve. Filling out the montage was a picture of James as lieutenant governor and another as president of his Kiwanis Club. When the uninspiring photo spread was shown to Moses, even he recognized the project's futility and canceled it.

On a stronger note, the *Inquirer* printed a comprehensive series, "The Migration of Industry," stating that Pennsylvania was rapidly losing jobs and industry because of tax policies instituted by the Democrats and suggested that ever more harmful levies were in the offing. The devastating impression left was that everything not nailed down in the state would soon slide south of the Mason-Dixon Line to states that didn't have similar tax structures. The man to stem the flow, of course, was Arthur James.

The Democrats retaliated, but instead of going after James, the target was the man behind him, Moses Annenberg. Stern's *Record* began referring to Moses as the new "big boss of the Republican Party," and on one occasion the *Record* reported what was reputed to be private conversations held by Moses. The man with such alleged information was Albert Greenfield, who told the *Record* about Moses' supposed Machiavellian designs for the future: "Next, I must get my man James elected Governor. I sold James to the Republican leaders and he will have to follow my bidding, because after I get him elected I have big things in store for him. While he is governor he can appoint some judges for me. We Republicans are strong for judges. They control the Constitution and that gives us control over everything. With Pennsylvania turned into the Annenberg column and labeled Republican, I can start work on New York and Illinois, where I know the ropes, and, in a few years, control the Republican national organization. It is badly in need of money and brains, of both of which I have more than I can use in this sleepy town. Thus I will nominate a Republican President and put him over and then I will really have something."

Greenfield ended his diatribe stating, "There it is. The American plan for Moe Hitler-Annenberg. He has taken a lesson from Europe." Though the vindictive blast was undoubtedly made up, people who knew Moses still had moments of doubt. He did have a tendency to talk that way at times.

Sometimes Moses was infuriated by such attacks. Other times, he looked wearily at his executives and said with a sigh, "Such are the penalties of wealth and position." His son, Walter, was dismayed at the mud slinging and wished his father wouldn't stoop to Stern's level. But, like Hearst, Moses loved a good newspaper brawl.

The Democrats were exceedingly worried about Moses in particular, because his *Inquirer*'s active political support and his own huge donations threatened to undo the tentative gains they had made so recently. In 1933, for instance, Democrats had won four top municipal offices in Pennsylvania and ten magisterial posts. Then the first Democratic governor in forty-four years was elected, and Joseph F. Guffey, a powerful political boss, became the first Democrat elected to the United States Senate since 1875. Much of the party's resurgence in Pennsylvania had to do with Roosevelt's popularity, so its members turned to the White House for aid in trying to keep the political grounds they had taken.

The first visible sign that the White House was willing to treat Moses as a serious political threat came in April 1938, when Senator Sherman Minton, at Roosevelt's behest, attacked Moses from the Senate floor because of his criticism of the New Deal. There were at the time forty million newspapers sold in the nation, and fewer than 10 percent of them treated the President or his policies favorably. The Administration felt it was a dangerous situation at a time when public confidence in government was deemed essential. Only Annenberg, of all the country's publishers, however, was mentioned by name and it was an ominous sign.

Moses responded on April 30 with a lengthy editorial entitled "The New Dealers Can't Muzzle the Inquirer," which stated, in part, with respect to the Democrats in Washington, "For a considerable time they have been whimpering and writhing under the lash of just editorial criticism that has followed their arrogant actions and their inflammatory speeches." For the first time in his life, however, Moses had grossly underestimated a situation that could harm him. He seemed to think he could fling editorial words back at the government much the way he did at David Stern and that would be the end of the matter until the next round of diatribes erupted. Unknown to him, he had already lost. The government began checking into his income taxes in earnest, and as he stepped up his editorial attacks on both the New Deal and the Earle Administration, Roosevelt's cabinet ministers became more adamant about demanding updates on the progress of what was now known as the "Annenberg case." He was irritating a group of as yet hidden enemies, and at least one of them, Henry Morgenthau, Jr., the President's friend and Secretary of the Treasury, found his preoccupation with Annenberg almost an obsession. He wanted to put Moses behind bars.

Statewide, Moses became the focal point of the gubernatorial election. Congressman Michael J. Bradley, who was running for reelection on the Democratic ticket, for instance, summarized the situation by saying the contest was between "the Roosevelt candidate and the Annenberg candidate." Senator Guffey escalated the drama of the race by trying to rally Pennsylvania Democrats with a stirring radio broadcast in which he campaigned on three issues: the New Deal, corrupt Republican judges and Moses Annenberg. Guffey had a particular ax to grind in that he had been embarrassed by the *Inquirer*'s handling of his being called before a Republican-instigated grand jury investigating state politics, and he never forgave the publisher. His broadcast stated that Annenberg's wealth was "largely derived from poolroom rackets" and that he was using his money to buy great political power. "There are some things money can buy," Guffey concluded. "It can buy newspapers and it can buy judges, but it can't buy the governorship of Pennsylvania for your hand-picked candidate Arthur H. James."

Moses responded with a half-million-dollar libel suit against the Senator. Others named were Samuel R. Rosenbaum, vice-president of Albert M. Greenfield & Company in his capacity as president of WFIL, the Philadelphia radio station that had aired the attack, and David Stern, whose newspaper had printed the speech in full.

The feud with Stern had heated up to the point where each publisher routinely wrote hyperbolic editorials slamming the other; newspapering in Philadelphia had never seen anything like it before. On October 18, 1938, for example, Moses wrote a signed message to his readers: "I am proud of the enemies I have made. . . . Political skunks can wear themselves out if they wish, airing their poison gas at me, but I shall continue to do my duty as I see it." The same day, Stern had a similar signed diatribe: "Is the underworld to govern Pennsylvania? . . . The Republican Party of Pennsylvania is controlled by men who are either of the underworld or traffic with the underworld, or who can derive their income from the underworld." There was such acrimony between the men that local and national Jewish leaders, who were embarrassed by the public spectacle of two publishers of Jewish background going after each other in such unseemly fashion at a time of Nazi persecution of Jews, tried to settle the dispute or at least smooth it over to some degree. Stern brushed aside their pleas for propriety, and Moses found their interference intolerable. "Religion is a racket," he told one group that approached him.

Greenfield wasn't taking a back seat in the political turmoil either.

Nicknamed "the Egg" because of his bald head, and also known as "Mr. Philadelphia" because he wielded so much economic and political power, he spoke out against Moses whenever the opportunity arose. His favorite theme was that Moses was like a European dictator. One of his eloquent addresses, for example, noted that

> We have with us in Philadelphia a self-appointed evangelist of power. His greed for recognition and dictatorship is his ruling passion. He is ready to cut down and destroy everything that stands in his way. It will be interesting to see how far the easy going good nature of American people will tolerate his utter perversion of our American creed of fair play, free expression, good sportsmanship and common decency. The man is Moe Annenberg.

The address was aired over two local radio stations, KYW and WFIL. Once again, Moses filed suits against Greenfield and the station managers and Stern, who, of course, had printed the speech in full.

Moses, however, faced a more serious problem. The Democratic Administration in Harrisburg was trying to harm him where he was weakest, the Nationwide News Service. The state legislature formed a group called the Thompson Commission, after its chairman Edward J. Thompson, which was intended to "study and report on the use of devices and methods of transmission of information of gambling." The type of gambling being examined was betting on horses and the transmission method, naturally, was Moses' wire.

All told, the commission took 1,300 pages of testimony from eighty-one witnesses, and a lot of unsavory information about Moses was given to the press. Men who had once worked for the organization gave evidence against Moses, including Hartley, the former *Tribune* editor-lobbyist who had had a falling out with his former boss. Another was Kelly, the Philadelphia wire man who had worked with the General News Bureau and who claimed to have been coerced into doing so. The damning testimony characterized Moses as a ruthless racketeer whose control was nationwide. When reading such accounts, Moses' son refused to believe them. He preferred to think that the witnesses were liars, who had greatly embellished some mildly rough tactics some of his father's men might have engaged in. Nonetheless, he was embarrassed by the whole business, because he was convinced that many people wanted to believe such stories out of resentment or jealousy.

As November 8, election day, neared, the exchanges between the *Record* and the *Inquirer* became more heated. The election no longer seemed to be a contest between two judges; it appeared to be a vindictive fight between rival newspapers and between Franklin Roosevelt and Moses Annenberg. The Democrats were particularly worried because Annenberg's candidate seemed to have more public support than theirs did. Part of the problem—a large part of it—was George Earle. The Democratic Governor had turned out to be pretty much a playboy who didn't take his job seriously and couldn't see projects through. At one time he had superficially looked like such a good politician that there was talk about his running for President after Roosevelt, but now the New Dealers hoped to get him out of office without a scandal breaking first. His government was as corrupt as the Republican administration it had replaced, and everyone knew it. Washington columnist Joseph Alsop, for instance, had already referred to Earle's years of "really nauseous government." Moreover, there were rumblings that Earle might be in trouble over some money. All of that was hurting the Democratic candidate.

On the eve of the election, the Roosevelt team decided to take bold action. The tax case against Moses was moving with glacierlike slowness, so that couldn't be used as an issue. But Moses' past could be, as Guffey had already shown. The cabinet decided that Harold L. Ickes, Secretary of the Interior and a Pennsylvanian, should go to Philadelphia and deliver a brutal attack on the *Inquirer* publisher. Perhaps, they thought, the loftiness of Ickes' office and the toughness of the speech would turn the tide in their favor.

On November 5, just three days before the election, Ickes had lunch with Morgenthau and they discussed the matter. "No matter how bad I am on Annenberg, can I libel him?" Ickes asked the Treasury Secretary.

"No, go the limit, you can't libel him," Morgenthau reassured him.

Morgenthau was already devising another way he could get at the Philadelphia publisher. After talking with Elmer Irey, the Internal Revenue Service agent who was heading the investigation of Moses' taxes, Morgenthau had decided to have the President, immediately after the gubernatorial election, appoint a special United States Attorney to the case as a way of speeding it up. He had mentioned his plans to destroy Annenberg to Herman Oliphant, Roosevelt's administrative aide, shortly before the lunch with Ickes.

That evening, Ickes, an eloquent orator, delivered a radio broadcast in Philadelphia that went across the state. It was titled "The Curse of Two Cities" and it was a no-holds-barred attack on Moses—I "come here to tell Pennsylvanians what I know about Moe Annenberg, the curse of two cities, because the prospects of turning the public contracts of Pennsylvania and the whole law-enforcement machinery of the state over to a man with the record of Moe Annenberg is the most alarming thing that has ever threatened my native state . . ." His voice dripping with sarcasm, the cabinet member claimed that he had been contacted by Judge James, who "has informed me by telegram that it is he and not Moe Annenberg, who is running for Governor of Pennsylvania. Tush, tush Judge James—that's only a technicality. Of course you are the candidate. But the point is—whose candidate are you?" Ickes recounted Moses' newspaper days, attributing Max's deeds to him. He spoke of the racing wire and the days in Miami, including quoting from the old *Chicago Tribune* story about impending gang warfare with Jack Lynch: "Gangsters, gang weapons and gang methods will decide the struggle between John J. (Jack) Lynch, veteran Chicago gambling boss, and Moe L. Annenberg for control of the vast system that disseminates racing news to the thousands of Chicago handbooks." The speech went on and on. The text of it jumped from the front page of the *Record* to seven full columns inside the paper.

There was a stunned silence at the *Inquirer* the next day, reflecting the fact that there was something awesome about the speech. People everywhere could talk of nothing else, however, and it appeared to be as effective as the New Dealers had hoped it would be. One person on whom it had exactly the opposite effect, though, was Walter Annenberg. To hear his father smeared in such fashion only drew him that much closer to him. He could never repudiate him.

There were now doubts in other people's minds, however, that James would win. The New Deal had played its last card and it was the strongest to date. Only Moses still seemed to think the judge would win. He referred to the attack as a "blow below the belt," but he felt sure that months of groundwork weren't erased overnight. Moreover, the speech had been such a desperate gamble that it might have been perceived by voters as an attempt to distract them from the problems of the Democrat Earle—at least Moses fervently hoped so. He was so confident that he was right that he didn't cancel plans for a victory party similar to the one held in May to celebrate James's getting the nomination.

On November 8, the flares and cannons once again were set off outside the *Inquirer* building. The parade of well-wishers began arriving. From the earliest returns it showed that James not only had won, but that it was a landslide. Nowhere were the festivities greater than in the overcrowded third-floor offices of Moses, who staged the evening's gala event just as many people thought he had staged the election. Reports of election returns were scattered everywhere. The exploding pop of champagne corks rose above the loud talk and laughter of politicians, editors and other men who filled the rooms. They took turns congratulating Moses, who sat at his desk in the midst of the excitement, listening to cheering that filtered down from the fifth-floor auditorium. The somber Victorian landscapes that, in heavy gilt frames, decorated his office walls were out of keeping with the merrymaking. Flushed with victory, he occasionally broke into a mocking laughter and shook his fist down Broad Street in the direction of Stern's *Record*. Whenever he did so, laughter erupted from the men jammed into the rooms. Stern had worked diligently for eight long years in Philadelphia to build a strong newspaper as well as a constituency for the Democratic party. Within the brief two years he had been in the city, Moses had undone much of Stern's political work and undermined the financial stability of his press. In the process, Moses was instrumental in unseating Pennsylvania's "Little New Deal," the first Democratic governorship in forty-four years. He had won.

SEVEN

HENRY MORGENTHAU, JR., met with President Roosevelt in mid-March 1939 to discuss the Moses Annenberg case. The Treasury Secretary was hearing disturbing reports of pressure to back off, and they were coming from unexpected sources—fellow Democrats. Attorney General Frank Murphy, for example, was complaining that high Democratic officials were suggesting that the government ease up on Annenberg. Morgenthau had already devoted considerable time to the case, and he was intrigued by it. The last thing he wanted was to see it slip away.

"Mr. President, what did Frank Murphy mean?" Morgenthau asked.

Roosevelt patiently explained that pleas for leniency had thus far come from several sources, including Mayor Ed Kelly of Chicago and former Governor Earle of Pennsylvania. Kelly's position was easy enough to understand since Moses had been one of his largest financial backers. Earle was a different matter; he represented a time bomb for the New Deal. The former governor was under investigation for unlawfully accepting funds from Matthew McCloskey, a politically active Philadelphia contractor, who received a sizable number of government contracts. Earle feared that Moses, through the *Inquirer*, would make his situation worse, and he had had word that if the government eased up on the publisher, there would be no need for the former governor to be further embarrassed. There was Moses' political power to worry him too.

Former "Governor Earle was afraid that with this new Republican Administration (in Pennsylvania), which Annenberg controls, that he would get a Moscow trial on his own case and go to jail," the President said. "Earle thought if this Administration could settle with Annenberg that, in return for that, Annenberg would see that Earle would not go to jail."

Roosevelt hastened to assure his cabinet member that Earle's concerns were of little consequence and that he was deaf to overtures on Moses' behalf. As much as anything else, Roosevelt was paying off his debt to Stern and his *Record,* but he himself still smarted from the editorial attacks upon him and his policies that had been carried in the *Inquirer.* "I know of no reason why you should not go straight through with this case, Henry, but that is where the pressure is coming from," he said.

Morgenthau could well understand Earle's fears. He had recently seen a confidential memorandum given to the President by William C. Bullitt, the socially prominent Philadelphian who was Roosevelt's ambassador to France. While he was home on leave, Bullitt had received a visit from Moses. Though the publisher insisted that he wanted nothing for himself, Bullitt, being far from naïve, found the encounter unsettling. He wrote a full report on what Moses had said to him, feeling that the President should be made aware of it. Ostensibly, the topic of the conversation was Earle's plight, but it was obvious that Moses knew that there was some sort of federal probe of his activities and that he was using the former governor's situation to hint at whatever might be affecting him.

"As a human being and a father of a family," Moses told Bullitt, he was "extremely sorry that Governor Earle, who has a charming wife and is the father of four fine sons, should find himself in danger of criminal prosecution."

Moses wanted the ambassador to assure the Roosevelt Administration that neither he nor his newspaper had had anything to do with starting the accusations against Earle. The man to blame, he said, was Dave Stern, who was the only person other than the former governor and McCloskey who had known about the money that had changed hands. Knowing that Bullitt would relay the conversation to Roosevelt, Moses cautiously said that he personally saw nothing wrong with Earle's having borrowed money from a friend. As far as he was concerned, the governor was a "well-intentioned 'sucker' who had fallen into the hands of clever and unscrupulous politicians who had used him for their own purposes," Bullitt related.

What the Ambassador found particularly ominous was the sentiment that Moses stated over and over, rephrasing the wording each time he did so. "Annenberg went on to say that he had recently said to the new Governor of Pennsylvania, Judge James, that *'if this transaction were all that Earle were guilty of*,* it was disgraceful to press for an indictment." Moses seemed to be telegraphing a warning that he might have another Earle-related bombshell to drop unless his own case was treated leniently. Otherwise, Moses wanted to assure the President that he had always considered himself a loyal Democrat, despite his recent Republican partisanship. The only reason he had broken with the New Deal, he said, was that he hadn't agreed with the President's handling of striking workers, since he personally felt that the only way to get the country moving again was to force men, who couldn't see how much harm they were causing, to go back to work. Before he left, Moses even told Bullitt that he still "loved the President" and that he intended to make the *Philadelphia Inquirer* an independent newspaper, rather than have it continue as a house organ of Republicanism. He felt bad about the way his rival Stern was able to get the government to turn on him, a course of events that he found most unfair.

The extraordinary encounter only confirmed what Morgenthau already believed. This case was a strange, strange affair—one of the most interesting that he had ever worked on. Sometimes everything clicked into place immediately; other times there was a frustrating slowness in accumulating evidence, and there were times when there seemed to be no evidence at all.

Early attempts by the government to put an end to Moses' wire by going after American Telephone & Telegraph Company, for instance, hadn't worked, because the government had underestimated the utility's profit motive. Since the Nationwide News Service sold its information to bookies, the government had simply asked A.T.&T. to stop providing the race wire with lines. The utility, however, insisted that under the law it had to continue serving Nationwide. The company pointed to a federal law requiring it to service anyone who applied, paid the company's rates, and complied with its regulations. No utility, of course, was bound to provide service for an activity that was illegal, but A.T.&T. executives disclaimed any knowledge that Nationwide customers put it to an illegal purpose. After all, the race wire was A.T.&T.'s fifth-largest customer.

More recently, Morgenthau had a fight with Thurman Arnold, the acting United States Attorney General, who had threatened to dilute

* Author's emphasis.

Morgenthau's case against Annenberg—or at least that was the way Morgenthau chose to perceive it. The disagreement centered on Arnold's wanting to use Morgenthau's grand jury to press an antitrust suit against Moses on the grounds that he had a monopoly on racing-wire information. Morgenthau was infuriated, because he felt that Arnold wanted the jury merely as a fishing expedition, which he believed would jeopardize his own case. When he found out what Arnold wanted, he blew up when talking with William H. McReynolds, an administrative assistant to Roosevelt. "I think it is childish and I think it is crackpot," he snapped. "We have a one hundred percent well-prepared case and because this fellow has a lot of dish water, he wants to dilute our case instead of going it alone."

What Morgenthau didn't realize was that F.B.I. agents had slowly, methodically been gathering evidence that could amount to a strong antitrust action. They had detailed a number of specific incidents whereby strong-arm tactics had been used to build up both the racing paper and the racing-wire business. There was, for example, the case in 1936 of Edward Burg, who had been the Houston, Texas, manager of the *Turf Bulletin*, which had been a rival of an Annenberg publication. A tough man, whose parent company, the Bulletin Record Publishing Company, had once provided racing information to the Capone syndicate, Burg had been summoned to the office of Joe Burns, the brother of Pat Burns and the Houston head of the Annenberg operations. As soon as he had entered, Burg was knocked down and he found Burns standing over him with a gun, accusing him of vandalizing Annenberg property. The last thing he remembered was being forced from a car and hearing the deafening roar of shots being fired. Early the next morning, a milkman making his rounds found Burg, who had been shot five times and left for dead. He had lived to tell his tale.

But Morgenthau would have no part of it. He felt that he already had enough to worry about and he hadn't wanted to take on new complications. Whenever there was a delay or a foulup, which wasn't infrequently, he used the reproach: "The Annenberg case is the biggest criminal case this Administration has ever had, and it was initiated by the President of the United States ..." Sometimes he added, "Now Annenberg is just a plain everyday crook ... the only difference is that he is a rich one."

Invoking the President's name usually had the desired effect, but there were problems at times that seemed insurmountable. Internal

Revenue agents, for example, were having a terrible time figuring out the amount of money that entered and left Moses' enterprises. They daily confronted a bewildering corporate labyrinth unlike anything they had ever encountered before. The racing holdings, magazines and newspapers were in the hands of sixteen corporations. The vast array of real estate, insurance, laundries, liquor stores and theaters he owned were under the auspices of an additional fourteen corporations. Moreover, there were seven other entities listed only as foreign corporations. Trying to unravel Moses' financial affairs was like shooting in the dark.

What appeared obvious to everyone was that Moses kept a separate set of books, a factor that the government agents agreed upon after they were given access to one set when they approached his headquarters on Dearborn Street in Chicago. The agents weren't greeted warmly, but they were given a small room in which to work and they were given cartons and cartons of records to go over. The agents kept encountering signs of fraud, such as smudged records that had been erased and penciled over and what appeared to be dummy stockholders and what could be payroll records of employees who didn't exist. The grueling work went on for months and was inconclusive. Finally, someone learned that there were other records, but they were kept in a garage at Moses' house on Long Island. Frustratingly, the agents could find no way to get them. For a while, they considered pretending to be fire inspectors from an insurance company, but a check revealed that Moses' fire insurance for the Kings Point manor was through an insurance company in which he was a partner. If the agents attempted such a ruse, they would surely be found out. In desperation, they tried questioning servants, but they were loyal, so there was no chance of getting them to open the garage.

Nels Tessem, the I.R.S. agent in charge of studying the books, was at a loss as to what to do. He maintained round-the-clock shifts in the office provided him. He was almost desperate in his eagerness to find something. Tessem was all too aware of the pressure on the case being applied from the very top. Upon entering the room one day, Tessem found the cramped quarters even more claustrophobic than usual. "What's wrong with this dump today?" he asked one of his men.

"It's probably those boxes in the corner," someone replied. "They were brought in this morning."

Tessem went to get a closer look at the new material. Suddenly he realized they had struck gold. The boxes contained the missing links to the tentative discoveries his men had made so far. The files were the elusive records that had been shipped from Moses' Long Island estate and inadvertently delivered to the crowded little I.R.S. bunker instead of elsewhere in the building. Tessem quickly got subpoenas in order to keep the files after Annenberg's men discovered their error. There was finally enough to take before a grand jury.

Yet another problem Morgenthau encountered was the manpower, or rather lack of it, that he had to cope with. The young prosecutor picked for the Annenberg case, Riley Campbell, had never tried a criminal case and he had never even tried a tax case. Morgenthau feared that amateurism on the prosecutor's part could blow a massive case that was already costing the taxpayers hundreds of thousands of dollars. He worried that a young, honest district attorney with limited experience would be no match for the battery of high-priced lawyers that Annenberg was sure to bring into court. Irey, he believed, simply had to come up with an airtight case. On occasion, he complained to Irey about Campbell's callowness and the fact that the assistant prosecutor, Austin Hall, was even younger and had even less experience. The choice had come down to the two young men only because a number of other potential prosecutors had been found wanting, mostly because there was a "taint" about them and a fear that Annenberg would be able to buy them off. Nationwide News Service already had a few former F.B.I. agents on its payroll. So, Morgenthau had few delusions that prosecutors wouldn't be susceptible to high-paying jobs with the Annenberg organization. Morgenthau's fears about the two young men weren't allayed after he met them on a trip to Chicago. In fact, the meeting made him more dismayed than ever.

"I was never more shaky about the whole business than when I sat out there and there were these two young fellows talking and acting as though they had it in the bag," he glumly told Irey. "Now, I don't like it, and I am saying that . . . depending upon Riley Campbell and one law student I think is just childish."

By mid-March, the case was solidifying, but there were still a number of loose ends that had to be tied down before the grand jury met the following month. Morgenthau was increasingly anxious and wanted everything in the hands of the Attorney General as soon as possible. He again got hold of Irey. "There must be some place where you say to the District Attorney 'The case is ready' . . . I mean there must be some time when the Treasury says: 'We have completed our investigation; we are ready to turn it over to the Attorney General's office for prosecution.' "

Irey had to slow him down, telling him that wasn't the way cases were handled, that the procedure was infinitely more complex. There was no such cutoff point when the I.R.S. had gone after other tax evaders. "In other cases, we complete the investigation and make our report and present it to the General Counsel, who sends it to the Department of Justice and says, 'We are through; here is the case.' " In such a case as this, he added, "our men are instructed to confer with the United States Attorney and give him what they have and go along with him in the prosecution of the case."

"I don't want to see this spoiled," Morgenthau said pointedly.

"It is not going to be spoiled," Irey reassured him.

By the end of March, the Treasury agents were wrapping up the case as quickly as possible so as to ready it for the grand jury. Morgenthau, the I.R.S. and the Attorney General were recommending criminal prosecution, not just because the facts warranted it but because the political pressures determined that that was the way it was to be.

The specific charges to be brought were varied: failing to report in excess of $200,000 in profits one year from the sale of wall sheets; deliberately not declaring $30,000 in profits from Canadian operations; manipulation of purchase of General News Company stock so the price appeared as $100,000 more than it actually was and with that sum in cash going to Moses and not appearing on his taxes; a wide variety of nondeductible personal expenses that were charged off to various companies. The largest item on the I.R.S. laundry list was two million dollars that Moses received from one of his corporations and was believed to be hidden income. Another major item was disguising ownership of about one million dollars' worth of stock in Cecelia Company, his chief holding company.

After receiving the findings, Attorney General Murphy phoned Morgenthau and told him the Justice Department was ready to move. He was prepared to make any Treasury agents special assistants to his department with jurisdiction anywhere in the country they wanted it. Moreover, he told Morgenthau he was looking for the right kind of judge, one who knew what to do in a case such as this. One man he had in mind was old Judge James Wilkerson, the jurist who had put Al Capone behind bars.

Eight

THE *Philadelphia Record* carried a front-page story on April 16, 1939, about the owner of the rival *Inquirer*. The story bore a Washington dateline and said that the Treasury Department had completed an investigation of income-tax returns of Moses Louis Annenberg for the years 1932 to 1936. The findings had been turned over to the United States Attorney General for presentation to a grand jury that was to convene in Chicago. The same story was carried in Moses' papers but in less detail.

News of the action struck the *Inquirer* like a bolt of lightning. Moses naturally was very worried; his son, Walter, was terrified. Verbal attacks by high-level government officials, no matter how damaging they might be, were harmless when compared with the seriousness of a grand-jury investigation. The quick-thinking executive editor, Dimitman, immediately issued an in-house memo to all employees, warning them not to discuss the publisher's business with anyone, especially federal investigators: "Efforts may be made to entrap employees of this newspaper into statements or actions, which, however innocent or well meaning, *could be twisted by government agents* to charges that attempts were being made by employees of the *Inquirer* to interfere with this case."

Within a week, lawyers representing Moses had descended on the Treasury Department, asking for a postponement of the grand-jury decision and wanting to make a tax adjustment that could put an end to the troublesome business. Morgenthau's agents brusquely said the case was no longer under their jurisdiction and was with the Justice Department. Then Attorney General Murphy made it clear that

Moses didn't stand a chance of being able to smooth over the charges quietly. On April 21, just five days after news of the grand jury broke, he issued a statement to reporters saying that he fully intended to press the charges and that he didn't foresee an out-of-court settlement as a possibility.

A few days later, an agitated Moses personally tried to stop the proceedings. Anyone who is charged with income-tax evasion has the right to a private, preliminary discussion of his case with federal officials. Moses, Walter, and the attorney representing them from Weymouth Kirkland's firm, Hammon Chaffetz, a former Justice Department lawyer who had made a name for himself in big antitrust cases, appeared before Murphy and representatives of the Treasury Department. Moses was so distraught that to some of the federal agents he seemed almost desperate. They believed that his concern stemmed less from his tax problems than from the possibility that other aspects of his affairs might be examined.

Chaffetz conceded that there were a number of inaccuracies in Moses' returns, but he tried to make it clear that they had been made inadvertently by accountants who worked for the publisher. The problem, he said, was that Moses ran a family business and much of the sloppiness was simply because bookkeeping hadn't kept pace with the growth of the company. Moses himself assured the officials that he was willing to accept full responsibility for the errors, but he let it be known that if the matter was pursued, he would engage the nation's top lawyers to defend him. Apparently, he had already been in touch with such prominent attorneys as Max Gardner and Homer Cummings, who had reputations for getting wealthy clients out of similar situations. From his icy demeanor, Murphy conveyed that he was unmoved by the arguments, and that he was continuing his efforts. The meeting ended, and further talks were scheduled, but both sides realized that the talks would most likely prove fruitless. In an update to Morgenthau, one of the agents present simply reported: "Very little need to be asked in order to satisfy the conscience of the Government officers that a criminal case exists and that no adequate explanation has been made which would exculpate Annenberg."

The grand jury convened on schedule in the old Post Office Building in Chicago's Loop. Precautions were taken to see that no one gained access to the jurors, a step that was necessary after it was discovered that several of Annenberg's men had attempted to talk with jurors. The government wanted nothing to jeopardize the case. Three tired deputy marshals wandered the halls outside Room 475, where the jury was in session. They were under orders to arrest loiterers and to search routinely the bathroom adjoining the chamber to make sure that no one had his ear glued to the connecting door.

At first, the case received little publicity outside Philadelphia, Chicago and Washington, but that ended as a result of several *Washington Dateline* columns of Drew Pearson and Robert S. Allen. The first column noted that the jury was in session and that the case "reaches down into the very roots of Democratic politics and it touches the sporting nerves of perhaps one-fourth of the American public. For the probe of Moe Annenberg's bizarre career has gone into every phase of the racetrack gambling racket." The columnists wondered what would happen to the Democratic party as a result of the investigation, since Moses had backed Chicago Mayor Kelly, who in turn had backed Roosevelt: "But now the man whom Kelly would re-elect apparently is bent upon pulling the machine which helped elect him in '32 and '36 down upon his honor's ears," they stated.

When Moses was asked by a reporter for his side of what was happening, he wearily said that he wished "the public reserve judgment until all the facts are known. . . . I keenly regret that the Government has found it necessary to place the blot of an indictment on the name of my son, Walter. . . . Since the tax investigation has commenced, I have been informed that our bookkeeping systems have not kept pace with the growth of the business and it may be that some taxes are owing to the Government." To the end, Moses would protest his innocence.

The minor irregularities that Moses spoke of, however, appeared monumental when presented as evidence. The government had told the grand jury that his net income for each year between 1932 and 1936 was six million dollars, while Moses' lawyers had insisted that it was only a little more than one million dollars a year. All told, 227 witnesses had been called during the nine exhausting weeks the jury sat, and on August 11 they had indicted Moses on ten counts of income-tax evasion; his son, as a top corporate officer, had been indicted as well.

After the verdict, Moses' lawyers again approached the Justice Department about the possibility of striking some sort of deal. When Morgenthau learned about the maneuver, he was determined to see it fail. "As far as I'm concerned, there's no difference between Annenberg and Capone," he said. "Just because Annenberg has millions and some other poor sucker has only a few hundred dollars, that poor fellow has to go to jail, but Mr. Annenberg can buy his way out."

Thus, Moses couldn't get a commitment that he would avoid prison, nor could he receive assurances of leniency if he pleaded guilty. There were too many people in high places whom he had offended, including the President. Nonetheless, the government's case still had two very weak links, the young prosecutors who were to try it. Everyone would feel much more comfortable if Annenberg simply pleaded guilty and spared the government the possible ignominy of losing to the publisher's smooth, high-priced attorneys. In this frame of mind, District Attorney William Campbell decided to play on the only weakness he found in the publisher—his son. It had been obvious, from everyone the prosecutors had spoken with, that Moses had shielded his son from the unsavory parts of his businesses. Moreover, the district attorney believed that Walter represented what Moses wanted the world to think of the Annenberg family. Thus, he tapped Moses' Achilles' heel and told him that if he filed a "plain unvarnished plea of guilty" and paid the taxes owed, the government would drop the case against his son. For his part, Moses stored the information away noncommittally; before he did anything he wanted to discuss his chances with Weymouth Kirkland.

To Campbell's annoyance, Moses' lawyers made one last bid to elicit sympathy for their client. They described the publisher as a poor old man who would be irreparably harmed if he actually went to prison. As they talked on, Campbell became increasingly exasperated. Finally, he lost his patience altogether. "Poor old man," the attorney snapped. "I'll give you the names of three people he had killed in the city of Chicago in the last five years." Looking directly at the lawyers, he told them they were defending "a murderer and a thief. Don't come down here telling me about the poor old man.... He ought to be hung."

On August 17, Moses and Walter appeared at the ornate Federal Building in Chicago. They went directly to the office of William H. McDonnell, the United States Marshal, where they were charged with evading taxes. The amount of money the government said they owed was more than three million dollars. Two other men from the Annenberg organization, who were similarly charged, surrendered with them, Joseph E. Hafner and Arnold W. Kruse, Moses' accountants.

The business at hand was humiliating to the proud publisher, and it mortified his son. The procedure they followed was as simple as it was degrading. One by one, like common criminals, they were finger-printed by John Kane, the young assistant marshal. A short while later, all four were released on bail bonds that were set by United States District Court Judge William H. Holly. The publisher's bond was set at $100,000. Those of his son and associates were $25,000 apiece. A trial was scheduled for April 23, 1940, the date the press and public would bear witness to what was uncovered behind the grand jury's closed doors. The judge assigned to the case was Wilkerson, the man who had unflinchingly put Capone away.

The distasteful business temporarily at an end, the Annenbergs returned to Philadelphia. The father showed little emotion. Walter acted as if the walls were closing in on him. The son had a strong sense of injustice, one that would remain with him for the rest of his life. With all that was wrong in the country, he wondered, why was the government harassing his father over taxes? Why allow his father's stubbornness and editorial barbs against the New Deal result in such a senseless, scandalous mess? Why allow this to happen to his mother and sisters? Walter was afraid of the crush of events. He had a sense of dread that had been building for months.

Abruptly, the tone of the *Inquirer* reflected the seriousness of the publisher's position. Attacks on the New Deal stopped. The paper soured editorially on Judge James's administration. The Sunday magazine became more proper and began carrying features and pictures on people of prominence, such as Dennis Cardinal Dougherty, the Archbishop of Philadelphia who was a friend of Moses. On October 14, the paper even showed signs of wavering on its traditional Republican heritage. The logotype on the front page bore a new slogan: "An Independent Newspaper for All the People." In a quest to depict Moses as a guardian of the community, the *Inquirer* became much more civic-minded in an all-out public-relations drive. The paper, for example, launched a call for legislation outlawing the indiscriminate sale of fireworks. The efforts of the news and editorial departments once again prevailed, and a law was passed. The following year, only one child was reported injured by fireworks compared with many in previous years. In the midst of the campaign, Jacob S. Clington, Pennsylvania's fire marshal, presented an honorary fire marshal's badge to Moses, which was front-page material in the *Inquirer*. The newspaper also began a program of public-service awards to police, firemen and park guards. A medal and two hundred dollars were given each month to public servants who had performed some meritorious service.

While such generosity improved Moses' standing locally, it didn't slow down the government attacks on him. He was indicted on a different charge, it seemed, every morning he woke up. The grand jury in Chicago indicted him next for operating a lottery because the "prizes" were held to be winnings off horse races. In Los Angeles, Earl Warren, the state attorney general and later Chief Justice of the United States, charged Moses and nine hundred bookies operating in California with unlawful conspiracy. In Philadelphia, the indictment was for conspiring to bribe a city detective. During the grand jury proceedings, a General News Bureau enforcer and one of Moses' sons-in-law had tried to bribe detective Clarence Ferguson in order to get him to change his testimony. The government was obviously moving against Moses with an awesome arsenal of weapons. His fears increased in proportion to the salvos being fired; and his son was beside himself with worry. To Walter, the government was mustering a nightmare of power with what appeared to be blinding speed.

On top of everything else, Walter was worried about his father's health and his state of mind. The son was increasingly fearful about the headaches that sent Moses into gloomy, silent retreats behind his locked office door, where he refused to admit anyone, including Walter. The attacks were becoming more frequent and were worsening in intensity. In addition, Walter and some of his father's aides were becoming concerned about Moses' irrational behavior at times. For example, he purposefully filled the street-level windows of the *Inquirer* building with a large number of weapons that had been used in a variety of crimes, as though he were showing the world that his own crimes were insignificant in comparison. The grotesque exhibition included a machine gun once wielded by the notorious bank robber Willie Sutton; the revolver found on Al Capone when he was arrested in Philadelphia in 1929; and a particularly horrible item, the bloodstained saw that a mother had used to murder her baby.

Next, Moses wanted to print a series of photographs of racketeers in the Sunday magazine; they were to be listed under a headline proclaiming: "Take a Look at Who Runs the Nation." The publisher suggested the layout to the magazine's editor Gauvreau, telling him, "Let's show the country who these bruisers are who get the votes and elect mayors, governors and presidents." A few minutes later, Walter told the editor to forget the spread; he would talk his father out of it. According to Gauvreau, Walter told him nervously, "It's dynamite. For God's sake, forget it." The son spent a lot of time putting out such brush fires.

On another occasion, Moses became obsessed with circulation schemes to make the *Inquirer* vastly larger than it already was. Whereas at one point he became so cost-conscious that he placed little tags on lights reminding employees to turn them off, Moses now disregarded expense. One scheme was to launch a daily rotogravure magazine, the first in the nation. The extravagant impracticality of the proposal upset his editors, who urged him to abandon it. "They think I'm crazy," he told Gauvreau. "They're not 'yessing' me now; everybody says 'no.'"

One reason for Moses' frantic behavior was that he knew his options were running out for the first time in his life. He was desperate to think of something, anything that would save his neck. The power of the press, which was one reason for his troubles, was useless. His political power—another reason for his misfortune—was useless too. But he still had one powerful tool, which had helped him leapfrog his way up in the world. He still had money. Men he had known all through his life, whether they were priests or politicians, were willing to break all sorts of rules if they could get enough of it, especially politicians.

Therefore, Moses decided to ask for help from a prominent local Democrat, one who was pragmatic enough to see the value in helping a political foe, and he was willing to reward him well. He turned to Matthew McCloskey, the clever millionaire contractor who lived by making his own rules. It was McCloskey who had given Governor Earle the money which was perceived by too many people as a bribe for government contracts. The Irishman knew more about politics than he did about the construction business, since projects he worked on seemed to have more structural problems than his political alliances did. Indeed, McCloskey was plugged into Washington as much as he was into Philadelphia, which, with the exception of Stern, made him unique. Moses knew that, above all, McCloskey, a prematurely white-haired man with a ruddy complexion, was a realist. He did a man a favor when he could, especially when the favor would be returned tenfold through construction contracts, which he got as easily from Republicans as from Democrats.

McCloskey later related the meeting with Moses in the following fashion: "Matt, do you see that suitcase over there in the corner," Moses said. "Well, I will put one million dollars into that suitcase and you carry it out of here and I'll never ask what happened to the money. But I don't want to go to jail." McCloskey told Moses he couldn't take the money, but that he would see what he could do to aid the publisher. He knew that everyone, from Roosevelt on down, wanted Moses behind bars, and he didn't believe he had enough pull to change the course of events.

After such dispiriting business, editor Dimitman came across Moses and his son sitting somberly one Sunday in Moses' office. The publisher had just returned from talking with his attorney Weymouth Kirkland in Chicago, and the news was grim. Upon seeing Dimitman, Moses told him that he would no longer fight the charges against him. He was throwing in the towel. "I've changed my mind, I am going to plead guilty," he said.

Dimitman, who in his own way was as competitive as Moses, demanded to know why there was such an abrupt change in plans. The editor had always looked upon Moses in a way that most people did; he considered him fearless, and he expected him to fight like a tiger when he was under pressure.

Slowly, Moses told the editor about the government's plea-bargaining. If he pleaded guilty, he explained, the case against Walter would be dismissed. The prosecutors had as much as admitted that the only reason Walter had been contaminated by events so far was so that he could be used as a weapon against his father. As Moses spoke, Walter, looking downcast, sat in silent shame and humiliation, never uttering a word as his father continued speaking in a low voice. "As you know, I have always had great ambitions for Walter. I purchased the *Inquirer* and have built it up with his future in mind. That's the only thing I'm interested in, and if I can spare Walter the trial, I won't mind doing a year in jail."

In order to distance himself as much as possible from the world in which his son would grow in stature, Moses wanted his name stripped from the *Inquirer* masthead as chairman and publisher. The suggestion, however, brought a vehement protest from his son. Never, Walter declared, would he turn his back on his father. Never would he cease to view his father with anything but affection and honor. He had reluctantly gone along with his father's guilty plea, only because it meant so much to Moses not to see his son's name besmirched. But while his father was alive, Walter would never try to usurp his role. Moses' name was to remain on the *Inquirer* masthead.

Though he was dismayed at his boss's decision, Dimitman, who was ever the newsman, immediately thought of the paper's coverage of Moses' impending appearance in court. "How do you want the *Inquirer* to handle the story?" he asked the publisher.

"You are the editor, that's your job," Moses replied.

Dimitman straightforwardly told his boss the story should receive full coverage, including page-one treatment, if only because Stern would try to build circulation by hammering away at the story. Moses considered the suggestion for a moment and he agreed. "All right, why don't you come along and write the story and decide how the paper is to use it," Moses said. He knew Dimmy would play the story precisely the right way. He could always count on Dimitman.

On July 14, both Moses and Walter received a brief respite from their problems. Ronny gave birth to a little girl, who became a symbol of hope in an otherwise bleak situation. Moses was glad, and Walter was beside himself with joy. Walter had yearned for a child, it seemed, from the very day that he had married, and his father doted on grandchildren. Indeed, after Walter and Ronny had returned from their two-month honeymoon, Walter had been dismayed that his wife wasn't yet pregnant and he had sent her to a doctor because he was afraid something was wrong. His fears, of course, had been unfounded, but since his father and he had come from such large families, he was anxious to get started on one of his own. The baby was named Wallis, a derivative of Walter. Her pleased father thought that a son could come later.

Meanwhile, Moses' lawyers were anxiously trying to get the most favorable deal from the government they could, once a guilty plea was entered. They swiftly found out there wasn't much of a deal to be struck. For this part of the ordeal, the case reverted to the Treasury Department. Throughout three full days, attorneys for both sides negotiated like diplomats drafting a treaty of surrender. Guy Helvering, the I.R.S. commissioner, first demanded that Moses pay eleven million dollars in back taxes and penalties. Moses' attorney Kirkland offered two and a half million. Helvering sneeringly dismissed the offer as "frivolous." Meanwhile, Kirkland begged for time and he hurriedly conferred with Moses by telephone, a tactic that became routine. Whenever he did, he upped the ante. Helvering was bartering and slowly inched his ceiling down. Prior to the negotiations, he and Morgenthau had agreed upon a figure that included penalties and interest for a full settlement of taxes due from 1932 through 1938. The figure was $9.5 million.

Kirkland, however, only raised his latest offer to $6 million and Helvering balked, insisting that the attorney name a higher price or his client would surely face a criminal trial. He knew that on this score Morgenthau backed him all the way; the Treasury Secretary was itching to see Moses go on such a trial. At one point, it looked as if that was the way the situation would be resolved. In any event, Helvering wasn't sure whether Moses even had enough money to pay what the government wanted, even if he agreed to the staggering sum. "I'm convinced in my own mind that he owes a great deal more tax, and I'm convinced also of this fact, that he can't really pay with what he's got what he actually owes," he had said to Morgenthau. He was right. Moses didn't have that kind of money. Nevertheless, on June 4, 1939, Moses' attorneys agreed to pay $8 million plus interest. The money would be paid with $3 million up front and then $1 million installments over the next six years. As collateral, the government was given first and second mortgages on most of Moses' properties, exceptions including the *Philadelphia Inquirer* and 240 shares of Cecelia Company stock that was owned by himself and members of his family.

Though his son wasn't to go through the humiliation of being tried, Moses still was to face a civil trial and a possible prison sentence. In one final effort to present a more respectable appearance to the court, Moses did something that he had been contemplating for years. On November 15, 1939, he simply walked away from the Nationwide News Service, which had been trouble from the moment he bought it, and which the son whom he believed so naïve had warned him against taking on. Knowing the wire was now a detriment, Moses had tried to sell it earlier in the fall for $5 million. Though the wire had received a deluge of unfavorable publicity, he still believed it was a viable operation. Moses thought the business should begin policing itself and eliminate the strong-arm tactics that were objectionable both to the government and to the public. One step he proposed was employing two or three Justice men who would advise the government agency of their appointments as a "board of directors" and keep the bureau informed of the company's activities. The plan, however, was impractical and never materialized, so Moses simply disassociated himself from the operation. Jim Ragen, the wire's manager, and Mickey McBride, another old friend from the turn-of-the-century circulation wars who became a powerful distributor in Cleveland, took over. The Nationwide News Service went out of business and five days later the Continental Press, as the wire service was renamed, rose from its ashes.

Moses' hearings opened in Chicago on Wednesday, June 5, 1940. Reporters representing newspapers from cities across the country, including New York, Philadelphia, Miami and Milwaukee—all the places in which Moses had amassed a fortune and lived his many lives—were present to cover the event. Moses, who had hoped to end his life as a gentleman publisher of a respected major newspaper, found his life being raked over by the press that he had always felt so much a part of. Each day he showed up about fifteen minutes early for the proceedings. His son, Walter, was always at his side. For the first few days, Moses bantered with reporters and photographers and patiently posed for pictures, but as the deliberations wore on and he read what was being printed, he became testy and finally refused to answer most reporters' questions. Since the civil claims of the government had been settled, Moses' nerves were raw as he had to deal with the hard part. What happened in the courtroom would determine his immediate future as well as how he would be remembered by history.

District Attorney Campbell had 109 pages of evidence prepared. Court officers, members of the press and the spectators who came daily settled in for a long haul. Campbell set about describing the Annenberg empire, an incredible spider web of more than eighty corporations which the aging entrepreneur operated as personal fiefdoms. Campbell contended that the income from these sources was tremendous and that Annenberg knew exactly how the profits from each threaded their way through his dizzying corporate structure. As proof, the District Attorney submitted letters written by Moses to subordinates that directed specific and relatively small overhead expenses to be paid or eliminated. Other letters criticized employees for not thinking up new money-making ideas. Such letters had been written from time to time, but what wasn't apparent in court was that they were penned only occasionally, when an irascible mood struck Moses. Far more often, he had operated on a laissez-faire basis.

As an indication of how quickly and enormously Moses' wealth had grown, the prosecutor submitted financial statements signed by Moses that showed his net worth in January 1930 to be $7,858,343. By June 1938, that figure had soared to $19,496,308. The government con-

tended that the gains were the result of his monopoly of the horse-rac-
ing-information field. The huge profits were made possible only by
Moses' organizational genius, his ability to bring systems and order to
what could far more easily have been financial anarchy because of the
thousands of bookmaking establishments dealt with and the number of
hands the funds passed through before getting to the heart of his kingdom.

As part of his presentation, Austin Hall, the young assistant prosecutor, read aloud a letter that Moses had written to his son-in-law J.
Stanley Kahn on May 11, 1936. The letter little showed that Moses
had knowledge of the minutiae of his business, but it gave a startling
indication of the size and scope of his far-flung empire:

DEAR STANLEY,

After my several letters Saturday, I want to come back to the
scratch sheet discussion. After carefully thinking it over, I come
back to the conclusion as I have related to you many times, that I am
reluctant to risk my present position for all the possibilities that
were offered in the way of additional earnings.

You complained that the scratch sheet has injured the sale of our
racing papers, and then in the next breath you say that we are ahead
of last year in circulation in spite of a raise in price. So, the last two
statements do not reconcile.

Besides, we simply cannot have everything, and, like Mussolini
when he started out to grab Ethiopia, he had to very carefully consider what he might be plunging into, but Mussolini had nothing to
risk, because Italy was on the bum, and those who might have opposed his ambition had by far and away much more to risk than
Mussolini.

Our position is similar to that of the English nation. We in the
racing field own three-quarters of the globe and manage the balance.
In other words, the few little nations that are left have to pay us tribute to continue. Now, why isn't that the most beautiful and most
satisfactory position to be in, which ought to satisfy even me.

Have you ever stopped to figure our earnings and how that might
be upset by a little mistake such as we are discussing. For example,
we have a number of enemies with unusual ability that are eager for
a chance to get even with us and upset the monopoly, who would be
willing to work for almost nothing just for revenge, and who would
contribute their talent more enthusiastically than our own people
just for a chance to upset our apple cart. There is Mr. Tolleson, for
example; Hy Schneider, John I. Day, Harry Budd, Davenport and

many others, who have unusual ability in the racing field and between a lineup like that which would include the Armstrong organization and bank roll, we might find ourselves with many regrets.

Let me have your reaction to this. I want to remain, with best wishes, sincerely.

M. L. ANNENBERG

A ripple of excitement swept through the courtroom as the letter, which was part of the documentary booty Tessem had discovered, was read. Reporters strained to catch every word, and Hall, who was well aware of the impact the particular piece of evidence was having, read it slowly enough that every word could be heard and taken down. The men mentioned at the tail end of the note were all in the race-information business and they all lost hefty pieces of their action to Moses at one time or another.

Several letters and telegrams sent by Walter were also read. If anything, they pointed up the fact that young Annenberg was a man without substantial business experience. They showed that he worked always under his father's supervision and that his responsibilities in actuality were light. There was only one dynamo at the heart of the Annenberg machine. "The evidence shows that in these instances as well as in other of his participations, usually superficial, in his father's business, he always acted on direct instructions from his father rather than from his own ingenuity and volition," Hall told the court.

The charges against Moses, however, went on and on. There were, for example, his living expenses that were charged against the company. He had the *Daily Racing Form* pay $350 a week into his household account in 1934 and 1935 and charged the payments as racetrack expenses. He had purchased building and loan certificates in Milwaukee and paid for them out of the petty cash of his Milwaukee News Company. False and predated stock certificates of the Cecelia Investment Company had been used to serve as a fraudulent basis for not reporting the greater part of the dividends from his company. He received income from companies that had never been reported. The government contended that Moses had charged anything and everything against his companies as a business expense. In May 1934, for instance, his daughter Harriet was married at a gala celebration at the elegant Hotel Pierre in New York. Two Pullman cars were chartered from the New York Central Railroad to bring guests from Chicago.

The government said that all of the wedding expenses, ranging from the railroad cars to $6,644.44 paid to the hotel, were written off as business expenses.

In 1932, Bert Friedlob, an Annenberg son-in-law, was paid $400 a week by the Cecelia Company and then $200 a week for months, but the government contended that he had never worked for Moses. In 1935, Moses cashed checks for $100,000, pooled the money and included it in a "fraudulent charge" of $850,000 for the purchases of 50 percent of the General News Bureau stock, but only $750,000 was paid, and Moses refused to say what had happened to the other $100,000. There were gambling debts charged off as "political contributions." Expenses for Ranch A were examined and found wanting. "He spent enormous sums of money improving the ranch by constructing swimming pools, riding stables, guest cabins, installing electrical cooking equipment, buying sheep liver for trout feed, groceries, riding clothes, sleeping blankets and many other expenditures," prosecutor Campbell declared indignantly.

Even the Cecelia Company stock that Moses had given to his children and the dividends from such stock were declared illegitimate. Although the charge was vigorously denied, and rightly so, the government contended the stock contribution was a ruse and that the Annenberg children turned over their dividends to their father.

After several days of such assaults, the prosecution rested its case. Moses appeared to have shriveled. His son looked as though he had been physically punished; he sat straight in his chair, however, and there was a certain dignity about his suffering, as one observer later recalled. There had been many times when Walter felt that he might wildly break his silence and scream out that his father had only done what other men who owned private businesses did. His father had never paid himself a salary, he wanted to tell the court, but he maintained both his silence and his self-possession.

Finally, Weymouth Kirkland took the floor. A stocky man in an expensive pale-gray suit, the lawyer presented a portrait of sleek corporate smoothness. His graying hair was combed back from his high forehead. His gold-rimmed glasses gave him the look of an intelligent executive. The man had always inspired a deep dislike in Walter, and he had urged his father to turn to another law firm. Walter hadn't liked the idea that the attorney had so readily urged his father to plead guilty; he had been certain that Moses could have beaten the charges.

Walter had convinced himself that his father had only been as guilty as the corner grocer who had dipped into the till to pay for what he wanted. Moreover, Walter distrusted Kirkland because he was a lawyer for the *Chicago Tribune* and he had heard rumors that the attorney had worked with Jake Lingle, the *Tribune* reporter who had been part of the underworld. Young Annenberg hadn't realized that the Trust, his father's wire, had had strong ties to the reporter. Despite his son's having urged him to seek other counsel, Moses had stayed with Kirkland. They were friends, he told his son, and he trusted him.

After the government's arguments, however, Kirkland's defense sounded weak-kneed: "According to our analysis and investigation, some facts therein stated are incorrect and a great many of the inferences we believe are unjustified," the lawyer began pompously.

Immediately, he launched into the publisher's background in order to elicit sympathy for the defendant. "You have heard something of the life of M. L. Annenberg. It has undoubtedly given you a better understanding of the man and his action. The father and mother of this defendant knew in the keenest senses what 'the struggle for existence' means." In broad brush strokes, he painted a verbal picture of the early days of the Annenberg immigrant family; the privations they experienced; the ambitions of the children. Kirkland traced Moses' career through Chicago, Milwaukee, New York, Miami and Philadelphia. The account was maudlin and not very accurate. For one, he had even aged the "poor old publisher" by a couple of years, telling the court that he was sixty-four, when he was really sixty-two. Moreover, the arguments turned out to be mostly rhetoric. At one point, the lawyer went so far as "to assure your Honor that in the future there will be no more effort made by anyone to evade the payment of taxes, we have placed in the company's office in Chicago, as an executive, a man recommended by the First National Bank of Chicago, and approved by Price Waterhouse and Company. This man, with the assistance of Price Waterhouse and Company, is opening up an entirely new set of books and putting in an entirely new accounting system with new accountants and bookkeepers. This is in accord with a promise Mr. Annenberg made to the Attorney General of the United States."

Often, Kirkland's defense bordered on the absurd. Discussing one large item of income that the government zeroed in on, for example, he commented: "Mr. Annenberg has only one habit—an expensive habit. He does like to play roulette, and he is not a very successful player. He has lost considerable sums in this manner. I believe that most of this

money was used in this way, and the rest went for household expenses."

The lawyer rattled on about the taxes that Moses paid and the fact
that he wanted to make restitution, and he took into account the suffering the publisher had already gone through. Then, to Walter's humiliation, Kirkland expanded at length upon the fact that Moses had
entered a guilty plea for the sake of his son. Young Annenberg had
been strongly opposed to his father doing so just to save him from
public disgrace; he would rather have been exposed to any insults or
slander at a trial if he could have saved his father. Now Kirkland, the
man who had urged Moses to take the government's offer of a guilty
plea in exchange for his son's avoiding being placed on trial, was
bleeding as much mileage out of the situation as possible, even indicat-
ing that Walter might have been guilty of something:

> The decision of Mr. Annenberg to plead guilty was definitely
> made when he learned the case against his son would be dismissed.
> For his son, Mr. Annenberg has had great ambitions. Truly, he be-
> lieved him to be innocent, as did I. Yet public trial broadcast
> throughout the land would leave a scar, even a verdict of not guilty,
> that might forever ruin the son. His father would not take that
> chance.
>
> Now your honor has occupied this bench for many years and has
> witnessed the drama of life as men vexed and torn with trouble have
> passed in and out of your court and knowing men as you do—the
> fears and hopes that move them—do you not sense that a powerful
> desire to shield that son and a poignant hope that he be spared, have
> played no small part in Annenberg's decision to interpose his plea of
> guilty?
>
> And if mistakes the boy has made, must not much be granted for
> his inexperience and immaturity? Perhaps his desire to please his fa-
> ther—to accept the responsibility without experience to back it up
> may account for any trifling mistakes that he might have made.
>
> Between every father and son there, of course, exists a relation-
> ship of deep affection, trust and confidence. But I say to your Honor
> from my own knowledge that the relationship which exists between
> M. L. Annenberg and his son, Walter, is something different from
> any such relationship I have ever known. They have been constant
> companions since the boy left school. His father entertains for him
> the deepest affection and hope for his future. Everything was built
> with the son's future in mind, and as the son's feelings toward the
> father I can only say this: That all the indictments, pleas of guilty

and prison sentences that could ever be inflicted upon the father would never cause the son to waver in the belief and confidence that he has in his father.

The father and I had, of course, discussed the case on many occasions, but his mental condition due to worry and suffering was such that it was hard to get decisions out of him; yet when I told him of the possibility of Walter being spared the ignominy of a trial and possible danger of conviction, he immediately said he would plead guilty.

The son's persistent objections to this sacrifice were of no avail—Mr. Annenberg stuck to his original decision although he knew when he made it that he might face a penitentiary sentence ...

People who looked at young Annenberg during Kirkland's exposition saw his eyes glistening with unshed tears. His face was a mask of despair, yet he never broke. Walter kept watching his father to see how he was reacting. The son had long since stopped caring about how he was being used by this lawyer whom he didn't like. He cared only about his father.

NINE

THOUGH IT APPEARED to most of the reporters and spectators at the hearings that the outcome was inevitable, the actual three-year prison sentence Moses received shocked his family and friends. The mood at the *Inquirer* in particular, because it was where Moses had spent most of his time within the past four years, was funereal. Men and women who were close to the publisher moved through the newspaper's corridors and stairwells as though in a trance. Many of them didn't think Annenberg was capable of all the dark stories being circulated. Others simply didn't care. For employees who had grown fond of their driven, exciting boss, it seemed as though he had been dealt from a stacked deck. Few of them believed there was a rich man in the nation who paid his share of taxes. In particular, some of the old Hearst men Annenberg brought to the paper believed that they had seen too much and knew too much to think their publisher was worse than other men; in their eyes he was better than most. They believed that a man like Moses, who shared the same tough, poor background that had spawned many of them, needed to use his fists and wits and ignore the law to get ahead.

Moses was given until July 22 to wrap up his affairs before having to enter a new life at the federal penitentiary at Lewisburg, Pennsylvania. He found some solace during that period because of the genuine sympathy that many of his newsmen offered. Stud Norton, the old Hearst crony he had hired to edit the Jackrabbit edition of the Sunday paper, for instance, came up with tears in his eyes and offered to serve his boss's prison sentence for him. It was all Moses could do to keep from crying himself. "Brace up, Stud," he said. "But don't forget the Sunday's got to hold that million."

The rest of the nation wasn't as sympathetic. One editor was given the responsibility of weeding out photographs and editorial cartoons that mocked Moses' plight before the publisher saw them. *Time* magazine, for instance, reprinted a cartoon by Daniel Fitzpatrick that appeared first in the *St. Louis Post-Dispatch;* it showed Moses being pursued by an enormous Uncle Sam, while the caption asked, "Anybody Making Book on This Race?" The *Christian Science Monitor* applauded his sentence in an editorial entitled "Money Cannot Atone." "Even Mr. Annenberg's going to jail cannot restore the damage done to the lives of customers of his business. It will give him time to think things over," the *Monitor* stated. And Westbrook Pegler, a rabid anti-New Dealer whose famous column had appeared in the *Inquirer*, wrote one that was omitted from that paper. "It will be hard," it said, "to find anywhere in the underworld of the United States a more vicious and dangerous example of ingratitude to the generous nation which opens her arms to the oppressed people of the world than Moses L. Annenberg. . . ."

Moses, however, was beyond worrying overly much about what was being printed about him in other publications. He spent much of his remaining time of freedom reflecting upon his life, wondering whether he should have done things differently. Once, when speaking with editor Gauvreau, whom he had always treated with ill-concealed disdain because he wasn't more ambitious, Moses told him that he now understood what he previously perceived as folly—"Nobody bothers you and you can forget everything—no worries—and you can sleep. And when you wake up, the sun shines. Jesus! You know, you're not such a god-damned fool after all! What is money for Christ's sake?"

Meanwhile, his son, Walter, moped about the *Inquirer* building like a sleepwalker. He had difficulty concentrating on anything, and employees who addressed him found him not responding. When an editor approached him to pick some cartoons for *Click* magazine, Walter pushed them away. "How the hell can I laugh?" he exclaimed.

His father, who had witnessed the scene, stepped forward and critically looked at the drawings, flipping through them until one finally caught his eye. The illustration was of two scrub women looking up at a group of bejeweled, elegantly attired women walking by. "What did virtue ever get us?" one wearily asks the other. Moses let out a cynical laugh. "Print this one," he ordered. "It's funny by God; it's the truth."

Before turning himself in, Moses made it clear that when he was in prison, he was still the man in charge of what was now Triangle Publications, the name of a subsidiary that he took as the new name of his holding company. Cecelia was associated with too much adverse publicity. No one, of course, doubted that he was the boss despite his erratic behavior of late. The one other matter Moses wanted tended to was the immediate future of Walter. He spoke with his son about the urgent need to get serious about the business. It was a conversation that he had all too frequently with Walter in the past, but now Moses didn't have to convey the importance of the situation. Moreover, he told his son that he wanted him to learn as much as he could from a young attorney named Joseph First, whom he hired only several months earlier. Moses, like everyone who met the thirty-eight-year-old First, was impressed by his steel-trap mind, and his not letting emotion get in the way of his intellect. When he met First, Moses felt he would be good for Walter.

The thin, round-faced little attorney, with his glasses, thinning hair and cardigan sweater worn beneath a conservative suit, looked scholarly and wiser than his years. Indeed, First, who came from a family with more ambition than money, had impressive academic credentials. He had been at the top of his class both at the Wharton School of Finance and the University of Pennsylvania Law School and, until he joined the *Inquirer* as general counsel, he was certain one day to become a partner in the law firm of Richardson Dilworth, the attorney Moses kept on a retainer since his first encounter with Dave Stern in court.

It wasn't an easy decision for the cautious First to come to work for the race-wire tsar, but he consulted with his old law school dean, who told him to accept the post. What had also swayed him was not only a good salary but the flattering nature of his own dealings with Moses. The publisher, for instance, had asked him about taking certain loans from Philadelphia banks. "What would you do?" Moses had asked. First told him not to apply and gave his reasons. Moses thanked him and followed the advice. The attorney was impressed that a man of such vast experience was willing not only to ask him what he thought but to heed his recommendation. Also, Moses always addressed him as "Mr. First." To a bright young Jewish lawyer who had already experienced his share of prejudice in the incredibly in-bred Philadelphia legal world, a man of Moses' position addressing him respectfully had helped win him over. Moses knew his man when he assigned him the task of watching over Walter. Joe First would always know only one duty: Do what is best for the owner of the paper.

With a dreadful quickness, the few weeks Moses was given to put his affairs in order sped by. In the midst of the confusing, depressing time, Walter's wife, Ronny, gave birth to another child, the boy both Moses and Walter wanted in order to extend the Annenberg line. The child was named Roger, and far from bringing joy at a time when it was greatly needed, the baby added to the pain all of the Annenbergs were feeling. He was born with a double cleft palate, which severely deformed his face. The deformity seemed to symbolize not only that Moses' luck had run out but that he had been cursed. Walter was overwhelmed by sadness, and Ronny, who had always dreamed of having a large family of her own, told herself that she would have no more children, because she feared that there might be something terribly wrong with them too.

On July 22, just eight days after Roger's birth, Moses and Walter traveled to Chicago, where Moses had to surrender to federal officials. The father and son managed to avoid newspaper reporters and photographers and the publisher gave himself up without fanfare to United States Marshal McDonnell. From Chicago, he was to be driven to the prison back in Pennsylvania; the process was roundabout, but it was what the law demanded. Walter was prevented from accompanying his father and the federal marshals on the trip. The two said goodbye in the Spartan government office. The tenderness of their parting and the genuine despair of the son probably embarrassed some of the lawmen present.

While Moses sat in the back of a stifling prison van speeding along a road, trying to steel himself for what he was about to confront, a specially prepared statement that had been signed by him appeared on the front page of the *Inquirer*. The message asked the paper's readers to withhold judgment of him, "pending a time when my whole story can be told." He insisted that he had never knowingly evaded any taxes. "That I pleaded guilty to one count of one indictment is a matter of record. In so doing, I invited the penalty that now confronts me, but I have the satisfaction of knowing that thereby I saved others, including my son, from a severe and unmerited ordeal." By insisting on his self-sacrifice, Moses may have felt as heroic as Sidney Carton, but the statement was of little solace to his son. When reading and rereading those words, Walter again felt shame and guilt for having been instrumental in the terrible act that had put his father behind bars.

At the Lewisburg Penitentiary, Moses was fingerprinted and his photograph was taken holding a card bearing the number "10197," which was how he would be officially known. His gray hair was cropped short and he was given a baggy gray uniform. Everything about the dull-gray prison was robbed of color. Several days later, a package arrived at the *Inquirer* from the prison. Marion Hoeflich, Moses' attractive secretary and, later, editor Dimitman's wife, opened the wrapping. It contained the clothing Moses had worn when he surrendered. The articles were so lifeless and represented such loss and finality that Miss Hoeflich began weeping.

Each week, Walter and his mother and sisters traveled the 110 miles to Lewisburg from Philadelphia to visit the head of the family. The encounters were painful. The sight of their father in such awful surroundings was enough to set his daughters crying, but Moses, with his cynical sense of humor, could always manage to make them laugh. "Better here than elsewhere," he said, looking ominously at the ground.

In the presence of his family, Moses was more relaxed, different from the man the rest of the world knew. He was loving and caring and made each of the women, who always vied for his attention, feel special. There was talk of business too, which was something the family expected. While giving Walter ideas for features in the *Inquirer*, for example, Moses told his son to get a photographer and a reporter into the Pennsylvania Dutch countryside near the prison, an area about which he was now curious. He had new promotional ideas as well, which he laboriously wrote down in longhand, no longer having a secretary at his disposal.

Moses was allowed to write only a limited number of times, and his letters weren't to his wife, daughters, friends or business associates; they were always to his son. He exhorted Walter to "apply yourself in every direction" and he told him to do whatever he could to console his mother and sisters. Often the handwriting was shaky and difficult to read, and Moses apologized for it in his sardonic fashion. "Maybe later I will recover from my current nervousness," he joked in one letter.

Ever competitive, he wrote his son about one circulation problem that he found especially annoying. The *Inquirer* was losing to several out-of-town papers right there at the prison. "Some New York papers arrive on Sunday, while ours do not arrive until Monday," he complained. "Please investigate and make corrections. Send earlier edition if necessary to make deliveries." Moses signed his letters, "Yours devotedly. Love to all. The Poor Old Gov." Walter kept the letters locked in a safe at his Philadelphia home.

At least once a week, Walter wrote to Moses besides visiting with him. The word "Father" was always capitalized in his letters. He kept his father abreast of family matters and he frequently enclosed pictures of his mother and sisters. He repeatedly promised that he was applying himself; he was always aware of the sacrifice his father was making for him.

As a way of retreating from the hardships that life had dealt him, Walter moved to Philadelphia's Main Line from a center-city apartment. His family had grown larger and he wanted a bucolic retreat. He bought a beautiful old stone mansion on sixteen wooded acres tucked off in a series of little lanes that wove between lovely estates, each bearing an imposing home. The property, which was in the town of Wynnewood, cost $40,000, but it was in need of extensive renovation. The estate bore the pastoral name "Inwood."

The Main Line, one of Philadelphia's poshest addresses, derived its name from the major artery of the Pennsylvania Railroad which swept westward from Philadelphia in the 1870s and 1880s. By the time the Annenbergs had arrived in the city, Main Line residents were frozen into an archaic life style that was British dowdy. Both men and women wore sensible clothing and loved horses and Republicanism with the same intensity. An incredibly in-bred group, they considered themselves the custodians of manners, good taste and local culture, which embraced such institutions as the Philadelphia Orchestra and the Philadelphia Museum of Art, even though many such patrons didn't believe a painting was art unless a horse appeared somewhere on the canvas.

What appealed to Walter was the area's quietly elegant life style. The beautiful estates blended as harmoniously into the countryside as did the manor houses in the Cotswold hills of Gloucestershire, after which many of them were modeled. An insular world that had little time for those not born into it, Main Liners even had their own peculiar accent, a lock-jawed speech that sounded much the way Demosthenes must have sounded when he first placed pebbles in his mouth. Their sureness about their right to rule held a fascination for many less socially secure people, including Walter.

Among his new neighbors, there had been a resentment when his father bought the *Inquirer*, which had been considered the paper of the

Protestant Establishment. Their antagonisms focused as much upon his ethnic origins as upon the sources of his income. There was much talk of Moses being a "pushy Jew" and worse, and the attitude didn't soften in many quarters when it came to his son. The prejudice was perhaps best personified by Joseph Clark, a patrician politician and later a liberal Senator, who lived in Philadelphia's exclusive Chestnut Hill, where residents liked to joke they "went slumming" when they visited the Main Line. Clark loathed Moses and he disdained his son. More than anything else, the Annenbergs disturbed his sense of social order. They lacked pedigree, but their money and ownership of the *Inquirer* made them powers to be reckoned with in the community. They were Jewish; it mattered little that they weren't religious. Clark, who needed the Annenbergs to further his political ambitions, treated them cordially in public, but dismissed them in private as "dirty kikes," thus giving credence to the definition of *kike* offered years earlier by the urbane Jewish banker Otto Kahn: "Any Jewish gentleman who has just left the room."

The determinant of social acceptability was the *Social Register*, known as the "blue book," which was a careful record of the social elite, their addresses, maiden names, clubs and social organizations. For Walter, who had been raised amidst wealth and private schools, a part of him had been bred to live on the Main Line, but his mistake was in expecting to be accepted for his good qualities and his failure to perceive that to most of the blue bloods he would never be one of them. "You move to the Main Line," Dimitman had warned him when he first bought Inwood, "and after two or three years, after people have gotten their names into your newspaper, things might open up a little. Maybe after four or five years, they might invite you out. The *Social Register* is what counts. But because you're seen as Jewish, you won't be accepted by the Main Line whether your name is Walter Annenberg or E.Z. Dimitman." To many Main Liners, he would always be the son of Moses Annenberg, who had gone to prison.

As a result of his father's imprisonment, Walter was involved more in the company's decision-making process, but most of the major directives from Moses were carried out by First and Dimitman, who visited the publisher in prison as often as possible. One area in which Walter became involved was trying to determine where costs could be shaved, a step that was necessary because of the heavy tax burden. Walter used the circumstances to get rid of his brother-in-law Stanley Kahn, who, in his estimation, only wanted to use his father. Soon after

Kahn's departure, Walter heard from his father's old friend, Joe Ottenstein, that Kahn was talking about starting a cut-throat competition with the *Racing Form* unless he was rehired at a salary of one thousand dollars a week. Moreover, Kahn was threatening to use whatever political influence he had to see that Moses was transferred from Lewisburg to Alcatraz, which was impossible but nonetheless a frightening prospect to Moses' anxiety-ridden son.

Walter was obsessed with the idea of getting his father out of jail, and such talk only made him more passionate. He started a frenzied letter-writing campaign to persons of power or prominence who might possibly have influence with the President. In his naïveté, he even wrote to Morgenthau in the hope that the Treasury Secretary may have softened. There were letters to Congressmen and Senators and cabinet members, letters that he had his mother and sisters sign, rather than himself, because he thought heart-rending pleas from women would be more effective. He even asked local dignitaries, such as Cardinal Dougherty, to intercede with the President. His desperation was fueled by other pressures that were being brought to bear. The United States Immigration and Naturalization Service, for example, was trying to drum up a case against Moses, including the possibility of deportation. Immigration officials had frightened Walter by saying they couldn't locate his father's citizenship papers. Young Annenberg knew that his grandfather Tobias became a naturalized citizen in the early 1890s, automatically making citizens of his children. But immigration agents were repeatedly interrogating his father at Lewisburg, threatening him with deportation. Both Annenbergs were shaken by the new frightening twist of events.

Eventually, Walter himself located the naturalization documents. They were in the clerk's office in the Federal Building in Cooks County, Illinois, the most obvious place for anyone to look if the meant to find them. He had a duplicate made and kept the copy locked in his office safe; he was taking no chances that the record might one day mysteriously disappear from the courthouse. In the interim, Walter was visited several times by immigration officials, who, he believed, were simply trying to harass him. During one such encounter with José R. Espinoza, then chief supervisor of the Immigration Department, Walter felt there was something insinuating about the agent's approach. It dawned on Walter that there were too many innuendoes in the man's speech and he came to believe the agent was trying to entrap him into offering a bribe in order to save his father. He believed the government wanted him in prison too. Finally, Walter stopped playing games with the official and he told him that he had a copy of the document in question. Feigning surprise, Espinoza asked him for a duplicate, which Walter complied with, but only after saying he believed the agent was "part of a conspiracy to harass my father."

Several days later, Walter was contacted by a man named McGoldrick, who identified himself as head of the Immigration Department's Philadelphia branch, and he asked Walter to come to his office in the city's old Customs House. When Walter arrived, he found himself again queried about the citizenship papers, only this time McGoldrick told him that he could be prosecuted for having tampered with government documents as a result of having made a copy for Espinoza. The agent pulled a law book from a shelf, flipped it open and told Walter he could be sentenced to five years in jail and fined $10,000. "But Espinoza told me to strike the copy off," Walter replied bitterly. The meeting clinched in his own mind that there was an overwhelming conspiracy at work to destroy not only his father but himself as well. "Christ I was terrified," he recalled.

The encounter encouraged him to redouble his efforts to get his father out of prison before the government dreamed up some other extraordinary method of persecution. In desperation, he turned to Matt McCloskey, the Democratic contractor who his father had hoped might be able to head off his imprisonment. McCloskey agreed to try to intercede, as he later recalled: "I asked the President if he could see that Annenberg was released after one year. You see, the judge who sentenced him said he made the term three years only so that he would be sure Annenberg would serve one year. Roosevelt gave me an exaggerated wink and said, 'I am a practical fellow.' He then gave me assurances that Annenberg would be freed after one year, but said that only could be accomplished with the strictest secrecy."

The President very quietly set the wheels in motion to release Moses. After his first year in prison, Moses learned that the Federal Parole Board had voted to parole him, and Walter was elated. The happiness, however, was short-lived. At the last moment, the decision was rescinded. The reason given was that Moses had been involved in the Chicago circulation wars thirty years earlier. When he learned of the excuse, Walter personally appeared before the board, explaining that the ruthless general of the newspaper battles was not his father but his uncle Max. His speech failed to stir them into reconsidering their position. In any event, Walter was powerless to sway them; the board was merely following orders. Under intense political pressure, the President had backed off from his original intent to parole Moses. Stern had found out what was happening and he had sounded a cry of alarm to block the move.

The President heard from a number of influential Democrats who claimed to be outraged at the prospect of Moses being paroled. Morgenthau was opposed and Harold Ickes, the Secretary of Interior, who had broadcast the "Curse of Two Cities" speech, wrote a dramatic note to Roosevelt, urging him to keep Moses in jail: "My information is that a carefully planned campaign is under way to bring pressure upon you to pardon Moe Annenberg. . . . In his much smaller sphere, Annenberg has been as cruel, as ruthless and as lawless as Hitler himself. We are in desperate straits indeed, if, in order to preserve our liberties, we must have recourse to our Annenbergs."

In the midst of the turmoil, Max Annenberg died, and the occasion created another great strain among the Annenberg clan. When Ivan was asked by one of Walter's sisters, during a telephone conversation regarding the funeral arrangements, whether he wanted to know how his Uncle Moe was doing, Ivan brusquely replied, "No." The response shocked Moses' daughter, who told her sisters, and never again would their cousin be considered part of their family.

On December 7, 1941, Walter was temporarily roused out of his preoccupation with his father's plight. The Japanese had attacked the American Naval Base at Pearl Harbor, and the next day the United States declared war on Japan and then on Germany. Walter had known for a long time that war was inevitable; it had long been a part of the consciousness of his household. His wife's brother, Ben Dunkelman, had joined the Canadian Army and was now a much-decorated hero. The Dunkelman family lived on the letters sent home by Captain Dunkelman, a large, ruggedly handsome man who, in his uniform, looked like a recruiting poster of the modern fighting man. Walter admired Ben tremendously.

The war made its presence felt in other ways. A number of men who worked for the Annenberg companies were drafted or enlisted. One of the first to sign up was the lawyer Dilworth. The handsome, fiery forty-two-year-old attorney joined the Marines, just as he had done during the First World War. Dilworth was a man whom Walter was alternately attracted to and irritated by. One day it seemed that they were good friends; the next day they were arguing about everything under the sun. Nevertheless, Walter was impressed that Dilworth had reenlisted. He wished that he could slip away from the myriad problems confronting him, put on a uniform and fight something as tangible and black-and-white as the armies of ruthless tyrants, instead of fighting an evasive action with his own government, which he had been raised to believe was not his enemy.

Meanwhile, the visits to Lewisburg were increasingly depressing. Moses' health was deteriorating, and Moses was having trouble with prison guards, some of whom were harassing him and insulting him with such epithets as "Jew bastard." The guards who were leaning on Moses were so blatant about it that some of their fellow guards thought that there was some deliberate plot to harm the prisoner. "It was quite obvious that instructions had been handed down that Annenberg should not be accorded the same treatment that other prisoners were to receive . . . every opportunity was taken to ride him," Russell H. Varner, a senior guard at Lewisburg told Walter. The son had Varner later dictate a formal statement to that effect, and he had it notarized. Walter began amassing a file of material showing that his father was not only the victim of a concerted government plot, but that, if he wasn't completely innocent of wrongdoing, he wasn't as terrible a man as the government tried to make him out to be. The file included correspondence with Espinoza, judges, cabinet ministers and even a letter from former Governor Earle, who stated, "I must tell you that the *Inquirer* under your father, while opposing me largely on New Deal differences, was journalistically fair." Such documents were of small comfort to Walter at the time, but as the years passed they took on greater meaning as he dedicated himself to removing the blot of shame from the name of Annenberg.

As the months passed, Walter was increasingly worried about his father's health. There were times when Moses was disoriented. He couldn't place his hands on objects he reached for, resulting in his groping, like a very old man who could barely see, until he touched what he wanted. He complained of the headaches, the painful migraines that made him wish he were dead. Walter pleaded with the prison doctors to do something to relieve his father's suffering. He also renewed his letter-writing campaign and urged his mother and sisters to do the same. His father was deathly ill. Walter knew it, even if the prison doctors dismissed his father's complaints. All of the Annenbergs were terribly worried about Moses' condition. He was the rock the family rested on, and they couldn't stand the thought of his dying. Who, Walter's sisters worried aloud, could ever take his place?

On May 27, 1942, an announcement came from the United States Parole Board. Moses was to be freed on June 11. Ominously the decision was arrived at as a result of "the prisoner's condition." Moses would have been automatically eligible for parole on November 11. On the day of his release, Moses had to be lifted off the train that had brought him to Philadelphia. He was confined to a wheelchair and was too weak to get out of it by himself. The strong, tough man who charged into town only six years earlier to take over the *Philadelphia Inquirer* and challenged all comers was grossly transformed by illness and adversity. He was sixty-four years old, but he looked seventy-five. His large frame seemed to have shrunk. His face was that of a wizened old man. Only his eyes were bright and alert with a sharp cynical gleam. Moses was surrounded by his family, an embattled circle of women and a young man who held their heads high and by their erect carriages defied anyone to utter a word against their father. Each of the Annenberg children displayed a steeliness, a protectiveness of the man who had done so much to shelter them throughout their lives.

Following a medical examination, Moses went to the Mayo Clinic in Rochester, Minnesota, where neurological tests revealed that he had a brain tumor. The head of the neurology department told Walter that further tests were needed, but results thus far weren't promising. Finally, the doctor told Walter, who with his mother and sisters had accompanied their father to the clinic, that Moses had an inoperable tumor. The best that could be done was an operation that would open the back of the patient's skull in order to relieve the pressure that had been building for years. Walter agreed. After the operation, the doctor informed Walter of something that the son suspected: his father's condition was hopeless. The surgeon told Walter to pray that pneumonia developed and took Moses quickly, otherwise the suffering in such cases was protracted.

Moses' son was filled with an unutterable sadness, and on July 15, he sent each member of the Federal Parole Board a note telling them about the brain tumor and that his father was dying. He wanted them to know the truth of what he had been trying to tell them for nearly two years—his father was a sick man who should never have been in jail in the first place. He wanted them to share in the guilt of his father's imprisonment.

Moses was confined to St. Mary's Hospital in Rochester. There were long periods of wakefulness before he drifted into unconsciousness, and Walter remained seated on a chair at his father's bedside.

When he could, Moses held long rambling philosophical discussions with his son. The talks weren't of business and money, but of life and death, and they made Walter uneasy. His father had always been a doer, impatient with people who philosophized when they could be accomplishing something. The pneumonia that was mentioned as a possibility, however, had set in, and Moses knew that death was near. In the midst of talking about the meanings of his triumphs and power, Moses looked at his son. Abruptly, his mouth twisted into a wry smile. "You know, Walter, it all amounts to *nothing!*"

The words chilled his son, who struggled and continued to struggle for the rest of his life against accepting such a terrible view of life. At other times, Moses tried to rouse himself to what he believed was his last gamble in the world. When he was rational, Moses was worried about what was going to happen to his family after he was gone. He felt that he had to do something, say something that would turn his ineffectual son into the man he wanted him to be. On the evening of July 20, the gaunt, pain-racked father asked his son to lean forward so that he could tell him something that he wanted neither Sadie, nor the girls, nor anyone but his son to hear.

"You know, Walter, who knows what is the scheme of things," he said softly. "My suffering is all for the purpose of making a man out of you!"

Moses died at 10:45 P.M.

Ten

ON THURSDAY JULY 23, 1942, Philadelphia's Chestnut Street outside the Oliver H. Bair Funeral Home was awash with a sea of automobiles, and the sidewalk was overflowing with people who came to pay their last respects to Moses Annenberg. Baskets of flowers, which had been sent from all over the nation, filled several rooms of the gloomy but imposing funeral parlor. The occasion was one of the largest funerals in the city's history and special detachments of police were needed to maintain order as more than fifteen hundred people were in attendance. There were employees from the numerous Annenberg holdings as well as state and local politicians. Their ranks included Governor James and Acting Mayor Bernard Samuel, Judges Harry S. McDevitt, Vincent A. Carroll and Eugene C. Bonniwell. Moses' old political mate Joe Pew was there looking sour and displeased that he had lost a supporter of great wealth and power. Joe Ottenstein, Moses' old friend who had marched in step with him from Milwaukee on, was cloaked in sadness.

Moses' son, Walter, stood like a protective rock in front of his mother and sisters as he received friends and acquaintances. His face was impassive, while those of his mother and sisters were masks of grief. The irreplaceable had been torn from their lives.

Ironically, Moses was mocked in the end by the presence of a religious leader standing closer to him in death than he would have dared in life. He was a rabbi, Dr. Nathan A. Perilman, of Temple Emanu-El, which Mrs. Annenberg attended in New York. Sadie had insisted on his presence even though she knew only too well her husband's disdain of religion. The rabbi read the Ninetieth Psalm and paid a glowing tribute to the publisher—"A man of great humanity, he felt very profoundly the hopes and suffering of other men. As some men have a genius for right living so indeed did Moses L. Annenberg. He is not lost to us."

The ceremony was covered by *Inquirer* reporter Fred Hyde, who looked at Rabbi Perilman in his cutaway and striped pants and tried to imagine what Moses would have made of the scene. He concluded that "Moe was probably laughing like hell."

In an unusual move, the *Inquirer* the next day carried pages of the sympathy notes the Annenbergs had received from people of prominence around the country. They included William Randolph Hearst, Herbert Bayard Swope, who was then special assistant to the Secretary of War; Philadelphia's Cardinal Dougherty; George W. Maxey, chief justice of the Pennsylvania Supreme Court, and Arthur James and George Earle, both former governors of the state. The list seemed unending. It was as if such testimonials to the deceased man's character were the beginnings of a campaign to shine the tarnished reputation that Moses had left his son as part of his legacy.

ELEVEN

WITH A DISPLAY of self-confidence that he didn't feel in the least, Walter immediately moved into his father's office in the *Philadelphia Inquirer* building. He assumed the title president of Triangle Publications, which included the *Inquirer*, the *Racing Form* and the magazines. As if to show that he wasn't usurping his father's role, the thirty-four-year-old publisher ordered the initials MLA—set in the curved lettering similar to that his father used for his monogram—placed in a small design on the covers of the magazines and M. L. Annenberg was listed on the *Inquirer* masthead as chairman and publisher 1936–1942.

It became readily apparent to everyone that much of the personalized style that had characterized Moses' running of the company had died too. The rough-and-ready give-and-take between Moses and his employees, the fishing trips and drinks after work with favored employees and the jokes and effusive friendliness the father had engaged in with everyone from truck drivers to top executives, weren't part of Walter's makeup. The new publisher was shyly self-conscious, and he quickly became aloof from the line operations on his holdings, preferring to deal only with ranking executives. He rarely visited offices and instead summoned people to him. When he did make an effort to get to know employees by name, likely as not he muffed it. For example, he invariably referred to an *Inquirer* editor named Alexander Joseph as "Mr. Alexander." "Some people felt sorry for him, but others felt he was a bit of a fool when he took over," Fred Hyde, the *Inquirer* reporter recalled.

What few people realized was how overwhelmed by his responsibilities Walter was feeling. He was faced with running a large corporation that was still under siege by the government. He had his wife and children to take care of, and he had to fill his father's shoes as leader of the Annenberg clan, a role that his mother and sisters had assigned to him upon Moses' death. To make matters worse, neither members of his own family nor the executives within his companies had much confidence in his abilities. To date he had shown little spark. He had never stood up to his father or shown any particular talents or managerial abilities. Cassandras were already saying that with Walter at the helm, Triangle might as well file for bankruptcy. "Few people believed that Walter had what it takes," Dimitman, the *Inquirer* executive editor, said.

The pressures were all the greater on the young publisher because he was only too aware of the general lack of confidence in him, a position that he found himself in since beginning to work for his father. Moreover, the weight of his responsibilities was made much heavier by his new sense of mission. Walter was using the terrible ordeal that he had gone through with his father as a source of inspiration. He believed that he had to turn his father's unhappy death into something of value and in the process erase the shame of the past years from the family name. Somehow, he had to measure up.

In search of guidance and a way to bring order to this chaotic period of his life, Walter sought solace in the sayings of essayists, poets and politicians, like Emerson, Wordsworth and Churchill. He seized snatches of their work that struck him as fundamental truths, wrote them down and committed them to memory and repeated them to others when he wished to stress a point, until the practice became an ingrained habit. One of the first such expressions was a line from a prayer for the dead. The words summarized the sense of obligation he was feeling as well as the strain of living for so long with the realization that he hadn't been the son his father had wanted him to be. They also articulated his sense of guilt for having been the reason why his father went to prison, and his firm belief that his father was a far greater man than he was credited with being by the world at large at the time of his death. The prayer stated: *"Cause My Works on Earth to Reflect Honor on My Father's Memory."* He had the line engraved on a bronze plaque and displayed it prominently on his desk. Implicit in the phrase was a challenge both to himself and to others, those who deemed Moses to be a man of little honor.

Moses had bequeathed his publishing properties in trust to his son, widow and daughters, but all voting rights on the disposal of the property or stock were entrusted to Walter. To just about everyone's amazement, the estate was listed as insolvent when the inheritance tax was filed. Assets totaled $2,700,016 and included bank deposits, cash, jewelry, two Cadillacs and five cases of whiskey. Debts totaled $5,582,-757, ranging from five million dollars still owed on the *Inquirer* to a bill for $28,197 for funeral expenses. Moreover, there was Moses' tax penalty, now about four million dollars still outstanding.

The once vast Annenberg holdings were a mere shadow of what they once were. The properties in Wyoming, Miami, Milwaukee and New York were long since mortgaged to the Treasury Department to pay the crippling tax fine, but real-estate values had plunged before the war, so their sale wasn't the boon it might once have been. The Long Island estate that had formerly belonged to George M. Cohan, for instance, was valued at about one million dollars at the time Moses had bought it. When offered for auction, the Kings Point manor brought no satisfactory bids. It wasn't simply that property values were eroded, but times were changing. There were few men of immense wealth who could afford such an estate. The gracious haven that was one of Moses' first brash manifestations of glittering success and had enthralled his wife and children with its majesty and beauty was a white elephant. The Treasury Department finally agreed that the property could be sold for as little as $70,000, but even that proved too much. The only offer was $24,900.

The tax return failed to list an estate executive commission to which Walter was entitled, but which he had waived, knowing his father would want him to serve the family without compensation. Always conscious of the way Moses had judged his actions while he was alive, Walter behaved as though his father was still watching him. The act was the first step he took in asserting himself as head of the family that was used to pampering him as the spoiled little boy who had grown up in a household of doting women.

Years later, when asked why he was so successful, Walter frequently laughed and replied, "because I had a rich father," or "because I had so much handed to me." The reality of the situation was far different. After inheriting the remnants of a smashed empire, he had to grow up in a hurry if he was to keep what he had, let alone create his own corporate kingdom. For any young man the awesome task confronting him would have been intimidating, but for Annenberg, whose insecurities and agitated state of mind were additional negative elements in the mix, the challenge appeared monumental.

His indecisiveness about his next step manifested itself in a confusion about where his loyalties lay in those first few weeks after his father's death. The horns of his dilemma were the sense of duty he felt about serving in the armed forces and his lifelong obligation to pursue the business career his father had expected of him. Adding to his consternation was the extreme sense of vulnerability he felt as a result of the government harassment he had experienced. He was now wary of the government that he had been raised to believe in so strongly, and which had become, as his father once had been, a force in his life that he had to try to appease. At times, he felt that he might never extricate himself from what seemed to be an unending and antagonistic problem. If he went to war, he would be deviating from the ambitious path that Moses had laid out for him, but if he stayed home, he would be shirking his responsibilities as a citizen and possibly offending his new oppressive master—the government.

His ostensible dilemma, however, was more a reflection of his anxieties than of reality. In truth, the military was bound to reject anyone with a hearing problem such as his, but after much deliberation, Walter decided to join the Marines. Once he had finally made a choice, he pursued it vigorously even though it readily became apparent that the option wasn't realistic at all. But Richardson Dilworth's reenlistment in the Marines probably was a factor in his decision, since their relationship was characterized by a competitively sharp edge, and he had the example of his brother-in-law Ben's heroics to make him feel that he should be in the thick of the action. Men of courage were placing their lives on the line. Honor could be gained—or regained—on the battlefield.

When he took his physical, however, he was turned down by a Marine doctor. With a single-mindedness that was to become one of his fiercest characteristics, he used his status as publisher to take his case to ever-higher authorities. After a number of rebuffs, he finally reached the top of the chain of command, General Clifton Cates, commandant of the United States Marine Corps, who wasn't overly impressed by civilian office and bluntly told the young publisher that he was wasting his time. "We have rules," Cates said. "We aren't going to break those rules for you." Like a bloodhound that picks up a new scent after scratching at an empty hole, Annenberg next pursued a commission in the Navy, where he met similar disappointing results. "Suppose we accepted you and you were on a ship and didn't hear an order or the hissing sound of a shell coming," a kindly medical officer told him. "It could jeopardize the safety of other men."

Finally realizing that he couldn't force his way into the military, he rapidly formulated another plan that, he hoped, would enable him to get overseas and was just as unrealistic as his bids to join the armed service. Though he had only superficial experience as a reporter on his father's old *Miami Tribune,* he told the local Selective Service board that he wanted to cover the war in Europe as a correspondent for the *Philadelphia Inquirer.* He was infuriated when forced to submit to a lecture by a local attorney on the board who chastised him for being "irresponsible" for turning his back on his company at a time when it desperately needed him, but he abandoned the notion of being a war correspondent. What no one realized was that his bids for adventure and to confront danger constituted a hope that he would be thrust into a situation where he could prove himself. No one knew better than he that in his absence Joe First, the man his father had installed in the company as his mentor, could run Triangle Publications far better than he himself could, and, indeed, was already directing the business.

The Selective Service board member, however, may have been more right than Walter himself realized. His attempts to place himself in the obvious perils of war may well have been an effort to run from possible failure in the business arena he had inherited, which, at the time, held greater terrors than anything he might confront in the trenches or at sea. For one of the few times in his life, Annenberg found himself in a frustrating position that he couldn't solve with the tools he took for granted, wealth and power. He was out of options and he had to try to come to grips with the job he had inherited. With Joe First at his side, he set about becoming head of Triangle in more than name only.

The sense of unease that he felt was partly relieved when he heard from two prominent men who offered to counsel him in the world of business and high finance. One was Bernard Baruch, the financier, who felt compassion for him as a result of discussions with Walter's mother Sadie who, like Baruch, was a philanthropist and gave to the same causes. The other was Edward Eagle Brown, chairman of the Chicago First National Bank, who had often advised Moses, as well as many other men of prominence. Both men understood the difficulties Annenberg was facing, especially Brown, who had known of Moses' disappointment in his son. Since he had known Moses, Brown must have realized that it was impossible for the son or anyone else to have become a dominant force in the elder Annenberg's businesses while he was alive; there had always been room for only one star in Moses' universe. Though Walter rarely sought their advice, Baruch and Brown's offers helped him stave off fears of failure that threatened to engulf him, making him feel less alone.

The easiest task confronting him, Walter found, was fulfilling one of his father's death-bed requests. Like a lord bestowing gifts on faithful vassals, Moses had asked his son to distribute news agencies to certain loyal employees who had managed them for years. There had been men who had disassociated themselves from Moses as quickly as possible when his troubles with the government had erupted; but there also had been those who rallied to his side and continued to be solicitous while he was imprisoned. From the grave, Moses was rewarding the men who had remained his staunchest troops. Because of such acts of generosity, which had characterized Moses in life as well as in death, Walter couldn't reconcile the public record of his father as a ruthless gangster with the loving, caring friend and father he had been. To confirm his own image of his father, Walter began writing to Moses' old friends and loyal employees, drawing from them reminiscences about his father's kindnesses, which, in his own mind, blotted out the darker side of Moses' past.

Knuckling down to the day-to-day responsibilities of learning the operation of a huge, unwieldy corporation, however, was a much more difficult and time-consuming task. One of the first steps that had to be taken was streamlining the vast, disorganized holdings that made up the company. Much of the rationale for the complex way the businesses had grown had died with Moses, and Walter and First spent long days poring over company records, ascertaining where money was coming in and where it had to go. They consolidated the eighty-odd companies that Moses had created, and they routinized ways of doing business within Triangle and with its suppliers. At this juncture, one of the most critical steps Walter took was breaking ties with any business that appeared in the least shady. He vowed that under his direction the company would never be associated with anything that gave a hint of scandal, a move that First embraced wholeheartedly.

As much as Walter, the cautious little First was worried about being associated with an organization that had criminal links. When he spoke with anyone about his job, the lawyer made it clear that he had accepted the position only after discussing it with his former law-school dean, who had encouraged him to take it, as though that advice had absolved him of any ethical problems that might have arisen by his having gone to work for the race-wire king. The attorney's sensitivity was so great that he even tried to loosen Walter's bonds with some of his father's most loyal employees who had been implicated in the tax scandal. Walter, for example, wrote often to Joe Hafner, one of the Cecelia Company accountants who had been found guilty of preparing false tax returns for Moses and had been sentenced to prison as well.

Hafner, a bright little man who looked like a racetrack tout, idolized Moses, as Walter well knew. To keep up the man's spirits while he was in jail, Walter sent him solicitous letters, asking him if he could send him anything to read or do anything else to help ease his plight. One such letter contained a sentence that Hafner never saw, because Joe First, whose influence over Walter from the time his father went to jail was enormous, even reviewed all of young Annenberg's correspondence.

After reading the note, First sent it back to Walter telling him to delete one section. It simply stated: "Please do not feel too bashful about any request, because after all, Joe, you and I have been friends and fellow workers for a good many years, and I know that if our positions were reversed, you would do anything that you could for me; therefore, I want you to assume the same attitude as I do." First thought the wording struck too familiar a note with a convicted criminal, ignoring the fact that Hafner had gone to prison only because of the man who also employed him. The fact that it might have eased the mind of one of the Annenbergs' most trusted employees was irrelevant. Walter gave unquestioning acceptance to First's decisions, reflecting his belief that he needed the lawyer as he had never needed anyone else in his life. Later, however, he made Hafner his personal accountant.

More often than not, in actuality, the recommendations made by First were exactly what were needed. The lawyer was naturally more suspicious of men's motives than the young publisher, and when some ruthless, tough men, including in their ranks men past friends of Moses, moved to take advantage of the weakened Triangle, First expected it, whereas Walter was not only dismayed but naïvely shocked that onetime friends would behave dishonorably. Shortly before Moses' death, for instance, Walter Howey, once one of Hearst's famed editors in Chicago and a poker-playing pal of Moses, began stealing information from the *Racing Form* and putting it into the

Boston American, another Hearst paper that he now edited. To add insult to injury, Howey threatened Kenneth Friede, Walter's brother-in-law, who ran the *Racing Form* operation in the Boston area. Angered after hearing of the matter from Friede, Walter became bitterly outraged when Louis Frohlich, a Triangle lawyer in New York, informed him that the Hearst editor not only refused to stop stealing the information but had actually threatened the Annenberg organization in the worst way Walter could imagine. "Howey said that if Friede did not get out of Boston," Frohlich relayed, "he would get Mr. Hearst to write editorials that would influence the Parole Board in not granting any consideration to your father."

Sickened by what he had heard, Walter wasn't sure what to do, telling Frohlich that such "a threat was as vicious and mean a statement as I had ever heard." Pressing what he believed to be his advantage over a disorganized company headed by a weak young man, Howey next tried to intimidate Walter with a phone call: "Laddie Boy, what's all the excitement about over our racing edition? You know, you're an out-of-state publication; and if you keep on trying to make trouble, I can easily have legislation introduced in Boston and Massachusetts keeping you out of the state. You know, you do not print up here; and this would be easy to do."

Furious about what Howey had said about his father, Walter stammered, "I resent your threats and, besides resenting your threats, there's still the Constitution of the United States which is a safeguard against your remarks."

Joe First urged Walter to make affidavits of the conversations with Howey and Frohlich and have them notarized, and he told him to sue the Hearst organization. Walter, however, believed Hearst a gentleman and thought if he presented the facts of the case to the aged publisher, Hearst would rectify the situation immediately. He intended to visit Hearst personally, but at the last minute he was prevented from doing so by other pressing business. Instead, he wrote him a friendly letter. Walter made it clear that "the *Boston American* has been systematically pirating copyrighted material from the *Daily Racing Form,*" and he outlined what Howey had said. "I write you this letter because of the high personal interest in which I hold you, and I am happy to conclude this letter with the hope that I may not long be deprived of the pleasure of paying you the personal visit which I had so much anticipated," his Victorian-sounding letter concluded. He enclosed copies of the affidavits he had made and sat back confident that the honorable publisher himself would be outraged by the actions of one of his top editors.

Instead of the response he expected, Walter was dismayed to see that the man who had treated him so kindly as a child now dismissed him as an inexperienced fool. As he read Hearst's letter, Walter's estimation of the man disintegrated. The terse note stated:

> MY DEAR MR. ANNENBERG,
>   Pardon me if I say that I think your affidavit is a lot of nonsense.
>   I have always been a good friend of your father's and nothing could induce me to say or write or do anything that would injure him.
>   Moreover, I do not for a moment believe that Mr. Howey made the statement attributed to him.
>
> Sincerely,
> W. R. HEARST

The tone of the note suggested that Hearst believed Moses' son to be incredibly naïve. He himself had always believed that one of the best ways, if not *the* best way, of getting anything was simply to take it until you were forced not to. He must have wondered why Moses hadn't taught that to his son.

For Walter, the brush-off was a bitter lesson that the seas of business were filled with sharks; it taught him to be more wary. But then Joe First was always warning him not to expect too much of people. As usual, First was right. The lawyer filed a suit against the *Boston American*, forcing the paper to stop its theft of *Racing Form* matter. The embattled young Annenberg began to realize that the competitive world was as harsh and untrustworthy as his father had always told him it was; he began to understand his father a little more.

With his own instincts having failed him so miserably, Walter naturally heeded what First told him after Moses died. Within the Triangle organization, First was respected, but he wasn't liked, and that was the way he wanted to be perceived. He believed in keeping underlings at bay, and the philosophy that he tried to instill in his protégé was simple: "Keep them in awe of you." "Them," of course, were the thousands of employees who worked for Walter Annenberg. Since he was ill at ease in his new role as head of the company, and because his stutter made him uncomfortable at large gatherings, and because he was essentially a modest man, Walter naturally adapted to First's motto. Moreover, the confidence of wealth had given him an intimidating edge: When angry, he was a very formidable man; he spoke sharply to employees who disappointed him, whether they were secretaries or executives and, with an icy look, could put an end to an argument.

To the vast majority of his employees, who rarely, if ever, saw him at all, Annenberg became in fact an awesome figure, about whom fact and fiction soon swirled, and legends about his father became attached to him. Several truths did emerge, however, and one was that Annenberg loved to live graciously both at home and at work. He moved his headquarters to the former Elverson apartment in the airy *Inquirer* tower, where he had a spacious, elegantly decorated office replete with steam and exercise rooms, and it became a symbol of both his aloofness and his lordliness. Visitors found the office all the more remarkable because Walter commissioned a self-portrait, immediately visible upon entering, which eerily contained a shadowy figure of his father in the background, the person who always had been so much a part of his life. Another truth that readily became apparent was that the publisher, who arrived daily at the newspaper in a black Rolls-Royce, expected his whims and orders to be treated like commands. As he gained more confidence over the years, Walter's employees came to believe they were working more for an emperor than for a tycoon, one who indulged himself by keeping Associated Press news wires in his homes, bought art objects from all over the world, and commanded legions of employees across the nation.

Before becoming at ease with his company, however, Annenberg had much to learn from Joe First. A tight-fisted man who equated waste with sin, First was, his subordinates found, a difficult executive to work for. A shrewd, exacting man with little—some colleagues said no—personality, First's primary characteristic was caution. He had a reputation among his subordinates for saying "no" whenever a question about entering new ventures, buying new equipment, or exploring new ways of doing business was raised. His response most often was, "No, we're getting along without it." On one occasion an executive worked up a painstaking cost analysis and had the report carefully typed and bound in a blue folder before submitting it to First. The next day, he received the cover and an introduction he had written accompanied by a cryptic note from the general counsel that sneeringly said, "I want the meat, not the frills."

Under the tutelage of "the Abominable No Man," as First was called behind his back, Walter learned to take a dim view of what he came to think of as extravagance. Although he himself was paid handsomely, and set about building a huge portfolio of stocks and bonds, First strongly believed that pensions and profit sharing and big salaries were a waste of money. Triangle salaries soon reflected his thinking and came to lag behind those in the rest of the industry. The executive didn't believe in keeping thermostats high in the winter or air conditioning in the summer, and he convinced Annenberg of the wisdom of his ideas, even when confronted years later by studies that showed employees in air-conditioned buildings were more productive than those toiling in sweltering heat. But, then, First's own home wasn't air-conditioned either. In those early days, First told Walter when he did something wrong and even criticized him on occasion. Having been catered to all his life by everyone, Walter chafed under the little lawyer's remarks. Nevertheless, he accepted conduct from First that he would never have tolerated from anyone else, because he recognized that he had to go through an ordeal of fire if he wanted to cling to the company he had inherited.

After all, the federal government was still monitoring his every move, waiting for him to jeopardize himself. His personal taxes and those of the company were routinely audited, and whenever he heard the slightest rustle of anything that could possibly harm him, he moved to head it off. "The government was trying to wreck us in those early days and we had to battle to save everything," he later recalled. Indeed, Walter developed an instinct to protect himself from anything the government might be able to do to him. On one occasion, for instance, an assistant alerted him to a rumor that J. Edgar Hoover believed an Annenberg-owned magazine was about to print an unfavorable article about the F.B.I. chief. Quick to go on the offensive and allay any fears Hoover might have, Walter wrote to the nation's top law-enforcement official that the rumor was unfounded. The letter illustrated the awful sense of vulnerability that Annenberg lived with and the lengths he would go in order to appease a man of such power:

"Rumors have reached me to the effect that publications which I direct are supposed to be critical of you and your efforts," Annenberg wrote. "Mr. Hoover, if it is true that you have been so informed, then I wish to take this opportunity to deny such allegations." Then with a strange twist of flattery that characterized his own identifying with established office and the men who held such office—even a man such as Hoover whose agents had such an active role in destroying his father—Walter sought to ingratiate himself with the F.B.I. leader: "As a matter of fact, if it should interest you, I consider your success phenomenal and a truly brilliant performance. I might add that, as a private citizen, I gain great comfort out of the knowledge that the Federal Bureau of Investigation is headed by so able an individual as yourself."

Far from viewing such a statement as a betrayal of his father, Walter had spelled out a position that he firmly believed. As part of his shielding himself from political harm, he came to identify with the men who could harm him. He had made up his mind that he would never antagonize anyone with the power to hurt him or his family. The missive was merely the first of many "keep up the good work" notes that he sent to the F.B.I. chief. For his part, Hoover acknowledged Walter's "thoughtful" letter, but he didn't lessen the intensity of his agency's scrutiny of Triangle, and many years later Walter would learn that he was on a master list of select Americans whose conduct was monitored by the F.B.I. even if it only meant routinely examining his tax returns.

Besides working to improve his knowledge of the business, Walter began an agonizing and often frustrating approach to conquering his terrible stutter. His early uncertainty at heading Triangle was reflected in the tentativeness of his speech. But even as he came to dominate his business world, his speaking pattern remained difficult, and it wasn't unusual for him to pause for painfully long moments before he managed to blurt out an order or discuss the business at hand. It was obvious to everyone that his sharp mind had a dozen ideas for each one his employees had, but his enunciating them was like a race horse pulling a cart, because the words came so slowly. Whereas his memos were clear and concise—rarely more than a page—his conversations were often tortuous. Now, with great determination, he began a speech-therapy program that had been devised by Dr. Edwin Twitmyer, a professor of psychology at the University of Pennsylvania. He had started the program while in college, but, as with everything that was difficult in those days, he had discontinued it. The exercises consisted of about twenty minutes a day of recitation, including works such as the Gettysburg Address and Robert Southey's poem "Cataracts of Lodore," which were therapeutic because of the rich range of vowel sounds. Even to this day, if Annenberg were to discontinue, his speech would rapidly backslide. Thus, to the bewilderment of others on occasion, Annenberg put himself through his lessons wherever he happened to be. While staying at the Beverly Hills Hotel during the

Second World War, for instance, his warblings panicked a guest in an adjacent room, who informed the management that a Japanese spy was barking orders at someone next door.

Ironically, a major factor in Triangle's ability to survive intact, and to grow, was the war that Walter was so anxious to become a part of. The public was seeking diversion from the uncertainties it faced, and reading was a cheap form of entertainment that was readily available. Triangle's *Detective* and *Screen* magazines, for instance, were selling better than ever, with some issues of *Detective* reaping a $50,000 profit. Even *Click*, which had always been only marginally profitable despite its enormous circulation, began making money, because advertisers who had once ignored it began buying space in the publication. One reason why they gave the once-sleazy magazine a second chance was that Walter had improved *Click*'s tone. Tentatively at first, but gradually with greater self-confidence, Annenberg put his long-dormant ideas into action. Having always disagreed with his father's Hearstian philosophy of going after mass audiences by groping for the lowest common denominator, Walter wanted to make quality the prime determinant of a publication's success. Quality, plus what he perceived as a publication that would serve an essential need, were the mix he believed the public wanted.

In *Click*'s case, he changed the format with the aid of Walter Dorwin Teague, a respected industrial designer who had served on the Board of Design of the 1939 World's Fair in New York. The magazine's revised look, coupled with editorial changes, enhanced the magazine's appeal. Mainstays, including profiles of celebrities and photos from upcoming motion pictures, like those of Fred Astaire from *South American Sway*, were retained. Gossipy stories and cheesecake photos of starlets were replaced by human-interest articles about the men and women behind the Allied war effort. Several years later, despite the time and care taken with revamping the magazine, Annenberg decided to kill it and the December 1944 issue was the last. Walter had an idea for a new publication, and he suspended publication of *Click* in order to let the new one come to fruition. During the war, publishing companies were allotted paper on the basis of what they were using before the war started. The only way to get paper for a new venture was to stop publishing another. Walter, like his father, was ready to risk a sure thing for a potentially better gamble, one the cautious Joe First warned him against taking. But as he had grown more confident, Annenberg was relying less upon First. He was trusting his intuition.

The seed for the new venture was planted one spring day in New York when Walter and his sister Enid Haupt were strolling along Fifth Avenue and looking at imaginative display windows containing dresses for teen-age girls. Walter absently remarked, "You know, there isn't a magazine for girls in that age group." The comment might have been the end of their concern about young women's fashions if, out of curiosity, Walter hadn't noticed, in his publishing data, that fashion magazines were so full of advertising that they had to turn retailers away in droves. Some magazines, including *Mademoiselle* and *Vogue*, were rejecting up to 150 pages of potential advertising per issue. Annenberg was determined to stand under the flow of ad dollars "with a bushel basket of my own."

Uncertain as to his next step, he contacted the owners of three leading Philadelphia department stores and asked them who best knew how to promote their women's clothing lines and who knew the fashion industry inside out. The unanimous response was Helen Valentine, the smart promotion manager of *Mademoiselle*. The publisher, who was becoming a man who never wasted a minute, immediately contacted her and asked her to come to Philadelphia to discuss a business proposition. When Miss Valentine, a dynamic little woman who knew her own mind, sounded him out a few days later, he told her he wanted to launch a fashion magazine, but other than that he wasn't sure exactly what kind it should be. "There's only one criterion," he told her. "It must be sensible and wholesome." Wholesomeness, of course, had become the goal that separated the new Annenberg company under Walter from the old one under Moses.

Miss Valentine had her own ideas and one of them was a magazine directed at teen-age girls. She ticked off her reasons: Teens were spending ever more money on clothing. Special lines were made just for them; and the clincher, as far as Annenberg was concerned, was that there was no publication aimed at the market that numerous advertisers wanted to reach. Walter thought back to his and Enid's stroll along Fifth Avenue and told Miss Valentine that he was willing to start such a publication; he asked her to be its editor. Several days later, she excitedly called him and said that, at a cocktail party the evening before, a friend had tossed off what she believed was the apt title for a magazine aimed at that age when a girl is no longer a child, yet isn't quite a woman. It was *Seventeen*. Annenberg liked the ring of it as well. To make sure there were no copyright problems, he wrote to Booth Tarkington, author of the novel *Seventeen*, outlining his plans, again emphasizing the wholesomeness of the magazine. The author responded with a letter telling him that there were no problems as far as he was concerned. Annenberg, one of the biggest publishers in the nation, was flattered that the novelist had taken the time to reply personally. He always kept the letter.

When retailers learned about the magazine, they stood in line to advertise, just as Annenberg had hoped they would. As the first issue rolled off the presses in December 1944, *Seventeen* was already operating in the black. The publishing community admired the courage and vision the new venture had demanded, but, perhaps more than anyone else, Walter's mother and sisters marveled at *Seventeen*'s overnight success; it was so much like what Boy's father used to do. And they were constantly being amazed at the transformation taking place in him. The happy-go-lucky young man was evolving into a no-nonsense businessman, who increasingly had less difficulty making decisions. *Seventeen* became the first of what they began to call "Walter's epiphanies," brilliant insights that led him into businesses that were bound to make millions of dollars. They relied more on his judgment as a result of it; they began to realize that, just as Moses had done, Walter could protect and care for them.

While the success of the magazine brought him to national attention, the place where he wanted to be accepted was Philadelphia, and more than that, he wanted to be liked. What time he could spare away from his business and family, Walter devoted to a wide variety of civic and humanitarian causes. While he wanted the esteem and recognition given to business leaders, he believed that it was through good works that he could redeem the honor of the name Annenberg. Soon, both he and the *Inquirer* were receiving numerous awards for a diversity of campaigns that Walter used his newspaper to promote. The *Inquirer*, for example, called for improving the city's water supply, cleaning up political corruption, and highlighting the problems of juvenile delinquency, a situation that Annenberg familiarized himself with by riding through the city's streets in police cars to gain firsthand knowledge of the conditions that spawned the crimes his paper wrote about. As part of his community services, he donned a waiter's jacket one night a week and worked at the Stage Door Canteen, a club in the basement of the city's Academy of Music, where prominent Philadelphians aided the war effort by waiting on military men and women who were on leave. Moreover, having joined the Pennsylvania State Council on Defense, he became a prime mover in the city's civil-defense efforts. Like many busy people, the more he did, the more he seemed capable of doing.

Annenberg didn't throw himself into social situations with abandon as he did in his work or other activities. For one thing, it was impossible in Philadelphia, where society was calcified into a small, but then important, circle. Newcomers, with the exception of a few with social pedigree in select other towns, such as Boston or New York, were usually treated to a frosty, forced politeness by those who considered themselves the social elite. Catholics and Jews, of course, were automatically excluded by heredity from such a crowd. The son of Moses Annenberg, who bore the double onus of being both Jewish and the son of a convict, never stood the whisper of a chance of being admitted to the tight little world. Be that as it may, Walter spent years of trying to strike some sort of rapprochement with Philadelphia society, but he made only the most modest gains in return for great effort. He developed individual friendships within the blue-blooded community, of course, but often as not he was rebuffed and sometimes humiliatingly so. For instance, he was blackballed from the Main Line's most exclusive golf clubs, so that he was always forced to leave the area in order to play. To ease his plight, he built a three-hole golf course at Inwood. He could have associated with Philadelphia's Jewish aristocracy, naturally enough, but Walter didn't perceive himself in terms of Jewish or Gentile. He always gravitated toward people of wealth and power. Unfortunately, he had blindly failed to recognize the insularity of the group controlling the Quaker City when he and his father arrived there. In a more socially relaxed city, even New York, with the aid of money spent on the right charitable and cultural causes, he might well have eased his way into the social hierarchy. But from the first day he set foot in town, any likelihood of becoming a social voice was lost to him.

When Walter encountered frustrations with people, whether they were socialites, employees, relatives, friends or business acquaintances, likely as not he simply removed any evidence of them from his life. His ignoring them took the form of not accepting telephone calls, not speaking in hallways or public or private places and not acknowledging letters. Life was too short, he felt, to bother with people who disappointed him. His erasing people in such fashion might last only a few days or it could go on for years. Almost superstitiously, he acted as if when he ignored someone's existence, he or she ceased to exist—which the ignored one did, as far as he cared. For Annenberg, this mode of dealing with problem people became strikingly apparent because he was a publisher and his reasoning extended to his publications. As often as not, people who offended him found that their names had vanished forever from the pages of the *Inquirer*, no matter what they did or said.

Thus, people who snubbed him socially found themselves snubbed editorially. Other times, people Annenberg found insufferable were twitted in the society columns. One prominent woman, for example, found herself referred to in the *Inquirer* society pages as "a Chestnut Hill housewife," as though she were the spouse of a postman rather than that of an influential attorney. Such indulgences on the part of the publisher, while rare, nonetheless raised more concern among the city's blue bloods than had Moses' blatant political use of the paper. Perhaps because the aristocrats were losing their grasp on the city's institutions, Walter's actions simply made them feel more threatened. But, in time, his policies would infuriate a much wider audience.

Walter's biggest headache at the *Inquirer*, however, wasn't the charge of editorial abuse that occasionally was made over a disappearing name—his major problem was executive editor Dimitman. For years, Dimitman had been Moses' surrogate in the newsroom, and the editor and the deceased publisher had understood each other like brothers. Often it seemed to other editorial employees that the two thought the same thoughts simultaneously. When Moses got around to telling Dimitman he wanted something done, he found the editor often as not had already tended to the matter. The two had been so similar that they had been like a pair of bookends, stalking through the building in loose-jointed strides, each with hands joined behind his back, his shoulders slightly stooped and his body bent forward at the waist. After years of being in charge, Dimitman was accustomed to having everything his own way; his way had been Moses' way, so it had made little difference. But Dimitman had adopted a habit from his former boss that was to become a boomerang. Like Moses, he dismissed Walter and his ideas as inconsequential.

Just what he could do with the editor was a puzzle to Annenberg. On one level he was pleased with Dimitman's running of the *Inquirer*, especially the paper's war coverage. E.Z. had dispatched Alexander Kendrick to Moscow, for instance, where the reporter's moving pieces on the struggles in the Soviet Union under terrible privation made the paper shine. He had sent another reporter, Ivan H. "Cy" Peterman to Europe, where his dispatches compared favorably to just about any other foreign correspondent's, and Peterman's own personal daring made for good reading. On June 6, 1944, "D-Day," for example, he joined the Allied invasion in a glider that was flown by the Airborne Infantry. He received a Purple Heart as a result of breaking his wrist when the glider overturned upon landing.

The *Inquirer* also was on top of the many local angles inherent to a newspaper in a state that had one and a quarter million of its men and women in uniform and where readers were well aware that many military leaders were home-town boys. General Henry Harley Arnold, who commanded the Army Air Force, for instance, was from the Philadelphia suburb Gladwynne, and his second in command, General Carl Spaatz, was from nearby Boyertown. The Army's youngest general, James M. "Slim Jim" Gavin, had sold newspapers as a boy in Mount Carmel. Thomas C. Kinkaid, who commanded the Seventh Fleet in the Pacific, was from Philadelphia as was Vice-Admiral Alan K. Kirk, who commanded forces in Normandy and Sicily. Even the nation's top soldier, General George C. Marshall, was a Pennsylvanian. Reporting the great events of the day most often meant discussing men many *Inquirer* readers knew intimately.

The mechanics of war generated much home-front news as well. The Philadelphia Navy Yard had round-the-clock shifts totaling 70,000 workers, who churned out battleships and aircraft carriers as well as repaired and outfitted hundreds of ships. The Philadelphia Quartermaster Depot was the central procurement agency for military uniforms, and the city's Frankford Arsenal cranked out millions of small-arms ammunition and trained workers for new plants. Westinghouse's Sharon plant developed an electrically powered torpedo that didn't leave the telltale bubbles that characterized compressed-air-power torpedoes; the Hershey Company created the D-ration chocolate bar; Philadelphia Radio Corporation helped develop radar, and the Banton Car Company of Butler developed the hardy jeep.

Besides keeping the paper on top of the story in the trenches and the factories, Dimitman rarely missed an opportunity for heart-warming tales that would sell more papers. At one point, for instance, the *Inquirer* raised $100,000 for a young Army Air Force sergeant named Jimmy Wilson, who was a quadriplegic as a result of his wounds. The gutsy young Wilson learned to walk, and the *Inquirer* followed his progress; one story gave a heroic account of the soldier attending a dance after a year of rehabilitation at a Philadelphia hospital. With the shortage of manpower, the paper had turned to a number of women to

fill its editorial ranks, and one of the *Inquirer*'s new feature writers
was Walter's sister, Enid, who worked hard and impressed editors by
taking the job seriously.

The war, of course, hadn't diverted the *Inquirer* from coverage of
local and state politics. Though the paper hadn't stopped being Republican, the *Inquirer* under Walter Annenberg lost much of its biased editorial partisanship. The paper supported Edward G. Martin, a
permanent fixture in Pennsylvania Republican politics whose military
career that dated back to the Spanish American War. As such, Martin,
who enjoyed the backing of the old G.O.P. warhorses Pew and
Grundy, epitomized the kind of simplistic man the public apparently
wanted at this complex moment in history. Not only was the *Inquirer*'s reporting fairer and the editorials less strident than they had
been in Moses' days as publisher, but Republican leaders were
shocked when Walter refused to give donations to the party. Walter
had seen how much trouble his father had gotten into as a result of
meddling in politics, and he vowed that that would never happen to
him. It soon became obvious to any fund raiser that the subject was a
testy one with the new publisher, although his father had given hundreds of thousands of dollars to the state party. Moreover, after the *Inquirer*-backed candidate won, Walter stunned Republican leaders by
saying he wanted nothing for his paper's support. Well aware of his father's lust for political power, the party chiefs settled back and waited
for Moses' son to make his move in the same direction. It was inevitable, they said, as though love of power was in his genes.

The man who was most surprised by Walter the publisher was Dimitman. Besides being more restrained politically than his father,
Walter was interested in the kinds of stories that had never interested
Moses, or Dimitman either. Walter, for instance, gave the editor suggestions for articles on the museum, the orchestra and other cultural
institutions but, likely as not, Dimitman disdainfully filed them in his
wastebasket. The editor also didn't like Walter's occasionally seeing to
it that somebody's name didn't appear in the newspages. Often as not,
Walter said, "Do we have to carry something about this son of a
bitch?" and the person's name never surfaced again, while on other
occasions, he quashed a story about someone he didn't like. Though
such actions were haphazard, word spread among staff members and
eventually around Philadelphia over the years that Walter Annenberg
had a blacklist—or "shit list," as it came to be known—that had names
of many of his enemies. In reality, there was no such compendium, but

whenever someone wanted to discredit the publisher he mentioned it. There were enough examples of Annenberg having ordered references to certain people deleted from the *Inquirer*'s pages that such a list seemed to exist. One of the earliest instances of a reporter being embarrassed by his publisher's whims came when Joe Van Hart was sent by a new city editor named Morrie Litman to interview Albert Greenfield, who, as everyone but Litman apparently knew, had been on the outs with Walter ever since the old Stern-Moses feuding days. "Will the *Inquirer* print the story?" Greenfield asked Van Hart at the end of the lengthy interview.

Only too aware of the bitter blood between the men, Van Hart decided to call Litman to double check. "Sounds like a good story," Litman replied. "Tell him it's O.K."

A few minutes later, Greenfield's phone rang. With a cynical glance, the millionaire told the reporter it was for him. Litman was on the line, and he explained that he had decided to run the story past Annenberg, who had killed it. Van Hart left Greenfield feeling foolish about having had to explain the change of plans. Greenfield merely laughed.

Whereas Dimitman hadn't minded pillorying a political candidate who was on the opposite side of his paper's political fence, he thought such business as striking names from copy and spiking stories because the publisher disliked a principal involved was petty. In turn, Annenberg was maddened by Dimitman's attitude. He respected the relationship E.Z. had had with his father, and he ran the company with the same paternalism that his father always had, which meant that many faults in a man could be overlooked as long as he was loyal to the Annenberg organization. But he had to run the company his own way and have everyone know it. Finally, he lost patience. He summoned Dimitman to his office, closed the door and told him that he had had it. Running down a list of stories that the editor had failed to cover even though he had ordered them, Walter told him he was tired of seeing his own ideas ignored. "I don't like doing this, but you'll have to take a walk," he told him. Like the names of people who disturbed him, Walter wanted Dimitman out of his sight.

Dimitman was taken aback. He had been so wrapped up in his own position he actually came to believe he held the power that in reality was the publisher's. He also took a new look at Walter. The reserved, stuttering young man who had always seemed to shrink a little in the presence of his father had disappeared. Dimitman found himself staring into the eyes of a tough businessman, who over the past few years had grown used to giving orders. There was a steely glint about the publisher's eyes that Dimitman recalled seeing before. It was the look that Moses had had.

After his sacking, Dimitman headed westward to Chicago, which was where he planned on going years earlier when Moses stepped into his life and made the *Inquirer* the kind of newspaper the editor enjoyed running more than anything else in the world. The greatest time of E. Z. Dimitman's life had just come to a close, and he would always believe that "M. L. Annenberg was the best thing that ever happened to the *Inquirer*." He went to Marshall Field's *Chicago Sun*, where he landed a top editing job. Ever the cynic, he realized what had happened. He philosophized that he had committed an unpardonable sin. When Moses died, he said later, "I forgot the old maxim: 'The King is dead; long live the King!' "

TWELVE

FOLLOWING THE WAR, Annenberg finally got a chance to play foreign correspondent. An intensely curious man, he had the money and position to pursue his interest, whether his fancy entailed traveling in a Philadelphia police car through crime-ridden neighborhoods or flying to Europe to witness the ravages of war. Thus, in his role of editor and publisher, he visited England, France and Germany, where he talked with political leaders, publishers and people in the streets. The gilded Continent of his youth had disappeared, of course, and he was alarmed by the vast numbers of homeless people living in squalor, understanding how they could be attracted to Communism, one of the alien "isms" that his father had abhorred, as he himself did. Wanting to add his voice to those already alerting the world to such a possibility, which he felt was his duty as a publisher, he sent back dispatches of his impressions that were printed under his byline in the *Inquirer*.

One article, for instance, warned of "the glacial inroads of Russia's Communism," which he believed was fueling "a rising tide of nationalism that has overwhelmed any serious consideration of a workable United Nations." He became convinced that the United States had to do something to defuse the tensions and rebuild the crushed cities and civilizations he encountered. Of paramount importance, he came away believing that the United States must be militarily strong, an opinion that he always maintained and that was perhaps best summarized by a headline that appeared over one of his dispatches: U.S. MUST ARM AND REARM TO KEEP THE PEACE. The need for constant vigilance, he wrote, was required in view of Russia's goal of world domination—"If this country were to abandon Europe, we would merely be hastening the day when the Dictator of the Kremlin could set in motion combined production facilities greater than ours, designed to defeat ours." Exhorting American leaders to "sell Democracy aggressively and affirmatively—we should not permit the Russians to be on the propaganda offensive alone," Annenberg became, as his friend Richard Nixon later admiringly said, "a hard-liner."

The voice of Walter Annenberg wasn't easily dismissed in the corridors of power in Washington. Whereas ordinary citizens have no automatic forum for their ideas, publishers do, and in the 1940s, newspaper publishers carried weight far beyond the geographic bounds of their circulation areas. Radio was still a relatively young medium, and television was an unknown quantity. The nation depended upon the press for most of its information, and politicians relied upon it to convey their ideas to the electorate. Major publishers like Annenberg were the kings of the communications business, and since many of them inserted their own biases in their newspapers' news coverage as well as editorial policy, they were treated by Congressmen as well as Presidents with as much wariness as deference. A large number of these publishing moguls echoed Annenberg's get-tough theme, and more than a few politicians of national stature likewise heard anti-Soviet warning bells and championed the cause themselves.

While traveling through Europe, Annenberg, who always considered himself a newsman, was drawn to headline-making stories. In Germany, for example, he observed the Nuremberg trials. Though he always bore being Jewish lightly at best, stories and photographs about Nazi concentration camps that were printed in the *Inquirer*—one of the first newspapers General Dwight D. Eisenhower had invited to inspect the camps—had stirred sympathetic Zionist feelings within him. He already had a firsthand familiarity with the Zionist movement—his war-hero brother-in-law, Ben Dunkelman, after the war had stunned family and friends by turning in his Canadian Army uniform and joining the underground forces in the Middle East fighting the British for the formation of an Israeli state. Dunkelman himself would later explain his complex motives in his autobiography, *Dual Allegiance.*

While in Germany, Annenberg visited Dachau, the prison where prominent Nazis were incarcerated. As he was shown about, he passed the cell of Herman Giesler, an architect of the Third Reich, who was imprisoned for having used slave labor. On impulse, Annenberg gave vent to one of the boyish urges that still gripped him from time to

Sarah and Tobias Annenberg.

Moses and Sadie with their children.

(*Left to right*) Enid, Jan,
Aye with baby Walter in
her lap, and Polly in 1909.

Moses and Walter fishing in
1915.

Sadie and Moses Annenberg.

Moses at his Ranch "A" in 1935.

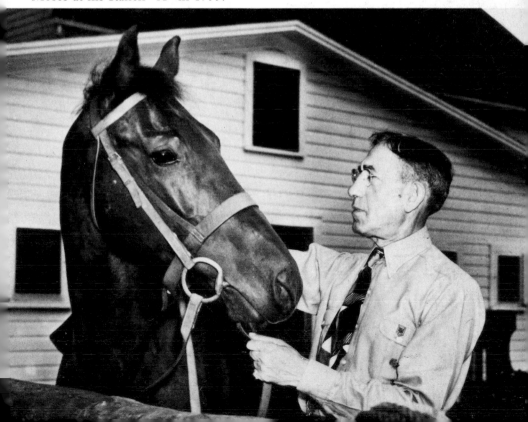

Walter seated second from left at Camp Yukon, Winthrop, Maine, in 1921.

Walter, standing by left pillar, outside a residence hall at the Peddie School, Hightstown, New Jersey.

(*Left to right*) Weymouth Kirkland, "Cissy" Patterson, Arthur Brisbane, Moses, and Bernie Gimbel.

Moses during his trial for income-tax evasion, emerging from Judge Wilkerson's courtroom.

Bernard Baruch
and
Sadie Annenberg.

Walter with Wallis and Roger in 1952.

Wallis Annenberg.

Walter Annenberg standing in the window of Hitler's mountain retreat at Berchtesgaden, August 9, 1946.

Walter and Lee at "Sunnylands," their Palm Springs winter estate.

LEFT Lee Annenberg. RIGHT Enid Haupt, the sister Annenberg placed in charge of *Seventeen* magazine.

Annenberg with long-time
friend Bob Hope.

Annenberg with Wendell
Willkie.

Annenberg with Harry Truman and Joseph Clark.

Walter and Lee with Tricia Nixon in London.

Nixon and Annenberg at Walter's baronial Main Line residence, "Inwood." The Vice President made this his first stop after a Latin American trip during which he was stoned in Caracas.

Walter in an extravagant bow to
his friend Queen Elizabeth.

Prime Minister Harold Wilson
and Ambassador Annenberg at
10 Downing Street, October 14,
1969.

Walter and Lee at Wynnefield House.

Annenberg with Lord Louis Mountbatten in May 1969.

Elizabeth

Elizabeth the Second,
by the Grace of God of the United Kingdom of Great Britain and Northern Ireland and of Her other Realms and Territories Queen, Head of the Commonwealth, Defender of the Faith and Sovereign of the Most Excellent Order of the British Empire, to The Honourable Walter Hubert Annenberg

Greeting

Whereas We have thought fit to nominate and appoint you to be an Honorary Knight Commander of the Civil Division of Our said Most Excellent Order of the British Empire.

We do by these presents grant unto you the Dignity of an Honorary Knight Commander of Our said Order and hereby authorise you to have hold and enjoy the said Dignity and Rank of an Honorary Knight Commander of Our aforesaid Order together with all and singular the privileges thereunto belonging or appertaining.

Given at Our Court at Saint James's under Our Sign Manual and the Seal of Our said Order this Eighth day of June 1976 in the Twenty-fifth year of Our Reign.

By the Sovereign's Command.

Philip
Grand Master.

Grant of the Dignity of an Honorary Knight Commander of the Civil Division of the Order of the British Empire to The Honourable Walter Hubert Annenberg.

The certificate attesting to Annenberg's knighthood.

(*Left to right*) Ronald and Nancy Reagan, Annenberg, Prince Charles and Lee Annenberg at Sunnylands.

Annenberg with Pope John Paul II at the Vatican.

Ronald Reagan, Gerald Ford and Walter Annenberg at the Palm Springs Desert Museum, 1979.

Dear Walter:

Happy and ? are so proud of you — as two American citizens who were shocked + distressed by what happened in B.H. to the Shah's mother + sister — when you in friendship and compassion reached

out to redeem this humiliation for us as a country, by inviting them to your home.

You're a great American and a true gentleman!

Thanks and very best wishes to you both for a very Happy New Year. Happy & Nelson

Correspondence between Nelson A. Rockefeller and Walter Annenberg regarding Annenberg's controversial offer to allow the family of the deposed Shah of Iran to take refuge at Sunnylands.

SUNNYLANDS

(C O P Y)

January 17, 1979

The Honorable Nelson A. Rockefeller
Room 5600
30 Rockefeller Plaza
New York, New York 10020

Dear Nelson:

I was touched by your thoughtfulness in sending me the handwritten letter concerning my housing the Shah's mother and sister, following the Beverly Hills tragic happening.

Not only was I enraged by the conduct of the so-called "students," but I felt it necessary to back up our government's hospitality.

My reference to so-called Iranian "students" underscores that an examination of the film footage reveals that most of the unruly mob constituted 40, 50 and 60-year-old characters who are always available for radical causes; I think it fair to describe most of them as "rent-a-mob."

Lee joins me in all good wishes to Happy and you.

Sincerely,

Walter Annenberg

WHA:h

"Sunnylands"
P. O. Box 98
Rancho Mirage
California 92270

Portrait of Walter Annenberg by Andrew Wyeth.

time. Pulling back the metal plate that barred the view of the prisoner's cell, he yelled, "Achtung!" The startled Giesler leaped as though he had been summoned to be shot. "I rather felt sorry that I had alarmed him," Walter noted afterward, but he savored the momentary amusement of witnessing one of the top Nazis, who had demeaned so many people, jump like a frightened rabbit. Days later, at Hitler's renowned retreat, The Eagle's Nest, Annenberg had his picture taken standing in the hideaway's vast windows, where he was acutely aware of the magnitude of fresh history enveloping him like the cool mountain air. As at all the stops along his whirlwind tour, there was a sense of urgency about him, he was making up for having missed the war, wringing whatever remained of the awesome experience that was rapidly becoming covered by time.

In Paris, the story of the moment was the Peace Conference. Determined that his newspaper should have thorough coverage of the historic event, Annenberg opened an *Inquirer* bureau and installed Francis Chase and Larry Klingman, two well-known former war correspondents, to be responsible for day-to-day coverage. Madame Suzanne Roquère, a noted French editor and wartime Resistance leader, wrote background stories and events that led up to the conference, and Mrs. J.P. McEvoy, an American writer and photographer, sent back weekly dispatches about personalities and stories behind the news, as well as photos. Opening the bureau was in keeping with the quality of coverage for which he wanted his paper to be known, and it reflected his sense of patriotism to chart the role his nation was playing.

Far from his and his father's enormous problems with his government making him feel bitter toward his country, Annenberg had become an unflinching patriot who wanted to prove himself just that. Thus, while he was in Paris, his sense of Americanism was grossly offended when he observed the disdain Charles de Gaulle exhibited toward the United States, and he became a lasting anti-Gaullist. In light of the number of American lives lost fighting in France, Annenberg found the French leader's posture insufferable. Referring privately to de Gaulle as "an ingrate," he resented practically everything about the man. When he saw the provisional president of the new French government sitting in an outsized chair like a throne, Annenberg thought he wanted to be "a king, and the arrogance of the man made me sick." Soon, criticism of de Gaulle became grist for the *Inquirer* editorial mill, a policy that remained in effect as long as Annenberg owned the paper. Occasionally indulging himself as only a man of wealth and large ego could, he paid to have his editorial attacks on the Frenchman reprinted in European newspapers in hopes that de Gaulle would see what Annenberg had to say about him. The price of the advertisements was small, he believed, to take to task an ungrateful ally.

In contrast, he was quite taken with General Dwight Eisenhower, the great Allied leader he had read so much about and finally got a chance to meet. Eisenhower's headquarters were outside Paris, where Annenberg casually met him through a mutual Philadelphia friend, Anthony Drexel Biddle. The publisher was as impressed by the general in person as he had been by him in print. Annenberg had long ago determined that he wouldn't live his life hiding in disgrace as a result of the shameful past, but that he would push himself along, meeting people who knew what his background was and who must have been wondering what he himself was like, this son of Moses Annenberg. With few exceptions, this persistence paid off. Eisenhower, for instance, became a friend, one whom he would later support politically.

When he returned home from Europe, Annenberg turned his editorial guns on a man he despised, old Joe Guffey, the Pennsylvania Democrat who had helped bring down his father. In 1946, Republican Governor Martin wanted to cap his political career by challenging Guffey for his Senate seat, and Annenberg immediately gave him his unconditional support. Walter had never forgiven Guffey, Stern, Ickes or any of the New Dealers for what they had done to Moses, and he would have supported just about any Republican who could breathe if he ran against one of those sworn enemies. The *Inquirer*'s campaign on behalf of Martin and his running mate, James H. Duff, the state attorney general who was running for governor, again lacked the sting and gross distortions that had characterized the paper's lopsided coverage of "Old Button Shoes" James's gubernatorial bid eight years earlier. The *Inquirer*'s endorsement of the Republicans actually mirrored a temporary resurgence of the party in Pennsylvania. Martin's conservative attitudes, particularly toward labor, which a few years later would be out of fashion, were in vogue. The governor had dealt sternly with strikers in Philadelphia and Pittsburgh, and, after years of war, the public was tired of change and out of sympathy with complex labor issues that edged on violence. Though the G.O.P. candidates had the support of Pew and Grundy, Annenberg could convince himself that he was backing men who had minds of their own. They were both staunch anti-Communists, which the publisher liked, of course, and Martin at least had shown his independence by bucking the Pew-

Grundy factions on several occasions, which also appealed to Annenberg, who was disgusted with the rampant corruption among Republicans on both state and local levels. In any event, the *Inquirer*-backed team won, and Annenberg was pleased to see Guffey's career smashed on the political rocks.

Guffey's loss wasn't the only victory Annenberg had to celebrate. After years of relentless hard work and ingenuity, he had paid off his father's tax penalties. The company, his company, was finally free of the enormous, troublesome burden, and the man who had saved Triangle Publications had become a tough, shrewd, respected businessman in the process. Making the payments had always galled Annenberg, who clung to the belief that his father had been the victim of a political conspiracy. When the final $1.5 million installment was made in 1946, he and Joe First met in Washington with the then Chief Counsel of the Bureau of Internal Revenue, J. P. Wenchel. Knowing the publisher's feelings of bitterness, Wenchel related to the pair an apocryphal anecdote about the old United States Treasury Building having been built on a plot of ground, which during the Civil War was used as an assignation point for camp followers ministering to homesick soldiers. Wenchel may have been trying to illustrate that the foundations of the mighty Treasury Department weren't very hallowed, or that time changes everything. But after much dissection of the comment with First, Annenberg, who seized anything that would exonerate his father, interpreted the tale to mean that Moses had been "screwed" by vindictive New Dealers.

Though he worked diligently at trying to restore the honor of his father's name—for example, by establishing the M. L. Annenberg Foundation, which gave generously to worthy causes—Moses' past continued to haunt Walter in unexpected ways. In 1946, for example, Jim Ragen, the former manager of the wire, was gunned down by hoodlums who were once more battling for dominance of the service. While in a hospital recovering from his gunshot wounds, Ragen was poisoned by an underworld killer who had slipped into his room. Moses' name was brought under the harsh glare of publicity when statements that Ragen had drafted regarding the Capone gang's assassination plot against his boss a dozen years earlier were found in his safe-deposit box. The documents, which Ragen intended as his insurance policy, failed to keep him alive and brought Moses' name back into the press.

Far from weakening in his resolve that his father was not a less honorable man than he had known him to be, Walter stood firm. Through the steely belief in his father, he had found the inspiration to believe in himself. The myriad problems he had coped with since Moses' death had changed him into the kind of resilient, creative businessman that Moses had wanted him to be. He could hardly deny his father now. Moreover, he had come to accept the fact that if he and his family were to survive in a world of potentially dangerous political adversaries, he had to put aside the bitterness of the past and concentrate on forming powerful alliances that would ease his life in the future. Thus, when a special F.B.I. agent named L.V. Boardman visited him in 1946, Walter treated the man cordially, but it was clear to the agent that what had happened to Annenberg's father still preoccupied the son. Boardman, whose visit had no specific purpose, wrote to Hoover that Walter was visibly upset when discussing his father and that he made reference to Department instructions that had been "to get Moe Annenberg at any cost."

"He immediately continued in rapid succession that he had long since decided to let bygones be bygones and that it was his intention to steer clear completely of politics and to lead such an exemplary life that the false wreath that had been hung around the neck of his father would be dissipated by the exemplary conduct of the son," the agent's letter to Hoover noted.

Walter's push for propriety had made him a very serious man. He joked with employees and friends with whom he was close, but to most people he presented a very formal exterior as he strove to meet life with dignity. The man who now autocratically ran Triangle Publications—and there was no question that it was Walter Annenberg, not Joe First, who now ran the company—wasn't the same person his mother and sisters had pampered and nicknamed Boy. At social functions, he appeared far too serious for his years, while at work there was the impatient brusqueness about him of a man who has all too few hours in the day as he gave orders, dictated memos and made quick decisions.

At home, however, he was a loving, caring man who doted on his children and would leap up from the breakfast table to chase a squirrel that his son or daughter had seen about to pounce on a bird.

Of all his cares, his most immediate was his son, Roger, whose cleft palate had made him shy and withdrawn. Walter, who knew only too well how a physical imperfection can prey on a child's mind, was protective of his boy and solicitous of his needs. He didn't treat Roger as if there was anything wrong with him, however, and as the child grew older, his palate mended naturally in a way that even doctors described as "miraculous." When he was old enough, Roger underwent plastic surgery, which reduced his facial deformity to a mere trace of what it had been, but the boy's ordeal had left its mark on him in other ways. Roger remained a brooding child, using his keen mind for reading literature, especially poetry, that was far in advance of his years, and spending much of his time listening to classical music. The Annenberg estate, Inwood, which Wallis found desolate and lonely with its huge manor house and stretches of sunless woodland, suited the boy's personality and he wandered for hours by himself over the sixteen acres with a book of poetry as his companion. From the time Roger was a young boy, his father doubted that he would succeed him in the business world and he didn't press him to do so.

Wallis, however, was another story. A bright, energetic child, she became her father's refuge of sorts. He played with her whenever he found the time, often boxing and wrestling with her in the yard or living room, and he took her to all the home football games at the University of Pennsylvania, an institution that Annenberg sentimentally identified with, even though he had been a bored student there for only a year. All institutions in his life, however, took on great meaning for him, perhaps again a way of defining his ties with established authorities. Wallis was content to be with her father no matter what he was doing, and she spent enchanted days off from school sitting in his office, marveling at the procession of important people who called up her dad and listening to telephone calls from and to the high and mighty, including politicians and celebrities. "It was very glamorous to sit in Father's office and hear him talking to everyone," Wallis recalled. "That's where the action is."

Wallis and Roger were nice, mannerly children, and Walter tried to make them realize how fortunate they were. To build his case, he frequently turned to the repertoire of sayings he had consciously absorbed from his own father, who had never forgotten the poverty of his youth. When the Annenberg family drove along a road and an obviously poor family was ahead in a battered old car, Walter said to his children, "There but for the grace of God we go," and "Don't ever forget that what you have is an accident of birth." He reinforced his homilies with the sort of lessons in thrift that can be devised only by the extremely wealthy. While growing up, for instance, the children had to travel second class, whether by plane or train, but their father's chauffeur-driven Rolls-Royce took them to the airport or train station and picked them up. Even as a little girl, Wallis grumbled about the incongruity of showing up in a Rolls but having to go the rest of the distance in tourist style.

Unlike his own father, Walter never talked business with his children, and he never discussed their grandfather with them. The past was simply too painful. Nevertheless, he had absorbed so many of Moses' attitudes that he passed them along unconsciously to his son and daughter. His wife, Ronny, for example, had gained his reluctant approval to send the children on weekends to a Jewish school, which was a major concession, since Walter, like Moses, had little use for religion. The school's rabbi, a pretentious man with an English accent, particularly grated on Walter's nerves. Thus, one day when Roger called his father at work, asking him what he should be doing for his "religious advancement," which the rabbi insisted he pursue, Walter couldn't restrain himself. "Tell him you're looking for a rich wife," he told the little boy.

Aside from the deep concerns he had about his son, Annenberg, as the years passed, encountered a trying time with his beautiful sybaritic young wife. Ronny dressed elegantly, wore clothes with more flair than any woman around, and she liked being admired. When they went out, she was flirtatious, a form of behavior that pained her husband. Ronny was charming and made other women's husbands feel wittier and more handsome than they were. Her own husband, who became accustomed to dominating thousands of employees, didn't seem sure how to dominate her. Because he expended so much energy forcing himself to impose his will on his companies, Walter had little left over to meet the challenges of a strong-willed woman at home. For Ronny's part, she believed that if she had spent her waking hours devoted to telling her husband that he was the most wonderful man in the world they would have no problems, but that was a role she couldn't accept. With all the pressures brought to bear upon them since they married, the Annenbergs' marriage, unknown to friends, was collapsing and eventually would end in divorce.

At the time, Walter's friends found him to be too hard on himself, and his self-consciousness had him behaving at times too effusively. When Robert and Ellie Wolf, a prominent young couple who had a close relationship with the Annenbergs visited Inwood one evening, for example, Walter asked them to try caviar that he had just bought. "Isn't that the best caviar you've ever tasted?" he asked them repeatedly. Ellie got the feeling that whenever they replied that it was, Walter didn't believe them, so he'd ask again. Mrs. Wolf, a strong-minded, attractive Southerner who never hid her intellectual curiosity as so many other wealthy women did, thought it was a shame that a man of Walter's brains and obvious abilities, a man who could have just about anything in the world if he only realized it, felt that he had to bend so much to please others. Like so many people who knew him then, she didn't realize what a toll it had taken for Walter to come to grips with the draining family and business problems of recent years. Only in his corporation did he now feel completely comfortable, where his role was unchallenged and his grasp was secure.

Unlike Ronny, Ellie Wolf was keenly interested in both publishing and politics, and she frequently engaged Walter in discussions of local, national and international affairs. She found him open to examining different sides of issues, seldom adopting a dogmatic, conservative stance and, when she disagreed with his newspaper, she told him so. In the summer of 1948, for instance, she had attended the opening address of the Republican Convention, which was held in Philadelphia. Believing that she had never heard a drearier speech, she was dismayed when the *Inquirer* splashed the story of the event across the front page, and the article said the oration was greeted by a roaring, enthusiastic crowd. "I remember saying, 'Goodness, what in the name of heaven is this,' " she recalled. "I told Walter I was appalled, and he said, 'What do you mean?' I said the place was dead, but your paper had a big banner headline about how enthused everyone was."

Walter, who was a diligent supporter of New York Governor Thomas E. Dewey at the time, amiably explained that since the convention was in Philadelphia and the *Inquirer* was the first newspaper delegates read, he believed it was terribly important that they had positive impressions. Believing it critical that the delegates felt the same way he did, Annenberg hadn't minded bending reality in his newspaper. The action was similar to what his father might have done, but Walter's motives were selfless, and he considered that an essential difference. Whereas Moses would have used the occasion to strengthen his own political hand, his son did it to ease the nomination of a man he considered a national need. In recognition of such support, Dewey invited Annenberg to have breakfast with him the morning after he received the nomination.

In the late 1940s, Annenberg began, at last, to believe in his own destiny. The seeds that Moses had sown in his boy many years ago not only had enabled Walter to stand on his own two feet, but had enabled him to become a man of vision. As restless as his father had been, Annenberg now wanted to create a media empire, and he realized that he needed responsible men to help him. Possessing a fairly accurate assessment of his own strengths and weaknesses, he was never averse to hiring consultants who specialized in whatever project he undertook. But for men who populated his executive ranks, he preferred smart hard-workers who could learn whatever job had to be done at the moment and learn it in a hurry. Above all, he demanded that men be loyal. "He's our kind of man," he said when introducing a new executive to others. And if there was doubt about someone, he asked, "Is he on our team?"

Annenberg found some of his executives through friends and associates, while others came inadvertently to Triangle through acquisitions that were made. In 1946, for instance, he had bought radio station WFIL in Philadelphia from the Lit Brothers department store, and with the acquisition came Roger Clipp, the station's manager, whom Annenberg recognized as an asset. The following year, he had bought the Philadelphia Arena; he wanted it because of its sporting events, which he believed could be aired on the new medium television someday. Several executives and men with executive potential came his way with that transaction, including a young man named Brian Bradfield, who would one day become general manager of *TV Guide*.

Typical of the young men he hired was Merrill Panitt, a veteran whom Annenberg asked to join him as his administrative assistant on the advice of another executive. A cordial, courteous man with a quick mind hidden beneath a congenial Midwestern manner, Panitt, like other Triangle executives, instinctively knew never to overstep the line that Annenberg drew between himself and his employees. Annenberg was very fond of many of his workers, and even called some by nicknames he made up, but Annenberg was "Mr. W." to most of them and Walter to only a few, and even they rarely socialized with him. There were no equals at the top of Triangle publications.

He found another executive while vacationing in Sun Valley. Through friends, he chanced to meet Frederick Chait, an intelligent young lawyer with sleek good looks and manners, who had been general counsel for the United Nations Relief and Rehabilitation Agency. Their friends were amazed when Chait, a sharp-tongued iconoclast with decidedly liberal leanings, and Walter, a naturally conservative reverer of institutions, struck it off. Almost to the point of ignoring everyone else, the two discussed the European Recovery Plan, better known as the Marshall Plan after the general who had drafted it. Chait, who was familiar with the subject, enthusiastically explained it to a serious, attentive Annenberg, who came to believe it meshed with the kind of drastic action he believed the United States must take to thwart Communism in Europe. Several days after their discussions, Annenberg handed Chait a copy of the *Inquirer* that was mailed to Sun Valley and which was open to the editorial page. The lead editorial called for implementation of the Marshall Plan; the *Inquirer* was perhaps the first newspaper in the nation to endorse it. The publisher was so proud of the editorial that he struck Chait as a Boy Scout who had done his good deed for the day.

Impressed by the lawyer's inquisitive mind and elegant manners, Annenberg recognized him as a man on the make and offered him a job as counsel for the *Inquirer*. Chait, who had let Walter know in a dozen subtle ways that he was casting around for a position, believed there were worse ways of making a living than working for this gruff young publisher who was so shrewd and forceful, but who also had a broad, somewhat naïve streak in him. Moreover, the lawyer recognized another quality in Annenberg, which was apparent to people who spent a little time with him—behind his domineering exterior, he was a man who desperately wanted to do the right thing. Ironically, Chait was lured to the job for another reason that had much to do with his own naïveté—he hoped that one day he would have some say in the *Inquirer*'s news and editorial process, the lure of the written word being a magnet for many liberals. Annenberg himself had a much more practical view of publishing. "Editors," he said on more than one occasion, "are a dime a dozen."

With the exception of Joe First and a very few others, the men surrounding Annenberg knew him only as a dynamic, resourceful boss. They had never known his father, or what a metamorphosis Annenberg had undergone. Far from ever considering him undisciplined or inconsequential, they found him one of the most self-disciplined, motivated men they had ever encountered. He was a tough, exacting boss, who worked hard and expected them to do likewise. They also had to cope with his moods. When he was angry, it was as if an arctic wind had filled the room, and if his displeasure erupted during a telephone conversation, the receiver seemed to frost over from the tone Annenberg used. When he was very angry with them, his executives found themselves treated to one of his deadly silences until the day came when they were inexplicably back in his good graces. But he was also courteous and thoughtful, and he worked easily with the men and women he got to know well.

At times he was completely unprepossessing, asking an executive to join him for lunch in his offices; likely as not he would serve mortadella, or bologna, which he had imported from Usinger's, a firm that he had become familiar with as a youth in Milwaukee, and he himself would cook the meat he considered a delicacy. The invitation, "Come on down and I'll fry some bologna," was one that many executives, who weren't quite as taken with the meat as their boss, wished they had an excuse to reject. Thus, the men who worked for Triangle found they were employed by a man who could be most charming or give them the equivalent corporate punishment of sending them to Coventry, depending on his mood.

Despite his contributing to the day-to-day insecurities of at least some of those executives, many found that Annenberg, because he let them develop to their fullest capacities and indeed expected as much, respected him and worked hard for him. Again, not all of them liked him, but many became quite fond of him even though they never quite understood him. Those who realized something of the insecurities and burdens he carried as a result of what he perceived as the all-consuming family tragedy in his past, became quite protective of him, not wanting to see him harmed further. No matter how they viewed Annenberg, however, once men came to work for him they generally stayed. Though his executives never verbalized it, Annenberg seemed to have selected them because they were men who hadn't wanted the top job in a corporation. They were content to remain within his shadow, although naturally some resented that role at one time or another. Thus, Triangle became populated with executives who were generally good at directing their operations, but who shied away from ultimate responsibility, a role that Annenberg never shirked. In truth, they worked well within the paternalistic atmosphere, knowing Annenberg was always there to protect them.

Moreover, he was willing to take charge of their entire lives. Many Triangle employees were retained long after retirement age, either because they couldn't afford to retire or didn't want to. A joke in the executive suite, for instance, was an aged black waiter named Archie, who was so slow that it was almost painful to watch his deliberate moves. When Annenberg was asked why he kept the old fellow on, he replied, "He's too proud to take a pension because he would view it as charity. What else can I do?" When the daughter of David Appel, the *Inquirer* book-review editor, was in an auto accident and her face severely damaged, Annenberg told Appel not to worry, and he had one of the city's top plastic surgeons care for her and bore the costs himself. Indeed, whenever he learned of misfortune affecting any of his workers, Annenberg quietly lined up doctors, paid medical expenses, or subsidized families until the time of hardship ended. In 1947, the staff of the *Inquirer* library decided to forgo the annual Christmas party and gave the money that had been collected to a co-worker whose young daughter was badly burned when she accidentally set her dress on fire. When he learned of the incident, Annenberg saw to it that the child received special medical attention and that the family wasn't financially harmed. He also saw to it that the librarians' party was held.

His generosity, like his father's, extended beyond the company as well. Frequently, he was moved to send money to people whose troubles he learned about in his paper or from letters seeking aid. After reading of the misfortune of a deaf-mute Chinese man, for example, he turned to his administrative aide Panitt, telling him to send the man a sum. "The poor son of a bitch needs it," Annenberg said. "He already has three strikes against him." Thus, there arose a feeling among many executives shortly after they arrived that they worked for a feudal lord who ran his kingdom in an unpredictable and very personal manner.

With the collection of bright, diligent men around him, Annenberg set about expanding his corporate kingdom, which the cautious Joe First warned him against doing too quickly. But *Seventeen* was doing fabulously well and the *Racing Form*, which Annenberg referred to as "the old brown cow that always gives milk," incessantly piled up profits, and the *Inquirer*'s advertising and circulation were strong. He needed new challenges, and he had a number of new ideas that he wanted to put into action. Having absorbed his father's gambling instincts, Annenberg realized that if he wanted to win big he had to play for high stakes.

One new communications field that intrigued him was broadcasting. He had some familiarity with radio, because one of his father's publications had been *Radio Guide*, a program-listing magazine that had never attracted a broad enough circulation to pay its own way. Walter, however, had seen how profitable many radio stations were, and he always believed that his father would have been smarter to get into radio. What Annenberg found far more interesting than radio, however, was television, which was touted by enthusiasts as the medium that would do away with radio, live theater, movies and just about everything else that took people out of their homes. While Walter didn't believe TV was the final word in entertainment, he immediately recognized its awesome potential, and he knew that he wanted in some way to become a prime mover in this new field.

Before entering any new venture, Annenberg wanted to know as much about it as possible. In the case of television, he asked his assistant Panitt to write a series of articles about the development of TV to date and the outlook for the future. When his aide had completed his task, Walter had him deliver the findings in a report before a meeting of Triangle's top executives, about a dozen men in all. Always thoroughly prepared, Panitt nervously gave a rundown of what he believed to be the potential of the young medium. There was no track record to go by, of course, but he believed there was a possibility for strong growth; Panitt's report was one of cautious optimism.

As his aide finished, Walter told the gathering that he had an option to build a television station in the city and he asked his officers whether he should exercise it. Somewhat to his surprise, to a man, from Joe First on down, they told him no. Basically, they believed the business was too risky and the return on investment would take too long. Television, they concluded, was a medium for dreamers, not for realists. Annenberg listened carefully to each man's arguments. Then he thanked them and told them he was plunging ahead with the project in any event. "Gentlemen, full speed ahead," he said before dismissing them. "We missed out on radio when we could have gotten in on the ground floor, and we're not going to do the same thing again." As his executives bemoaned their boss's folly, Annenberg in 1948 sent a two-cent post card to the Federal Communications Commission stating that he would construct TV station WFIL, the thirteenth station in the nation.

Since he knew so little about broadcasting, Walter turned for expertise to Roger Clipp, the feisty little manager of radio station WFIL, which Triangle had acquired two years earlier. Clipp was notorious for treating his staff harshly, even cruelly. He publicly humiliated his employees, and on the infrequent occasions when he complimented them, he did so in private. If he didn't like music that was being played over the air, he thought little of walking into the control booth and smashing records, while the dismayed disc jockey looked on. He had ripped so many telephones out in fits of rage that the telephone company had notified him that service to the station would be cut off if it happened again. "Clipp was one of those men that people are afraid of," Dick Gideon, who had worked at WFIL, said. "He intimidated everybody, even people outside the organization."

But Roger Clipp was an absolutely loyal employee, and there was something else about him that his subordinates found fascinating. He was afraid—deathly afraid—of Walter Annenberg. No one ever knew why. Indeed, there seemed to be no reason other than that something within Clipp, who bullied everyone around him, feared his master the way a beaten dog does. For his part, Annenberg didn't like either Clipp or his methods, but he put up with him because he was hardworking and his operations always showed a healthy profit. Moreover, Clipp knew the broadcasting business. What struck everyone, however, was how Annenberg could put Clipp in his place with a glare—rarely a harsh word or raised voice—just an icy look that made the little tyrant tremble. "He has a pretty good temper," Clipp said quietly when discussing his boss. Then he made the unmistakable motion with his right hand as though he were being driven by whip. Yet that never kept Clipp from lashing out at his subordinates. His cruelty was so disdained that when he was named a vice-president, Panitt wrote him a note of congratulations, but criticized his treatment of employees. Laughing, Clipp showed it to others.

Nevertheless, Annenberg tapped Clipp to be the emissary who would acquire broadcasting properties for him. The station manager had many connections in the field, so Walter gave him a free hand. What Annenberg hadn't counted on was Clipp's small-mindedness. A naturally mean-spirited man, who personally signed every requisition at his radio station, even if it was only a few dollars for hand towels for the bathroom, Clipp was tight-fisted when it came to buying television stations. Instead of pursuing properties in major markets, he kept his horizons low. Over the next few years, he bought stations in out-of-the-way places, including Binghamton, New York; Altoona, Pennsylvania; and Fresno, California. In all, he acquired a group of sixteen radio and television stations, and when Annenberg came to be more familiar with the industry, he would be disappointed with the quality of the stations. Annenberg simply thought in grander terms. Clipp had had some chances to make more significant purchases. For instance, he was about to buy a station in Baltimore for $4 million, but he backed out when the price escalated to $4.4 million. Less than a year later, the same station was sold to Westinghouse Electric Company for $6.5 million.

Clipp also didn't know how to maximize the profits of the stations, which Annenberg allowed him to oversee. His nature led him to cut costs to the bone in an industry where profits often increased exponentially in relation to the amount of money reinvested. Little money, for instance, was spent on local programming, and the only program on any of the Annenberg stations that was of consequence was spawned by Annenberg himself. While trying to think of ideas to fill up air time, Annenberg told Clipp to try a dance program aimed at teen-agers. The show was called *Bandstand,* and later was broadcast nationally as *American Bandstand,* which was avidly watched by teen-agers from coast to coast.

While Annenberg's hand in the creation of the highly successful *Bandstand* went relatively unnoticed, he started another innovative use of his television station WFIL that gained him national recognition. He told Clipp to program college courses during the day. Thus, the Philadelphia station became what was perhaps the first in the nation to seize directly upon the vast, untapped educational potential of the medium. Education—or rather, innovative ways of learning—was one of the issues that preoccupied the publisher from time to time and was one of the areas where he quietly lavished philanthropic gifts. He wondered how poor people could receive an education and, in one of his flashes of insight, he saw television as being the conduit. With his now characteristic directness, he simply put the idea into action rather than step back and try to evaluate whether it would work. He was sure that it would. Called the *University of the Air,* the program was hailed by both educators and broadcasters as boldly innovative, and resulted in a flood of commendations from universities, educational associations and broadcast committees.

Ever continuing his search for executive talent, Walter took note of a man who was working for Clipp. He was James Quirk, a tireless, tense, brilliant man who had once been an aide to General Omar Bradley. Annenberg filed Quirk away in his mind as the kind of man to whom he would give major responsibilities one day. He believed in what he called "interior line management," by which he meant developing talent within the company, rather than looking outside. The practice was similar to that of his father, who called it counting on men of proven loyalty. Thus, with his expansionist plans in full swing, Annenberg made up his mind to rehire a man he knew well and about whom he had always felt somewhat guilty. He placed a call to Sam Newhouse, the head of the newspaper publishing chain, and asked him if there were objections to his hiring one of the top editors at the *Newark Star-Ledger*. With Newhouse's reluctant blessing, Walter telephoned E.Z. Dimitman. "How would you like to come back to the big leagues?" he asked.

Walter had always felt bad about Dimitman's departure. During his father's troubles, there had been executives who declared they would stay with the company only if there was something extra in it for them, and there had been those, such as his former brother-in-law, Kahn, who had lashed out at both his father and him. But Dimitman had always displayed a remarkable degree of loyalty and compassion during the terrible period, and he had been one of Moses' most ardent defenders. When he reflected upon such loyalty, Walter knew that his father would want him to bring the editor back into the Triangle fold. Besides, Walter needed someone to oversee the editorial side of the business, and he had always respected E.Z.'s abilities. Moreover, he knew that the canny editor was open to the prospect of coming back. Dimitman had shrewdly kept in touch by writing periodically critiques of the *Inquirer* for Walter, and his foresight was rewarded.

Dimitman, of course, accepted the offer immediately. His roots were in Philadelphia, and his heart was at the *Inquirer*. He was tired of living in strange cities, having restlessly moved to the Newark paper after Chicago. The moves had been difficult, primarily because he felt he was too old to start making his life over. He was fifty years old and yearning for the familiarity of his home town, which more than a decade earlier he had been willing to chalk off. Philadelphia's society and politics were second nature to him, and he could call a source to find out just about anything he might need to know. For an editor of a Philadelphia newspaper, his knowledge of such things was invaluable, but it was useless elsewhere. Moreover, Dimitman had learned the most valuable lesson of his life. He now understood his relationship with Walter Annenberg. A line was drawn, and he would never trespass it again. Annenberg was the publisher, and it was his duty to please him. Thus, E.Z. Dimitman returned to Philadelphia. Outwardly, he appeared to be the same self-confident, somewhat sardonic and unflappable man who had left. But he himself knew that he was different. He had been taught a lesson.

CHAPTER

THIRTEEN

SHORTLY BEFORE THE mayoral election in Philadelphia in November
1951, Michael A. Foley, the Republican candidate for district attorney,
delivered a blistering broadcast over radio station KYW. His speech
was a vicious attack on Walter Annenberg, and its tawdriness illustrated the depth of both anger and resentment that the city's Republican hierarchy harbored against the publisher of the *Philadelphia Inquirer*:

> A journalistic Dr. Jekyll and Mr. Hyde. He is a knight in shining
> civic-minded newsprint on the one hand, and on the other, the
> black-robed boss of the racing-news empire without which big-time
> gambling could not exist in America. In Philadelphia, Walter H.
> Annenberg is the publisher of a great newspaper dedicated to and to
> quote from the *Inquirer*'s own platform—"fight and never cease
> fighting to maintain the sanctity of personal liberty and the inviola-
> bility of human rights." In crime and gambling circles, Walter An-
> nenberg's racing tip sheets help keep alive what Senator [Estes]
> Kefauver calls a multimillion-dollar industry for the underworld—a
> National Crime Syndicate which violates every human right there
> is, including the right to life, liberty and pursuit of happiness. To-
> night, I ask you fellow Philadelphians, which Annenberg do you
> want in Philadelphia—the righteous publisher Annenberg, or the
> racetrack publisher Annenberg?

The broadside was merely the latest fired at the publisher. He and
his newspaper were embroiled in a tough, mudslinging political contest the likes of which Philadelphians hadn't seen since the 1930s,

when Moses Annenberg and David Stern were battling like dinosaurs. The reason for the Republican furor was all too obvious. Walter had thrown his editorial might behind two liberal Democrats, Joe Clark, the elitist patrician, and Richardson Dilworth, the former *Inquirer* lawyer, who were running on a reform ticket for mayor and district attorney, respectively. The *Inquirer*'s support of the pair had sent shock waves through the Republican party; this was the first time in the paper's 123-year history that the *Inquirer* had backed a Democrat for mayor, and the action had earned Annenberg a host of bitter enemies.

If the Republicans had had any foresight, however, they would have anticipated the inevitability of what had happened. Two years earlier, the publisher had proclaimed the *Inquirer*'s independence of all political parties. The news had exploded like a bomb in the ranks of the Republican organization, but, even then, there had been far too many Republicans who could not believe it was true; they could not conceive of the *Inquirer* as being anything else but theirs.

The decision to create an independent publication had been arrived at only after much deliberation on Walter's part, and for anyone whose political antennae were attuned to changes taking place at the *Inquirer*, the path Annenberg was traveling was obvious. For instance, there had been a series of articles in the paper that had probed deeply into the local municipal power structure and had disclosed numerous examples of corruption. The *Inquirer* had editorially called for a thorough housecleaning by the Republican city administration, but the advice had gone unheeded. Finally, Walter Annenberg's voice had thundered in an editorial on October 27, 1949, that the paper was independent:

> The political misrule of the present [Republican] administration in Philadelphia cannot be condoned. . . . It is time for a change. It also appears to me the logical time to declare our journalistic independence.
>
> No political party should be able to take any newspaper for granted. On October 14, 1939, my father, M. L. Annenberg, put on our logotype "An Independent Newspaper for All the People."
>
> He meant exactly what he said. I am sure that if my father were alive today, and had the same opportunity, he would have done as I have done. Unfortunately, he could not take the action I did because of a competitive newspaper situation in Philadelphia and the Federal government's campaign of using every resource against him.

Fortunately, through the mills of the gods, I have been completely free to take whatever stand is necessary in the interests of all the people. There is no question of the *Inquirer* going Republican or Democratic. As far as our editorial approach is concerned, we are going to support an individualistic philosophy against any collectivism.

The editorial had opened a Pandora's box. An unprecedented flood of letters had swamped the *Inquirer*, all of them emotional and either praising the stand as bold and progressive or condemning Annenberg as a traitor to the Republican party. More than anything else the editorial pointed out that the *Inquirer*'s publisher believed that a new era was dawning. He felt comfortable making the move, because two years earlier, in 1947, David Stern's *Record* had closed its doors as a result of bitter labor troubles. Thus, Walter felt that the *Inquirer* didn't have to be editorially polarized any longer.

The step wasn't an easy one, but it was important for him. Several years earlier, his instincts for independence had cost him membership in one of Philadelphia's most prestigious clubs, the Union League. A friend, General Milton Baker, headmaster at Valley Forge Military Academy, had proposed Walter for membership in the exclusive League, which was founded in 1862 by maverick, though prominent, men who were reacting against the city's then Democratic leaders, who were opposed to President Lincoln. As an affirmation of their faith in the President, the new club's members fielded a brigade of the city's wealthiest young men for the Union Army. By the middle of the twentieth century, the club was a bastion of economic and political power, and its membership rolls included the kind of men Walter wanted to be accepted by. Nevertheless, he withdrew his application when he learned of one of the League's requirements, one which other newspaper publishers in town had for generations accepted blindly— an oath of loyalty to the Republican party. Walter, with his father, had voted Democratic in the 1932 Presidential election, and he could foresee the day when he would vote Democratic again. "My independence is the most important thing in my life," he said. Even if he hadn't withdrawn his application, however, anti-Semitism might have blocked his membership.

The proper Philadelphians were at a loss as to where to place Annenberg on the political spectrum. On occasion he appeared to be a rock-ribbed conservative Republican, as in his stand on the Soviet

Union and his belief in individual initiative as the basis for solving the problems of the poor. Yet, there were many positions he adopted that were being espoused only by left-leaning liberals. For example, his *Inquirer* had printed numerous articles that were critical of United States aid given to Chiang Kai-shek, the Chinese general, who had retreated to Formosa. "Until and unless Chiang could be induced or impelled to use American aid more honestly, more faithfully and more efficiently, our help was not only certain to be wasted but worse, to entangle us disastrously in Chiang's inevitable defeat," one opinion column in the paper in September 1949 had stated. Annenberg even went so far as to warn Henry Luce, the founder of *Time* magazine, that he was being duped by Chiang. Not unpredictably, Luce, who considered Chiang the savior of Asia, was antagonized. And in 1950, when Senator Joe McCarthy proclaimed his famous list of "205 State Department officers that are known" to be Communists, the *Inquirer* didn't mindlessly take up the cry as many newspapers did, but in its editorials coolly demanded that the Truman Administration determine whether there was any truth to the charges. "This newspaper has criticized Senator McCarthy's failure to back up his sensational charges with evidence and his irresponsible use of smear tactics," the *Inquirer* intoned on April 14, 1950.

Thus, in 1951 Annenberg decided to support the Dilworth-Clark ticket simply because, like a lot of people, he was disgusted by the Republican rule. The city's G.O.P. machine was corrupt and inflexible and had long contained the seeds of its own destruction. But when Walter threw the support of the *Inquirer* behind Democrats, the Republican party immediately contended that his motives were far more devious than what could be perceived on the surface. The G.O.P. bosses made veiled references to Dilworth being in Annenberg's pocket, because of the retainer the lawyer once received from the *Inquirer*. Men who knew both Annenberg and Dilworth realized that such a charge was ridiculous. Walter Annenberg as a publisher had never sought political reward. As for Dilworth, he was an extremely independent man, whose judgment at times was clouded by passion, but no one had ever questioned his integrity. He had postponed entering politics just because of the hefty retainers he had received from local companies, such as the *Inquirer*, and he had bided his time until he could do without them.

Walter, however, was paying a severe price for his independence. The Republican Foley and his running mate, Daniel A. Poling, the candidate for mayor, indulged in a sleazy campaign that attempted to tar Walter with his father's past. They rehashed Moses' links to organized crime and implied that his son had the same ties. The attacks by Poling, who was a minister, were so low that they shamed more temperate Republicans, especially when he made much of the fact that Senator Kefauver hadn't called the Philadelphia publisher before his famed hearings on organized crime, implying that Walter and Kefauver had struck a deal whereby the publisher would support the Senator in a Presidential bid in return for not being summoned before his investigative panel. The tale grew to such proportions that an embarrassed Kefauver felt forced to deny publicly there was any basis to the innuendoes. "We never made a deal," Kefauver said at a press conference he called. "I have never discussed the campaign with Mr. Annenberg or anyone from the *Inquirer*."

Upon being confronted by the malicious tactics, Walter was dismayed. The charge was an especially sensitive one, of course, and called into question the positive steps his life had taken. For months the televised committee hearings had dragged mobsters before the American public, and dozens of times the name of Moses Annenberg and his racing wire were tied to illicit activities. Men like Dan Serritella, the pal of Al Capone and former partner in one of Moses' publishing enterprises, made repeated references to the elder Annenberg and the history of the racing wire, including Jim Ragen's violent death. Walter retaliated by denouncing Poling and Foley as "liars," and he was outraged that they stooped to using the hearings for their own ends. Dimitman urged him to use the *Inquirer* to get even with the pair, and, at length, Walter was so maddened by the charges that he gave the shrewd editor the green light to go after the "bums" and "parasites," as the publisher took to calling the two Republicans.

Soon, the candidates found out what it was like to be hounded by the press in the hands of a master. Dimitman began running stories that dredged up whatever was unsavory about the basically bland politicians' pasts, even to the point of telling readers about old traffic violations that Foley had received. The *Inquirer* cited conviction records of the New Jersey Motor Vehicles Department that revealed Foley had been arrested for speeding in 1945, 1946 and 1950, and that he had been indicted for drunken driving in 1936, a charge on which he was later acquitted. The *Inquirer* went all out. Even old John Cummings, the political writer who had never written anything nasty about Republicans in his life, found that the candidates "aren't fit for office."

Almost daily, the pair had to defend themselves against attacks in the *Inquirer* rather than try to get their platforms across. Meanwhile, Walter himself even penned an editorial denouncing the traffic violator Foley who "so arrogantly had broken the law and now wanted to act as its defender." *Inquirer* staffers knew when their boss had a hand in the preparation of an editorial when the word "arrogance" appeared: it was one of Walter's favorite words when describing someone he detested.

In the final days of the campaign, Clark and Dilworth were almost forgotten. The Republicans made Annenberg the main issue, even dubbing him the "ghost candidate." One day more than a million handbills denouncing the publisher swept across the city like a blizzard: "The VOICE of the INQUIRER is the VOICE of ONE Man: Walter H. Annenberg who alone dictates and controls its editorials and news policies. Richardson Dilworth is ANNENBERG'S LAWYER. Do you want ANNENBERG to control your city? If not, VOTE REPUBLICAN." The words echoed diatribes made more than a decade earlier against Moses, but now the political parties were reversed.

While scratching for issues, Poling even went so far as to question Walter's patriotism by implying there was a sinister connection between the fact that both the Communist newspaper the *Daily Worker* and the *Inquirer* were opposed to his candidacy: "I am the chairman of the All-America Conference to Combat Communism which is the official voice of 63 national organizations whose membership totals 83 millions," Poling declared at a rally. "The Worker charges me with everything from Fascism to a 'purge of labor.' Last night, in the bull-dog edition of today's Philadelphia *Inquirer*, a front-page editorial calls for the election of the Democratic ticket and my own defeat. . . . Incredible that these two publications should now bed down together. . . ."

Calling Annenberg's patriotism into question was sheer lunacy. Over the years, he had proven his loyalty at every turn whether it was wholeheartedly supporting the war effort or backing the Marshall Plan. Moreover, much to his pleasure, he had received a reserve commission in the United States Navy following the war. He had been assigned light duties at the Philadelphia Naval Base, which had to do with the surveillance of potential subversives. While occupying himself with such matters, he had come to see how people could be implicated through circumstances in what appeared to be possibly traitorous situations, and he was wary of condemning anyone on flimsy evidence. That may have been one reason for the *Inquirer*'s strong condemnation of Senator McCarthy for not being able to back up his charges. Still another was the sense of injustice he still felt about his father, a man who, he believed, had been convicted on little other than political vindictiveness. The Naval commission meant much to Walter, however, because it was a sign that the government was accepting him, a status he had desperately wanted since the days of his father's troubles. By 1951—the year of the mayoralty election—he held the rank of lieutenant commander, and he had recently served on the battleship *Missouri* on a tour of Europe and the West Indies, which had given him a greater feeling than ever of belonging to the service—and his country.

In the Republicans' desperation to attack Annenberg, they enlisted the support of the Republican candidate for mayor in New York, Edward Corsi, who likewise was running an uphill battle. In a reckless charge, Corsi contended that "Mr. Annenberg of the racing interests" had visited the prison cell on Rikers Island of Frank Erickson. Erickson was the bookmaker who twenty-two years earlier had suggested that a national racing wire service be operated by the gang leaders in attendance at the underworld conference in Atlantic City. Determined not to let the incident pass unchallenged, Walter immediately fired off a telegram to Corsi: "I am the only 'Mr. Annenberg of the racing paper interests.' I state unequivocally that I do not know Erickson, have never visited him and would have no reason to visit him. I feel you owe me a public apology, which, as the Republican candidate for Mayor, you should be big enough to make immediately." Corsi never responded. He had served his purpose. His charges had created a stir in Philadelphia.

On the eve of the election, however, the *Inquirer* and Walter Annenberg had the last word. Walter ordered a front-page editorial that was two columns wide and ran from the top of the page to below the fold. The editorial naturally endorsed Dilworth and Clark but it pitilessly mocked the Republican candidates, in part saying:

> Independent Republicans are not falling for that specious line on behalf of politicians who care nothing about their party in the State and the Nation—as their weak efforts in past elections have shown—but only about keeping their own fat jowls hanging over the feeding troughs at City Hall. . . .

More than anything else, the electorate vindicated Walter. On election day, Clark and Dilworth swept into office by a comfortable lead of more than 100,000 votes apiece, and a great deal of the credit was given to Annenberg. Few people underestimated the importance of the editorial shift his paper had undergone, and national publications, such as *Time* and *Newsweek*, honored the publisher with the victory. Ironically, years later he would fall out with both Dilworth and Clark and come to resent having helped place them on the political map. But in 1951 he was pleased with his role of kingmaker, and when the pair showed up in his office to find out what he wanted, much as Republican leaders had done in the past, he was about to reply "nothing." Instead, he paused for a moment and told them he wanted "four good seats" at the Army-Navy football game which was traditionally played in Philadelphia. "That's all I want," he said, and he insisted on paying for the tickets, so that no man could say Walter Annenberg had benefited personally for his editorial support.

The victory had shored up Walter's image in the community as an incredibly powerful force, but unknown to anyone else, he had been considering ways of sharing that power. He had come to believe that Philadelphia wasn't large enough for the only two major newspapers that remained, his *Inquirer* and the *Bulletin*. The number of newspapers going by the wayside because they couldn't afford to compete for advertising and circulation in cities across the country was alarming; Annenberg believed that only one newspaper could successfully survive in Philadelphia. Therefore, he contacted Major Robert McLean, publisher of the *Bulletin*, to discuss merger possibilities. Both papers' profits were diminishing as a result of their competition, and Walter believed he had found a solution whereby each publisher could turn a profit of $5 million to $6 million a year. He wanted the *Inquirer* and the *Bulletin* to merge into one morning, one evening and one Sunday paper.

Walter outlined his thoughts to Richard Slocum, the *Bulletin*'s general manager and chief operating officer. Slocum, who too was worried about the future, immediately grasped what the *Inquirer* publisher was saying and became excited about the prospect. Costs of newsprint, labor and sundry other items were increasing, and competitive pressures between the papers had precluded major price hikes for advertising linage. At the time, the *Inquirer*'s daily circulation was 644,000 and the Sunday paper was 1,125,000, while the *Bulletin*'s daily was slightly under 700,000 and the Sunday edition was about 680,000 Since his Sunday paper was an advertising gold mine, Annenberg believed it more than offset the differences in the daily circulation figures. Nonetheless, he told Slocum he was willing to split profits fifty-fifty with McLean. Several days later a long-faced Slocum nervously appeared in Annenberg's office. He was embarrassed and didn't know where to begin what he had to say. Eventually, he found his tongue and said that his boss wanted the profits from the proposed merger to be 60 percent for himself and 40 percent for Annenberg. Believing he himself was being more than fair, Walter pressed for an explanation.

"McLean says he is bringing his name to the venture, which he believes has more prestige than the name Annenberg," Slocum said quietly.

With a start, Walter looked up from his large desk and dismissed the plan from the realm of possibility forever. Of all the reasons that could have been offered, this was the one that was bound to cut him to the quick. "Dick, the deal is off," he said. "The pig will wind up in the slaughterhouse."

Years later Annenberg would see his prophecy come true. In 1980, after sustaining heavy losses resulting from intense competition from an *Inquirer* no longer under Walter's control, as well as from lack of foresight, the *Bulletin* was sold to Charter Company, the huge oil and communications conglomerate. The *Bulletin* by then was a dying paper.

Though Walter had been the object of the two Republican mayoral candidates' hatred as well as that of certain party bosses, he still had the support of more temperate party leaders as well as Democrats in another cause that he had devoted himself to. Throughout the waning months of 1951 and early 1952, Annenberg chaired a group called the Citizen's Committee, which was created to try to convince the Democratic and the Republican National committees to hold their next Presidential conventions in Philadelphia. Aside from being the publisher of a powerful newspaper, Annenberg was a good choice for the chairmanship for a number of reasons. While expanding his alliances, his Democratic city victory gave him clout with the party. Moreover, Walter had befriended a large number of G.O.P. leaders. He personally knew men like New York Governor Dewey, Senator Robert A. Taft and other Republicans of national stature. In addition, he was one of Philadelphia's most enthusiastic boosters. The convention, he believed, could prove to be the shot in the arm the city's economy needed.

After the war-induced economic boom, both Philadelphia and Pennsylvania were seeking ways to expand economically and needed something to bring them to the consciousness of the nation's business leaders opening new plants. Annenberg had introduced a feature in the *Inquirer*, "Delaware Valley Column," which reported on promising business developments in the area, and he coined the title "Delaware Valley U.S.A." for the region in an effort to shake off Philadelphia's reputation for stodginess. Through a massive marketing effort begun by the *Inquirer* and picked up by the Chamber of Commerce, national magazines, including *Time, Business Week* and the *Saturday Evening Post,* were soon reporting on the flowering of the newly named region. In light of his efforts, Annenberg was inundated with awards from local universities, civic societies and the Chamber of Commerce. With a touch of cynical humor that would have pleased his father, Walter packed up the plaques and scrolls and other honors and shipped them to Harry Brand, an old friend he had known since his days gallivanting around Hollywood, now living in Beverly Hills. Quick to see the absurdity in Walter's gesture, Brand, a public-relations man for a movie company, placed the items in his recreation room, which over the years would become filled with awards bestowed on his publisher friend, who had little use for such "clap-trap."

Nonetheless, Walter threw himself into the task of bringing the conventions to town. After a great deal of planning, in May of 1952 he and a score of Philadelphia's leaders and newspaper reporters boarded a sumptuous private railroad train that was headed for Tulsa, Oklahoma, where competing cities were to submit applications to the Site Committee of the Republican National Committee. As the day of reckoning arrived, Walter was extremely nervous. The two leading contenders, according to general understanding, were Philadelphia and Chicago. Walter had in his pocket a certified check for $250,000 that was to be given to the committee if it opted for his city. In addition, he was empowered to offer the use of Convention Hall free of charge, and the city would spend an additional $30,000 just entertaining delegates and their wives.

As Walter well knew, his competition was formidable. Old Senator Taft, who was known as "Mr. Republican" because of his clout, was working on behalf of Chicago, which naturally also had the strong support of Colonel McCormick, who at the age of seventy-two was still dictating policy at his *Tribune*. While trying to shore up his own support, Walter placed a call to Tom Dewey, a move which cost him the friendship of the man he had so ardently backed for the Presidency four years earlier. Walter said that he didn't want the delegates exposed to the editorial philosophy of Colonel McCormick's newspaper during the week they picked the man who was likely to be the next President. Dewey, who was probably already committed to Chicago, expressed annoyance. "What makes you think I want them exposed to the *Inquirer*'s?" he asked. Without further ado, Walter slammed down the phone and he never mentioned Dewey again.

When the private train headed home, the mood aboard was subdued. What the Philadelphia contingent never realized until much later was that its members never really had a chance of convincing the G.O.P. leadership to return to their city. The same proved true of Democrats. "You're a nice young man and you've been through a lot, but you're wasting your time," Harry Truman told Annenberg, when the publisher was visiting Washington. After their conventions were held in Philadelphia in 1948, both Democrats and Republicans had been thoroughly disgusted at the way the affairs had gone. The city's fathers had lied about everything, including the number of first-class hotel rooms that were available and a listing of good restaurants. Many delegates had found themselves in rooming houses that were not only fleabags but were inconvenient to boot. Restaurants had proved almost nonexistent and taxicabs were almost as scarce. Philadelphia's dreary image couldn't be overhauled by Annenberg's efforts.

Walter's throwing himself into the project with such intensity was a way of distracting himself from the fact that his marriage had disintegrated. He had been extremely bitter when Ronny sought a divorce in 1950, and he resented it when their mutual friend William Wolf had advised her as an attorney. Wolf's action was probably unwise in such a delicate situation, and to Walter the man was no longer his friend. The publisher manifested his anger in his usual way of dealing with people he believed had treated him shabbily—he stopped speaking to the lawyer, and for years, no matter what Wolf did, his name didn't appear in the *Inquirer*.

Such use of his press made many Philadelphians wary. People who witnessed Annenberg's attacks and needed the support of his newspaper watched what they did and said around him so they could stay within his good graces, especially since there was concern about certain of his actions that affected institutions as well as people. In 1948, for example, the local National League baseball team, the Phillies, was banished for several weeks from the *Inquirer*'s sports coverage except for scores and team standings. The order to ignore the team came after Walter failed to exact an agreement from the Phillies to re-schedule a hastily called evening game that conflicted with a charitable event, the Music Festival, which was one of numerous sports and cultural endeavors the *Inquirer* supported. The Festival usually attracted 40,000 to 50,000 people, but the crowd that year was much smaller. Walter blamed the low attendance on the baseball game, a problem he had foreseen. He believed that it was selfish of the team to compete with a charitable endeavor, especially one in which he had had such a large hand.

Thus, Annenberg became an oddity in Philadelphia. His name was associated with numerous good works, and he was often the first prominent citizen anyone seeking charitable donations approached, but the whimsical use of his paper on occasion to punish those who offended him made many people uneasy. There was also at times an aloofness, an icy reserve, which was a steely façade that he had developed as a protection against the barbs that came his way as a result of his father's history. No matter what the reasons, however, Walter was becoming a man to fear.

There were numerous people he befriended, of course. Usually they were men of prominence, and most often they were business leaders or fellow publishers. Locally, there were figures such as John T. Dorrance, head of the huge Campbell Soup Company, and Frank McGlinn, a fund raiser for the Republican party, who was well connected both politically and socially. The publishers included Eugene Meyer of the *Washington Post* and Norman Chandler of the *Los Angeles Times*. They were men who had never felt the sting of Annenberg's attacks, and some of them agreed with his arbitrary editorial actions. McGlinn, for example, was always grateful that Annenberg had seen to it that a story in which his schoolgirl daughter was an innocent victim wasn't printed in the *Inquirer*.

For his part, Walter was convinced that he ran his paper with a sense of fair play, and he dismissed criticism as the inevitable griping that publishers encounter. So intent was he on having the *Inquirer* considered evenhanded, especially politically in Presidential elections, that he told his editors during the 1952 contest that he wanted the same coverage given to each political party. No President would ever complain of his treatment at the hands of the *Inquirer*. In their effort to please, the editors determined that one day they would give prominent coverage to the Democrats and the next day such coverage would shift to the Republicans, thus ensuring the balance their boss wanted. But while the plan may have seemed laudable at first glance, it was fraught with problems, not the least of which was that the policy was shortsighted. No matter what was said by the Republican or Democratic candidate on his particular day, no matter how dull or unnewsworthy, it was treated as momentous. And if the candidates were unfortunate enough to say or do something newsworthy on their day off at the *Inquirer*, the newspaper's readers found the event treated in a trivial way, or not at all.

There was another problem as well. Though the *Inquirer* was officially independent, the editors knew their publisher's sympathies were Republican and they cynically referred to the paper as being "independent Republican." As such, they tried to second-guess Annenberg, a policy which E. Z. Dimitman had come to believe was essential. Thus, both the problems of rotating major coverage and editors trying to outwit their publisher dramatically came to a head on September 18, 1952, in the midst of the contest between Dwight Eisenhower, the war-hero Republican candidate, and Adlai E. Stevenson, the scholarly former governor of Illinois. As Eisenhower was rolling across the Midwest making platitudinous calls for an "honest deal" and quoting Scripture, Stevenson was in Connecticut seeking "ethics in politics ahead of victory." Senator Richard M. Nixon, Eisenhower's running mate, was making a whistle-stop train trip in his home state of California where, as the only visceral candidate, he was blasting Democratic "corruption" and demanding high ethical standards in government. The campaign's plodding predictability was suddenly shattered when the *New York Post* revealed the existence of a private slush fund that was operating for Nixon. Dubbed the "Millionaires' Club," its purpose was to ensure the Senator's financial comfort. The disclosure naturally put a crimp in the Republicans' "crusade" to clean up Washington and had Nixon fighting for his political life.

At the *Inquirer*, the revelation posed a monumental headache. For one thing, it came on a day when the Republicans were to be played down. Furthermore, the editors were all too aware that their boss was an admirer of Nixon. The publisher had liked Nixon's activist role on the House Un-American Activities Committee, finding the young Republican a tenacious fighter for America. Another factor the editors considered was that Walter's mother, Sadie, was known to be an ardent supporter of the California Senator and had given him large campaign contributions. The last thing the editors wanted to do was offend the publisher's mother, whom Walter revered. Their response was business as usual. They kept the hottest story of the campaign off the front page, and readers certainly could have been excused for missing the impact of what happened if they noticed the article carried on the second page. The headline stated: FRIENDS' GIFTS TO NIXON DRAW DEMANDS. The following day, a Saturday, the editors were again true to their formula and this time placed the story on the front page, but again the story lost most of its impact. The four-column headline declared: NIXON'S EXPLANATION OF FUND ACCEPTED BY EISENHOWER; PUBLIC TO GET ACCOUNTING. A related story reported Stevenson saying it would be wrong to condemn Nixon "without all the evidence."

Despite such waffling, Annenberg believed the *Inquirer*'s overall coverage was responsible, and compared with many papers in the nation that were much more partisan in their coverage, it was. When the election was over, the editors surveyed their stories and found that during the campaign the paper had devoted 764 columnar inches of news space to the Democrats and 737 inches to the Republicans. A full-page ad in the paper told readers of the findings, and many *Inquirer* staffers themselves were quite pleased, especially those who had been with the paper for a long while. "Moe would never have given a damn about such a thing," Bill Grover, a former editor, said. "He would have brought out his big guns for the guy he liked. You have to give Walter credit."

Over the years, however, the *Inquirer*'s policies once again became the creation of E. Z. Dimitman. Annenberg was ever a delegator of authority. Occasionally, he picked up the telephone and slashed through the *Inquirer*'s levels of management in order to tell the fashion editor that a particular photograph looked awful. More frequently, he told Paul McCurdy Warner, who for decades was the editorial-page editor, that he wanted a particular topic written about, but most of the time he relied upon Dimitman's judgment. Dimitman, by his own acknowledgment, was much more politically conservative than his publisher, and many of his ideas were mistakenly assumed to be his boss's. Soon, for example, a scathing attack on Charlie Chaplin, "The Case Against Chaplin," which explored motives behind the federal government's barring the movie actor's reentry into the United States, appeared in the *Inquirer*. "Charlie Chaplin was held in such high regard by Communist party leaders they ordered editors of the organization's official publication, the *Daily Worker*, to defend the comedian's morals when he became involved in paternity charges. . . ," one article in the ten-part series began. There was no byline on the articles. They had not only been placed on the front page by Dimitman, but they had been written by him as well. Liberals, however, accused Annenberg of having orchestrated the Chaplin attack.

FOURTEEN

FOLLOWING HIS DIVORCE, Walter was at odds with himself. He felt a terrible sense of loss, and he had told Ronny, who had moved to Washington with the children, that he would never remarry, so devastating was the experience. Almost daily, he talked with Wallis and Roger by telephone, but it wasn't the same as having them with him, and the big house in Wynnewood seemed lonely and depressing.

Occasionally, he was linked romantically in gossip columns with prominent women, including Dorothy Schiff, the publisher of the *New York Post*. Their being seen together generated speculation about the possible merger through marriage of two powerful publishing empires, but in reality the two were friends and they dismissed any suggestion of emotional entanglement.

On the social circuit, the Philadelphia publisher was considered a prize catch. He had power and wealth and he was an attractive, extremely vital man in his early forties. Moreover, women had always found him appealing. He was a curious mixture of modesty and self-assurance and his manners and taste were elegant. While he was brusque and demanding at work, he was charming and courtly with women. But there was another quality about him that was readily apparent as well. He was guarded. The painful memories from his marriage made him wary about getting serious with anyone, and he wanted to fend off the kind of woman who was more interested in his money than in him. There were many in that category, a problem he didn't need.

According to habit, Walter sought inspiration in his time of adversity, and he threw himself into both his work and his civic projects with great determination. One thought that gave him comfort was an encounter that he had had several years earlier with Winston Churchill. Bernard Baruch, who had continued keeping a kindly eye on Sadie's son, had given a dinner for the British leader, and he had invited Walter. Fortunately for Annenberg, the seating arrangement was alphabetical and he sat near Churchill. But for all the stature he himself had gained, Walter was still intimidated by people of great prominence and for much of the meal he could do little but utter a few pleasantries, although he was extremely anxious to make a good impression upon this man whom he considered a living monument. It wasn't until about one o'clock in the morning, after being well fortified by wine and brandy, that Annenberg summoned the nerve to address the great man in his own Victorian way: "Sir, I hope you will not find me presumptuous, but I have to tell you how saddened I was when the electorate rejected you after you saved the Empire and a way of life, and the only tools you had to do it with were oratory and spirit."

Churchill looked at Annenberg long and thoughtfully, and much to the publisher's delight, replied with the kind of pithy remark that Walter came to memorize as his golden rules for life. "Look not for reward from others," Churchill said, "but hope that you have done your best." The statesman thanked Annenberg for his sentiment and upon reflection said, "I'm going to do something I never do. I'll give you my autographed picture." The gesture was small, but the publisher found it great. Walter placed the photograph on his desk and ever after recalled the man's spirit whenever he himself was facing difficult times.

Unexpectedly, Walter was abruptly brought out of his post-divorce doldrums. One evening in Boca Raton he attended a party that was given by Colonel Henry Crown, the wealthy Midwestern financier whose affairs brought together people of prominence and power. There Walter was introduced to a stunning blonde named Lee Rosenstiel. She was the wife of Lewis Rosenstiel, even though she was young enough to be the Schenley liquor king's daughter. Lee had attended the party with Harriet Simon, a lifelong friend, and her husband, Sylvan, a film producer at Columbia Pictures. Rosenstiel hadn't been able to go to the party, and he hadn't cared whether his young wife attended. Their marriage wasn't the soundest around, and, at the age of thirty-one, Lee was wondering what she should do. This was her second marriage, and it was as dismal and unrewarding as her first had been.

There was a specialness about Lee that people who met her remarked upon. She was always gregarious and vivacious, rarely ever displaying publicly any private sorrows that she might be experiencing. Rooms that she entered suddenly seemed brighter and crowds became more enlivened. The nickname "Lively Lee," which she had acquired during her coed days at Stanford University, continued to describe her personality, but obscured the misfortunes of her past.

When she was a child, her mother was killed in an automobile accident, and she and her sister had been sent from their native Connecticut to live with an uncle in California. The uncle was Harry Cohn, the tough movie mogul at Columbia Pictures. The girls had attended a private academy, and Lee had received a degree in political science from Stanford, but their upbringing had left much to be desired. A man who wasn't known for his delicate sensibilities, Cohn had treated the sisters as "second-class citizens," as Walter later said. Thus, Lee was raised with many insecurities, and she had turned for comfort to her aunt, Rose Cohn, who was a devout Christian Scientist; Lee adopted the religion as well. Though she hadn't any money of her own, Lee had been raised in the midst of great wealth, and it was natural that she would marry someone who was rich. Soon after graduating from college, she married Belden Katleman, a wealthy dilettante and later owner of a Las Vegas gambling casino. When that marriage ended in divorce after the birth of a daughter, Diane, she again married and her husband was the forceful Rosenstiel.

As soon as Walter and Lee met, it was obvious that there was a deep mutual attraction. He found her enchanting and appeared to be captivated by her. For her part, Lee was charmed by the serious young publisher, who by his very presence demanded attention. Over the years, Walter had evolved into the kind of man who filled whatever space he entered. As his businesses succeeded and he came to take for granted his powerful role of newspaper publisher, Annenberg became a man of conviction, which was manifested in a strong personality and strong opinions. He knew what he wanted and how to get it. It swiftly became apparent that he had fallen in love with Lee Rosenstiel and that he wanted her.

What worried everyone who knew Walter and Lee was the reaction of the unpredictable Rosenstiel, who though sixty years old, was a dynamic man and strong as a bull. He had fought his way to the top of the often deadly liquor business during the Prohibition Era and, after the repeal of the Volstead Act, he had created a company that in North America was second only to the Bronfman Seagram empire in the liquor industry. It was inevitable that Lee should become disenchanted with him. For one thing, the aggressive tycoon was paranoid, especially about the subject of Samuel Bronfman, his arch rival. He constantly thought that "Sam the Bronf," as he called his competitor, had him followed, and he was forever seeing Bronfman agents lurking about. But Rosenstiel was so distrustful even of men within his own company that he tapped their phones, and his townhouse at 5 East 80th Street in Manhattan was a veritable spy center equipped with eavesdropping equipment, including concealed microphones, wiretapping paraphernalia and tape recorders.

The liquor lord's bizarre behavior resulted in many often-told tales. On one occasion, Rosenstiel was determined to test the loyalty of his subordinates. He sent word to them that he was dying, requesting that they convene at the townhouse for his final moments. When the men had gathered in a downstairs room, Rosenstiel sat in bed wearing pajamas, a robe and dark sunglasses, as was his habit, and monitored their comments. Finally, he had a bodyguard tell the executives that he had died. As his anger mounted, he listened while they expressed their elation in various unflattering ways. When he had heard enough, Rosenstiel stormed downstairs and had his bodyguards throw the men out, telling them they were finished working for him.

Living with such a man was an impossibility, and Lee had long thought of leaving him. There was the problem of her two daughters, which held her back. When she was pregnant with her second daughter, Libby, Rosenstiel had promised her one million dollars in the child's name, but he had reneged after his daughter's birth, even though newspaper stories had referred to the "million-dollar baby." Rosenstiel appeared determined to antagonize his wife at every turn, and after Lee met Walter, her dilemma intensified. She found herself in love with another man, but she had her daughters to consider first. Throughout her life, she had relied upon the strength she was able to summon as a result of the Christian Science faith she had embraced as a child and which had helped her through times of turmoil and indecision. Now she was confronted with perhaps the most difficult problem of her life.

A man who monitored his wife's moods as closely as he did competitor Seagram's sales, Rosenstiel quickly perceived that something was amiss. He began listening to Lee's telephone conversations, including those with Walter. When he learned there was another man in her life, Rosenstiel had all his wife's phone calls tape-recorded and he had her followed by detectives. Eventually, she couldn't stand the tension any longer. She asked Rosenstiel for a divorce, and much to her dismay, he refused. Instead, he tried to dampen her attraction to the Philadelphia publisher, making up stories about him and telling Lee that she was merely one of numerous women Annenberg was seeing. In an effort to find out something scandalous about Annenberg, Rosenstiel had him followed, and he apparently hired Ben Javits, the brother of the New York Senator Jacob Javits, to try to uncover unsavory facts about the man Lee loved.

When he in turn found out what Rosenstiel was doing, Walter treated the matter with amusement. "My friend I. D. Levy got a call from Ben Javits one day and knew what he was fishing for, so I told him, 'Look, tell Rosenstiel that I'm keeping three women at a certain hotel downtown,'" Walter recalled. "Javits did, and I heard that he eventually got $75,000 out of Rosenstiel for his snooping."

At last it became clear to the liquor magnate that Lee's involvement with Annenberg wasn't a passing infatuation, and he relented to the point where he allowed her to file for divorce. Nevertheless, in his anger he wanted to make the experience as humiliating for her as possible. He told her that he would see to it that she left behind every bit of clothing and jewelry that she had received as his wife. Thus, Lee went to Bergdorf Goodman's and purchased a complete outfit and had it delivered for her departure; the bill was paid by Annenberg, not Rosenstiel. As she was about to flee the townhouse, Lee suffered further ignominy at the hands of the man she was escaping. Rosenstiel had one of his hulking bodyguards search her, ostensibly to make sure that she wasn't taking anything of value. She had to accept the insult. The valuables were inconsequential, Walter told her. He would always give her whatever she wanted.

Walter had also soothed her mind about a much more important matter—her children. He said they would soon be with her. He had relayed to Rosenstiel through intermediaries that the girls belonged with their mother, and he would do everything within his power to see that they were. Rosenstiel believed him and he relented.

After leaving Rosenstiel, Lee immediately flew to Reno, where she obtained a divorce on grounds of mental cruelty. She and Walter had already made plans to marry, and everything was in motion when she returned to New York several days later. Walter and Lee were married at his mother's home at 2 East 88th Street in Manhattan. Sadie was supportive of the couple during the traumatic period. She had stood behind her son when he had been divorced, and she blessed his decision to marry again. After meeting Lee, Sadie had known instinctively that the beautiful young woman could make her son happy. For her son's part, he believed Lee would make his mother happy as well.

Well aware of the life their father had led, all the Annenberg children were extremely protective of their mother. They doted on her, always treating her as though she were much more fragile than she really was. Throughout her life she had weathered her own misfortunes and those of her children, including the many marriages made by her daughters, a turn of events that she at first had disapproved of but later accepted with a flicker of cynical humor that would have pleased her husband. "I'm the only one I know who has three times as many sons-in-laws as daughters," she once remarked in exasperation.

But to the children she was always Little Woman, her husband's pet name for her. In their memories, Walter and his sisters pictured her walking down the street with a child ever attached to either hand, a wonderfully kindly mother who was always there when they needed her. The extent of her children's concern for her well-being was illustrated when they were thrown into a panic after the death of Sadie's oldest and dearest friend, a woman named Anna Granowitz. Fearing what the news would do to their mother, the Annenberg brood went so far as to clip Anna's obituary from newspapers in their mother's apartment. At length, they realized they had to tell her when Sadie began asking why she hadn't heard from her friend lately. Walter, as head of the family, was given the unenviable task of delivering the sorrowful tidings, but before he did so elaborate precautions were taken, including having a doctor and a nurse waiting out of sight. Upon hearing that Anna was gone, Sadie accepted the news matter-of-factly. To Walter's relief, she carried on as before, including insisting on doing her own grocery shopping while her chauffeur-driven Rolls-Royce remained parked outside the supermarket.

That Sadie stood by her children was always taken for granted. But whereas she was always concerned about her daughters and made sure she spent an equal amount of time with each of them, staying in the special "Mother's Room" that each had set aside for her visits, it was Walter who was always her pride and joy. Boy, as she never stopped calling her son, could never do wrong in her eyes. As the male child, he was the one who carried on the family name and was her favorite. Throughout his life, she never criticized him and always made him feel the specialness that she felt toward him, and he loved her for it. So intense was her pride in him that whenever a baby was born in the family, she said, "It looks just like Walter." It mattered not whether the baby was light or dark, male or female; she had bestowed her greatest compliment, and everyone knew that the remark was a sign of great joy at the child's birth.

More than anything in the world, Sadie wanted Walter's happiness. She, more than the others, knew what a tremendous effort of will it had taken on his part to fill the roles of head of the family and head of the company after her husband died. Of all people, she knew too well her stubborn husband's fears about their son's ability to carry on, and she knew the harsh way he treated Walter at times in order to make him more manly. After his father's death, Walter had told his mother and no one else about Moses' deathbed words to him, and she had tried to console him. Sadie had reassured him about his father's love, and she could think back upon letters that Moses had sent her in which he had unabashedly referred to "our son, the light of our life." Over the years, she had become tremendously proud of the transformation that had taken place in her son, but then, unlike Boy's father, she had always been sure of her son and that he would find his rightful place in the world. Her confidence in Walter had never wavered, and she never hid from anyone that Boy meant more to her than anyone.

A simple woman who was always at home in the kitchen no matter how much money she had, Sadie expressed her love in traditional ways. It wasn't unusual for her to cook one of Boy's favorite dishes, such as Chicken Spanish, place it on the cushion next to her in the back seat of her Rolls and have the driver take her to Walter's home, Inwood. Thus, she had insisted that he have his second wedding at her home.

The wedding ceremony was performed by Dr. Carroll Oscar Morong, headmaster of the Peddie School, Walter's alma mater. The school had always meant a great deal to the publisher, and, after he had paid off the last of Moses' tax penalty and had extra money to give to charity and other worthy causes, he had embarked upon what seemed like a singlehanded effort to transform the small prep school into one of the best of its kind. His sentimentality was reflected in the choice of the man performing the ceremony. The affair was simple and there was a reception in the elegant apartment for the family afterward.

Both Walter and Lee were extremely self-conscious and wary when they took up residence at Inwood. They resolutely ignored the initial barrage of gossip that they realized was bound to greet them. Their marriage was grist for delicious stories on the Main Line, most of which were based on fancy rather than on fact. Above all, Annenberg's neighbors were curious about this person whom the publisher described to his friends as "a wonderful girl." Divorce itself was frowned upon, and now Walter was bringing home someone who was divorced twice and whose previous husbands were controversial characters. While some people privately found their tale akin to a storybook romance in which love conquers all, the prevailing sentiment was one of disapproval. Nevertheless, even people who were prepared to dislike Lee intensely found that upon meeting her they couldn't. She was somewhat guarded, as Walter was, but it was clear to everyone that she knew instinctively what her husband wanted and needed in a mate. Walter meant everything to her. "Here was this very desirable woman who looked up to Walter and there was no question about it," Ellie Wolf, who herself later divorced and remarried, recalled. "Lee took care of Walter. She knew the troubles that Ronny and Walter had been through. She made it her business to make Walter happy."

Lee, however, wasn't a vacuous woman whose only role in life was that of helpmate. She had a mind of her own and was interested in politics and the arts and she had strong opinions about both.

Politically, she was more conservative than her husband, though their views were similar on law and order. But more than her husband, she feared the country was in great danger from the Left. Over the years, Walter's increasingly conservative views became more like hers.

In order to succeed in Philadelphia, Lee vowed that she wouldn't let gossip about the past disturb the present or the future. She had an undaunted determination, knowing before she arrived that she wouldn't be welcomed with open arms. She also knew, though, that she had useful talents that would help her to succeed socially, which was important both for her sake and for her husband's. There was her interest in art and cultural affairs, which was essential for any claim to social standing in Philadelphia, and just as importantly, she was a very organized woman who knew how to get things done. Such traits could open doors if one worked hard and was persistent. Thus, she was willing to risk venturing into the tight little world of Philadelphia society if that was what it took to pursue her interests. With a determined steeliness, she threw herself into the business of working for a number of cultural institutions where her talents, the prominence of her publisher husband, and the openness of his checkbook to causes that interested her eventually ensured her a seat on the board of a number of prestigious institutions, including those bastions of Brahmin society, the Museum of Art and the Academy of Music.

Before stepping beyond the front door of her new home, however, Lee got her husband seriously interested in collecting art. Walter had always liked paintings, but he had never pursued this inclination beyond occasionally buying a work that appealed to him. Lee had a more professional interest, making her husband recognize what a sound investment the shrewd collecting of art could be. He had become a man who examined many sides of every issue, and in what swiftly became his new hobby, he found that he could indulge his artistic sensibilities while appeasing his nature as a canny businessman as well. As always when undertaking any new venture, he boned up on the subject so that soon he could discuss knowledgeably the techniques of Cubism or French Impressionists with much the same authority with which he could dissect an annual report of a Big-Board company.

What Lee found more difficult than pursuing cultural interests in Philadelphia was resigning herself to the climate. For someone who had grown up in California, that wasn't undertaken easily. The city's winters in particular she found cold, dismal and gray. Recognizing his wife's disenchantment with the drearier months in town, Walter saw to it that they spent each winter in Palm Springs, where the sun was brilliant and living was more in keeping with the relaxed life style that Lee preferred to Philadelphia's rigid formality.

Lee was bothered by the town's notorious social reserve even more than by its weather. She found the tiny, inbred society that still controlled most of the cultural institutions both infuriating and, yet, oddly beguiling. Like Walter, she was intrigued by a set of people who never for a moment doubted that their world was the right one and that they were the only ones fit to rule. To the Annenbergs, both of whom had grown up in the midst of first-generation money that wasn't earned in the highly respected professions or occupations, such as banking or law, the very sureness of Main Liners was enough to increase their insecurity. What amused and depressed Lee at times, though, was how insufferably stuffy the Main Line could be. Lee was a woman who needed chums, and she lived in an area where people who fit that description were difficult to find.

There were other preoccupations that the Annenbergs faced, and one far outweighed all others. Ronny, who had since married a wealthy Washington automobile dealer, Benjamin Orisman, asked

Walter to take their son Roger to live with him. Ronny was worried about the boy, and she didn't think she could control him the way his father could. At the age of eleven, Roger had slashed his wrists in what his parents and sister Wallis tended to dismiss as an attention-getter rather than a serious suicide attempt. But that incident, together with other troubling behavior, worried everyone. He had stopped going to school in Washington, and he wouldn't listen to his mother. She believed that he needed the firm hand of his father, to whom Roger paid more attention than to Ronny.

A tall, thin, brooding boy, Roger's often erratic behavior made his sister think of him as having a Vincent Van Gogh type of personality, by which she meant artistic and unpredictable. To Walter, Roger needed structure and the highly disciplined father believed he could offer that. He never forgot for a moment how a physical deformity can intrude upon a boy's life, but he decided not to make special allowances for his son. He gladly took his son back into his home and saw to it that Roger's days were fairly routinized. He was enrolled at Episcopal Academy, a nearby preparatory school, and his father saw to it that he set aside time for study and tried to get him interested in sports.

Walter's solution to his son's problem seemed to work. Roger did extremely well at his studies. His music and books, though, continued to be the mainstay of his life to such an extent that his troubled father tried to get him to take a more practical view of life. At times it seemed that Roger was more suited to a different century. As a teen-ager, he was a lithe, graceful youth who stood six feet tall. Much of his time was spent alone, a book of poetry in his hands and a look of Byronic melancholy on his face. He played classical music on the piano, and for his sixteenth birthday, he asked for a harpsichord. Instead, his father, trying to break through the wall of music and literature which Roger was erecting to the exclusion of just about everything and everyone else, gave him a Dodge automobile, hoping the boy would use the car to travel off the Main Line estate.

There was never any question of taking the boy to a psychiatrist, because of the stigma attached to such treatment in the 1950s, and because Walter truly believed that his son would outgrow his moods if given the chance to do so. He tried to create those chances. One summer, for example, he had Roger work at the *Inquirer* under the direction of E. Z. Dimitman, but the exposure to the paper and to the shrewd editor did little for such a boy, whose interests were far from those of the men and women he came into contact with at the paper.

Newsmen lived for the moment, while Roger seemed lost in time. Dimitman would ask whether the boy wanted to work for a few days with a police or a courthouse reporter, and Roger listlessly responded, "If you want me to." He trudged off to the assignment as though it were a chore instead of the kind of opportunity that Dimitman believed any other boy would have been overjoyed to have. Dimitman wondered what kind of publisher Roger would make and shook his head over the prospect. But Walter was abandoning the idea of leaving the *Inquirer* to his son. The boy was too artistic, too out of touch with the fast-paced events that one had to be interested in to run a newspaper. Roger's interests and sentiments were those of a Romantic poet, not a publishing mogul. He lived in his own world.

FIFTEEN

ONE NOVEMBER EVENING in 1952, Walter was skimming through a late edition of the *Philadelphia Bulletin* when he came across a full-page ad for a publication called *TV Digest*. Though it was late, he placed a call to Merrill Panitt, his administrative assistant, wanting to vent his annoyance at seeing the *Bulletin* get the advertisement and wanting to learn more about the advertiser. When he had an irksome issue on his mind, Annenberg never thought twice about contacting an employee at home, although he generally refrained from doing so between midnight and 7:30 A.M.

Accustomed to his publisher's habits, Panitt had come to expect such interruptions of his evenings. Although Panitt was only ten years younger than Walter, the latter treated him in an almost fatherly way. For example, he frequently placed his hand on his assistant's shoulder and introduced him to others as "Young Panitt here . . ." He thought no more of telling him that he should plant more trees in his yard and what kind they should be than he did of giving him business directions. As usual, Walter curtly dispensed with formalities. "Why was that full-page ad for *TV Digest* in tonight's *Bulletin* instead of our newspaper?" he demanded.

Panitt himself wasn't really sure, but the *Bulletin*'s daily circulation was larger than the *Inquirer*'s, and it was a handy excuse he frequently used, so that was the reason he gave his peeved boss. Annenberg calmed down a bit and questioned the magazine's circulation, which was listed at 180,000 a week. Since he wrote a television column for the paper and perhaps from instincts he had developed to second-guess his ever inquisitive boss, Panitt had done a little homework on the publication. He told Walter that the Audit Bureau of Circulation had verified the figure; he also knew that the publishers of *TV Digest* had taken out the ad to lure retailers into advertising with them.

There was a silence on the telephone and anyone other than an Annenberg confidant would have thought the line was dead. But Panitt, conditioned to his boss's ways, knew the silence meant that Annenberg was thinking, and that meant he could be hanging uselessly onto his receiver until the publisher let an idea blossom. Finally, Walter asked him if there were similar magazines published elsewhere. Panitt replied that he knew of one in Chicago and another in New York, and he thought there might be several others in existence. As far as he could determine, he said, there was little connection between them. They all dished up local listings of TV shows and their articles were generally gushy, fan-type fare about local television personalities. If one had an especially good cover or article that boosted circulation, the others were likely to copy the idea the following week.

Slowly, Annenberg began thinking out loud. Supposing, he mused, there was a national editorial section that could be bound around local TV listings. He thought that he could print such a section in color at a huge rotogravure plant that he had constructed next to the *Inquirer* four years earlier. Such editorial matter could be shipped to various cities around the country where local television listings could be printed and bound inside the national section. As he talked, the details of the venture he was imagining kept tumbling out in his broken, stuttering fashion. There would be staffs in each city, and the emphasis of the editorial content would be network shows. Advertising could be sold both nationally and locally. By the time the publisher hung up, he had outlined in broad brush strokes the basis for what he would call *TV Guide*, a strange little magazine that was to make publishing history. In essence, his concept was similar to what his father had done nearly thirty years earlier when he had envisioned the *Daily Racing Form* as a national publication.

The idea was simple enough, but it was a great vision when compared with the existing local magazines whose worlds stopped at their city limits. As part of his plan, Walter felt that it would be wisest to buy the magazines as the nucleus for his national publication. The venture, however, was fraught with risks, because what had sold in a few sophisticated major markets might die elsewhere. Moreover, the chancy plan would cost millions. Nonetheless, Annenberg foresaw the magazine as an opportunity to become a power in television. By now he realized that the stations Roger Clipp had acquired, while sound, weren't prestigious and would never give him the stature that he yearned for. Before committing any money to the publishing venture, however, he decided to test his gut instincts by personally conducting a market survey in the three cities with the largest TV magazines—Philadelphia, New York and Chicago. Thus, in late November and early December, Walter Annenberg, an imposing figure elegantly clad in a dark suit and charcoal overcoat, stood by newsstands in those towns monitoring sales of the publications he was interested in. Whenever he saw someone buying one, he formally introduced himself and asked why he or she had made the purchase. Listening attentively, he kept mental notes on what the buyer said.

In Philadelphia, people bought *TV Digest*. In New York, it was *TV Guide*, and in Chicago, it was *TV Forecast*. The reasons he was given had a similar ring. Consumers liked the magazines' accurate listings, their convenience, and they enjoyed reading articles about the burgeoning world of television. Annenberg realized that he was onto another way of enhancing his fortune. The instincts that had told him to launch *Seventeen* and exercise a license for TV station WFIL now told him that a publication catering to what was happening in television could be a bonanza.

When he informed Joe First of what he was planning to do, the cautious little lawyer was again dismayed. The risk was too great, he said, and the costs of starting up such a venture were monumental. Once again, however, Walter chose to disregard First's advice and trust his own intuition.

The first problem he encountered was convincing the publishers of the three major TV periodicals to sell. Each was a seat-of-the-pants operation run by free-wheeling, rambunctious entrepreneurs. In every instance, the owners had faced tough early years that were now bearing fruit. Moreover, the publishers had gained a certain measure of status once their program guides started doing well, because they were wooed by TV personalities who were anxious to get their names and faces in them, especially on their covers. In New York, even such big stars as Milton Berle, Arthur Godfrey and Ed Sullivan promoted the city's *TV Guide* in return for plugs in the magazine.

The original idea for a magazine listing TV programs belonged to a New Yorker named Herbert Muschel. In 1947, the scholarly-looking Muschel was a book salesman who was always thinking of new ways of selling things or inventing new services. (Years later, he founded

PR Newswire, an important and profitable public-relations service that efficiently distributed publicity releases to the news media.) Muschel designed his *TeleVision Guide*, as he called it, but he didn't know how to get it published. When he approached publishers with the concept, they told him he was foolish. No one, they said, would pay for such a service. At length, a friend introduced him to Lee Wagner, a brash young lawyer who was quick on the uptake. Wagner immediately seized Muschel's idea, expanded it, and believed it could be the hottest thing that he had ever touched.

The first edition of their publication appeared on June 14, 1948, but several months later, Muschel left the magazine after a falling-out with Wagner. Wagner in fact had more faith in the idea than Muschel did, and he spent several hard years staving off creditors and paying staff salaries from the backing of several silent partners and the three-dollars-a-year subscription fees that trickled in. But publicity agents gradually recognized the value of the magazine, telling their clients to support it on the air and grant interviews to the little publication. As a result, a picture of an entertainer on the cover of *TV Guide*, as the magazine's name was later abbreviated, became so coveted that stars themselves called Wagner seeking the honor. Top TV personalities, such as Maury Amsterdam, and Dorothy Kilgallen and John Daly, who were panelists on the popular TV quiz program *What's My Line,* asked to have covers made of them. Often, Wagner asked the stars to write an article for him so that they both got something out of it. The magazine became so popular that Eleanor Roosevelt even asked to be on the cover, and while Wagner acquiesced to the former first lady, he later wished he hadn't. Covers are supposed to boost newsstand sales, but the Eleanor Roosevelt issue didn't sell well. "People hated to look at her," Wagner recalled. "Kilgallen had the same kind of face."

Sometimes stars reneged on promises they had made to promote the magazine in exchange for publicity that Wagner gave them, but he was always able to outwit them. "We put Berle on the cover and he said 'Watch me Tuesday and I'll show the magazine,' " Wagner recalled. "Then he showed the Chesterfield cigarette ad on the back cover. He did this twice, which he thought was funny. The third time, I pasted another front cover on the back of the copy we gave him. When he held it up, people finally saw our cover."

By the time Annenberg was interested in acquiring his publication, Wagner was having problems. The state attorney general was breathing down his neck for alleged kickbacks involving the magazine,

charges that Wagner claimed were the fault of an unscrupulous partner. Moreover, Muschel was suing him because he had never been
compensated for his idea. Thus, when Wagner heard that Walter
wanted his operation, he decided to sell. The terms he worked out
with Joe First came at the same time he was dealing with Muschel,
who had no idea the magazine was being sold. Wagner received about
$1.5 million from Triangle Publications plus a fat consulting fee. He
gave Muschel $10,000. For years, whenever a *TV Guide* commercial
came on television, Herb Muschel, the man who first thought of the
idea for the magazine and who now knew how much Wagner had received, became physically ill and had to leave the room.

In Philadelphia, the magazine Annenberg wanted belonged to two
brothers, Irving and Art Barowski, who operated North American
Publishing Company. In 1948, they were in the printing business
when they dreamed up the idea of putting out a little TV program
guide that could be used as a promotion piece to increase television
sales. They received a commitment from local Philco television distributors to pay half the publishing costs as well as provide them with
TV ownership lists, which were then prized, because owners were
still such a novelty. For a three-dollar subscription fee, the brothers
mailed their guide to set owners, printing on different-colored paper
each week in an effort to appeal to housewives. By 1953, the magazine
was selling well and advertising was expanding beyond TV dealers.

When Walter expressed an interest in the publication, the brothers
at first balked. They had heard that he was in the market, but they had
agreed with Wagner and the owners of the Chicago publication not to
sell. Suddenly, however, they were confronted with the fact that
Wagner had sold his magazine. The Barowskis decided it was useless
to try to buck a big publisher and they sold as well. Walter questioned
them thoroughly about the business, but he left the negotiation of the
sale up to First. He disliked negotiating firsthand; he felt that as long as
he wasn't the man on the front line, there was always room for flexibil-
ity and face saving on both sides if need be. The Philadelphia deal was
nailed down for about one million dollars.

In Chicago, *TV Forecast* was the most free-wheeling of the operations. Launched by four young ex-G.I.s who were casting around for a
way of having fun as well as improving their lot, the magazine's history was the strangest. The notion for starting it occurred to one of the
four, Les Viahon, when he heard a comedian on the radio say, "How
can you tell the players without a scorecard?" He didn't hear the

punchline because the question stirred an idea. He had never seen television, but he had heard about it, and he wondered how people knew what to watch, since Chicago newspapers, which viewed TV as a competitive threat, refused to carry listings. He mentioned the idea for a TV programming guide to three friends, Norbert Dempke, an accountant, John E. Groenings, a makeup man for a publishing company, and Roy V. Whiting, an ad salesman. The four friends chipped in $250 each and started the magazine in the basement of Abbot Hall on the campus of Northwestern University. They were so broke they had to borrow staplers from offices in the building to bind the first issue. By December 1952, they were making so much money they held a lavish Christmas party at the Rainbow Room in New York and flew the entire staff there.

When a representative of Annenberg approached them about selling, the young publishers were apprehensive. They knew nothing about Walter Annenberg, but his father's reputation in Chicago was legendary. After Wagner sold, the idea of trying to fight off an Annenberg seemed to them unwise at best. To consummate the sale, they flew to Philadelphia, where they intended to ask $500,000 for their property. On the flight, the more they drank, the higher they pushed their asking price. By the time the plane landed, they had decided to ask for $1 million. They went to the *Inquirer* building where they were ushered into Joe First's large office. They found First and several other Triangle executives they came into contact with to be tough but fair. "First can count faster than you can think," Viahon whispered to one of his partners while dealing with the shrewd attorney. With their fingers crossed, they asked for the million dollars. Dealing with Triangle, they found, was like being in the position of owning a designer salon. "Rich customers don't haggle when a dress costs $1,200—they just pay it," Viahon said. There was no haggling. As the jittery Chicagoans listened in near disbelief, they got their asking price. At the conclusion of the deal, they were led into Walter's office, where they were awed by the vast, elegant airy chamber that seemed to them like an office designed for a movie. The room had a view of the city and the drapes enchanted them, because when they were drawn they had, depicted on them, the same view of the city that would be visible through the window if they were open. They were further impressed when Walter's secretary interrupted her boss, although he had requested not to be disturbed. The publisher had a telephone call from President Eisenhower, a man who couldn't be placed on hold.

In the process of acquiring the magazine, Walter had asked Roger Clipp to find an executive to run the new venture. Clipp shuttled constantly to New York, lining up prospective candidates, but his boss found something wrong with each of them. Clipp privately told people that Annenberg was driving him to distraction because he was being so picky, but Triangle men who knew the little martinet well believed he deliberately nominated men Walter was bound to reject in order to gain the job himself. Eventually, Annenberg did ask Clipp to take the task on. Recognizing the difficulties of juggling his broadcasting duties with the new venture, Walter offered the conniving executive a bonus consisting of a half interest in an edition of a *TV Guide* that he planned for Rochester, New York. Feigning surprise at being asked to expand his duties, Clipp asked time to think it over. "Fine," Walter replied. "Tell me tomorrow morning."

Other executives grumbled about the brash Clipp being given the task, especially since he knew nothing about magazines. Annenberg, however, hadn't chosen him for either his editorial experience—or his personality, for that matter. He gave him the job because Clipp knew everyone in broadcasting. He was the only person at Triangle who knew the right person to call when there were problems getting listings, or whom to contact for advice on how the new publication could best enter the new markets that were selected. There were other people around who knew how to put a magazine together, not the least of whom was Annenberg himself. Clipp provided a more valuable expertise at the moment.

To outsiders viewing the latest Annenberg venture, however, there seemed to be little rhyme or reason to what was taking place. Walter's management team as much as anything else raised serious questions among other publishers as to whether he knew what he was doing. Clipp looked like a professional compared with the rest of the hodgepodge of men Walter had drawn from elsewhere in his organization to launch the periodical. Merrill Panitt, for instance, was named national managing editor, a man who had never edited anything but his high-school yearbook.

The new advertising director didn't inspire much confidence either; he was Michael J. O'Neill, a big, beefy Irishman who had previously managed the *Philadelphia Inquirer* Charities, which didn't seem to anyone but Walter to qualify him as the top advertising man for a publication. Jim Quirk, then the *Inquirer*'s promotion manager, was given the additional duty of promoting the magazine, which worried publishing analysts; until now, the background of the intense Quirk was promoting an old established institution confined to one region, not a new magazine. Alex Joseph, a gruff assistant managing editor of the *Inquirer*, became Panitt's assistant only after he badgered the publisher into giving him a letter guaranteeing him his job back after the magazine flopped. Though the motley executive crew struck others as the officers of a new *Titanic*, Annenberg believed they would work out. He was a shrewd assessor of the men he hired. In this case, each man was exceptionally bright, and Annenberg felt that they would rise quickly to their new tasks.

As his publication plans raced along, Walter received little encouragement and a lot of unwanted advice. Almost universally, fellow publishers told him to abandon the venture, that he was tossing money away. They sounded like Joe First and their well-intentioned offerings annoyed him. Gardner Cowles, head of the communications giant that owned *Look* magazine as well as newspapers and broadcasting properties, told Walter the idea for a magazine that was simultaneously local and national was frankly absurd. Besides, his company had briefly tried a local TV magazine several years earlier and had met extremely disappointing results. Norman Chandler, Walter's friend and publisher of the *Los Angeles Times*, told him it was inevitable that newspapers all over the country would soon carry TV listings and that alone would kill his venture. Other publishers called with similar messages. Such lack of faith proved unsettling, of course, but Walter believed in what he was doing. He thought back to how his father would have played it and he plunged ahead. "If you want to get anything, you've got to take chances," he said. "The quarterback who wins is usually the one who runs or passes on fourth down, not the one who punts."

The only voice of dissent Walter heard that actually offended him came from an unexpected source. Alice Thompson, the woman who now edited *Seventeen*, was balking at letting *TV Guide* establish an advertising sales office on the premises of her magazine. Walter, who was shaving costs wherever he could, wanted to utilize extra office space at *Seventeen*. When he heard she was resisting the idea, he personally explained the situation to her, believing she must have misunderstood.

Miss Thompson unwisely said that the proposal had been crystal clear to her all along. "I don't agree with tenement journalism," she haughtily told Walter.

"Too bad," he replied. "You're fired."

She should have known better. Miss Thompson had succeeded Helen Valentine several years earlier and had witnessed her predecessor's less-than-graceful exit. Walter had been insisting that *Seventeen* run fashions and articles aimed at juniors, a line of clothing that was becoming increasingly popular. Editor Valentine had dogmatically ignored the advice, finally threatening in a moment of pique to walk off with the entire staff unless he let her run *Seventeen* her own way. "Keep walking," Walter told her. She did. Her staff didn't, and Miss Thompson, who had always appeared to be Miss Valentine's closest confidante at the publication, was elevated to the role of editor.

Thus in the midst of the fast developments with *TV Guide* Walter was stuck with finding a new editor for the magazine. He wanted someone who had his confidence, who was capable and who possessed a great deal of energy, verve and artistic sensibility. Explaining his problem one day to his sister Enid Haupt, who was his closest sister chronologically as well as emotionally, Walter had a thought that made sense to him, even though again it didn't make sense to anyone else.

"Enid," he said, "I want you to become the editor of *Seventeen.*"

At first she demurred, saying, rightly so, that she didn't know anything about running a magazine or young girl's fashions. Moreover, she didn't want a full-time job. Her final argument was that the suggestion was silly. But her brother persisted. She was as smart as any man he knew, and she had worked at the *Inquirer*. In addition, she had style, and her exquisite sense of what was beautiful was exhibited in her devotion to prize-winning flowers, which had gained her considerable renown. Perhaps most important of all, he could trust her. In the end, with a great deal of trepidation, she agreed to give it a try. She hoped Boy knew what he was doing, but even she wasn't sure that he did.

With that problem dispatched from his mind, Walter's attentions were again focused on *TV Guide*. His plans called for the magazine's first issue to be available in ten cities. The new editions were started by Clipp, Lee Wagner in his role as consultant, and Joe Bodkin, who had been one of Wagner's top men. The deadline for the first issue, April 3, 1953, was rapidly approaching. Typical of the Triangle blitzes was Bodkin's in Detroit. With the help of some of his old staffers from New York, he raced into the city, hired editorial and advertising staffs, found office space, and performed thousands of other chores, including softening up local TV station owners and managers so they would be receptive to the needs of the little publication. The Detroit edition was ready to roll six weeks after Bodkin arrived. "It was incredible, but we got all ten editions together in time," he said.

Like a general mapping out strategy behind the front lines, Walter pored over fact sheets, prodded operations that were going less than smoothly and offered words of encouragement as well. "When I was busy setting up the Atlanta edition, he called from somewhere out West," Bodkin recalled. "I finally located him and asked him what he wanted. He replied that he was just concerned about how I was doing. He told me I was a good soldier. I know it doesn't sound like much, but it made me feel good." Eventually, Bodkin quit his job because of the hectic, driven pace that characterized so many Triangle operations. "One day, I told my wife that I just had to get out or I would die," Bodkin said. "People who work for Walter Annenberg work very, very hard."

The problems didn't lessen after the magazine began publication. O'Neill in his job as ad director was having an extremely difficult time getting advertisers to take the magazine seriously. There was simply no faith in the new venture. The advertising community was accustomed to glamorous big slick publications such as *Life* and *Look*, and when *TV Guide* salesmen entered with their dinky product, a number of advertisers thought it was preposterous. "They laugh at us," O'Neill glumly told Annenberg.

After the first edition appeared, the Cassandras knew they had been right. Although 1,560,000 copies were sold, advertising was negligible. To make matters worse, the circulation slipped the following week to 1,492,000 and during ensuing weeks, the sales went down and down. The offices at *TV Guide* headquarters, then atop a popcorn distributor on Philadelphia's Broad Street, were hot and gloomy throughout the summer. Each week brought worsening advertising and circulation news, and the spirits of employees were flagging. O'Neill, for instance, was ready to bail out. "But Walter hung in there," O'Neill recalled. "He was like a pilot staying calm during stormy weather when everyone else is edging on panic."

Walter kept telling the staffers that the trials were to be expected. Then, to the amazement of everyone but Annenberg, in early September, circulation began climbing. The magazine's executives had just learned a painful lesson. Each summer there was to be a significant circulation drop, due to vacations and TV's summer-rerun programming. Now, the numbers climbed each week. A bell shaped like the

Liberty Bell was installed when the magazine moved in 1957 to new modern headquarters in Radnor, only minutes from Walter's home. Whenever circulation jumped by 100,000 copies, the bell's gong resounded throughout the building. Eventually, it wore out. The growth of the magazine paralleled the increase in the number of TV sets being sold in the nation. There were still advertising problems however, and in the first year ad revenues totaled only $760,000, which was a pittance compared with what Walter had invested. Despite the growing readership, the advertising community was slow in recognizing *TV Guide*'s potential, and it wasn't until 1956 that the first back cover was sold to a national account.

From the magazine's earliest days, Walter strongly said that *TV Guide* wasn't to be a fan magazine. His unrealistic concept of the publication was that it should become the *"Time* magazine of the television industry." Both the publication's tiny size and the frivolous nature of the medium it covered, however, precluded it from achieving the level of a serious magazine. Moreover, the early years of the publication's editorial content set a tone that was later difficult to shake. There were no hard-hitting articles about the TV industry, and much of the content was the fan-type pieces the publisher had contended that he hadn't wanted. Nevertheless, editor Panitt was being very cautious. When young editors and writers asked him when they could report on matters of substance, he told them "when circulation hits three million." Then it was four million. As a result, many writers came and went, because they despised the puff they churned out about stars' successes or birthday parties for TV puppets.

Panitt also had his hands full trying to change the attitude of entertainment press agents who were used to buying their way into fan magazines with offers of cases of liquor, trips to Hollywood and even call girls. Triangle editors were forbidden to accept favors, but some felt the policy of purity was carried too far. Two early writers, Bob Caniff and Tom O'Malley, for instance, felt the brunt of Triangle's code of ethics in a way they didn't think was fair. Caniff and his fiancée were strolling in New York one Sunday when for laughs they became part of the audience of a TV program called *Break the Bank.*

"We sat there like all the other yahoos trying to look like a nice eager couple and to our surprise they picked us," Caniff recalled. They were told to bone up on musical comedies and return the following week. If they did well, they had a chance of winning the grand prize of $4,755.

That Thursday Caniff was asked to report to the magazine's Philadelphia headquarters. There he found Panitt and Jim Quirk waiting, and they told him that he would have to give any winnings from the TV show to an Annenberg charity or face getting fired. The publisher didn't think it was proper for one of *TV Guide*'s employees to benefit from a TV show, because it might look as if it were a payoff for a future story that was favorable to the program. Caniff replied that if he didn't break the bank, he would do as requested, but if he hit the jackpot, he would quit. He and his fiancée won and he quit.

To show there were no hard feelings, the magazine gave him a going-away party in New York, with Panitt and a few other *TV Guide* executives in attendance. Caniff's pal O'Malley thought the whole business was unfair, and the more he drank at the party, the more vehemently he insisted on telling everyone that it was unfair. "If winning money on TV was supposed to be a conflict of interest," O'Malley said, "then I want to know why Triangle owning TV stations doesn't constitute a conflict too?" He left too and blamed Walter Annenberg.

The television industry itself in those early days was marked by a lack of sophistication. Many station owners had gotten into the business by accident, and the networks were groping for the kind of material they should put on the air. The farther from metropolitan centers, the clumsier were efforts to provide entertainment by local stations. *TV Guide* salesmen visited tiny stations where they shot the breeze with owners and lived in a much more leisurely world than the frenetic one that television was destined to become. Bob Saunders, who started as a salesman and became a *TV Guide* regional manager, liked those fresher times when "stations weren't sophisticated and grabby." In Hot Springs, Arkansas, for example, he spied a mirror in the corner of a dance floor the station manager used for a local teen-age show and he asked what it was doing there. The manager explained that by fixing the TV camera at a certain angle that took in the mirror "it looks like there are twice as many people dancing."

As the magazine grew, Walter kept in touch by telephone and written reports from his officers. He suggested ideas for articles and editorial comment, and if a particular story pleased him he asked Panitt to send the writer a note complimenting him. He also criticized. Typographical errors infuriated him, and if the color of a cover wasn't true, he complained mightily. Other times, he called Panitt and asked him if he hadn't a better cover photograph to use. After venting his spleen, likely as not he concluded the conversation by saying, "Don't worry. Babe Ruth struck out once in a while."

As his corporate kingdom grew, Annenberg found himself under pressure to hire relatives. His sisters always seemed to have husbands or sons who needed jobs, and, as the family patriarch, Walter felt obligated to place them somewhere in his organization, much the way his father had done. His nephews, Gilbert and Donald Kahn, for example, were made promotion directors in New York and Philadelphia respectively. Another nephew, Ronald Krancer, became promotion director in Cleveland, while another relative, Frank Wolf, entered Triangle and eventually rose to become publisher of *Seventeen*. There were others, most of whom brought no better qualifications with them than family links. Many stayed for a while and moved on, either out of boredom, wanting to prove themselves in a non-family-related business, or divorce, which gave Walter an excuse to get rid of them. Some were thrown out; Walter didn't tolerate much more from his relatives than he did from other employees. For instance, he sacked a nephew who embarrassed him by placing a political ad in the *Philadelphia Bulletin*. As soon as he saw the ad, Walter gave the young man the boot. It was bad enough that Annenberg was on the opposite side of the fence from the political candidate, but he couldn't forgive his nephew for placing the full-page ad with a rival paper instead of his own.

Of all the relatives who were brought into the company, however, the one who proved most valuable was Enid Haupt. When she had assumed the job as editor in chief, no one knew what to expect, least of all Enid. To her great surprise and her brother's relief, she turned out to be an excellent editor and *Seventeen* began thriving under her direction as never before. She was quick to spot flaws in copy, and her instincts for stories were sound, and, being an Annenberg, she never doubted herself when she had an idea. One of the most self-possessed women to walk the face of the earth, Enid was easily able to delegate authority, and she felt no compunction about her acknowledging her ignorance of the new world that she had entered. Quick to learn, she worked harder than anyone around her, expecting more from herself than she did from her employees.

Moreover, it rapidly became apparent to everyone that Enid knew how to deal with problems. When she first came to the magazine, one of the top women executives obviously resented her presence, apparently feeling that she was just a rich, spoiled dilettante who came to create havoc for a while before flitting off to some other pastime. Thus, when Enid asked the woman to give her a tour of the publication so that she could meet some department heads and familiarize herself with the operation, the executive perfunctorily replied that she was "too busy." The insolent woman realized a moment later that she had just committed an unpardonable sin. "You don't know it," Enid told her pleasantly. "But you have just written your epitaph." The executive was off the premises within hours.

A slender woman of medium height, Enid radiated an imperious air, and for a woman who was beside herself with worry that she not make a fool of herself, the façade was impressive and served her well. Her editorial experience was limited to having written features for the *Philadelphia Inquirer* during the war. She didn't know anything at all about magazines or how they were published. As she well knew, she had taken the job blind. But when she assessed her strengths, she believed that she might not fare badly. That she had a keen artistic sense there was no doubt at all; her floral arrangements were considered stunning by everyone. Her art collection was exquisite, one that she and her husband, Ira, a top Wall Street broker, put together themselves. They had, for example, been among the first, if not the first, collectors to seize upon the unknown artist Robert Rauschenberg years earlier. Moreover, she loved magazines and good layouts.

What convinced her to take the job more than anything else was Walter. All too often, he had proved that his judgment was correct even in the face of incredible odds. "My brother always had these brilliant ideas that nobody else thought were going to work," she recalled. She believed that she was one of them.

There were moments of doubt—fleeting, of course—in those early days when it dawned on her that the magazine was primarily a business, not just a pleasing compilation of words and pictures. A department-store representative visited Enid on her very first day on the job and talked and talked about such things as storewide promotions, national advertising and ad linage. Enid nodded sagely and politely while her stomach curled into a knot because she hadn't the faintest notion about what the other woman was discussing. After the executive left, Enid rushed to the telephone and called a friend who knew people who owned department stores, thinking surely she would know about such matters as advertising. She made an appointment to meet with the friend and when she did, she set about picking her brains. Above all else, Enid was a very determined woman. "Everyone must have been laughing to high heavens at my brother's nepotism, and I vowed I would not embarrass either myself or him," she recalled.

Like everything she did, Enid immersed herself in the business, which swiftly became her life to a far greater degree than she had ever realized it would become. In retrospect, years later she felt that if she had known what she was getting into, she doubted that she would have accepted the responsibility. For the first two years of her editorship, for example, she was constantly exhausted from working so hard that she and her husband didn't go out to dinner socially. Fortunately, her diligence and effort paid off and *Seventeen* bloomed like one of her prize-winning floral arrangements. Surprisingly, even her ignorance of the business worked to her advantage, since she wasn't hampered by adhering to the ways in which the business always had been conducted. When she became interested in certain sports clothes while on a trip to the West Coast, for instance, she told the manufacturer that she would like to introduce the line to her readers. Out of compassion, the head of the firm explained to her how wrong she was, that the particular style she liked sold well only in California. She introduced the style anyway, and soon the clothing was selling briskly all over the country.

While directing the magazine's operations, Enid also learned that the top job anywhere is a lonely business, just as the cliché always said it was. Sometimes while working late, she overheard other women laughing or holding intimate conversations and she wished that she wasn't excluded, that she could sit and chat with them in the same vein. But she too had her brother's sense of dignity of office; such desires simply couldn't be indulged. Enid, however, was liked and respected by her staff, and she tried to be fair. There were occasional situations that confronted her, however, when she reacted the way her brother would have, and for much the same reasons. She and her husband, for instance, always spent several weeks in Paris each September, and the first year she was working she and Ira encountered one of the magazine's editors who was vacationing there as well. Wanting to do something pleasant for a woman alone in a strange city, they invited the editor out to dinner. In the middle of the meal, the woman told Enid that she would like to take on a higher editorial job that had just become open.

"We'll talk about it back in New York, not while we're here on holidays," Enid replied.

The editor persisted. "No, I want to know whether I'm to be the editor or not," she said.

"I shall remember then," Enid answered firmly, "and look for someone else."

Enid had been appalled at the bad manners and gall of her employee. She hoped that word of the encounter would spread around the office, and she was gratified when it did. She always believed that bad manners were intolerable and she didn't want rude people working for a magazine directed at "our girls," as she affectionately referred to the readers.

For their part, most staff members enjoyed working with her. There was nothing drab or dreary or predictable about their editor, either at the magazine or in her personal style. When Enid felt like walking to work, for example, her chauffeur-driven Rolls-Royce glided along behind her at a discreet distance until she indicated she was tired, and she would have the chauffeur pull up. If she felt like buying a scarf to wear with one of her expensive designer outfits, such was her self-confidence that she felt no compunctions about entering a five-and-ten-cent store and buying a few scarves that appealed to her. And the front office suddenly bloomed with beautiful plants, which took away from the stuffiness that was peculiar to so many corporate offices. "Flowers are my religion," she told her staff.

But mostly, the staff liked working with her because she sought and accepted their advice. "Show me the ropes," she said when confronted with something she hadn't met before. And she gave a free hand to most of her editors, as long as they stayed within the bounds of propriety. The magazine's fiction department, under her guidance, won numerous awards, and Enid herself wrote an advice column for teenagers. The humor of her success at working for such a magazine also constantly struck Enid. Her staff was not aware that at the age of seventeen she had angered her father by running off with the thirty-nine-year-old Norman Bensinger, whose family made billiard tables. When Weymouth Kirkland, her father's lawyer, had caught up with the couple, the marriage hadn't been consummated, but the naïve school girl simply hadn't known how to get rid of her new husband just as she hadn't known how to escape eloping with him. Confronted by Kirkland, she was afraid of what her father would do to her, so she had remained with her husband. Later, her sisters had looked at her in dismay and said about Bensinger, "But he's so old." She thought so too and found herself stuck, until it dawned on her one day that divorce could solve her problem, which it had. In any event, she found it amusing that she now wrote an advice column, telling girls how to avoid far less dangerous pitfalls than she had stumbled into at the same age. But never one to denigrate experience, Enid believed that she was qualified to give such advice.

Unfortunately for Walter, she didn't mind giving him advice either. She spoke her mind and if he disagreed, she was bound to have the last word. While everyone else stood in awe of the head of Triangle Publications, Enid never forgot that he was her little brother, Boy, and Walter was forced to accept behavior from her that he wouldn't tolerate from anyone else. At times, she told him he was wrong or, even worse, what to do. "You know," he said, "I've never had a completely satisfactory working relationship with any woman, including my sister Enid."

SIXTEEN

WITH ALL HIS properties prospering smartly, Walter's itch to expand his empire still needed scratching. Oddly enough, the man who gave him an unexpected opportunity was Matt McCloskey, the millionaire contractor who had unsuccessfully tried to intercede with Roosevelt for Moses. At the end of 1957, McCloskey asked Annenberg if he wanted to buy another newspaper, the *Philadelphia Daily News*, which had proven to be a financial sinkhole in the three years the contractor had owned the tabloid.

This wasn't the first time Annenberg had been asked to buy another paper, of course; publishers routinely asked one another if they were in the market. In 1954, for example, Colonel McCormick, who owned the *Washington Times-Herald* as well as the *Chicago Tribune*, was ill and decided to give up his Washington paper. The Colonel had asked Annenberg whether he was interested in acquiring the property. The *Times-Herald*, however, was losing about $35,000 a week, and Walter, who saw the paper as useless to himself, had declined. Annenberg turned around and contacted Eugene Meyer, owner of the *Washington Post* and advised him to buy the paper, figuring the *Post*'s publisher was the only logical candidate to benefit from the move. Annenberg suggested to Meyer that he merge the paper into the *Post* as a way of strengthening his paper and simultaneously hurting the *Post*'s biggest competitor, the *Washington Star*. Meyer had liked the idea, and the deal had gone through, with the *Post* emerging with four additional pages of comics and thirty special features, helping it to engulf the *Star*, just as Annenberg had predicted.

The request to take on the *Daily News* on the surface appeared

stranger than other offers Annenberg had received. The wily McCloskey had operated his newspaper as a voice of the Democratic party,
and he had frequently locked horns with Walter's *Inquirer*. Whereas
the *Philadelphia Bulletin* traditionally shied away from taking political positions, the other two newspapers loved to do so. Walter's pledge
not to get politically involved in attacking Presidential candidates remained in effect, but that left a vast array of other political targets.
Since the paper had campaigned for Dilworth and Clark in 1951, the
Inquirer had become highly active in state and local politics. Besides
being frequently on the opposite side of the political fence from the *Inquirer* publisher, McCloskey had made personal attacks on Walter and
his paper, which added to many people's wonder about why he had
asked his rival to buy the *News*. McCloskey, however, was used to
rearranging his alliances, whether political or business, with the self-
assurance of a Mississippi riverboat gambler shuffling a deck of cards.
He always believed that pragmatism won out. For his part, Walter
agreed. To him, the paper represented a challenge to his ingenuity as
well as a way of muting an irksome critic.

There was little doubt that much of the criticism of Annenberg in
the 160,000-circulation tabloid was scathing. The paper's editor was
none other than David "Tom" Stern III, the son of Moses' bitter rival
who rarely missed an opportunity to attack the son of *his* father's
sworn enemy. Shortly before the sale, for instance, there was a damning editorial in the *News* entitled "Gutter Newspapering":

> Newspapers are strange. When they begin playing dirty they can
> play dirtier than the seamy side of a slave trader's soul. Philadelphia
> these days is being subjected to some of the dirtiest newspapering in
> recent history. The muck is being hurled by Walter Annenberg and
> his unhappy Inquirer. . . .

The subject of the hyperbole was a series of articles that had appeared in the *Inquirer* about the Pennsylvania Board of Pardons. The
Inquirer stories had concerned a convict who, after serving eleven
years, was released a year before he normally would have been, thanks
to the intercession of Democratic Congressman William A. Barrett.
The criminal, who had been captured after accidentally being shot by
members of his own gang during a holdup, was from Barrett's district,
and the *Inquirer* made it appear that the Congressman would do anything for a vote, that he had gotten the Pardons Board to do something
unethical. Annenberg had always harbored a grudge against the way

the Democrats had reneged on his father's original release from prison, and he was quick to see other parole abuses, real or imagined, on the part of Democrats. His paper continued its hue and cry about pardons and even attacked the Democratic Governor George Leader for profligate use of his pardoning power. The *Inquirer*'s assaults, though, didn't stand up under scrutiny. In 1956, the governor had granted the lowest number of pardons since 1915. But the paper had created an anti-Leader climate, and the pardons campaign was held responsible for ruining Leader's bid for a Senate seat two years later, in 1958.

Taking the *Inquirer* to task wasn't unusual for the *News*. The paper had crusaded against the *Inquirer* in 1956 on another matter that appeared much more explosive than any of its carping about pardon stories. Following the death of Henry J. Turner, a fifty-four-year-old *Inquirer* truck driver, the *News* launched a month-long series of articles that indicated there was much more to the man's death than the *Inquirer* was willing to divulge. Turner had been beaten to death one night on his paper's parking lot, and the murder had been treated by the *Inquirer* as a minor story and then dropped. The *News*, though, contended that Turner was slain because of a fight with loan sharks, who were "believed to be minor executives" of the *Inquirer* and who were supposed to be exploiting their own men. The *News* further made the startling allegation that Philadelphia police knew who murdered the driver and were doing nothing about the case.

Annenberg was furious when he read the *News*'s charges and he ordered Dimitman to investigate to determine whether there was any truth to them. In the past, there had been cases of numbers rackets proliferating at the paper, a problem that flared up periodically. On occasion, management had allowed police to plant an undercover agent on loading docks or in a supervisory job to observe truckers until the numbers runners were spotted, collared by police and hauled before a magistrate, where they were usually fined, and their illegal activity stopped for a while. The *Inquirer*'s unions were never told of the plants for fear of such knowledge sparking a walkout. The charges in the *News*, however, were obviously far more serious, and the district attorney's office was under pressure to investigate, because the tabloid was demanding swift action. Both Dimitman and the district attorney, however, came up empty-handed. No arrests were ever made, and later there was conjecture that Turner may have been the victim of a mugger, not a loan shark. He had had an artificial leg and would have had a difficult time escaping any attacker.

Because of such campaigns in the *News,* Annenberg had had McCloskey's name stricken from the *Inquirer.* Since the contractor was prominent in the Democratic party, his name was often tied to the news, but neither his name nor his face appeared in the *Inquirer,* since the ban extended to photographs as well. A clever man of no small ego, McCloskey tried to devise ways of insinuating himself into Annenberg's paper. At length, he believed he had found the answer. As a picture was being taken one day of two prominent politicians, McCloskey squeezed between them, thus apparently guaranteeing himself a spot in the *Inquirer.* When he cheerfully picked up the paper the next morning, however, there was nothing between his politician pals but a gray smear. The contractor's image had been airbrushed out.

During McCloskey's tenure as publisher, the Democrats were riding high in Philadelphia. The Republican corruption had largely been swept away several years earlier by Mayor Clark, who had almost eliminated patronage from government jobs by filling posts with able men and women who were well qualified and who, in many cases, were Republicans. Municipal services increased, and additional revenues were raised equitably through modest real-estate and business taxes. The city administration also, through the efforts of District Attorney Dilworth, came to be associated with urban renewal. Dilworth had moved to the city's downtown Society Hill section, a once elegant but deteriorating neighborhood of historic importance. Dilworth's presence had much to do with an urban renaissance that slowly lured middle-class families back into the city. Philadelphia's progress under the new administration was so dramatic that officials from cities like New York and Detroit studied methods used to keep traffic flowing on narrow streets, and New Haven city fathers studied the urban-renewal program. In light of their achievements, the *Inquirer* in 1955 backed Clark for the Senate and Dilworth for Mayor and they won.

For all the good he did, Clark remained a waspish-tongued, arrogant man, and he didn't have the foresight to maintain all the political alliances he had developed during his campaign. Clark was comfortable only with the city's blue bloods, and while he wrote Annenberg gushing notes of thanks for editorial stands that helped ease public acceptance of his programs, he privately told people that he didn't need Annenberg, a message that eventually filtered back to the publisher. As much as ever, Clark resented Annenberg's money and his intrusion into the city's power structure. When he reminisced years later, Clark faulted Annenberg mainly for his lack of pedigree, the family ties that he himself considered so important. He believed, for instance, that he and his friend Dilworth had "learned the American way on the beaches of Southampton in our youth," a world far from that of the Annenbergs. With a gesture of ill-concealed disdain, Clark dismissed Walter Annenberg as "a social climber who tried to get himself infiltrated into the higher level of Philadelphia society. He opened his checkbook for people he wanted to influence."

McCloskey, being Irish and Catholic, was as much an outsider to Clark as Annenberg, and the then Senator disdainfully expected little else when the contractor turned to the *Inquirer* publisher when he wanted to sell the *News*. McCloskey, however, knew he needed someone who was a gambler to take the paper off his hands, and there were few such men to be found in the conservative, tight-fisted world of Philadelphia's moneyed movers and shakers. In the few years of his ownership, McCloskey had pumped five million dollars into the *Daily News* and although losses were trimmed to $40,000 a month from $225,000 at their worst, McCloskey couldn't see a turnaround in sight. Never a man who liked bad tidings, McCloskey didn't tell anyone that he was selling out. Only four days before he did so, he told his editor Stern that he would back the paper for another year.

Annenberg accepted stewardship of the newspaper after he agreed to eat the losses the *News* incurred. Immediately, E. Z. Dimitman was given the task of determining what should be done with the paper. One of the first steps Dimitman took was visiting Stern's office and sacking him, which he did with relish in light of the insulting editorials that Stern had penned against the *Inquirer*. The *News*'s problems were clear-cut enough as far as Dimmy was concerned. The drab makeup had to be made sprightly, and instead of being published around the clock, there should be only one shift of printers for a first edition and a few minor replates. Finally, Dimitman recommended that a Sunday edition be scrapped.

With Dimitman's report as a springboard, Annenberg himself came up with ideas to make the paper profitable. He believed the *News* should be devoted primarily to entertainment and sports and that serial rights to popular books should be obtained in order to draw new readers. News coverage would rely heavily on the old Hearst formula of sex, crime and greed. Knowing it to be critical to his efforts to revitalize the paper, Annenberg ordered an aggressive advertising and circulation campaign. Results were soon obvious as both ad linage and circulation began creeping up. Eventually, the paper added about 90,000 readers and advertising linage almost doubled from the 7.2 million a year that it was when Annenberg took over.

Perhaps the man who benefited most by the change in the paper's ownership was a tough Philadelphia policeman named Francis L. Rizzo, who was becoming something of a folk hero as a result of the press coverage he received. Both the *Inquirer* and the *Bulletin* had already gone a long way toward turning Frank Rizzo into a heroic, outsize figure. Stories informed readers that the officer dealt effectively with rising crime, disorderly ghettos and those who didn't properly respect the law. The *Daily News*'s new emphasis on crime reporting, a tendency to disregard facts in order to have a colorful story, and a thirst for sensationalism inevitably led the paper's reporters to Rizzo, as war correspondents had flocked to General Douglas MacArthur. Rizzo's flashy style, for example, won him the sobriquet "Cisco Kid," which *Daily News* headline writers found irresistible. Quick to cultivate the press because it was useful, the policeman also liked a lot of the city's newsmen and they liked him. It wasn't unusual for Rizzo to call the city desk of one of the town's newspapers to say that he had tucked away one of the senior editors who had been on a bender and that he would have the man driven home after he slept it off.

Among the city's papers, the *Inquirer*, not the *Daily News*, was where Rizzo was most appreciated. The editors who ran the *Inquirer* were basically a conservative group. The fact that Rizzo's arrests were frequently trailed by reports of police brutality bothered them little, since they believed that was the price for doing the job right. Several of them routinely ate dinner with him as a way of keeping their fingers on the pulse of the city. But often as not, they simply liked being around the big cop, who was built like a fullback. Rizzo had a certain roughhewn charm, and it was obvious that he knew the city, the hookers, racketeers and panhandlers, and he could regale the newsmen with tales they could never print in their newspaper. It wasn't unusual even for top editors to have such a close relationship with a cop. Many of them had served as police reporters when they first entered the business and had maintained contacts with the police force over the years. *Inquirer* managing editor John Gillen and City Editor Morrie Litman, for instance, routinely dined with Police Inspector Clarence Ferguson, who several decades earlier had pointed the finger at Moses Annenberg for a bribery attempt during the course of grand-jury investigations.

What was surprising was that Rizzo boasted among his friends at the *Inquirer* the publisher, Walter Annenberg. Publishers, too, cultivated police if only because it was good business sense. They have fleets of trucks on the streets, many of which raced through city streets at breakneck speed, trying to deliver bundles of newspapers in time for newsstand sales and home deliveries. Their schedules were often met only because policemen turned a blind eye as the trucks whipped through yellow lights, broke the speed limit and made illegal U turns. The reason for the largesse of the police was the fact that the relationship between newspapers and the force was a strong one. Annenberg's friendship with Frank Rizzo, however, went beyond the practical. The publisher was a strong law-and-order advocate, and Rizzo was a walking example of what he believed a policeman should be. Rizzo was fearless, he knew his job and he was loyal—qualities that Annenberg respected. Moreover, the police captain may have reminded the publisher of the tough rough-and-ready type of man his father had frequently associated with.

In turn, Rizzo was shrewd enough to court the publisher. He was never overly familiar and always called him "Mr. Annenberg" or "sir." When Annenberg expressed an interest in resuming the rides in a police car that he had taken during the Second World War, Rizzo was quick to accommodate him, personally touring the millionaire through the city's seamier side, the police radio crackling and danger lurking around every corner. For Annenberg, the rides were a form of boyish fun, and Lee would roll her eyes and wonder when he would outgrow such impulses. The publisher even had a standing offer to ride a fire truck as well, and though he always meant to, he never got around to it. But for Rizzo, the presence of a powerful publisher sitting at his side boosted his already inflated ego. The policeman was an ambitious man and he carefully stroked people who were useful to him. Throughout his career, Rizzo had needed allies, as he well knew. There was the case years earlier, when he and another officer were accused of beating six enlisted men who were orderlies at the Philadelphia Naval Hospital, but the charges were dismissed and the incident hadn't been covered in the *Inquirer*. Long after the affair, Thomas J. Gibbons, Philadelphia's police commissioner from 1952 to 1961, told two *Bulletin* reporters that Rizzo "beat those sailors for no reason," but he hadn't spoken out against him at the time.

When around men like Annenberg, Rizzo suppressed his unrulier side. Over dinner with the publisher Rizzo earnestly outlined his beliefs about how to make the city a better, safer place, and he often took his cues from the publisher before voicing his own opinions. Thus, not surprisingly, Rizzo's concerns were tailored to the same sense of obligation that Annenberg felt toward the city. Moreover, it was an open secret that Rizzo didn't get along with Senator Clark, who privately referred to the police captain as a fascist. To the publisher's way of thinking over the years, however, a Clark slur was likely to become a recommendation.

When a crippling strike hit the *Inquirer* in 1958, Rizzo saw to it that Philadelphia police were out in force to make sure that those who crossed the picket lines weren't harmed. The forty-day strike, which began in the third week of May, was only the second since an Annenberg had owned the paper, the first being in 1946, when truck drivers had walked off the job for several days. The second strike, however, was far more serious and would have lasting implications for the quality of the paper. The truck drivers, who belonged to the International Teamsters Union, hit the bricks and they were soon followed by members of the Newspaper Guild. The strike was ugly and in retrospect unnecessary, with charges and countercharges being made by management and labor. The basic disagreement was a job-security clause in the Guild contract and the strike tore the *Inquirer*'s staff apart. The Guild had come to the paper in 1938, when Moses signed an agreement with union members, many of whom were still with the *Inquirer* and believed the Guild was a sacred institution. Others, who believed they had no quarrel with management and that they were treated fairly, crossed the picket lines. The polarization was epitomized by the smashed, once close friendship of two copy editors, Gerard Chapeau and Max Spindel. Chapeau was an intense unionist; Spindel continued working. When the strike ended on July 1 and for years afterward, they were both desk men on consecutive shifts. They left written notes for one another if they had to communicate about stories or issues developing, but they never talked to each other again.

In an effort to increase pressure on management, union members had sought the backing of longshoremen and other unions, and quickly the crowd of marchers outside the *Inquirer* building took on a tough, menacing look as traffic on Broad Street was frequently stopped and men shouted their demands through bullhorns. Annenberg established a monitoring post on the newspaper's second floor, and he routinely checked to determine how the situation was progressing. Surprisingly, little hostility was directed at the publisher. To most of the strikers, Annenberg was so aloof from their operations that he was more of a figure of awe and mystery than an object of hatred. Moreover, enough of them knew of his paternalistic kindnesses to fellow employees that they didn't hold him responsible for what was happening. When his chauffeur-driven limousine pulled in front of the paper every day, it wasn't the mounted policemen who made way for him; it was Annenberg's employees, shouting, "Let the publisher through! Let Mr. Annenberg through!"

What dismayed many observers was that the real issue was the elimination of dead wood, not any alleged attempts by management to clamp down on employees' job security. The contract made it almost impossible to fire anyone without "just and reasonable cause," which was so open to interpretation that it was almost meaningless. Over the years, a number of reporters and editors had been hired at high salaries and higher expectations, but they hadn't turned out to be the professionals that they had appeared to be. The result was a fifth column in the newsroom of overpaid not extremely talented men, who found themselves with a sinecure for life.

The strike finally ended when Sadie visited her son at the paper one day. The obvious bitterness of the men on the big picket line alarmed her and she was heartsick that such a situation existed. With great dismay, she stood in her son's office and told him, "Those are your people down there. You can't let them do this." Walter never refused his mother anything, and he wasn't about to start.

Management backed away from trying to get rid of any employees, and the men returned to work. Annenberg, however, was so angered by the senselessness of the strike that he wanted to buy out the militants who started it. He offered double severance pay to anyone wishing to leave the paper, fully expecting that the troublemakers were the overpriced, untalented dead wood. As it turned out, most of the union stalwarts were also the most able newsmen, and several hundred *Inquirer* men took their publisher up on his offer, including about thirty of the best writers and editors.

When the dust of the exodus settled, Walter had Dimitman survey the news operation to determine what it would take to rebuild the staff, what was needed in terms of plant and equipment, both of which were aging, and he wanted to know how to improve the paper's efficiency. Several months later, Dimitman was back with a thorough study of the *Inquirer*'s needs. His analysis concluded that restoring the *Inquirer* to the level of a major, sophisticated metropolitan daily newspaper would be a very costly endeavor. More than the few hundred workers who had left, for example, would have to be replaced. The newsroom alone needed at least fifty new people, not just the thirty who had resigned. Printing presses had to be replaced, and the paper needed a new fleet of delivery trucks. When Annenberg calculated the amount of money that would be required to make a strong paper, it merely confirmed what he had thought for years. He should sell the *Inquirer*, because it wasn't economical to spend as much money as it needed. But he again avoided the issue. The *Inquirer* was the cornerstone of the legacy that he had from his father. The paper was the instrument that could bring social prestige and respectability to the Annenberg name. Without the *Inquirer*, Annenberg would not have a powerful voice or the special status that belonged to major newspaper publishers. He would lack an essential tool with which to redeem his father.

Following the strike, the *Inquirer*'s newsroom never settled down. Key reporters and editors, the strong anchors any worthwhile newspaper needed, were missing. Many editorial employees who remained were third-rate—such as one, who was a poor reporter and a poor writer who had carved out a niche for himself by running errands for editors, driving them to dinner and generally currying favor. Joe Miller, the old warhorse in the Harrisburg bureau, remained with the paper, but his partisan style of reporting had gone out of fashion over the years as journalism tried to become more responsible. Nevertheless, Miller was regarded fondly by the publisher, whom he kept informed of the political machinations in the state capital. John Cummings, the aged political reporter, still ground out his columns.

Not only had the staff deteriorated, but the paper suffered because the way it covered news hadn't changed with the times. The bulldog, or first of the half dozen editions, still carried an eight-column headline across the front page, a practice dating back to when there were many papers to choose among and sensational headlines were needed to catch readers' attention.

Other than Dimitman, the man most responsible for shaping the day-to-day newspaper was Morrie Litman, the city editor who had been hired in the 1940s from the *Evening Ledger*. A hard worker who put in fourteen-hour days, Litman loved newspapers, but his idea of what one should be was frozen in the era of sex and crime, and murder was the hottest story. The idea of fairness that was creeping into

American journalism didn't make sense to Litman when it meant telling two sides of a story. There was only one side, he believed, and anything else tended to confuse issues. Litman's concept of news was exciting, but not necessarily accurate. He was also the conduit that Dimitman used to see that stories the publisher wanted—or those Dimitman himself wanted or he believed Annenberg probably wanted—got into the paper. Sometimes such stories were of a political nature, and Litman turned to Miller or Saul Kohler, another Harrisburg reporter who didn't mind what task he was asked to carry out.

After the strike, another reporter came to the forefront. His name was Harry Karafin, who had started as an $18-a-week copy boy, and graduated to police reporter and an investigative reporter under Litman. Karafin was a street-savvy little man who had been among the first reporters to break the picket line. A braggart who freely mixed fact with fantasy when talking about himself, Karafin claimed, for instance, that he had been an O.S.S. agent during the war and was dropped behind enemy lines to distribute hundreds of thousands of dollars to French Resistance leaders. He described his daring exploits in such vivid detail that even though the men who worked with him knew he was an inveterate liar, they were never sure whether his war feats were true. They weren't. Merrill Panitt, Annenberg's *TV Guide* editor, had worked with Karafin during the war; they had both been public-relations men.

Nevertheless, Litman recognized Karafin's value. He played rough, telling everyone, from City Hall politicians to the city's top bankers, that if they didn't cooperate with him, he would smear their names across the front page the following day. Karafin could shade a story so that it looked as though a parish priest was skimming his Sunday collection. His method of operation was like that of a tough cop. I'll do you a favor, if you do me one, he said; or else he threatened. Because of his broad range of sources, including top-ranking policemen and politicians, Karafin got good stories, and people who played ball with him received good copy. What made everyone more than a little wary of the reporter was his insinuating that he had a direct line to the publisher. Everyone between Harrisburg and Philadelphia knew that Joe Miller said he could call Annenberg directly whenever he wanted. There was that edge of doubt about Karafin. Perhaps he could too.

Following the strike, Litman relied even more heavily on Karafin for many of his sensational front-page stories. As an investigative reporter,

Karafin broke more hot stories than anyone in the city. Litman liked the reporter, because he was plugged into what was happening and could enhance the editor's knowledge about activities at City Hall or within the police department. A cherubic little man with a fringe of gray hair, who packed a revolver under his ever-present blue sports coat, Litman was obsessed with what was going on within his city. He was always talking secretively on the telephone with callers. He knew at least as much about what was happening at the state level as Miller did, and Miller's knowledge was formidable. After a rewrite man had taken a story from the Harrisburg reporter, for example, Litman often penciled in enhancing details that made legislators whom Miller dealt with believe he was far more perceptive than he actually was. Thus, Miller gained a reputation for being knowledgeable but pro-Republican. Since he worked for the most political newspaper in the state, he could send for legislators when they were speaking on the floor of the state house and they came—not walking, but running. His true power, legislators knew, wasn't his at all. They recognized him as Walter Annenberg's emissary.

Though a strongly partisan paper in both city and state politics, the *Inquirer* again refrained from showing any bias when the 1960 Presidential election was held. The decision hadn't been as easy for Annenberg as it had been in past elections. The reason was that the Republican contender was his friend Richard Nixon. The two had met in the early 1950s, but it wasn't until 1957, when Nixon had addressed the Poor Richard Club in Philadelphia, that the two became close. Walter and Lee had sat near the Vice-President during his address, and when they spoke later, Nixon was impressed by how closely he and the publisher agreed on domestic and international issues. The politician was also struck by Lee's beauty, finding her "simply stunning." The encounter had led to their visiting each other socially, and Nixon won the publisher's eternal friendship when the Vice-President gave a dinner in his home for Sadie Annenberg. But as much as he admired Nixon, Annenberg adhered to his policy of refraining from giving him any campaign contributions. In keeping with Annenberg's long-standing Presidential-campaign policy, the *Inquirer* editors decided not to give his friend more intensive news coverage than his rival, John F. Kennedy. Adding to the difficulty of the resolution was the fact that Annenberg believed that Kennedy lacked the experience to be President. In any event, wire-service copy, not *Inquirer* reporters' accounts, were used for coverage as further insurance against partisanship, and each candidate was given an equal amount of space. Like three quarters of the nation's newspapers, however, the *Inquirer* editorialized on behalf of Richard Nixon.

In his efforts to strive for fairness, Annenberg was appalled when Dr. Norman Vincent Peale, the powerful Protestant religious leader, raised the issue of religion during the campaign. Dr. Peale headed a group of ministers and laymen who questioned whether a Roman Catholic President could separate his responsibilities to church and to state in the performance of his duties. The issue was a smoldering one, and Annenberg felt that it was unseemly for someone of Peale's stature to fan the flames of bigotry. The act merely confirmed the publisher's opinion that mankind would be far better off without religions. To show his displeasure, Annenberg dropped Dr. Peale's weekly column, which the *Inquirer* had carried on Sunday for years, a move that stunned Philadelphians and was reported by other newspapers across the nation. On September 11, 1960, Annenberg wrote a signed note to his readers explaining why the column would no longer appear:

> When the Inquirer several years ago began publication of Dr. Norman Vincent Peale's weekly article, we regarded it as a non-sectarian feature, strongly inspirational to men and women of all faiths. To our regret, Dr. Peale has impaired this public image and distorted the non-sectarian character of his writings by his approach to the so called "religious issue" in this political campaign.
> For this reason we are discontinuing publication of his column with the issue of Sunday, September 18th.

When Nixon lost the close election, Annenberg was more disappointed than he had been by the outcome of any Presidential contest that he could remember. His dismay, however, had more behind it than mere friendship with Nixon or questions about the ability of Kennedy. Annenberg had long harbored a deep resentment of Kennedy's father, Joe. While his own father had been thrown in prison, Joe Kennedy, a man Annenberg considered dishonorable, had been made the ambassador to Great Britain by Franklin Roosevelt. The injustices that he perceived at work never ceased to anger the publisher. "Joe Kennedy was the most ruthless operator I ever saw in my life," he said. "He once was given $100,000 to bring in a report on what should be done with Paramount Pictures when it had just come out of receivership. His principal recommendation was that there were already too many Jews in the movie industry and that the company should be given to him."

To illustrate further Joe Kennedy's character, Annenberg related to friends an incident that had involved Frank Sinatra, who was to become a friend of the publisher. Sinatra had invited Kennedy to stay with him during the campaign when he came to California, and Kennedy had accepted because Sinatra was a major contributor to the Democratic party. Old Joe, however, heard that one of Sinatra's friends was in trouble with the gambling commission in Las Vegas and he had told his son to stay at Bing Crosby's home for propriety's sake. "He told his son 'brush the Dago off,' " Annenberg related. "That's the kind of man Joe Kennedy was."

Nonetheless, Annenberg, as always, was anxious to help any new President if he sought his support and he didn't have to wait long. Shortly after taking office, Kennedy let it be known that he wanted the Philadelphia contractor Matt McCloskey to be his ambassador to Ireland. The appointment wasn't unexpected in light of all the work McCloskey had done for the party, including serving from 1955 on as treasurer of the Democratic National Committee, during which he had come up with the idea of the $100-a-plate dinner as a clever party fund-raising ploy. That alone, in political circles, merited appointment as ambassador to Ireland. McCloskey, a professional Irishman, was anxious for the job, so anxious that he began hosting celebration parties for himself before the post was nailed down. When he was thinking of offering the job to the Philadelphian, Kennedy had called Annenberg to see if he could gain his support.

"Mr. Annenberg, I want to appoint McCloskey ambassador to Ireland," the President said. "But I want to know if you will attack the appointment editorially."

"Mr. President," Annenberg replied, "I certainly recognize the value of sentimental appointments, and I will be as helpful as I can."

There was a pause on the line and then Kennedy broke into a laugh and asked Annenberg's help in easing the appointment. "Can you think of any way of getting Senator Hickenlooper off my back?"

The President then explained how Republican Senator Bourke B. Hickenlooper from Iowa was threatening to throw a monkey wrench into the McCloskey appointment. The Senator had a long memory, and instead of making the Philadelphia millionaire an ambassador, he felt the public would be better served by having the contractor thrown in jail. During the Second World War, McCloskey had gone into the business of making cement boats for the government. They cost the taxpayers a fortune, and when they were launched, the boats cracked in half and were useless. Moreover, Hickenlooper believed that the buildings McCloskey had erected under government contracts were inferior, and none of Kennedy's emissaries had thus far been able to change his mind. The issue was beginning to embarrass the President. McCloskey was telling everyone the appointment was in the bag, and Kennedy had even found himself one evening at a party at the Mayflower Hotel in Washington that had turned out to be yet another of McCloskey's celebrations.

In any event, Kennedy in desperation turned to Annenberg as a member of the Republican power network. After hanging up, Annenberg thought about the problem for a moment, and with his characteristic directness came up with what seemed like a good course of action. He called his friend Gardner Cowles, head of Cowles Communications, which owned the *Des Moines Register* and the *Tribune*, the most powerful newspapers in Iowa. Explaining the President's problem, he asked Cowles if he thought he could persuade the Senator to back off. A short while later, Cowles called Annenberg back, telling him that Hickenlooper wouldn't object when the Senate Foreign Relations Committee moved on McCloskey's ambassadorship. Annenberg didn't ask how the Senator's consent was gained. When Annenberg informed Kennedy, the President was delighted. Eighteen months after Kennedy took the post, however, neither he nor McCloskey was smiling. The Philadelphian returned from Dublin to Washington as one of the main witnesses in the scandal involving his friend Bobby Baker, who had used his job as Democratic secretary to the Senate to line his own pockets.

The Hickenlooper incident wasn't the last time that Annenberg heard from the White House. A short while afterward, the President's wife, Jacqueline, called him and explained her plans to refurbish the White House, including her goal of making it the home of an exquisite art collection. As she talked, Mrs. Kennedy made several flattering remarks about Annenberg's own art collection and then she got down to business.

"I have heard that you have a great portrait of Ben Franklin done by David Martin," Mrs. Kennedy purred.

As he listened, the publisher began getting a better fix on why she had called. She was so charming, so gracious, that he felt that it was as if she had him up against the wall; he could see what was coming next, and it did—"Do you think a great Philadelphia editor like you could give the White House a portrait of Philadelphia's greatest citizen?" she asked.

The beleaguered Annenberg asked her for a few days during which he could think over her request. When he hung up, he realized that he was dealing with a genius when it came to getting what she wanted. He liked the painting and it had cost a fortune, but he found himself not only ready to hand it over to her but anything else she might ask for as well. An hour later, he called her back.

"Mrs. Kennedy, you have very effectively twisted my arm," he said. "You're right. The picture is more appropriate in the White House than it is in my home." He had it delivered to her the next day.

Out of gratitude, the Kennedys invited the Annenbergs to the White House for dinner and the only other guests were Mr. and Mrs. Charles Englehard, who were friends of the Kennedys. Mr. Englehard had large interests in gold and platinum and was an art authority as well. By the end of the evening, Annenberg had enjoyed himself thoroughly and he found that Kennedy was an extremely engaging personality. Thereafter, the voice of the *Inquirer* wouldn't be raised against Kennedy, even when other conservative publishers ranted against the costly social programs the President wanted to introduce, or his bungled Bay of Pigs attack on Cuba.

Shortly after aiding the Kennedys' efforts to build a White House art collection, Annenberg had cause to celebrate another effort that involved him and works of art. The *Inquirer*—after a long, nine-year campaign—had successfully ended a battle to open to the general public a strange art gallery on the Main Line called the Barnes Foundation. Late in 1951, at the publisher's bidding, the newspaper had begun editorializing for public access to the Barnes gallery. On February 16, 1952, the *Inquirer* had gone so far as to start legal action in the Court of Common Pleas of Montgomery County to force the opening of the institution, which operated under a tax-free status "to promote the advance of education and appreciation of the fine arts." The Barnes collection was thought to be massive, containing perhaps 200 Renoirs, 75 Matisses and 25 Picassos, as well as numerous Seurats, Rousseaus and pictures by other artists. The rambling twenty-three-room mansion housing the paintings was also supposed to contain a priceless collection of African tribal sculpture.

No one within the art community, however, was sure exactly what the gallery contained since the man who put the collection together,

Dr. Albert C. Barnes, an eccentric who made a fortune by inventing the antiseptic Argyrol, kept the enjoyment of the works pretty much to himself. When art critics or connoisseurs called, the doctor had his servant unceremoniously tell them to "go away." When the famed author and critic Alexander Woollcott sent a telegram requesting admittance, he received a telegram in response: "Dr. Barnes was out on the lawn singing to the birds. . . . It would cost me my job if I should disturb him at his regular Sunday-morning nature worship." The signature was that of a "Secretaire de Dr. Barnes," a "Fidèle de Port-Maneuch," which was the name of the good doctor's dog. Sometimes the responses were laced with obscenities, since the doctor was a student of the subject, a practice that had brought him to the attention of the United States Post Office and the threat of being dragged into court for sending obscene literature through the mail. Thereafter, the doctor had his chauffeur hand-deliver his mail.

The number of people who were upset by the doctor's behavior were legion, and after his death in July 1951, they had further cause for dismay when his will established the foundation, which banned anyone from seeing the collection with the exception of a tiny number of art students. Among the people who were upset was Walter Annenberg, who had found Barnes's antics funny, but believed his postmortem admittance policies to the gallery a crime against democracy. In any event, the publisher made the gallery one of his paper's causes, and soon, whenever there was the slightest chance of attacking the gallery, there was a major story in the *Inquirer*. The fight, however, wasn't easy. The doctor had laid down the principles of the educators John Dewey and William James as the restrictive guidelines for allowing anyone into the gallery. Thus, a relatively few art students could study the masterpieces in the doctor's "laboratory" in order to see how the artists had created their works with elements of light, color and symmetry but, as an educational laboratory, the gallery didn't have to be open to everyone.

Over the years, Dimitman saw to it that Barnes stories were relentlessly hard-nosed, and on occasion he had reporters write bogus letters of outrage, which were printed to further the paper's cause. Periodically, there had been verdicts and appeals in courts, and the case was finally taken to the Pennsylvania State Supreme Court, which years earlier had ruled that the Barnes facility was an educational institution, not an art gallery. On the second time around with the issue, the court had again dismissed the *Inquirer* suit, contending there was no apparent public need to gain access, and it wasn't necessary to reconsider the decision. One justice, though, dissented from his colleagues' opinion. He was Judge Michael Musmanno, a feisty little man whose dissent presented the restriction on admission as a serious infringement of the rights of Pennsylvania's taxpayers.

Grateful for anything that would bolster their flagging fight, the *Inquirer*'s editors, who had already devoted hundreds of inches of news space to blasting Barnes's policy, used Musmanno's remarks to fuel the cause. The little judge himself became the rallying point to rouse public opinion and, surprisingly, the last-ditch effort succeeded. The state attorney general's office, which had felt the heat of the *Inquirer*'s blasts, reexamined the foundation and discovered some hazy wording that called the restrictive policy into question. Under the renewed onslaught, the beleaguered foundation agreed to broaden its admission policy starting in the spring of 1961, after which the number of visitors to the gallery was vastly increased.

The hero of the hour, at least as far as the *Inquirer* was concerned, was Justice Musmanno, who combined the characteristics of a distinguished jurist and a circus barker. He was known for ardently pursuing noble causes and for calling attention to himself in the process. In his younger days, he had fought to outlaw brutal coal and iron police in the coal region of western Pennsylvania, where he had grown up. In the 1920s, he had gained renown for having helped defend Sacco and Vanzetti, the two Italian radicals tried and executed for the 1920 murder of a Boston shoe-company paymaster and a guard during a $15,000 holdup. After the Second World War, he was a judge at the Nuremberg war-crimes trials. In his later years, the judge was a staunch patriot who wrapped himself in the flag, defended Democracy in flowery prose at the drop of a hat and devoted a great deal of time to defending yet another Italian he believed under false attack: the "Noble Genoese," as he called Christopher Columbus, who the jurist defended against scholars who contended Vikings actually had discovered America before Columbus had done so.

Since the judge's stand had so greatly aided the *Inquirer*'s efforts, the newspaper's editors inadvertently rewarded him by letting Musmanno use the paper as a personal platform for his self-aggrandizement. The turn of events started one day when the judge called the paper with a story about a speech he had given before an American Legion post. The bewildered editor on duty believed someone had asked the judge for the story, so he let him give it to a rewrite man.

When other editors read the story, they thought that the judge had Walter Annenberg's permission to weigh in with his own stories. Soon other Musmanno speeches before patriotic organizations were called in, then came his Flag Day and Christopher Columbus speeches.

Eventually, the jurist became an institutionalized joke. An editor on the city desk yelled to a rewrite man, "The judge wants to unload a story," which the writer dutifully took down and tried to make coherent, often a very difficult task. The stories always appeared in the paper. The practice illustrated how far removed from their publisher the editors felt, and it showed how much the paper's standards had slipped since the 1958 strike. Any strong editors who might have questioned the publisher about the judge's access to the news columns had left, and those who remained were either too lazy or too afraid to approach him. Moreover, the editors found turning to Dimitman for an explanation was useless. He saw little wrong with giving someone like the judge a little free publicity every now and then.

CHAPTER

SEVENTEEN

ON AUGUST 7, 1962, Walter Annenberg's world came undone. After several weeks in Europe, he and Lee arrived in the afternoon at Philadelphia International Airport. They were both weary after the trip from Paris, but Walter immediately realized that something was dreadfully wrong. The reason for his anxiety was that Joe First was waiting to meet them, something the efficient little executive never did, since he tried to intrude as little as possible into the publisher's personal life. This day was obviously different, and Joe First, for perhaps the only time in his life, didn't know how to articulate the problem that he had to tell the man he had served these many years.

First could easily be excused his uncertainties. The sad duty that he had to perform was telling Walter that his son, Roger, had committed suicide earlier in the day. The young man was only twenty-two years old.

When the lawyer learned the terrible news, he was unable to contact Walter in Europe, so he elected to go to the airport to tell him personally. As well as any man in the Triangle organization, First knew how much Annenberg had worried about his son and how much suffering the boy had caused the father. He had seen his employer go through many changes over the years. Of the company's executives only he and E. Z. Dimitman knew the full extent of the pain and sorrow Walter Annenberg had suffered as a result of Moses' ordeal and death, and now he feared the way the publisher would react to his son's tragedy. He tried to determine what would be the best course of action to adopt and how the publisher should be treated by members of the staff. Thus, before coming to the airport, First had gathered together the company's top officers and related what had happened. Then he outlined what he believed was the best course they could follow. Instead of mentioning the tragic death to Annenberg, he told them to avoid discussing it. As an alternative, he suggested they give the publisher as much work to do as possible and to make sure that he was always kept occupied at this time of grief.

A religious man who valued family with the Old World intensity of the Jewish patriarch he was within his own family, First believed in the rightness of the path that he had laid out. In this instance, however, more than a few of his executives felt that he was wrong. Though Joe First was a canny businessman, he had few sure instincts when it came to matters of the heart. His proposal that they avoid mentioning, let alone sympathizing about, such a terrible loss seemed bound to affect their boss adversely, and no benefits to him could come of it, other executives believed. Nonetheless, all of them did as they were asked; not one felt he had the authority to dispute First, especially regarding such a delicate matter. In days and even years to come, many Triangle men believed that their boss never had an atmosphere in which to grieve properly for his son, and that much of the bitterness, anger and sense of despair that are the normal reactions accompanying any such tragedy remained bottled up in him, causing him at times to lash out in misdirected rage.

Walter had been all too aware that his son's problems were worsening, and he had feared Roger's self-destructive impulses. After graduating *magna cum laude* from Episcopal Academy, Roger had gone to Harvard. At the university, however, the boy's school work had suffered and at first his father had ascribed it to the young man's being away from home with too much money in his pockets. Walter needed only to scratch his memory to readily understand that. When he gave his son funds to furnish his rooms, for instance, Roger had spent it all on clothing at J. Press. Moreover, his son assumed a life style at Harvard that would have been more appropriate to a nineteenth-century student attending either Oxford or Cambridge. Roger had established a literary salon of sorts, where he entertained fellow students with sherry and poetry readings. Within several years, his behavior became more erratic than eccentric, and finally the university had contacted his parents, because he could no longer function at school. Doctors had diagnosed the student as schizophrenic, and they told his parents that he needed professional psychiatric help.

At a loss as to what to do, Walter had sought the best care that he could find. He settled on an exclusive psychiatric institute in Tinicum, a township in the gently rolling hills of Bucks County, Pennsylvania. The facility was run by a Dr. John Rosen and was extremely expensive. The hospital provided a homelike environment for its patients, who lived in cottages and were supposed to receive constant attention. Because of its cost, the sanitarium had as its patients only the children of the very wealthy, including members of the DuPont and Rockefeller families. Walter had chosen the particular institution because the doctor enjoyed an excellent reputation and because of the stated practice of constantly monitoring patients.

Walter had visited his son frequently, and whenever he did, he became upset. The signs of improvement that he hoped to detect were never there. For a man who was used to ordering his world at will, he felt an acute sense of helplessness when he was around his boy. As months passed, Roger's condition worsened. During some of Walter's visits, he had a sense that his son was so withdrawn from reality that he didn't even realize his father was with him, talking with him, trying to encourage him. On such occasions, Walter attempted to engage his son in conversations about home, past vacations together, school, or Roger's mother, sister or grandmother, Sadie, but the efforts appeared to be useless. Roger had lost interest in company of any kind, including that of his father. Worse than anything else, Walter was deeply disturbed by his son's frightening flights of fantasy; they bore no relation to any reality that the father knew. At other times, Roger fled into another world, one where he only listened to music, and he had left his father far away. On the day of his death, Roger had managed to get his hands on drugs and had overdosed, escaping his problems forever.

Upon being told by Joe First what had happened, Walter was shattered. Ever after he would not be able to recall precisely where he had been returning from, or why he had been in Europe, which had actually been a vacation to Deauville. Roger's mother, Ronny, likewise plunged into a state of shock when she was told, and his sister, Wallis, was terrified. Since Wallis and her brother were only a year apart, the sister had always believed she was closer to him than anyone else. Two years earlier, Wallis had married Seth Weingarten, a young medical student. In reacting to what happened, Wallis became deathly afraid. She worried about whether there was a possibility that she was also susceptible to the disease, and she, like her father, blamed Dr. Rosen for her brother's death. Father and daughter believed, and would always believe, that the doctor was responsible for letting Roger get his hands on the drugs.

At the *Inquirer*, there was a great deal of indecision as to how to disclose the boy's death. The matter was so intensely personal that even Dimitman wasn't sure what to do. Finally, on August 15, or eight days after the tragic event, the world learned that Roger had died; a five-paragraph obituary was carried in the newspaper. The publisher himself had given final approval to the little story. The reason for more than a week's delay in the disclosure was Walter's fear as to how it would affect his mother, Sadie. She was traveling, and her son had had difficulty in reaching her. Walter would never cause his mother the harm of having her learn about what had happened from reading about it in a newspaper. Thus, he had held up the announcement until he had been able to locate her and tell her himself. Upon hearing the terrible news, Sadie predictably thought first of her son, her Boy.

In accordance with Joe First's dictate, Walter was given little chance to shed tears. Triangle executives steadily streamed through his office, and they constantly talked of balance sheets, advertising rates and revenues, newsprint orders and editorial matters. In each instance, the executive did indeed perfunctorily tell his boss how sorry he was, but then he launched into a litany of particular problems and needs, many of which were marginal at best. The men deliberately sought Walter's advice or approval on an ever-widening circle of business matters.

"Don't let him grieve," First constantly cautioned the other executives, and none of them went against the instinct of Walter's right-hand man.

It was obvious to everyone that Annenberg was in a daze, and for a long while, his officers found it next to impossible to get any reaction from him. Eventually, though, he began responding. He discussed the magazines, newspapers and television stations, but there was no enthusiasm about how well a project was going or the typical edge of impatience to improve upon whatever project was at hand. His replies were hollow, and he wasn't offering new ideas, new ways of doing business. Walter Annenberg wasn't challenging his executives, which had always been his forte.

Employees who had far fewer dealings with the publisher than did his top executives treated the tragedy from a careful distance. Since Annenberg was an aloof figure to most men and women, they didn't know how to express their sympathy. "Many people wouldn't offer their condolences, because there was a feeling that they simply couldn't do that," recalled Rubye Graham, who was at the time the *Inquirer*'s fashion editor. Thus, throughout the *Inquirer* building for a long time an eerie silence greeted Walter when he walked down corridors.

A telltale sign that the publisher wasn't himself was that he had lost interest in local politics, a subject about which he had always exhibited a great deal of active concern. His disinterest was all the more obvious because Walter, just prior to Roger's death, was a central figure in an organization called the Republican Alliance. The aim of the organization was to reinvigorate Philadelphia's Republican party and demote some of the party's bosses who seemed to Alliance members more of a hindrance than a positive force. The group formed after the last Presidential election and consisted of Nixon supporters who were dismayed that their candidate had lost the city by a narrow margin in 1960. Many of them blamed William A. Meehan, the leader of the Philadelphia G.O.P., for what they perceived as an embarrassing loss.

Walter became involved with the Alliance as a result of the efforts of Robert Johnson, a friend and neighbor who was the president of Temple University. A charming man, who with Henry Luce had founded *Time* magazine years earlier, Johnson started the Alliance out of the conviction that a big city could still be Republican, a premise that Walter shared. A persuasive man, Johnson soon lined up a number of the city's rich and powerful Republicans who wanted to do something to see that their party was strengthened. In addition to Annenberg, their ranks included Thomas McCabe, chairman of Scott Paper Company, and Philip T. Sharpless, the millionaire founder of Sharpless Company, a manufacturer of centrifugal pumps.

With the support of the Annenberg newspapers and the contributions of other wealthy men, the Alliance tried to wrest power away from Meehan. The strategy was to run an Alliance candidate for chairman of the City Committee, and some $500,000 was raised to defeat the city boss. Much of the money was funneled to Republican ward leaders, assuming they would spend it to help the cause. Although Annenberg didn't contribute financially, his *Inquirer* was planted firmly behind the movement. The newspaper daily carried stories bearing headlines such as "Alliance Attacks Meehan Role in GOP 'Dynasty,'" referring to the fact that Meehan's father, Austin, had been the party boss before him, and "Vigor Is Deemed Vital for GOP." In the end, though, the movement proved to be a case of the blind leading the blind. The ward leaders took the money, but they spent it helping Meehan, to whom they were indebted for patronage and numerous favors from the very beginning.

Meanwhile, Annenberg was showing that his political causes were wide-ranging and not confined to any one party. While fighting the established Republican machine, he was also using his *Inquirer* to block Dick Dilworth's quest to become governor. The two had fallen out a year earlier over what was known in the *Inquirer* as the "Frankford El Scandal," which involved possible kickbacks from construction work done on the city's elevated train line. At Annenberg's bidding, the *Inquirer* had demanded a grand-jury investigation of city officials who appeared to be benefiting from El-related contracts. Dilworth, as mayor, had become incensed by the attacks and he was afraid that the grand jury would turn into a fishing expedition that might rope Democrats into an embarrassing situation.

In the heat of what he felt to be righteous indignation, and perhaps to show once again that he had not favored the election of Dilworth because the lawyer once worked for him, Annenberg hotly demanded that action be taken in the case. The dispute at times seemed much like a personal brawl publicly aired by two stubborn men, as the bullheaded publisher and the argumentative mayor squared off against each other. Dilworth aides had found themselves frantically responding to the editorials appearing almost daily in the *Inquirer*. "The *Inquirer* was a very powerful paper in the state and I spent half my time writing letters to the editor," recalled Cliff Brenner, one of Dilworth's top lieutenants. In the end, the *Inquirer* prevailed and a grand jury was convened, but no one was ever sent to prison.

In turning away from his former friend, Annenberg had no trouble finding a candidate to support for governor. He was William Scranton, the scion of an old Pennsylvania family. In actuality, the similarities between the two candidates were striking. Both Dilworth and Scranton were wealthy men who had graduated from Yale Law School after interrupting their studies to serve in the armed forces. Each was articulate and personable, and each was married to an attractive woman of high energy. Moreover, each was the descendant of a distinguished family. The city of Scranton was named for the Republican candidate's great-grandfather while Dilworth's great-grandfather had been one of Pittsburgh's pioneers. The chief difference between them was that Scranton was cool and colorless compared with the combative, hotheaded Dilworth.

The gubernatorial campaign proved to be bitter and hard fought as each party called upon powerful allies. President Kennedy, for instance, campaigned for Dilworth as well as for Senator Clark, who was seeking reelection. Former President Eisenhower spoke out on behalf of Scranton. Walter Annenberg, who had temporarily stopped speaking with Dilworth, used the *Inquirer* to promote Scranton's cause, and after Roger's death, the newspaper's voice hardened into a vindictive tone. Stories, such as one bearing the headline "City GOP Aide Calls Dilworth 'Evil Old Man' " began appearing and, on October 31, an editorial appeared on the front page entitled "A Balance Sheet," which left no illusion about where the newspaper or its publisher stood. Scranton, the *Inquirer* declared, was a "man of integrity . . . modesty, stability and decisiveness. . . ." But Dilworth's sins were many and included his "mistakes in judgment . . . his egotism . . . his instability."

The most damning *Inquirer* assaults on the mayor came from the pen of the old political writer John M. Cummings. Cummings, who had smarted from 1949 to 1959 while his boss backed Dilworth and he himself had been forced to write positive columns about the reform Democrats he so despised, now unleashed the venom that had long been welling up within him. Unfortunately for Dilworth, he was going through a period of his life when he drank to excess on occasion and got carried away in a frenzy of emotional rhetoric that would have been better left unuttered. Cummings seized upon the weakness and began carping in his columns about the mayor's "lack of self control," and, on one occasion, he made reference to Dilworth's mother having placed his "inheritance in trust for him for fear he did not have judgment enough to manage it for himself." On October 29, however, Cummings outdid himself. He penned a torrent of abuse that resulted from Dilworth's having made an innocuous statement about Pennsylvania needing a "strong" governor at this moment in history, which was marked by the Cuban Missile Crisis that had the nation sick with worry. Cummings's column began, "Megalomania as defined by the Century Dictionary: A form of insane delusion the subjects of which imagine themselves to be very great, exalted or powerful personages; the delusion of grandeur. It may be of some interest to the people of the State to know that the solution of the international crisis growing out of Russian domination of Cuba depends almost exclusively on the election of Richardson Dilworth to the Governorship of Pennsylvania. . . ."

On election day, a series of events worked to defeat Dilworth. The Democratic machines in both Philadelphia and Pittsburgh—the party's two strongest cities—remained cool to his campaign because he hadn't followed traditional party methods in seeking the nomination. Dilworth had further hurt his own efforts by his volatile outbursts and by honestly stating that he would call for new taxes in order to bring about certain educational and other programs he wanted. Finally, political analysts cited the role of the *Philadelphia Inquirer*, which no one could actually measure, but which many people ultimately blamed for the mayor's defeat. "When Annenberg was against you with his paper, it could be bad . . . very bad," said James H. J. Tate, who had followed Dilworth as mayor. There were many liberal Democrats as well as Main Line conservatives, who were socially close to Dilworth, who bitterly blamed Annenberg for what they perceived as vicious editorial attacks on their friend. Many of them would later resurrect the *Inquirer*'s opposition to Dilworth in 1962 as a reason why they disliked Walter Annenberg.

Just a month after the gubernatorial election, Annenberg found himself embroiled in yet another controversy. Though it was one much more of his own making, it surprised him more than the criticism of the *Inquirer*'s behavior toward Dilworth. This time the man in the center of the storm was his friend Richard Nixon. Although Annenberg had always believed that Nixon was generally treated unfairly in the press, he had nonetheless felt it necessary to rebuke the former Vice-President in an editorial after Nixon had lost his bid for the governorship of California and he had blamed his defeat on the media. Walter's problem occurred, however, when he tried to redress the rebuke by coming to his friend's aid at a time when he thought he should. His act was one of alarming authoritarianism. Annenberg censored a television program about Nixon that was to have appeared on two of his stations that were affiliates of the American Broadcasting Company, WFIL-TV in Philadelphia and WNHC-TV in New Haven. His other four TV stations were CBS affiliates and would not have carried the programming the publisher found offensive.

The ABC program that Annenberg found himself strenuously objecting to was entitled "The Political Obituary of Richard Nixon," a half-hour show that was to have aired on Veterans Day and preempt another documentary, "The American Fighting Man." On the Saturday before the program was scheduled to be broadcast, Walter read a story that came over his Associated Press wire at Inwood. The news report was about the Nixon show and noted that the documentary included interviews with four people who had played significant roles in shaping the former Vice-President's political career. They were Murray Chotiner, Nixon's longtime campaign aide; Gerald Ford, a Congressional associate; and Jerry Voorhis, the first person he had defeated for political office. The fourth interview was with Alger Hiss, the controversial former State Department official who was found guilty of perjury in 1950 when he denied that he had turned over secret government documents to Communists. The case gained notoriety when Nixon, a prominent member of HUAC, was Hiss's principal interrogator. That role brought Congressman Nixon to such prominence that it served as his springboard to the Senate and placed him in the position of becoming Eisenhower's Vice-President.

Annenberg didn't like the idea of such a show, believing that his friend had already been placed through enough hardship and denigration in his Presidential and gubernatorial defeats. What he found most unfair, though, was that Hiss, a convicted perjurer, was allowed to sit in judgment of the former Vice-President for all America to watch. Thus, he contacted John Gillen, the cool and compliant Irishman who was the *Inquirer*'s managing editor, and told him to print a brief explanation from the publisher in the newspaper about why WFIL would not air the program. The story appeared on the *Inquirer*'s front page the next morning in a small box under a headline stating "TV Show Is Killed." The statement simply said, "I cannot see that any useful purpose would be served in permitting a convicted treasonable spy to comment about a distinguished American." Though another editor had pointed out to Gillen that Hiss hadn't been convicted of spying, he ordered that the statement stand as it was. John Gillen was a man who had "yessed" his way to the top, and he wasn't about to tell his publisher that he was wrong about such an issue. The managing editor knew that Nixon was a close personal friend of his boss, and he also knew how moody and irritable Annenberg was ever since his son's death.

The managing editor was a vain, handsome man, who was nicknamed the "silver fox" by his staff because of his carefully combed mane. His particular talents were his ability to lay out a sparkling front page, which he often took the time to do on Saturdays for the huge Sunday newspaper, and his ability to unquestioningly follow orders from Annenberg and more often Dimitman. He had a partiality for Irishmen on his staff, giving raises that often as not were based more on a reporter's Celtic name than on his craftsmanship. A veteran of four Pulitzer Prize committees, Gillen's major claim to journalistic achievement had occurred three years earlier, in 1959, when he had negotiated the rights to reprint Soviet Premier Nikita S. Khrushchev's memoirs, at the time making the *Inquirer* the envy of other big newspapers. The Khrushchev story had amounted to an international scoop for the paper, and newspapers and magazines everywhere had tried to strike deals to share in printing the material. But the *Inquirer* had kept the first rights to itself. There was so much speculation surrounding the memoirs that it was erroneously reported that *The New York Times* had offered Walter Annenberg two million dollars for the rights, leading Orvil E. Dryfoos, the *Times* president, to write Annenberg a note asking, "Walter, Would you really have turned down $2 M?" Annenberg had replied:

> DEAR ORVIL:
> I was in Europe when somebody dreamed up this drivel, but if you want to make the offer I am sure that Khrushchev, Menshikov and the Council of Ministers will be happy to have me negotiate a fast contract.
> WALTER ANNENBERG

The censorship of the ABC program couldn't be treated as casually. It had created a fire storm of publicity, and most of it was critical of Annenberg. WFIL was inundated with more than two thousand telephone calls, most of which condemned the cancellation, and the *Philadelphia Inquirer* was besieged by callers protesting the action as well. John Gillen realized that he couldn't ignore the fact that his boss was making news, but his natural instincts for self-preservation took over. The editor chose to avoid the negative side of the reaction. A headline on Monday's front page declared, "Veterans Groups Hail Decision Not to Air Hiss TV Appearance," which only generated more criticism, including from ABC, which contended that Annenberg had stopped the program to help Nixon.

Stunned by the backlash, Annenberg felt compelled to explain to his readers why he had adopted his position. He certainly didn't view his own motives as ruthless or manipulative as his critics contended. Quite simply, he was offended by the appearance of Hiss, and he assumed that just about anyone who gave the matter a little thought would agree. Thus, he prepared a "Letter from the Editor" that appeared in the *Inquirer* on November 14. More than anything else, he tried to express his belief that he hadn't just tried to suppress a show that treated an old friend in a manner that he didn't like. The letter illustrated how Walter Annenberg believed himself the judge of what was good for the public, and how his media complex enabled him to arbitrarily censor a news program on television and then explain in print why he had done so:

> I am taking this means of acknowledging the many messages, pro and con, which came to me from the valued readers of the Inquirer, with respect to my action in the matter of the American Broadcasting Co.'s telecast on Veteran's Day.
> I appreciate the thoughtfulness and the interest of those who wrote, telephoned and telegraphed, and I feel that an amplification is in order . . . It seemed to me that the use of a spy, convicted of perjury in the infamous Chambers-Hiss episode, to sit in judgement on a distinguished American who loyally served his country in war and in high public office, would be repugnant to most viewers. This was especially so in light of the Veterans' Day holiday we were observing . . .
> The American Broadcasting Co. in its radio network has since sought to establish that my decision was based on a pro-Nixon attitude only. This is untrue and can be underscored by the fact that the Philadelphia Inquirer, in its editions of Nov. 9, censured Nixon editorially for his attacks on the press following his defeat in the California Governorship race. This editorial comment was written at my direction, for what I regarded as bad judgement on the part of Mr. Nixon.
> It is my belief that both these decisions of new evaluation were valid and in the public interest.
>
> WALTER H. ANNENBERG

The open letter did little to mute the criticism, so several days later the *Inquirer* printed a telegram from Nixon to Annenberg which was meant to reaffirm the publisher's stand. In part, the Nixon missive stated, "There is no more striking example of this truth than the events of the past week. What does an attack by one convicted perjurer mean when weighed on the scales of justice against thousands of wires and letters from patriotic Americans?" No matter what Annenberg or Nixon said, however, nothing quelled the concern of Philadelphians who were appalled by the censorship. Reflecting upon such an action, for instance, Thatcher Longstreth, a local blue blood who was active in Republican politics before becoming president of the Philadelphia-Baltimore-Washington Stock Exchange, told a reporter for the *Washington Star* that the *Inquirer* was a "second-rate newspaper that the publisher uses for his own ends." As a result, Longstreth's name was stricken from the paper for years.

Most *Inquirer* staffers took such activity in stride. More than a few of them were men of the old school, to whom a paper meant getting out a flashy product that people found attractive, rather than one that contributed to an understanding of the world. Many of them firmly believed that a publisher should be able to do with his paper just about whatever he wanted, even when that conflicted with what might in journalism schools be considered the fairest or most accurate coverage. Men like Paul Hayes, a tough, cynical copy editor who became an assistant managing editor, had kicked around at a half dozen or more papers before winding up at the *Inquirer*, and they accepted as a publisher's right the ability to manipulate news coverage, just as they on occasion bent reporters' stories out of shape to fit their own view of the world. Every paper, they knew, had its drawbacks and even some of the younger men, such as Joe Goulden, a burly Texan, found it funny, at least for a while, to work for a publisher who often involved his newspaper in his personal feuds. The attitude of many *Inquirer* staffers was later summarized by Goulden: "If you can't buy the paper and you're going to work there, then don't bitch."

Although it often didn't show, Annenberg himself, of course, knew what constituted a good newspaper. In a nutshell, he believed that a paper should perform a service and show a profit. He also thought a newspaper should be fair, telling both sides of a story and be a constructive voice in the community. After the 1958 strike, Annenberg periodically went through the motions of rebuilding the paper, such as hiring from the *Bulletin*, as city editor, Phil Schaeffer, a man with a strong reputation for being a responsible journalist. When Schaeffer was interviewed by Annenberg, the publisher lectured him on reporting and editing in a way that sounded much like a professor from Columbia Journalism School. The reality of the *Inquirer*, though, often proved to be a far cry from the philosophy Annenberg espoused, and sometimes the paper was made to look foolish.

In 1962, for instance, the year in which Schaeffer was lured away from the *Bulletin,* Annenberg was feuding with Gaylord P. Harnwell, the president of the University of Pennsylvania. A new facility at Penn, which was to house the Annenberg School of Communications, an ambitious undertaking that the publisher had funded, was dedicated that November. A vast, elegantly modern structure of theaters, offices and open spaces, Walter had named the school not after himself, but for his father. He had originally proposed the school to Penn about 1958, but because the institution was to be dedicated to M. L. Annenberg there had been loud opposition from faculty members who objected to Penn's honoring a man of Moses' past. Moreover, many faculty members believed that Annenberg wanted to retain control over the school by appointing faculty members himself, a situation they considered intolerable. The plan was eventually approved, but Annenberg hadn't believed Harnwell acted decisively enough to mute the criticism, and that left a bitter taste in the publisher's mouth. For a while, Harnwell's name wasn't mentioned in the *Inquirer;* he was simply referred to as a "university spokesman," and people around the city lamented Annenberg's highhanded use of his paper.

The issue of the communications school was an especially delicate one for Annenberg, of course. The *Inquirer* Charities and the M. L. Annenberg Foundation, which he had established as well, generated vast sums for worthwhile causes, but because such giving was generally done quietly, neither of the charitable organizations had done much to remove the blemish from his father's name. Thus, Walter viewed the school as a grand gesture that would not only serve the public well but would finally make the name of M. L. Annenberg respectable. "I've had such inspiration for citizenship that it takes on almost a religious fervor as I tried to reflect credit on my father," he said.

Once again, however, an incident occurred that tainted the moment. After Penn accepted millions of dollars for the new school, a facility that would come to enhance the university's stature, a story appeared in the *Evening Bulletin* that angered and dismayed Annenberg:

> Four or five persons believed to be former friends and associates of the late Al Capone are anxious to establish the "Al Capone Chair of Taxation" at the University of Pennsylvania.
> Isador Ostroff, a Philadelphia lawyer, wrote to Dr. Gaylord P. Harnwell, president of Penn, saying that he had been approached by some people interested in establishing the chair in either the

Wharton School or the Law School, depending on the university's needs.

Ostroff said he had been asked to find out what the prerequisites were for establishing the chair "from the standpoint of money and other inducements which the university will require . . . ."

Ostroff, a 1927 graduate of Penn and a 1930 graduate of its Law School, said the group he represents apparently wants to "correct the impression" people have concerning Capone.

The group wants to "create an aura of respectability about a name that has been dragged through the mud."

The story was such a blatant hoax that no one was ever sure how *Bulletin* editors allowed it to get into the paper, and it was yanked after several editions. Nevertheless, the damage was done and people at Penn as well as elsewhere in the city chuckled over the obvious effort to discredit Annenberg's new communications school. But while many Philadelphians laughed, Annenberg was humiliated. The Ostroff in the story had been a member of the 1938 Pennsylvania legislative commission that had investigated the racing wire. The lawyer himself had reason to believe that Walter Annenberg had never forgiven him for the role he had played, especially after he was prominently featured in a series of *Inquirer* articles critical of a $1.6 million incinerator deal with which he was involved in a Philadelphia suburban community. For his part, Annenberg bitterly wondered why people were miserable enough to attack him through his father. As a protection, he developed a philosophy that others were envious of his wealth, position and power, and that they would do anything to undermine him. Certainly just about every man of wealth and power feels this way at one time or another; Walter felt so most of the time. "There are people who try to throw mud at me," he said. "You know one of the tragedies of life is to discover the amount of envy there is."

Such a setback merely fueled Annenberg's desire to be recognized for the positive steps he took, but the ways of attracting such attention were limited. Most of his charitable donations were very low key. His political influence in the city invariably drew the wrath of either one or the other of the political parties, sometimes both at once, because he cared little about adopting popular positions. In 1964, for example, the *Inquirer* printed a series of articles that challenged a previously impregnable bastion of corruption that even Clark and Dilworth hadn't been able to do anything about when they wielded their clean political broom in the early 1950s. The *Inquirer* took on the magistrate-court system, and the stories shook the city's power structure. The articles detailed wrongdoing to the extent of giving names, dates and places. Within three weeks after the first article appeared, the state Attorney General sent a task force, spearheaded by Arlen Specter, formerly staff counsel to the Warren Commission, which had investigated President Kennedy's assassination. The Chief Magistrate, John P. Walsh, made a desperate bid to get his house in order, but the local district attorney cracked down on constables involved with the magistrate's activities, and the governor even proposed bills to eliminate the magistrate system. In the end, four magistrates were indicted, and ten other public servants, including a constable and bailbondsmen, were indicted as well.

Thus, late in the spring of 1964, when Walter Annenberg found that national attention was about to be paid to him, he was both flattered and extremely nervous. Annenberg was about to be honored by Lyndon B. Johnson, the President of the United States, who was to stop at the *Inquirer* specifically to see the publisher. Annenberg was overwhelmed at the thought of the occasion and by 7 A.M. on the day of the visit the *Inquirer* was bustling with activity, a time when the building would normally not even be rousing itself to its daily tasks. A number of top editors were already on hand as was Joe Goulden, a reporter who was given the special assignment of covering the event. The publisher had summoned Goulden to his office the day before and told him to sleep overnight at a downtown hotel rather than chance being late the next day. Annenberg himself slept in the *Inquirer* building that night.

Presidents don't ordinarily stop at newspapers to see publishers; publishers call on them. But the visit came on the heels of an election year, and Johnson was extraordinarily grateful to Annenberg. For the first time since Lincoln's Presidency, the *Inquirer* had endorsed a candidate other than a Republican for the office. That man was Lyndon Johnson, who well knew the symbolic importance nationally of the *Inquirer* with its strong Republican heritage backing him, a shift that was highly publicized around the country. Annenberg could just as easily have sat on the sidelines, or have given a tepid endorsement to the Republican party, if not the party's candidate, Arizona Senator Barry Goldwater. But that wasn't Annenberg's style.

The publisher hadn't immediately endorsed Johnson. The move came only after he was part of a coterie of powerful Republicans who had tried to work within the party to block Goldwater. In a last-minute gamble, they had tried to make William Scranton, the Pennsylvania governor and friend of Annenberg, the candidate. Annenberg had raised the possibility of Scranton's candidacy in his paper's editorial and news columns, and the cry was quickly taken up by other Republicans who were disenchanted with Goldwater. More than $800,000 was rapidly collected on the governor's behalf and much of it was raised by three of the publisher's friends, Frank McGlinn, a party fund raiser, who was a senior vice-president of Fidelity-Philadelphia Trust Company; Tom McCabe, Sr., of Scott Paper Company; and Thomas S. Gates, Jr., chairman of the executive committee of Morgan Guaranty Trust Company. The movement had the backing of other well-heeled moderate Republicans such as CBS's Bill Paley and Campbell Soup Company's William Murphy, as well as a fair sprinkling of Du-Ponts, Mellons and Whitneys. Generally, they believed that Goldwater's policies were both simplistic and radical and could do nothing but harm the party. Goldwater's support, however, was tremendous and crushed the Scranton move before it got off the ground.

Thus, Annenberg swung his backing to Johnson, a man he felt comfortable with. He knew the President since the middle 1950s, when he printed editorials supporting Johnson's Senate campaign, because he agreed with the politician's moderate, pragmatic stances. As a result, Johnson contacted the publisher to express his thanks, and Annenberg was struck by the raw force of the shrewd Democrat's personality. Following President Kennedy's death a year earlier, Annenberg was impressed with the way the Vice-President quickly settled into the demanding role of President, perhaps reminding Annenberg a little of what he himself was forced to do when he took over as head of troubled Triangle Publications after his father died. He well knew the strains a man was under when confronted by critics contending he was in a job beyond his abilities. Moreover, he knew the additional problems confronting Johnson because of the popularity of the man he replaced.

Like most people, Annenberg was deeply affected by Kennedy's death; he had grown fond of the man who had beaten his friend Nixon out of the White House. On the day Kennedy died, the publisher sat in his office weeping for both the man and his country. He was at a loss as to what he could do personally, but as a gesture of Americanism he had quietly sent a check to Mrs. J. D. Tippet, the widow of the Dallas policeman who was slain while trying to capture the President's assassin. The money equaled the amount still owed on the Tippets' mortgage. "This is the hour of good deeds," Annenberg said at the time.

When Johnson visited the *Inquirer*, his motorcade stopped outside the Elverson Building and Secret Servicemen didn't allow the President out of his car for fear of his personal safety. Therefore, Annenberg with reporter Goulden tagging along behind him approached the President and wished him well. Their words were lost, because Goulden couldn't get close enough to listen to the conversation. Nevertheless, the story that appeared in the next day's paper did little to reflect the level of nervousness and painstaking care that had gone into its creation. In keeping with the publisher's policy of not calling attention to himself, the three-paragraph story appeared inconspicuously on page three of the *Inquirer*. Despite its brevity, Goulden's copy had been worked over carefully by a group of top editors, including E. Z. Dimitman, who had devoted much of the day to their task.

The *Inquirer*'s dramatic political shift in its editorial endorsement showed that the paper's publisher was a lot more flexible than the newspaper's editors themselves. The paper's drift that started after 1958 continued and worsened, and the *Inquirer*'s failure to change with the times was illustrated several months after Johnson's festive visit. In the summer of 1964, Philadelphia was rocked by a race riot that frightened the city's residents and caught the newspaper as well as its rival, the *Bulletin*, off guard. The *Inquirer* was unaware of the black community's needs, joys and sorrows, let alone conditions that might spawn a riot. The only time a Negro was likely to be mentioned in a story or have his picture in the paper was if he was a criminal.

The riot starkly illustrated the city's problems and reflected the newspaper's ignorance of a large segment of the community. On a hot August night, an intoxicated quarreling couple caused a traffic jam with honking horns and flaring tempers, and the man and woman refused to allow police to move their stalled car. A crowd gathered, a melee erupted, and before the North Philadelphia neighborhood settled down again 2 people were killed, 339 were injured, and fire and looting claimed more than three million dollars in property. Like many newspapers in cities where similar riots occurred, the *Inquirer* lacked sources in the black community who could vocalize what was truly the reason behind the violence. There was no black reporter who might have been able to interview people from the neighborhood without arousing fear or suspicion. The *Bulletin* fared just as poorly.

If anything, the press's coverage of the event served to exacerbate white Philadelphia's fears of the city's black residents. Moreover,

Frank Rizzo, the tough cop, once again appeared in heroic proportions; the press reports again helped his career climb to the top. The special- ness of the police department's relationship with the *Inquirer* was ap- parent in other ways. Police reports were routinely taken at face value; for example, the most notorious instances being stories that were tele- phoned to the paper by Detective Clarence Ferguson. The friend of top *Inquirer* editors, including managing editor Gillen and city editor Litman, Ferguson in the 1960s called to the paper various arrests and raids he personally made. Like Justice Musmanno, the detective was a standing joke among the *Inquirer* rewrite men, who took down notes of his cases, always making sure they asked "Fergie" if it was his big- gest seizure to date. "Yeah, this is the biggest," Ferguson invariably replied in his droning voice.

One of the few editors who tried to bring about changes in coverage was Schaeffer, a quiet, reserved ex-Marine who taught Sunday school. Though he had been hired to replace Litman, the soft-spoken Schaeffer hadn't the political instincts to quash the canny Litman, so the *Inquirer*, in effect, wound up with two city editors, although Lit- man was then called executive editor. A long city desk was placed in the middle of the newsroom, and Litman sat at the south end while Schaeffer sat at the north. Litman controlled political reporting and criminal investigations. Schaeffer ran the rest of the day-to-day cover- age and features. As a result of Schaeffer's efforts, stories about blacks, their leaders and the problems of their community began appearing in the *Inquirer* and, in coming years, stories about the Peace Movement and protest demonstrations against the war in Vietnam appeared as well, even though the paper's editorials firmly supported the Adminis- tration in Washington. As a whole, however, the paper increasingly appeared anachronistic with its streamer headlines and lack of in- depth reporting. One reason why the paper didn't have to change, of course, was that its competition, the *Bulletin*, wasn't a strong paper either.

In 1966, Annenberg again toyed with the idea of improving the *In- quirer*, a process that usually entailed hiring a few new men as editors and after which the costly plans were placed on the back burner. In this instance, Michael Pakenham, who had been an assistant foreign editor of the recently folded *New York Herald Tribune*, was hired. Pakenham was reluctant to join the paper, because he knew of Annen- berg's reputation for interfering with the *Inquirer*'s news columns. Nonetheless, he was assured by Gillen that such occurrences were rare and that Annenberg was greatly interested in improving the *Inquirer*'s Sunday magazine, the department that Pakenham was to preside over. Once he began working for the paper, the new editor concluded that in actuality the publisher had very little to do with the paper.

Pakenham never saw the infamous blacklist and began wondering how much of the notorious catalogue of enemies was manufactured by editors trying to second-guess the publisher out of laziness or fear. What he found was a number of people who traded on what they claimed were close ties to Walter Annenberg. "There were mystical references to people's links with Annenberg," he recalled. There was Dimitman, of course. Others who frequently made such allusions to the publisher included Litman and reporters Joe Miller, Joe Trachtman and Harry Karafin. As a result of invoking Annenberg's name, such men created a "chilling effect . . . the inferred imperative," Pakenham found, and the result was the publishing of some questionable stories or the dropping of names. The abuses in the paper weren't all attributable to Annenberg.

The strength of the concern about the publisher's supposed desires was brought home to Pakenham when he suggested a change in the layout of the Sunday magazine. A courtly, elderly editor named Arch Luther, who had worked on the publication for many years, piped up with the objection, "I don't think we ought to do that. The publisher doesn't like it." When Pakenham suggested another design alteration the following week, Luther again scotched the idea, repeating how "the publisher wouldn't stand for it." Annoyed at seeing his ideas dismissed, the new editor pressed Luther as to how he knew the publisher wouldn't like it. The elderly man shuffled over to a filing cabinet, rattled around inside until he found a copy of the magazine, which he pulled out and showed to Pakenham. Scrawled across two pages was a note saying, "Arch let's not do this!" The initials under the notation were "M.L.A."

In actuality, Annenberg rarely appeared in the newsroom, and he depended upon Dimitman to oversee the paper's operation. On occasion, he critiqued a layout or berated the quality of a photograph that had appeared, but he didn't know what was going to be printed in the paper on any given day. More often than not, he was so circumspect in his editor's role that when he had a special interest in a story in the paper, his editors played a cat-and-mouse game with him until they figured out which article it was. Annenberg was likely to call the operations desk and begin by asking the assistant managing editor on duty what was on the front page, even though the editor knew the publisher had the same paper in front of him. The responsibility for divining the story Annenberg had in mind frequently fell to Andy Khinoy, an assistant managing editor who had started working on the copy desk in the 1930s. Khinoy began the ritual of frantically racing his eyes over the front page and calmly mentioning one story after another to Annenberg until he hit the one in question. "Do you think that belongs on page one?" the publisher would ask. By the next edition, the story surfaced elsewhere in the paper. Paul Hayes, a testier, gruffer editor than Khinoy, on occasion wasn't as compliant when he got the publisher on the line. "I'd tell him 'Yes, I think it belongs on page one,' if I did think so," he said. "That was that. He never ordered me to move it."

Once in a while, however, Annenberg was more direct. For example, he ordered an exclusive interview by reporter Harry Karafin with Angelo Bruno, the head of the Mafia in Philadelphia, off the front page. And when Sonny Liston was heavyweight boxing champion, Annenberg ordered that the fighter's picture not appear on the front page because of his alleged criminal associations. In each case, the publisher's reasons were the same. "I don't want to give a lot of free publicity to a bum like that," he told his editors.

The *Inquirer* editors and reporters, generally speaking, expected Annenberg to quash a story that came over the Associated Press wire on February 8, 1966, in which his nephew, Robert Friede, the twenty-five-year-old son of his sister Evelyn, was charged with homicide. The tale was sad business. Friede's girl friend Celeste Crenshaw had died of an overdose of narcotics, and Annenberg's nephew had been arrested after he was stopped by New York police while driving in a daze, and the girl's body was discovered in the car's trunk. The publisher had long been worried about the young man, who two years earlier had been arrested on drug charges. Friede, a graduate of Choate and Dartmouth, was an example of what Annenberg feared happened all too often to the young who had too much money. He lived a useless life, receiving $25,000 a year in unearned income, which would soar to $100,000 a year on his thirtieth birthday. As wire copy related to the tragedy crossed the *Inquirer*'s news wires, David Umanski, a copyboy, rushed it to Annenberg's secretary, who immediately gave it to her boss. The next morning, the *Inquirer* carried the story.

By the following summer, however, all the Annenberg critics had concrete proof of what they perceived as the publisher's irresponsibility and even vindictiveness. The reason was the *Inquirer*'s coverage of a gubernatorial contest between Raymond P. Shafer, the Republican lieutenant governor, and Milton Shapp, a Democrat and the founder of Jerrold Electronics, a Philadelphia concern and one of the main forces behind cable television. The paths of Annenberg and Shapp had crossed a few times, and the publisher had taken an instant dislike to the businessman, whom he took to calling "a sleazy son of a bitch." Because the *Inquirer* editors knew of the publisher's feelings toward Shapp, the man's name never made the pages of the *Inquirer*.

In the years just before he ran for office, Shapp had attracted a good deal of recognition throughout the state. A self-made man, he had solid liberal credentials, having established college scholarships for Negro and Puerto Rican students. Shapp also liked to take credit for having suggested the notion of the Peace Corps to John Kennedy, and he had even proposed an imaginative educational experiment that entailed selling $5.5 billion in bonds to provide free education to state residents, an experiment that never got off the ground. But while Shapp's proposals sounded good, he didn't impress Walter Annenberg, who considered the man a self-aggrandizer who created impractical issues, such as the bond offer, just to call attention to himself. "I thought he was an oily windbag," Annenberg said.

Shapp's quest for the governorship was an uphill battle from the very beginning, a fact that initially had little to do with Annenberg. While the Republicans had few problems picking the man they wanted to succeed William Scranton, the Democrats were in a quandary. The party had no strong candidates, and the Democratic Policy Committee eventually gave a tepid endorsement to a state senator, Robert P. Casey from Scranton, who immediately found himself being challenged by Shapp. The electronics millionaire launched a vigorous, costly campaign in which he attacked Casey as a pawn of the Democratic organization while casting himself as the "man against the machine." Shapp spent a fortune filling the airwaves with radio and television commercials, having thirty-four half-hour telecasts in prime time alone. His thorough campaign included a direct mailing that reached 1.6 million homes, which were inundated with pamphlets and position papers on everything from crime prevention to a milk-control program.

Meanwhile, Casey's campaign proved lackluster as a result of limited funds and squabbling among Philadelphia's top Democrats.

Nonetheless, it came as a surprise to just about everyone that Shapp won the primary contest in a fashion that even brought the praise of the *Inquirer* political reporter Joe Miller. In the May 19, 1966, edition of the paper, Miller, in his usual hyperbolic style, called the victory a "political feat unparalleled in modern intraparty warfare. . . . In typical David vs. Goliath style, Shapp trounced the so-called Democratic 'bosses' from one end of the state to the other. His victory was regarded as so decisive that the party leadership must make peace with the gubernatorial nominee, recognize his new political stature, and close ranks towards a victor in the Nov. 8 general election."

Though he didn't care for Shapp, Annenberg hadn't intended to take a strong stand in the election. There were many aspects of Shapp's campaign that Annenberg, who monitored the campaign closely, didn't like. For one thing, the candidate had spent more than a million dollars of his own money during the heated contest, and Annenberg was incensed by the thought of someone "buying an election." But what he found far more upsetting was Shapp's controversial stand on an issue of grave importance in the state, a stand that would have turned the publisher against Shapp even if he hadn't previously disliked him. The Democrat had struck a blow at a venerable Philadelphia institution, one that Annenberg not only strongly believed in but had heavily invested in. Milton Shapp had criticized the proposed merger of the Pennsylvania Railroad, a symbol of corporate greatness in Philadelphia, and the New York Central Railroad. Whereas Annenberg believed the merger was not only necessary for the public good but also represented the best interests of two major transportation forces in America, Shapp saw the linkage as the "greatest single threat to the economic future of Pennsylvania." In the heat of his campaign rhetoric, the Democrat even went as far as to castigate the merger as a "multi-million-dollar swindle by robber barons." Annenberg, the reverer of institutions, believed the attacks on the merger constituted an assault on Establishment values. Moreover, he was concerned because of what Shapp's words would do to the reputation of the Pennsylvania Railroad's chairman and chief executive officer, Stuart T. Saunders, a close personal friend of Annenberg.

In response, the *Inquirer* publisher told Dimitman that he wasn't going to "let that bum Shapp destroy" the railroad, and he ordered the editor to see that the paper did everything within its power to prevent him from becoming governor. Dimitman, of course, needed little encouragement. He loved such frays, and he had as little use for Shapp as his employer did. Thus the *Philadelphia Inquirer* embarked on one of the most brutal attacks on a politician that journalism in a major metropolitan area had witnessed for years. The *Inquirer*'s role in the campaign more than any other act revealed the lengths to which Annenberg would go to harm someone. The coverage showed his autocratic nature; he indulged his emotions at the expense of his responsibilities as a publisher. It was the act of a vindictive man.

For his part, Dimitman turned to political columnist Cummings; the two Harrisburg reporters, Miller and Kohler; reporter Harry Karafin and the editorial writers. Soon, anyone who voiced criticism of Shapp, no matter how absurd, found his statements repeated in the *Inquirer*. On August 21, a story quoted Republican boss William Devlin as saying the Democratic nominee was "intellectually dishonest" and that his campaign was based upon "grandiose promises, 'kooky' programs and false issues." Another article bore the headline "Bloom Calls Shapp Drive 'Maniacal,'" referring to George I. Bloom, chairman of the State Public Utility Commission, who objected to Shapp's proposing that utilities pay real-estate taxes on certain holdings. Kohler's story stated that "Bloom took off the gloves in a reply" to Shapp, but a more accurate assessment was that the *Inquirer* had taken off the gloves.

The *Inquirer*'s assaults were fast and furious. Also in August, reporter Kohler wrote a three-part series with the headline "An Unholy Alliance." The articles were irresponsible. Kohler, for instance, contended that Shapp, a "self claimed liberal and civil rights advocate," was in bed politically with Harvey F. Johnston, the founder and president of a racist organization known as the National Association for the Advancement of White People. In fact, Johnston had briefly worked on the candidate's campaign staff, but he was dismissed when Shapp learned who he was. Shapp himself denounced the "Hitler-like views" of the Johnston organization, but that curiously hadn't found its way into the *Inquirer*. In yet another attempt to brand Shapp a racist, the newspaper on August 29 bore a story with the headline "Shapp Accused of Picnic Snub of Negro" in connection with a Negro Democratic candidate for the state legislature in Delaware County not having been invited to a Citizens-for-Shapp picnic. Then in a reversal, the *Inquirer* tried to alarm white voters by charging that Shapp had bought the services of a hundred black ministers to campaign for him. Shapp was in a no-win situation as far as the *Inquirer* was concerned.

The *Inquirer* never made any pretense of being fair. Miller, Kohler and Karafin ferreted out whatever damaging information they could. Karafin for one boasted that he was going to "smear" Shapp for having changed his name from Shapiro, and he and Miller contacted numerous people who knew the Democrat, asking about his business dealings and his "mental problems." When he became aware of the reporters' tack, Shapp was infuriated and threatened to sue the paper. The threat merely touched off another round of abuse. Miller called Shapp and asked whether he would sue, and the candidate assured him that he would. Going for the jugular, Miller then asked if he denied the patently false charge that he had once been in a mental institution, which of course, Shapp did deny. The following day, Miller had a story in the paper saying the candidate denied that he had ever been in an asylum, thus publicly raising the issue. Not to be denied a hand in the journalistic overkill, old John Cummings continued the theme. "Shapp had denied, in response to inquiries, that in the summer of last year he had been sent by his doctor to a Philadelphia hospital for psychiatric examination," the columnist wrote on October 30, only nine days before the election. As a parting blow, his column referred to Shapp as "unknown, unhonored and unsung."

Despite the *Inquirer*'s mailed-fist approach, Annenberg believed the Democrat was merely getting what he had deserved. Shapp and his campaign aides, however, were aghast and reeling from the shock waves of what seemed to be almost daily editorial bombs. At one point, Shapp and a mutual friend tried to intercede with Annenberg in an effort to silence the *Inquirer*. During a telephone call, the candidate and his friend were on one end of the line while Walter and Lee were on extensions at their home. The conversation, of course, proved fruitless, especially because of the slights Shapp had made with regard to the Annenbergs' friend Saunders. Walter Annenberg would never back away from a friend. Thus both Walter and Lee told Shapp in no uncertain terms what they thought of him and his stand against the merger of the railroads. "I'll never forget that you called our good friend Stuart Saunders a robber baron," Lee said before hanging up.

The Annenbergs, of course, weren't the only Pennsylvanians who were dismayed by Shapp's charges. The area's moneyed Republicans quickly made contributions to Shapp's opponent. The Democrat later charged that Republican Shafer received directly and indirectly some $81,000 from Richard King Mellon, a Pennsylvania Railroad director, but official campaign records indicated that only $21,000 in Mellon money went to the Republican's campaign war chest. John Dorrance, Annenberg's friend and head of Campbell Soup, who was a director of two of the railroad's subsidiaries, gave Shafer more than $5,000, while a prominent Philadelphia stockbroker, Howard Butcher III, contributed $3,000. In Philadelphia, the Pennsylvania Railroad wasn't to be trifled with.

While the *Inquirer* waged war with Shapp over the merger, many people faulted the publisher for not revealing publicly that he had a stake in the venture—an enormous stake. Walter Annenberg was the Pennsylvania Railroad's largest single shareholder. At the time, he owned 177,000 shares of stock, valued at about $13.5 million. There were covert charges that the publisher was seeking vengeance upon the Democrat in order to protect his financial interests. Annenberg, however, was able in his own mind to distinguish between his stock holdings and his editorial policies. He felt himself above any form of public accountability, and there was no one who could demand that he disclose his personal finances. It wouldn't be until several years later, when the merger proved disastrous and the then Penn Central filed for bankruptcy, that Annenberg's integrity of the moment would be redeemed. Even though he was a member of the Penn Central Board, he remained the railroad's biggest shareholder and lost a fortune when the carrier filed under Chapter 11. In truth, he had believed wholeheartedly in the merger and it became one of his few bad business calls.

Annenberg's views were best summarized in an editorial that appeared on October 19, 1966; it was entitled "The Choice in Pennsylvania":

> The office of Governor of Pennsylvania is not a plaything nor a rich man's hobby. It is not something to be grasped and held, for the cynical exercise of personal power. Its duties are stern and demanding; its responsibilities heavy. In the hands of the ignorant and the incompetent, it could wreck the Commonwealth ... The balloting will represent not merely a choice between two individuals and two parties; but a choice between the sane, the prudent and capable administration of the State Government by Raymond Shafer and the reckless irresponsibility of Milton Shapp. . . .
>
> The men and women of Pennsylvania are not stupid. They know that a Milton Shapp, as Governor, contains the promise only of erratic and unstable management of their affairs. It is beyond belief that they would take this road to disaster.

When the election returns were tallied, Shapp had lost, and he blamed Annenberg. "The *Inquirer* smear campaign cost me a minimum of 125,000 votes," Shapp told reporters for the *Evening Bulletin.* "We would have won if it hadn't been for Annenberg." His statement, however, wasn't accurate. Shapp's opponent, Raymond Shafer, won by 240,000 votes. By the end of the election, both Shapp and Annenberg were considered losers. Many Philadelphians as well as newsmen elsewhere were shocked by Annenberg's use of his paper in such a fashion. The excesses were those of a man to be feared.

CHAPTER

Eighteen

IN MARCH 1967 Annenberg was so disgusted that he wished he had sold the *Inquirer* years before, when he had first contemplated doing so. The reason for his foul mood was the revelation that one of the newspaper's reporters had abused his position, and the ramifications of the man's actions were sure to reflect badly on both the *Inquirer* and its publisher. The reporter was Harry Karafin, who was nothing more than a cheat, a crook and a liar.

Philadelphia Magazine, then a small-circulation periodical that was trying to shake its image as a house organ of the Chamber of Commerce, was about to expose the reporter in a painstakingly prepared, devastating article. Before the magazine was even edited, *Inquirer* managing editor John Gillen was told by a friend at Mid City Printers, which printed *Philadelphia Magazine*, that a hot article was coming about Karafin. Several weeks later, the same man slipped Gillen a copy of the story, which was even worse than the managing editor and a few other editors he had alerted had imagined. Karafin not only was reporting about the region's hoodlums—he was working with them. He used his journalistic credentials to shake down local companies, including a major bank, by threatening to smear them with damaging stories in the *Inquirer*. Moreover, he had manufactured a mythical relationship with Walter Annenberg in order to enhance his own credibility and prestige, and make it appear that he had the paper at his disposal to do his bidding.

When Gillen demanded an explanation, Karafin tried to lie his way out of the charges; he told his editor that he was going to sue the magazine. On March 1, the reporter did sue *Philadelphia Magazine* for having fraudulently obtained his tax returns. When Gillen demanded to see those returns, the slippery Karafin failed to produce them. Editor Dimitman, however, obtained copies through friends at the regional I.R.S. offices, which were directly across the street from the paper. The matter was finally brought before the publisher, who read the article, looked at the tax returns, and gave a quick, heated response. "Get rid of the bum," Annenberg ordered.

When Karafin and the *Inquirer* severed relations, the magazine bearing witness to his dishonesty still wasn't on the newsstands and only a few people on the *Inquirer* staff knew why the reporter was gone. Rumors abounded, however, and when word leaked out that he was no longer employed by the paper, the *Philadelphia Dispatch*, a City-Hall-oriented gossip sheet, stated on its front page:

> For years, lawyers cringed, city officials winced and politicians prayed when Harry Karafin walked into their offices. He broke more exclusives, triggered more 72-point streamers and spearheaded more journalistic crusades than any other newsman in the long history of the Philadelphia Inquirer.

What the *Dispatch* noted was only too true, which dismayed the *Inquirer*'s editors that much more. Karafin had often attacked corruption with the zealousness of an avenging angel, and his wall was full of awards for his exposés—the magistrate system, an auto-accident racket, nursing-home abuses. His enterprising reporting was grudgingly admired by colleagues, even those who disliked his brash, egotistical, loud-mouthed style. When a stock swindler who had jumped bail and fled the country finally returned to the city, it was Karafin who climbed off the plane with him and had an exclusive story. Whereas other reporters had fruitlessly devised every scheme they could concoct to gain access to Jack Lopinson, an accused murderer who had been held under incredibly tight security, Karafin had gotten the exclusive story. And it was Karafin who had the contacts and the brass to meet Angelo Bruno in Boston, when the Philadelphia crime boss was returning to the United States from Rome, while federal officials were searching everywhere for him.

The *Philadelphia Magazine* article, however, made no bones that Karafin was living a double life. The gutsy, enterprising crime reporter was also a hoodlum. For instance, Karafin was the original president of something called Twin State Distributing Company, which was ostensibly a home-remodeling and heating firm. In reality Twin State was a clearing house for millions of dollars of merchandise that was being disposed of through a fraudulent bankruptcy scam. Police observers noted that the major customers going in and out of the company's headquarters were Philadelphia's leading underworld figures. Other than Karafin, the key man in the operation was a 600-pound behemoth named Sylvan Scolnick, who was a pal of Karafin and who had gone to jail before Karafin's role in the crime was revealed.

The reporter's racketeering, though, wasn't confined to Twin State. There was also Karafin's "public relations" work. He and Scolnick visited home-repair companies with sleazy reputations and told the owners they needed public-relations counseling, the kind that could keep the firms *out* of the news. If a company they approached needed convincing as to the kinds of benefits Karafin offered, the head of the firm was told to think it over. A story then appeared in the *Inquirer* warning about "high pressure salesmen" who preyed on "unwary home owners." The story usually ended with a spokesman for the Better Business Bureau saying his office believed the best way to fight such a racket was "to expose it." Karafin's customers took the hint and signed on. Such public-relations advice was given to finance companies, aluminum-siding concerns, and a number of fly-by-night operations that couldn't withstand public scrutiny.

Karafin's success proved so great that he wasn't intimidated about going after bigger fish. He had stumbled onto some information that had led him to believe that officers of the First Pennsylvania Banking and Trust Company might be interested in protecting the bank's image with the kind of service he alone offered. First Pennsylvania was holding millions of dollars of commercial credit paper, including that of a New Jersey home-repair company run by a wheeler-dealer who had been expelled from the New York Stock Exchange. There were special Pennsylvania Senate investigative-committee hearings on the upcoming sale of debentures, and Karafin suggested that the bank hire him as a public-relations consultant. The bank's officers, however, were unaware of what was being proposed, and they dismissed the notion, saying they saw no need for Karafin's services.

A short while later, two First Pennsylvania vice-presidents testified before the Senate committee. The *Evening Bulletin* carried the essence of their testimony: they urged a state licensing system for credit and finance agencies. The next morning's *Inquirer* carried a picture of the vice-presidents beneath a headline: "Bank Admits Paying Dealers for Sales-Loan Business." In contrast with the *Bulletin*, the *Inquirer* focused on a banking practice called "dealers' reserve funds," which was a common inducement to get business, but sounded quite different in Karafin's story, which began, "Bank kickbacks to dealers for bringing business was admitted. . . ." It didn't take long for the bank to hire Karafin for his public-relations talents.

Thanks to the rewards of his illicit activities, Karafin lived well beyond his $11,000-a-year *Inquirer* salary; yet no editor at the *Inquirer* had ever decided to question how the reporter paid for the big purchases he frequently bragged about making. For instance, Karafin had bought a new home, which he had decorated with $20,000 worth of new furnishings. He drove to work in a new flashy red Buick, which had a twin at home for his wife to drive, and he had paid cash for both. If any of his colleagues on the reporting staff took note of his affluence, Karafin was always ready with a fast answer. Like Jake Lingle, forty years earlier, he had stories about inheritances and gambling winnings.

When the *Philadelphia Magazine* article reached the newsstands, the rest of the *Inquirer* staff learned what had happened, and morale, which hadn't been high since the Shapp election, sank lower than ever. The story detailed in thousands of words all of Karafin's corrupt dealings. In the strange world of Philadelphia journalism, the *Bulletin* chose to ignore the story, the editors of the paper assuming that that was the proper, gentlemanly posture. The press elsewhere, however, wasn't bothered by such reserve, and it leaped at the story. Reporters from *The New York Times*, the *Washington Post, Time, Newsweek*, and other publications flocked into Philadelphia. The story of a reporter for a major metropolitan paper gone wrong was the shame of the profession, and one that editors of national publications felt they could not in good conscience ignore. In light of the attention, *Philadelphia Magazine* prospered as never before. The periodical's circulation jumped to 90,000 from 19,000. People all over town tried to get their hands on a copy and the magazine's editors reveled in the kind of recognition they long had yearned for.

At the *Inquirer*, however, the editors weren't sure about how to confront the dispiriting business. Annenberg, of course, was shamed, and Dimitman was disheartened, to see the paper so sullied. Only managing editor Gillen seemed not to have fully understood the importance of the damage that had been done to the newspaper. He glided about the newsroom with the same look of aloofness that he always wore, and the only outward display of concern that he indulged

in was a childish gesture. He sent *Philadelphia Magazine* publisher
Herb Lipson a carved wooden hand with the third finger upraised, as
though the terrible disclosure was more of a joke than anything else.
The inscription on the carving stated "Nice Wishes to You Too."
Basking in the glory of the moment, Lipson placed the offering on a
shelf in his office, where it would remain a trophy symbolizing the
power of his press.

If Gillen found moments of levity in the situation, his publisher
didn't. Annenberg was mortified by the attention the story was receiving. Moreover, the inevitable rumors linking Karafin's dreadful
deeds to the past of Moses Annenberg began circulating. Karafin could
only have gotten away with what he had, the rumor mill went, because
of the unsavory ties of the past publisher, and some people speculated
that the present publisher had them as well. Why hadn't anyone complained to Walter Annenberg about the reporter's activities, they
asked, especially a big bank like the First Pennsylvania? The critics answered their own questions. Because Annenberg condoned what
Karafin was doing, even encouraged him, they said.

The reality of the situation, of course, was far different. The last
thing Walter Annenberg wanted or needed was to be linked to the
kind of scandal Karafin had created. He had spent his life trying to
atone for the sins of his father, and he wouldn't knowingly have tolerated any criminal activity at his publications. His problem was the
aloofness he had cultivated since his father died. With the exception of
friends, close business associates and the Triangle executives he had
come to rely upon, many people in town simply did not know how to
approach him. What was more, to most Philadelphians, Walter Annenberg was a fearsome figure. Since the Shapp campaign, many people's wariness of his publishing power had intensified.

"If there is anything Philadelphia businessmen have in common, it
is that they don't stand up to anyone," *Philadelphia Magazine* publisher Lipson said later. "Half the town was cowed by the *Inquirer*—
no one would say a word."

Annenberg himself resented immensely how the Karafin scandal
tarnished his reputation. Even worse, the story had spread across the
nation, and he and his paper were being scorned everywhere for the
misdeeds of one man. "One rotten apple and it comes to this," he remarked to Dimitman. The publisher, of course, wanted to shut the
critics out of his life, but he couldn't, even though he tried. He wrote
letters of complaint to fellow publishers, being especially resentful to-

ward them because he and Lee knew and liked so many of the nation's publishers and they had always got along well at publishers' conventions and other gatherings. In the case of Katharine Graham, he was so disappointed at the coverage of the story in her *Newsweek* magazine that he threatened to cancel advertising in the publication for both *TV Guide* and *Seventeen*.

Though the press everywhere else was covering the story, there was no public response from the *Inquirer* for nearly a week. Finally, Annenberg told his editors that the readers were owed an explanation. He told Dimitman to verify the details of the article and prepare a story for the following Sunday's paper. The staffer who was given the task of writing the heartbreaking story was Joe Goulden, who among all of the *Inquirer*'s editors and reporters was probably the angriest about what had happened. He most frequently was Karafin's rewrite man, possessing a flair for spinning dramatic copy out of the investigative reporter's findings. A restraining force on Karafin, Goulden doublechecked his facts whenever he could, and he sometimes even accompanied Karafin on reporting assignments. But under the pressures of a half dozen deadlines daily, this kind of policing of Karafin, who had a reputation for being loose with his facts, was frequently impossible.

Thus, Goulden felt a sense of outrage and betrayal that he had been a party to Karafin's manipulation of the paper, and when he turned in his story about the reporter's crimes, his anger showed in his scorching prose. "This is the story of a liar and a thief," the article began. The lead was dropped after the paper's lawyers read the story. The rest of the blistering prose, however, was retained and it left little doubt that Goulden considered Karafin a disgrace to the profession. After the story was in type, Gillen had four proofs pulled, one each for Annenberg, Dimitman, the lawyers and himself. The type itself was locked in the composing room foreman's office until just before printing time, so that the contents of the story didn't leak out ahead of time. On Sunday, *Inquirer* readers found the article on page one under the somber headline "With Sadness and Regret," and throughout the tale there were repeated assertions that Karafin had managed to do what he had done only because he was a "remarkably adept liar." The story spilled over ten columns of the paper, but it did little to restore the badly damaged image of the *Philadelphia Inquirer* or that of its publisher.

Another man deeply wounded by the scandal was executive editor Litman. Karafin had long been one of the editor's major sources, filling him in on what was happening in the back rooms of City Hall and the board rooms of big companies. Litman, who prided himself on knowing what was going on just about everywhere, even though he never left his desk, liked to refer to Karafin as "my eyes and ears." Thus, when the news broke, Litman began weeping and said it had never occurred to him to be suspicious of the man whom he had known for nearly twenty years. "Hell, we're not clairvoyant," he remarked. When called to testify at Karafin's trial, Litman made a simple statement that people who knew and liked the editor believed to be true. "I would have trusted him with my life," he said of Karafin. Still, the two had such a close relationship that many *Inquirer* men wondered; they thought back over Karafin's "exposés" that Litman brought into news conferences that were yanked after one edition, because they hadn't been strong stories. Yet, Litman's defenders noted that the editor never had extra money, never even accepted gifts from anyone, and was always quick to lend a friend five or ten dollars to tide him over. The question of the executive editor's role in the mess would never be resolved.

Annenberg was so embittered by the turn of events that he wanted assurances that Karafin had been in the crooked schemes by himself. The last thing he wanted was an ongoing scandal whereby Triangle employees would be uncovered periodically and accused of being partners in the crimes. Thus, the *Inquirer* story recounting Karafin's sins contained a box asking readers who might have any "knowledge of any improper or unprofessional acts by any editorial employees" to step forward. The notice dispirited further an already disheartened staff, and the Newspaper Guild objected on the grounds that the plea reflected poorly on all the good men and women working for the paper, and that it could even result in a witch hunt. But Annenberg was insistent that the problem, or potential problems of an employee's wrongdoing, be dealt with once and for all.

One of the reasons that Annenberg was disgusted by what happened was that, in his own way, he was always wary of ethical considerations such as employees taking money or accepting favors. This was something that he was watchful about at all of his publications. *TV Guide* writers and editors, for example, were not allowed to accept anything from anyone in the television business, and *Seventeen* was just as scrupulous. The publisher was always giving warnings to *Racing Form* editors as well, especially with regard to their employees' betting habits, and a number of *Form* writers had been fired over the years because they showed too much of a penchant for playing the ponies. "If you see any of them at the hundred-dollar window at a track, ask the son of a bitch about it," he told the *Racing Form*'s top editors.

The *Inquirer* was a different matter. For some reason, he wasn't as strict with the paper's employees. For instance, travel writers were allowed to accept free trips from air lines and foreign governments in return for blatantly favorable articles. Far worse, reporters were actually encouraged to work on a free-lance basis for local public-relations firms, a practice that was of long standing because salaries were traditionally low in the newspaper field. That was a way of supplementing income, but it raised a host of potential ethical conflicts about stories generated by public-relations firms. A real-estate reporter was even a practicing realtor. While such activities weren't uncommon in the business, they were becoming embarrassing as papers increasingly tried to instill more integrity in their staffs.

On occasion, Annenberg himself made a stab at keeping *Inquirer* employees in line. Once, for example, he queried Rubye Graham, the fashion editor, who was usually draped in furs, jewels and expensive clothing, how she managed to maintain herself in such opulence on her not overwhelming salary. He feared that she had been bartering space in the paper for such touches of elegance. "On the day I was called to Annenberg's office, I was wearing a Valentino leopard-skin pants suit," she recalled. "When you got called up there, it was for a good reason and I was shaking." As she entered the publisher's office and found out what Annenberg wanted, she was suddenly relieved. She pleasantly explained that she received gifts "from husbands and other men." Knowing her popularity with wealthy men, Annenberg accepted the explanation.

To show that he meant business after the Karafin scandal, the publisher ordered Gillen to get rid of two editors, Litman and Schaeffer. There was little that could be said in Litman's defense and Gillen didn't try, but, to his credit, John Gillen did try to get the publisher to rescind his decision to fire Schaeffer. Like everyone else in the newsroom, Gillen viewed Schaeffer as a decent man who had gotten caught up in an unfortunate set of circumstances, and he told Annenberg that Schaeffer hadn't been involved in any way with Karafin. Rightly or wrongly, however, the publisher believed that both Litman and Schaeffer as city editors were the front-line watchdogs of the staff's behavior. Therefore, he reasoned, both had been remiss. Moreover, he was disappointed in Schaeffer for not having moved Litman out of the newsroom long ago. The publisher was tired of Litman's secretiveness and quiet phone calls and appearance of knowing so much. If he knew so much, Annenberg thought, he might have known what Karafin was doing. A fatalist, Litman accepted the publisher's judgment with an outward show of equanimity, even though more than thirty years' work had just been torn from him. Schaeffer, in the end, displayed more backbone than anyone who worked with him had expected. Instead of quietly "resigning" as Litman did, Schaeffer refused and was fired. The act at the time managed to keep his self-respect locally, but nationally he was blacklisted from working for another newspaper. He was tarred with the scandal.

Getting rid of the two editors happened so quickly that they were gone almost before the staff realized what had happened. Moreover, their departure pointed up just how weakened the paper had been since the 1958 strike. There was no one capable of taking their places, and into the breach was thrown a man named Harry Belinger, who had been the editor of the *Daily News*. The *News*'s forte, of course, was crime, sex and violence, and Belinger was good at the blood-and-guts approach to news. So good was he that he made Dimitman look like a paragon of progressive journalism. Quickly the *Philadelphia Inquirer* began to look like, and sound like, another *Daily News*. But while his editorial taste and talents would have pleased Max Annenberg, Belinger was an honest and open man who was greatly concerned about the integrity of his news columns. He had heard many stories about the way Annenberg interfered with the paper, including the notorious blacklist. Thus when he took on the new job, he asked Annenberg to let him run the paper his own way with no second-guessing, and the publisher agreed.

The first thing Belinger did was destroy a shibboleth as to who were the publisher's fair-haired reporters. Men like old-timers Joe Miller and Joe Trachtman had long traded on their alleged close ties to the publisher, and their stories, even those of dubious merit, were printed because of their perceived closeness to Annenberg. Belinger, however, decided to test the notion that the publisher stood behind such men. "When old Joe Trachtman came up to me and said, 'Here's a story the publisher wants,'" Belinger recalled, "I always learned that Annenberg never had any knowledge of the story." The way Belinger found out was simply not printing the reporters' stories, something other editors had long been afraid to do.

Therefore, when Miller and others came to the new editor with their "publisher musts," as such stories long had been known, Belinger began replying to them "Bullshit"—which is what he thought of their stories. The city editor began questioning other long-standing practices, such as anonymous sources from City Hall and the state capital, who usually had nasty things to say about Democrats. Miller, for instance, found it difficult to admit that a Democrat was even a human being, let alone that he could be a responsible politician. Here, too, Belinger found the sources evaporated when he raised questions about them. Overall, "There were a lot of journalistic crimes committed in Annenberg's name over the years," Belinger recalled.

A prime example of the kinds of Annenberg-ordered shoddy journalism, however, appeared shortly before the new editor took over. It was the coverage of the last campaign of Senator Clark. Clark's opponent was a young Republican Congressman, Richard S. Schweiker, a decent hard-working liberal whom Annenberg liked and admired. By then, it was an open secret that Clark and Annenberg disliked each other, the publisher referring to the Senator as a "nasty little man," when he was in kindly moods, and a "son of a bitch" when he was feeling less amiable. The *Inquirer*'s editorial guns naturally were trained on the Senator, but so was the typewriter of Joe Miller, even though he was still a Harrisburg reporter, not a Washington reporter. Miller, for instance, joyfully wrote that support for the Senator was slipping and that he was hurting for campaign funds, and his stories often contained nettlesome remarks about Clark's personal life. In one campaign funding story, for example, he noted that Clark's personal fortune had declined in 1967 to an estimated $600,000 from $1,134,983 in 1965. The reason for the drop, he made sure he told readers, was the "result of the settlement he made upon his second wife, the former Noel Hall, prior to their divorce the previous summer. He subsequently married the former Iris Cole Richy, a former Pennsylvania state government employee."

One of the oddest aspects of the *Inquirer*'s campaign to unseat Clark was the attention given to State Supreme Court Justice Michael Musmanno. The aged jurist hated Clark, who had supported another Democrat in a state contest that Musmanno had participated in. Musmanno was appalled that Clark was an opponent of the American involvement in the war in Vietnam. The judge accused the Senator of being a racist and giving "comfort to our Communist enemies," and his remarks invariably found their way into the *Inquirer*'s news col-

umns, including nonsensical phrases he made up, such as Clark being a
"feather stained dove," which he failed to define. When Clark called
the war "wasteful and stupid," Musmanno fumed, "He uttered defa-
mation of the memory of American soldiers who gave their lives for
American freedoms while he was traveling deluxe at American taxpayers' expense." Not only did *Inquirer* reporters take down Musmanno's
remarks, which the little judge called in to the paper, but on occasion
he was allowed to have by-line articles. On October 3, 1967, for instance, Musmanno under his own name castigated Clark—"As a loyal
American and a war veteran wounded in the service of my country, I
love our democratic institutions and particularly revere the office of
the Presidency of the United States. Thus, I am shocked at the manner
in which Sen. Clark treats that exalted office. . . ."

To make matters worse for the Senator, Musmanno had a big following in Pennsylvania, especially among Italian Americans. Clark's
campaign aides cringed whenever they picked up the *Inquirer* and
read the judge's blasts, knowing they could have an effect on the coming election. For his part, Annenberg never ordered that the judge
should be given such easy access to the paper, but his editors didn't
find him objecting either. The editors simply put together their own
two and two and came up with the fact that Annenberg didn't like
Clark and enjoyed seeing the Musmanno copy berating the Senator. It
became an unspoken dictate that editors had to run as much anti-Clark
material as possible from the judge.

On Columbus Day of all days the judge's attacks came to an abrupt
halt. He died, and for some reason Walter Annenberg apparently got it
into his head that Clark's antiwar activities had so angered Musmanno
that they had hastened his death. Reporter Goulden remembered Gillen telling him that he had had to talk the publisher out of inserting
into the judge's obituary that Clark was the cause of his death. Annenberg denied the tale, and it may well have been Gillen simply ela-
borating upon the mythology of Walter Annenberg, the boss he was
afraid to stand up to. Whatever the case, within a few scant years the
story would return to haunt Annenberg at a critical time in his life. In
any event, Clark lost his seat to Schweiker, and he resented deeply
having to give up the patrician privileges of the Senate, which he had
so enjoyed. When he ruefully sought a scapegoat for his demise, he
chose Walter Annenberg and the coverage he had received in the *Inquirer*, a factor which also would one day threaten to undermine Annenberg's chance to receive the greatest honor of his life.

While Annenberg's critics were quick to find fault with him, his unpredictable nature made it difficult to criticize everything he did, though many people would have liked to. Even during the trying time of the Karafin mess, Walter Annenberg was still one of the most generous men in the city. There were few charities in the city that weren't receiving his support, and the Communications School at Pennsylvania University that he had endowed was a model of its kind. But since his charitable works were seldom publicized, the popular view of Annenberg—that of tyrannical newspaper publisher—came to prevail in the city because of the people his press had offended.

On one occasion, however, Annenberg's generosity did receive much public attention. The notice came after the Six-day War, in which Israeli military forces stunningly controlled the Sinai peninsula, captured Jerusalem's Old City and gained a hold on the strategic Golan Heights; the world was amazed at Israel's display of strength. What was obvious, however, was the financial toll of such a victory on the tiny nation, and Jewish organizations across the United States began appealing for funds to send to Israel. One of the major contributors, perhaps the largest donor to the cause, was Walter Annenberg. Though he himself didn't call attention to his gift, the enormity of it soon leaked out. Following the war, he had coolly written a check for one million dollars as his donation. He had done it in the name of his mother, Sadie, who had always looked upon Israel as one of her causes.

Oddly enough, during the same period of Karafin-induced turmoil, there was a new feature at the *Inquirer* that even Annenberg's detractors couldn't help admiring, and they wondered how it was allowed to exist under such a publisher as Annenberg. The addition to the paper was a column entitled "Passing Scene," which was the effort of two young writers, Joe McGinniss and Rose Dewolf, and it was the most exciting innovation in Philadelphia journalism in years. The column specialized in deflating the high and the mighty, particularly in the hands of McGinniss, a colorful writer who skillfully skewered politicians, debunked local institutions, and even bloodied the publisher's pal, Police Commissioner Frank Rizzo, who bellowed like a wounded bull whenever the columnist turned his attention on him. While people everywhere marveled at the young writer's freedom to attack a wide variety of subjects that the publisher obviously held sacred, Annenberg not only enjoyed most of the columns himself but also liked the circulation boost the controversial pieces created. The publisher even attended promotional lunches for advertisers at which McGinniss was the featured guest.

McGinniss, a former sports writer for the *Bulletin*, was a find of *Inquirer* managing editor Gillen, who had liked the reporter's writing style. When he hired him as a columnist, he promised him freedom of expression, and the editor rotated him with Miss Dewolf, a reporter with a breezy, less acerbic style. As McGinniss' confidence grew, he pressed his limits to such an extent that he traveled to Vietnam to write about the war, or flew to California to write about the assassination of Robert Kennedy, one of his idols. At times, Annenberg was dismayed by what the young man wrote, such as a column in which he referred to America as a "cess pool," following Kennedy's death, and several times he replied with editorials criticizing the columns. But he didn't censor him. "On the morning one editorial ran, Walter Annenberg called me and told me not to take this personally," McGinniss recalled. The publisher told him that he felt his action was necessary "because some people expect it." Eventually, McGinniss quit to write the best-selling book, *The Selling of the Presidency*, about the marketing technique used during the 1968 Republican campaign to sell Richard Nixon to the public, and the column, after being written by a series of other reporters, died.

Besides discovering McGinniss, the *Inquirer* scored another coup of sorts, one that could be considered so only in socially self-conscious Philadelphia. The paper hired away the *Bulletin*'s society columnist, Ruth Seltzer, at a hefty salary and an unheard-of fifteen-year contract. Miss Seltzer, a heavy-set, frumpy woman, who was called "Twiggy" behind her back by reporters in the *Inquirer*'s fashion department, was given not only a big salary but a healthy amount of overtime as well, so that managing editor Gillen complained that she took home a bigger paycheck than he did. Nonetheless, she knew everyone in society, she considered them all her friends, and her lusterless, discreet columns never offended anyone. She wrote about the Devon Horse Show, the Philadelphia Charity Ball or the Main Street Fair for Chestnut Hill Hospital. Her most sparkling word was "amusing." She was perfect for Philadelphia, and Lee Annenberg wanted her for the *Inquirer*. "Walter personally didn't give a damn about Ruth Seltzer, but Lee felt that maybe the paper should lure Seltzer away to improve the *Inquirer*'s society coverage," Dimitman recalled. "Gillen didn't want her. Walter didn't want her. Lee wanted her."

Despite the addition of the columnists, the *Inquirer* continued to decline. Because its competition didn't spend money on a large Washington bureau, overseas bureaus, or highly paid, well-trained staffs, the *Inquirer* didn't either. Few beats were covered well, other than medicine and sometimes education, and the old habit of accepting the police version of crime news was so ingrained that editors rarely questioned the practice. By the late 1960s, the presses were antiquated, the news staff was grossly undermanned, and the turnover was enormous. Nevertheless, Annenberg couldn't bring himself to part with the newspaper, even after the notoriety of the Karafin scandal. Despite all the paper's problems, he was still aware that it was a vehicle of power and social prominence, no matter how much it was criticized, a factor that he and his father had understood since the day Moses bought the paper. "Without the *Inquirer*, I'd be just another millionaire," Walter remarked on more than one occasion. An office much more prestigious than a publisher's would have to come along before he would be able to part with the paper his father gave him.

CHAPTER

NINETEEN

ON A STEAMY morning in July 1967, Annenberg strode into the large, modern Los Angeles offices of *TV Guide*. Such an unannounced appearance was unusual, and it was obvious from the publisher's demeanor that he was very angry. He immediately began questioning executives about one of his top lieutenants in the region, and it readily became apparent that a not very discreet affair the hapless man was having with an attractive secretary had come to his attention.

The publisher didn't care what his employees did in their private lives, but he didn't want his publications associated with crass behavior, a position that he felt even more strongly since the Karafin scandal. The previous night a fight had erupted at a company party, a fight that Annenberg thought was both juvenile and unseemly. The executive he was asking questions about, normally an amiable, easygoing fellow, had gotten into an argument with one of his colleagues, and he had hauled off and punched the man so hard he had dislocated his own shoulder. To Annenberg, such behavior was intolerable and no matter what anyone said in the executive's favor, the publisher had made up his mind to get rid of him. Annenberg didn't want to do the job himself; instead, he demanded that Brian "Brad" Bradfield, who had risen over the years to the position of *TV Guide*'s general manager, be summoned to the telephone at the Radnor headquarters. When Bradfield was located, Annenberg told him, "Brad, get out here on the next plane; I've got someone I want you to fire."

Firings of any kind were highly unusual within the corporation, but Annenberg believed that he had to protect the company's image. The only other employee that anyone at *TV Guide* could recall the pub-

310

lisher having sacked was an executive who had had the audacity to keep Annenberg waiting for ten minutes, after his boss had come specifically to see him. Since everyone in the organization knew of the publisher's concern about his dignity, they never understood what had possessed the executive. When the man finally emerged from his office, he amazed everyone by looking brightly at his secretary and saying cavalierly, "Well, here goes nothing." The publisher gave him a humiliating dressing down about courtesy and dismissed him.

Triangle employees were seldom treated to such high drama. Of Annenberg's holdings, only the *Inquirer* was marked by controversy, probably because it was the only platform from which he delivered statements on public or political affairs. The newspaper's very character and visibility made it unique among Triangle publications. Far more typical was *Seventeen*, a model of understated taste, and a publication where money was lavished on top writers, artists, art directors and editors—as long as Enid agreed. The *Racing Form* over the years had become a technological marvel, since so much money had been reinvested in computers and new printing processes to improve the paper's productivity; the *Form* was so respected in the industry, its information so accurate, that it had assumed the official status of the recognized publication of the racing industry. Of all the Triangle publications, however, *TV Guide* most reflected Annenberg's vision and generated the greatest financial rewards. It was known throughout his empire as "Walter's baby." Thus, Annenberg's concern for propriety at *TV Guide* was sparked as much by his inordinate pride in the magazine as by his having been sickened by what Harry Karafin had done, or being angry about the executive's fight with a colleague.

Since its founding in 1953, *TV Guide* had moved from being the tiny magazine advertisers sneered at to the most powerful publication having anything to do with television. The listings in *TV Guide* were considered an essential service, and as the temperamental, high-priced programmers for the three big networks made their frantic schedule changes, the little publication was always in the back of their minds. They well knew that if they missed *TV Guide* with a program shift, they missed a huge proportion of the television-viewing audience. Moreover, television personalities and executives alike craved favorable mentions of their shows in the magazine, because the impact was enormous. Like the *Racing Form*, *TV Guide* had gradually come to be the leading authority in its field, and just as necessary.

Probably no one was more grateful for *TV Guide*'s rise in fortunes than Merrill Panitt. He had shepherded the magazine through the early years, making sure for the most part that few people within the industry were offended by the publication. Better than his writers during that period, he had understood that the publication needed the industry more than the industry needed *TV Guide*. There had been exceptions, of course, to the magazine's penchant for looking at only the bright side of the business and its personalities. *TV Guide*, for example, had carried an article about Milton Berle that depicted him as an egomaniac, leading the comic to contact the Annenbergs to vent his rage. The incident hadn't bothered the publisher; he didn't even get around to telling Panitt about the Berle phone call until several weeks after it occurred when he happened to think about it.

By the 1960s, Panitt had moved to enlarge the publication's scope. Both Annenberg and Panitt were concerned about the broader societal implications of the medium, believing such issues as sex and violence on television, and how important a role TV played in the American culture, should be examined. Thus, serious articles increasingly were sprinkled among the flattering portraits of stars, directors and producers, and Panitt began soliciting free-lance work from such well-known writers as Arthur Miller, Alistair Cook and Arthur Schlesinger, Jr. Moreover, the *TV Guide* staff writers were no longer under restrictions about what they could write, and some of them gained fearsome reputations in Hollywood. Rod Serling, for instance, bitterly referred to one staff writer, Edith Efron, as the "lace-covered hatchet." Jack Lord, the popular star of the show *Hawaii Five-O*, banned *TV Guide* reporters from his set, because he was livid over an article that made him out to be other than the nice guy his publicity people insisted he was. "He proved sensitive," Dwight Whitney, the *TV Guide* bureau chief, recalled.

For all the power *TV Guide* attained, it remained an unpretentious magazine and reflected another side of the publisher's personality than the one exhibited by his *Inquirer*. Whereas the newspaper was the product of a highly opinionated man who became combative when he believed he was in the right, the magazine was a little naïve, unsophisticated, and above all wholesome. Nowhere was *TV Guide*'s personality better personified than at the Radnor headquarters, where the publication had been since 1957. That was no elegant editorial cocoon housing intellectual editors who spent their days coaxing copy from temperamental writers. The physical plant looked just like those housing nearby pharmaceutical or electronics concerns in an area that was a big industrial park. *TV Guide* was a vast workshop where people matter-of-factly hammered out a utilitarian and well-crafted product. The location was very suburban and nondescript, leading author George Plimpton to refer to it as "that strange place in the middle of nowhere." The men and women who populated *TV Guide* offices were generally a provincial lot, who liked their work and enjoyed Triangle's paternalism. The editors as a group had little to do with the frantic, fast-paced Los Angeles–New York axis that made up the world of television. A National Broadcasting Company executive, for instance, was taken aback when Alex Joseph, the managing editor, informed the man that he was only the second network executive he had met and he couldn't recall who the first one was. Joseph enjoyed the look on such men's faces when he told them things like that, just as he delighted in going to elegant restaurants with them and ordering a ham sandwich and a beer, a touch that Annenberg appreciated.

By the late 1960s Annenberg was seeing more of his Los Angeles operations than he ever had seen, and the reason was Sunnylands, the gracious desert estate that he had built. Although his base of operations was Philadelphia, the publisher never considered himself a regional power. His many businesses and offices were scattered across the country, and he had a national perspective that made him as well acquainted with the tax structures in California and Connecticut as he was with those in Pennsylvania. Since he was a very private person and so very wealthy, it mattered little where he lived. There were servants to do his bidding. His private jet could take him in short hours wherever he wanted to go. Thus, he had created Sunnylands on an oasis in the desert, where he could live in the isolation he enjoyed, could run his businesses by telephone (as he invariably did anyway), and where Lee could enjoy the California sun and life style for nearly half the year.

The desert retreat had come about somewhat haphazardly. As early as 1962, Annenberg began acquiring land in Palm Springs, but at the time he thought of the property simply as an investment. The same instincts that had told him to start *Seventeen* and *TV Guide* had told him that there would be a great demand in coming years for second homes, and that Palm Springs was a logical place for such a boom. Once he had embarked upon buying land, word spread swiftly, and because his name was synonymous with big money, he often paid twice as much for land that would have cost anyone else $1,400 an acre. Because Palm Springs hadn't been growing of late, and the land

Annenberg wanted was a half dozen miles east of the town itself, there were many people who believed he was buying foolishly. A local exception was Frank Bogert, the mayor of Palm Springs. Out of curiosity, Bogert had watched Annenberg's career for decades and had perceived "what a smart son of a bitch he had turned out to be."

The mayor had first met the publisher in the 1930s when, as young bachelors, they had both dated the starlet June Travis. At the time, Bogert owned a riding stable in Palm Springs and, through his business, he had gotten to know many people in the movie crowd and had circulated in the same circles as Annenberg. At the time, he had viewed his rival for the starlet's attentions merely as a stage-door Johnny, "another of those Eastern millionaires who came West to have a good time." Since then he had admired the way Annenberg had taken over his father's company and built his corporate empire. Thus, when Bogert heard that Annenberg was buying acre after acre of what seemed like useless land, he believed that "the people who were talking about how foolish Annenberg was would soon wish they were that foolish." The mayor was right, of course; soon enough land near the Annenberg holdings was selling for $40,000 an acre.

Walter and Lee didn't think of building a winter home on the Palm Springs land until 1964, but when they did the scale they considered was magnificent. By then Annenberg had acquired a square mile of desert land and with it he had received the rights to buy the Tamarisk Water Company, which would supply the precious water needed for the project he had in mind. He wanted nothing less than a true oasis. As usual, he turned to experts for assistance in an area where he was lacking in knowledge. He sought out Quincy Jones, dean of the school of architecture at the University of Southern California, who had gained renown for his "California desert house" designs, which were in harmony with their environment. Other consultants on the project were William Haines and Ted Graber, who were Los Angeles decorators known for their elegant taste and powerful clients. Haines, a former silent-film actor who had starred in *Alias Jimmy Valentine*, and his young partner Graber left the environmental considerations to Jones, but they played a key role in developing the concept behind the house. After a great deal of thought and listening to what Walter and Lee said they expected, Graber suggested that they should consider a "great tent." The idea of a tent for Annenberg appealed to Graber, since the tycoon always reminded him of some Arabian sheik who could command whatever he wanted to appear. Thus, plans for

Sunnylands began to take shape, foremost being a tentlike ceiling that was to cover a living room area of 6,400 square feet. The house's total living area was to be 32,000 square feet. Several walls were to be cut from a deep rust-colored volcanic rock, and vast windows would overlook lakes, springs and brooks, as well as a swimming pool, two tennis courts, and a golf course that would surround the house.

The Annenbergs were both perfectionists, and they had the saving grace of instantly being able to make up their minds about whether they liked or disliked a particular plan. Numerous meetings were held with Jones at Inwood or at his Los Angeles offices. On such occasions, Walter and Lee were always together, neither wanting to make a decision that hadn't included the other. When at Jones's office, Walter always took time out to call his mother, who was in her middle eighties and very ill, and on July 7, 1965, Sadie died. Walter had hoped that one day she would be able to use the home he was building, knowing her unbounded pride in his achievements. Plans for Sunnylands, of course, had included a special "Mother's Room." The loss was felt by all Sadie's children, who were well aware of the depth of suffering in her life—the pain that her husband had caused her.

Thus, when Sunnylands was completed in 1966, the only sad note for Annenberg was his mother's absence. The home itself was breathtaking and was noted nationally as one of the architectural wonders of the country. In Palm Springs, residents could hardly contain themselves, they so wanted to see the residence that they had heard so much about for the past two years. Most of the area's people, however, were destined to be disappointed. Annenberg remained aloof from the town's social activities, spending his time working at his office or playing golf on the compound. The first guest was his old friend Dwight Eisenhower, who marveled at the golf course. When they had a dinner party, the Annenbergs' guests most often were friends from around the nation who flew in for the occasion and were house guests for several days. There were people such as the Nixons and the Reagans, and businessmen whose company Walter enjoyed, including millionaire Leonard Firestone, who published one of the local newspapers in Palm Springs as one of his many interests.

Oddly enough, one of the local people Annenberg became friendly with was Frank Sinatra, who also maintained a retreat in Palm Springs. Sinatra had called upon Annenberg while soliciting donations for one of the charities the singer helped support and, somewhat to their mutual surprise, the two men liked each other. They shared many political attitudes, and both liked intense privacy. Annenberg, of course, was well aware of all the rumors about connections in the underworld that Sinatra was supposed to have, but he had long ago made up his mind that he would judge people for the way they treated him—and little else. He found that he and the singer shared another trait, one that he respected in any man. Sinatra was devoted to his mother, just as Annenberg had been to his and, like the publisher, Sinatra gave huge charitable donations in his mother's name. Moreover, though of disparate backgrounds, the two probably recognized in each other that they were men who carried with them painful pasts.

When Annenberg acquired the Tamarisk Water Company, he hadn't realized what he was taking on. The utility supplied not only his property but others that made up Rancho Mirage, as the now growing community east of Palm Springs was known. His prediction about the area being bound to grow was coming true, and along with it came the headache of having to supply the water for homes owned by Sinatra, George Burns and Gracie Allen, Danny Thomas and others. People began calling him personally when their supply was disrupted. On one occasion the whole system suffered a failure and Annenberg had to hire someone to deliver bottled water to his irate neighbors. Eventually, he sold the shares in the company because, he said, "It became a pain in the ass." As usual, however, he came out ahead. He received for his water company not only more than he had paid for it, but an amount almost equal to the original purchase price of the land he had bought.

Such disruptions of the idyllic life at Sunnylands, however, were infrequent, and the house in the desert suited the publisher. Surprisingly, it was Lee, the Californian, who was disquieted at first. The house was so enormous that it took her awhile adjusting to living where a maid, answering phone calls, at times couldn't find the lady of the house. But despite being so vast, the house was marked by a formal serenity that both Annenbergs found appealing. Pale pinks and yellows and celadon-green–colored walls and furniture blended with the Annenberg collection of Impressionists. The home easily held a host of art treasures, including the Steuben glass, known as the Asiatic collection, consisting of thirty-six etched pieces set into blue-velvet–lined shelves, each piece being specially mounted so as not to be disturbed by earthquake tremors. There was also the Chinese jade buffalo, reputed to be the finest jade animal ever carved, which dated to the Ch'ien Lung period of the Ching Dynasty. Annenberg was so enthusiastic about the piece that his friends started calling it "Walter"; it stood discreetly on a graceful ebony stand.

If anything, the grounds were perhaps even more magnificent than the house. There was a sculptured garden; a private meditation garden for Lee; a cactus garden, and two hothouses, one of which was restricted to growing orchids. One of Walter's prizes was a huge, rare beaucarnea tree that he had purchased from Estelle Doheny's estate in Los Angeles and had transplanted. There was the pool, and the tennis courts, and the golf course, which though only nine holes was laid out so that it could be played as twenty-seven. Walter and Lee and their guests frequently dined outside, with their butler bringing them picnic lunches encased in insulated hot and cold picnic baskets. In the evening, movies were shown in a recreation room. The life was one that other people could only dream about. Thus, when Richard Nixon broached the subject of the ambassadorship to the Court of St. James, the Annenbergs talked of how much Sunnylands meant to them when they discussed together the prospects of taking the appointment. But there were other much more important considerations, which both of them knew only too well.

CHAPTER

TWENTY

SEVERAL DAYS AFTER he was offered the ambassadorship, Annenberg called his friend Nixon and told him that he and Lee would accept the assignment. The decision hadn't been an easy one. Both Annenbergs were anxious, of course, to spend more time at Sunnylands, which was still a novelty for them after the years of planning and building. That paled, however, before the serious problems the appointment could pose. There would be the inevitable charge of cronyism, which the publisher foresaw as fodder for Nixon's critics; but of even greater importance was the likelihood that the past events in Annenberg's life would be dredged up. His father's history once again would return to haunt him and possibly injure him further. Nonetheless, he accepted the President's offer, knowing that he was about to be exposed to more publicity than he ever received.

For all their apparent sophistication, the Annenbergs were fairly simple people, and the prospect of holding down the most prestigious ambassadorial job that the United States had to offer was intimidating. They were all too aware of the lofty social rank the job held both within and outside diplomatic circles, and the publisher found it awesome that so great an honor was now within his grasp. Walter and Lee were conscious of their lack of pedigree in taking a position that traditionally was assumed by representatives of the Protestant Establishment. The post held both a fascination and a fear for them. Walter knew how the task could redeem his family name, and he didn't like to dwell too much on it because of the possibility that it would slip away from him.

As weeks rolled by and Nixon didn't announce Annenberg's candi-

318

dacy, he and Lee became a bit edgy. They wondered whether the President decided to sidestep the problems the appointment would pose and now wanted to give the job to someone else. Indeed, their concerns were justified, because Nixon was under pressure to do exactly that. While some of the President's men, like William Rogers, the new Secretary of State, knew Annenberg and stood behind the nomination, there were others who told Nixon that the publisher was unwanted trouble. They suggested brushing Annenberg off in favor of someone whom they considered much more acceptable. It was inevitable that such dissension should leak back to Annenberg, who then reluctantly sent word to the President that he was willing to withdraw his acceptance in order to save him any embarrassment. Nixon, however, hadn't taken the time and effort to win his friend over just to give him the back of his hand when it looked as though the appointment would be treated roughly. He flatly rejected Annenberg's offer to back off. Finally, on February 20, Lee's fiftieth birthday, Annenberg saw the story of his nomination come over his AP wire at Sunnylands. In his elation, he had the wire copy mounted and gave it to his wife as one of her gifts.

As expected, criticism was quick in coming, and stories cropped up that the nomination would never be approved by Senator J. William Fulbright, chairman of the Foreign Relations Committee that passed on ambassadorial assignments. In fact, Fulbright had already voiced his objections, telling a *Washington Post* reporter that Annenberg was "simply not up to the standards we expect of our premier diplomatic post." Then an editorial in *The New York Times* denigrated the choice and contended that Annenberg bought the appointment with huge campaign donations.

The publisher had fully expected the attacks, but they added to the agitation he had been feeling for weeks, ever since Nixon had approached him about the assignment. The *Times* editorial in particular grated. Shortly before the piece was printed, he had been contacted by someone on the *Times'* staff who had asked him if he had made any financial contributions to the Nixon campaign, and he had replied that he hadn't. (His relatives had been big donors.) After the editorial's appearance, Annenberg believed that it was part of a malicious attempt to discredit him. He refused to accept arguments from aides that the phone call could have come from a reporter, not an editorial writer, and the information wasn't relayed from one department to another. Annenberg found it impossible to believe that the news and editorial staffs wouldn't know what each was doing, especially when it came to what he considered such a delicate and important issue as an ambassadorial appointment. No—he believed that someone well placed in the *Times* hierarchy had it in for him. Nixon thought so too.

"I wanted him for the reasons the *Times* opposed him," Nixon later said, when recalling the paper's negative criticism. "They wanted someone like Paley. The *Times* felt he frankly wasn't in the first rank of the social order to go to the Court of St. James. They were concerned about what his father had done. To them, Annenberg was too candid at times and not diplomatic . . . not the typical soft-headed diplomat. The *Times* is basically a snobbish paper. I wanted somebody who would go to the mat, somebody who was not part of the social elite, somebody who could express himself at times.

"But it was a tough fight," Nixon continued. "There were those— some—in those early days who indicated they didn't want to see the fight through. But I insisted. People on our own staff . . . people who are weak-kneed . . . said he was an embarrassment, and word came back that he was willing to pull out. But I passed word back that I was going to fight it and stand by him."

Even with Nixon's assurances of support, Annenberg's anxiety was growing. One source of worry was the caliber of the popular man he might replace. The current ambassador, David Bruce, was a career diplomat; but, more than that, he epitomized the best of the Protestant Establishment that for so long dominated the Foreign Service. Highly regarded in all the capitals of Europe, Bruce had perhaps the most finely honed diplomatic skills of any of his peers. A raconteur, he was as good at conversation with a glass of cognac in his hand as he was at drafting a diplomatic treaty. His specialness had been noted by all Presidents, no matter what their political coloration. Harry S Truman made him ambassador to France; Dwight Eisenhower sent him to Germany, and John Kennedy gave him Great Britain.

In London, Bruce's genteel elegance had charmed the British, and the fact that his wife, Evangeline, was half British certainly hadn't proven a handicap. Evangeline was known for her taste and beauty and her biting wit. She loved her husband's assignments abroad, and she had become especially attached to their life in London, where they had been posted for the past eight years. There she was the center of a sophisticated circle of admirers who paid court to her as one of the most powerful women in London. It was all too difficult for her to leave such a position. Leaving London and the glamorous duty as the

Ambassador's partner was more than just a matter of filling boxes with personal belongings. For Evangeline Bruce, it meant discarding her identity, and she resented it.

Lee Annenberg had already experienced the hostility Mrs. Bruce was feeling. When Annenberg's appointment was announced, Evangeline invited Lee to London to see Winfield House, the stately London residence of the American ambassador. Evangeline was curious to meet the woman who would replace her. After all, she told friends, she had "never even heard of these strange people" before. For her part, Lee was grateful for the opportunity, because she was dying to see where she might soon be living, although she too shared Walter's trepidations as to whether he would be confirmed. She flew to London without attracting any attention to herself. She didn't want to seem to be claiming the prize before the Senate committee had even held its hearing on her husband's controversial nomination. Nevertheless, she was excited at the prospect of being an ambassador's wife—a heady wine just from the sip of it that she had had so far. It was almost inconceivable to her that the niece of Harry Cohn and the son of Moses Annenberg could have come so far. Perhaps presumptuously, though, she brought with her Haines and Graber, the tasteful decorators who had had so much to do with making Sunnylands an elegant retreat. Their advice would once again be valuable, she believed, because both she and Walter had been told that the ambassador's residence was in need of redecorating and even some repairs.

Once Lee was in London, her meeting with Evangeline Bruce seemed on the surface to go well enough. What struck observers immediately was that physically the women were in stark contrast to each other. Evangeline was a tall, lithe, darkly beautiful woman, who through her years of entertaining as an international hostess had acquired the nonchalant grace of performing the duties of her office without any longer having to think about how to act or what to say. She did everything by the book, including inviting the wives of junior Foreign Service officers to tea or lunch the correct number of times a year. The fact that many of the wives found her patronizing bothered her little. At her level, they didn't count. Her real social life, the one she so valued, was in the lofty ranks of London society. On the other hand, Lee Annenberg was a small, slim, radiant blonde, who had spent years cultivating people of power and prominence, a role she thoroughly enjoyed.

Though Lee found Evangeline's welcome polite enough, she

thought she detected a disappointment, a feeling that Lee herself didn't
fit the image that Evangeline had fancied a Mrs. Annenberg should
look like. "I believe she thought she was going to meet a dumpy little
Jewish matron," recalled Lee. "Instead, she got me!"

As she was shown through Winfield House, Lee found that it was
her turn to be dismayed. Her feelings had little to do with Mrs. Bruce,
but with the state of the three-story, thirty-five-room mansion itself.
She and Walter, of course, had been warned that the roof was leaky
and some wiring was in need of repair, but as she strolled through the
many vast rooms and hallways her practiced eye told her that a vast
amount of work was needed—the residence verged on being a disaster.

Indeed, little had been done to the Georgian-style mansion since it
was built in 1937 for Barbara Hutton, the American heiress to the
Woolworth fortune, who named it after her maternal grandmother.
The property, situated off the outer circle of London's historic Regent
Park, one of Henry VII's hunting forests, had served some wearing
years for just causes. During the Second World War, Miss Hutton and
her husband, Count Haugwitz von Reventlow, had turned it over to
the Royal Air Force, which had used it as a headquarters for a balloon
barrage unit. Though so much of London was damaged during heavy
bombing, Winfield House had escaped with only a few broken windows. Following the war, the heiress had donated the property to the
United States government, and it had become the ambassador's residence in 1954.

Lee wasn't just dismayed by the physical deterioration, she was
shocked by signs of carelessness. There were water stains on tables
under plants, floors were marred, and the overall general appearance
was one of drabness. Not knowing what else to do, Lee had braced
herself and called her husband and she tried to prepare him for the
glum news she had to report.

"Walter, I hope you are sitting down, because I have quite a shock
for you," she told him. "The place is a mess. The wiring is shot and is
pulling plaster out. The roof has very serious problems. The whole
house needs repainting. And I don't know what to do about the furniture. There is some lovely furniture, but it will leave with the Bruces."

As she expected, Walter reassured her that he would see to it that
the problems were all tended to if the job actually became his. The
news was disconcerting, of course, but it was the least of his many
worries at the moment. Knowing that Haines and Graber were with

Lee, Annenberg told his wife to see to it that the decorators compiled a thorough study of the mansion's needs as well as an estimate of how much the apparently monumental job would cost. Thus, Lee told the two men that within a few days they had to try and get a fix on how to renovate the residence. The cost mattered little. Lee, as well as Walter, knew the budget for running an embassy wasn't nearly enough to allow them to live the kind of life style they were used to leading. Walter was more than prepared to make up the difference out of his own pocket, a small enough price, he believed, for the honor of holding the post. When he thought of being in a position to repay Nixon in some small way such as that, he was more than willing to do so. "Hell," he said later, "if you can't spend your own money doing something worthwhile for your country, then what can you spend it for?"

The few days in London proved trying for Lee. Mrs. Bruce, who probably found the experience trying as well, made her feel like an intruder, and Lee, who had expected to be treated quite differently, was humiliated. When she called Haines and Graber to ask them to come to the house to give their opinions about what was needed, she began crying and briefly explained the situation. "Let us take you home and we can do this later," Graber suggested. Like his partner, he truly liked Lee and considered her more a friend than a client, since they had gotten to know each other so well during the years of developing Sunnylands. He didn't want to see her hurt.

Lee insisted, though, that the task be completed. Thus, to Mrs. Bruce's understandable annoyance, the decorators carefully went through the residence taking notes and snapping pictures of all the defects so that they would have a very accurate record of what was needed. When they completed their task, the men and Lee prepared to leave London and Lee sent Mrs. Bruce flowers in appreciation for her having asked her to come. Even though the experience had proved so unpleasant, Evangeline hadn't had to invite her before the appointment was a reality. On the flight home, she excused herself from any conversation with Haines and Graber, explaining to them that she was in need of her Christian Science meditations after the ordeal she had been through. "If I don't," she explained to them wearily, "I'll be a real bitch by the time we land."

A short while after she was home, Lee began to believe that Mrs. Bruce resented the plans to redo Winfield House to a far greater degree than she had even believed in London. Her reasons for concern were items that began cropping up in both British and American gossip columns, insinuating that Lee had invited herself to London. Then there were references to the Annenbergs' plans to hire "Hollywood decorators" for the renovations, and snide references to ceilings being lowered and music piped into rooms. Lee was simmering.

One day Mrs. John L. Loeb, wife of the New York investment banker, called. Mrs. Loeb knew both Evangeline Bruce and Lee Annenberg and she didn't like the nature of the reports she was hearing. "I called to ask you a question," she said. "I'm just curious. That residence is beautiful." Mrs. Loeb implied that what was good enough for the Bruces should be good enough for the Annenbergs.

For Lee, the call was the final straw. The sneering references to Hollywood decorators and the rest of the business about taking herself uninvited to Winfield House and the other slights had been rankling her for weeks. "You just sit down," she told her friend. "You don't know a damned thing about it."

Trying to remain calm, she told Mrs. Loeb exactly what was wrong with the house, the host of repairs that had to be made, and the amount of time the work would consume as well as how worried she was about the project. Moreover, she expressed her irritation over the spreading of so many malicious rumors; their only possible source, she felt, was Evangeline Bruce.

Finally, with Nixon's assurances that he was doing everything within his mighty Presidential power to ease the appointment, the Annenbergs arrived in Washington on March 5, two days before the publisher was to appear before the Senate Foreign Relations Committee. Walter was extremely nervous and agitated, and, on the morning of March 6, he was in such a state that Lee became alarmed. At one point he clutched at his chest, gasping for breath; for a moment Lee thought he was dying.

The source of his suffering was an article in that morning's *Washington Post*. The paper printed a Drew Pearson column, and it bore out Annenberg's worst fears. The column's headline proclaimed "U.S. Will Ask: Is Annenberg Fit?" Pearson declared that "Annenberg's publishing empire was built up on the gang wars of Chicago and the illegal race wire ... Annenberg's father went to jail for cheating the government out of over $3 million and the ambassador was indicted for aiding and abetting him." Pearson further said that members of the

Foreign Relations Committee were "loath to tangle with a powerful newspaper publisher [who] has shown every disposition to throw the weight of his publishing empire against anyone who opposes him." Several Pennsylvania politicians who had felt the sting of "Annenberg's revenge," as the columnist put it, were listed in the article. One was Senator Clark, who had been a member of the Foreign Relations Committee until he lost his Senate seat.

With so much hanging in the balance, Annenberg was convinced that the Pearson column's appearance in the *Post*, much like the *Times* editorial, was part of a calculated effort to undermine him. The more he thought about it, the more furious he became. He finally decided to call the *Post*'s publisher Katharine Graham, who—despite *Newsweek*'s Karafin coverage—was an old friend. Now he felt that she had betrayed him. He and Lee had admired the forbearance Kay Graham had shown during the years of her husband's much-publicized mental illness and his tragic suicide in 1963. In light of the terrible time he himself had had as a result of Roger's suicide in 1962, Walter could well understand the agony she had suffered. Therefore, following Phil Graham's death, the Annenbergs had gone out of their way to console Mrs. Graham. They took her to dinner in Washington and had her as a weekend guest at Inwood, where they held a party in her honor in hopes of shaking her from her melancholy. Moreover, Annenberg thought the *Post*'s editorial stands showed more common sense under her direction. Like the *Philadelphia Inquirer*, the *Post* had supported Lyndon Johnson's Presidency in 1964 as well as his war effort. The *Post* too had supported Nixon in 1968.

The Pearson column, however, abruptly altered Annenberg's feelings toward Kay Graham. When his call got through to her, his words shot across the line like a hail of angry bullets. "God damn it, Katharine, what are you trying to do to me?" he demanded. "This is a vile attack on me and you know it." Walter went on and on, demanding to know how she could possibly allow the column to be printed, why she was trying to harm him. He saw his prospects for bringing greater honor to his name than he could ever have dreamed of being shattered like a crystal goblet struck by a sledge hammer. He spoke to the *Post*'s publisher so rapidly that his stammer worsened and that only made him angrier.

When she finally received a chance to speak, Mrs. Graham tried to soothe her fellow publisher's feelings. They were friends. Walter and

Lee had always been considerate and she especially appreciated their sympathy at the time of Phil's illness and death, a time when she was in pieces. She knew that Drew could be unfair at times. Nonetheless, she hadn't had anything to do with the column's appearance, which she tried to explain. The decision to print it was made by Ben Bradlee, the *Post*'s audacious editor. Bradlee was intent on turning the paper into one of the best in the nation, and his aggressive reporters were turning Washington upside down. The Pearson column was typical of the hard-nosed, irreverent stories he liked from his own staff as well as from columnists for hire. Despite, or perhaps because of, his brashness, Ben Bradlee had his boss's confidence. So when Annenberg asked Kay Graham again why the article was printed, she replied, "I went with Ben's judgment."

"God damn it, I know better than that," Annenberg snapped back. "That's not the way I run my paper."

"But it is the way I run mine," Mrs. Graham replied firmly.

He didn't believe her. Annenberg was editor as well as publisher of his *Inquirer*, and he took both jobs seriously. If the *Inquirer* launched an attack against someone of great prominence, Walter Annenberg not only knew about it and approved it, but often ordered it as well. His style of highly personalized journalism had fallen out of favor over the years, however, so that by the late 1960s the publisher's imprint had vanished from most metropolitan newspapers.

Mrs. Graham suggested that if he wanted to pursue the matter he talk to Ben Bradlee. The incident was embarrassing to the *Post*'s publisher. In a few days, she was to give a dinner for the Annenbergs in honor of the ambassadorial appointment, a way of reciprocating the hospitality they had shown her. She didn't want them upset with her. Therefore, she tried to make the impending party as pleasant as possible, and when she heard that David and Evangeline Bruce were arriving from London on the evening of the party, she asked them to attend. Bruce was an extremely gracious man. Unaware of any Annenberg-Bruce friction, Mrs. Graham believed that he and his wife would have a great deal to discuss with the Annenbergs. She saw Annenberg's appointment as inevitable, even if he didn't. Perhaps the unpleasantness would smooth over after Annenberg officially had the job, she thought. At least she fervently hoped so.

The Philadelphia publisher, of course, called Bradlee, but the conversation gave him little satisfaction. In his anger, Annenberg referred to Bradlee as a "dime-a-dozen editor" and in a lengthy harangue questioned his abilities as well as his credentials. Bradlee remembered years later that Annenberg "berated me for just about everything, every kind of failing an editor can possibly have." In truth, the *Post* editor hadn't spent much time weighing the delicate decision to print a column that was critical of another newspaper's publisher, and he was "glad that Katharine supported me when Annenberg complained." All told, Pearson wrote three columns that lambasted Annenberg, and Bradlee saw to it that all three were printed in the *Washington Post.*

Unfortunately for Annenberg, the Pearson columns weren't too different from what was being printed elsewhere. Since the announcement of his appointment, the press on both sides of the Atlantic had expressed dismay. Columnist Marquis Childs, for instance, found that "When the President named Walter Annenberg, the Philadelphia publisher and one of the most-valued clients of the Nixon law firm, to be ambassador to Britain, a muffled outcry arose from the professionals and those who looked on the Court of St. James as the star at the top of the diplomatic tree." Some publications even speculated that Nixon had made the appointment in retaliation for Prime Minister Harold Wilson's naming of John Freeman, a bitter Nixon critic, as the British ambassador to Washington. Worse, other periodicals depicted the appointment as a slap at the British nation. "If President Nixon had a sense of humor, he might have conceived of the designation of Walter Annenberg to be Ambassador to London as a monumental joke," the English magazine the *New Statesman* had snapped on February 28, 1969.

The chorus of press criticism only added to the anxiety Annenberg felt already. His terrible worries about Moses' past being made an issue were a reality as the *Washington Post* had made all too clear, and he concluded that former Senator Clark, his old political enemy, had had a hand in the Pearson column's preparation. Clark and Fulbright were friends, so Annenberg braced himself.

Thus when he appeared shortly before 10 A.M. on March 7 at Room 4221 in the New Senate Building, Annenberg's state of mind was one of turmoil. He hadn't slept well, and his head was ringing with the charges made in the Pearson column. Having no idea for the past several months what kinds of questions he would be asked, he had spent the time trying to prepare himself thoroughly on every aspect of the United Kingdom he could think of. He had read innumerable books, magazines and newspaper articles on the British economy, geography, history, society, culture and politics. There was little about Parliament, the monarchy and the monetary system that he didn't know. He had studied with a far greater intensity than he had ever studied in school, and his concentration on the subject matter was as singular as that which he focused on his businesses. Annenberg felt comfortable that he could field just about any question that might be thrown at him. Still, there was always the unexpected that never could be taken into account, and Walter Annenberg's life had prepared him to expect the worst.

When the committee convened, the first appointment on the agenda to be considered was that of Annenberg. Two other prominent men were to be judged for ambassadorial appointments as well. They were Jacob D. Beam, who was recommended for the ambassadorship to the Soviet Union, and John S.D. Eisenhower, the former President's son, who was slated to become ambassador to Belgium. The appearances of the latter two, of course, were considered *pro forma*, as the large number of spectators and members of the press who had convened well knew. But then there was Annenberg, the reason for the greater than usual turnout at such a committee hearing. There was still much uncertainty about his appointment, and everyone present realized that.

Speaking on Annenberg's behalf were two Republican Senators from Pennsylvania, Hugh Scott, who had always had cordial but not extremely close relations with the Philadelphia publisher, and Richard S. Schweiker, a liberal, who was relatively new to the Senate, since it was he who had toppled Clark a year earlier. Both men counted on the support of the *Philadelphia Inquirer* and they were grateful to Annenberg.

In paving the way for the publisher, Scott rattled off numerous awards Annenberg had received over the years, including such arcane honors as the Order of the Lion of Finland and Commander of the Order of the Crown of Italy, apparently in an attempt to show the candidate in an international light. Next, Senator Schweiker pointed out that Annenberg was "a hard-working editor for his paper and has taken upon himself the responsibilities of news editing, including an intensive knowledge and interest in international affairs." After the other two ambassadorial candidates were introduced in similarly glowing terms, Senator Fulbright settled into the serious business of cross-examining Annenberg. He skimmed over a few questions about the publisher's attitudes toward British politics and why he wanted to be an ambassador. Then Fulbright zeroed in on the Drew Pearson columns, which had made the publisher both heartsick and angry, and which had already ruined his friendship with Kay Graham.

> FULBRIGHT. That brings me to another matter which has appeared in the *Washington Post*. You are familiar with the *Washington Post*, I take it?
>
> ANNENBERG. I am, sir.
>
> FULBRIGHT. In recent days there have been articles about your appointment, in which it has been alleged that you have taken more than a casual interest in political matters, particularly in recent races in Pennsylvania. I think it would be good for the record to clear up some of these questions. I will read one or two items.
>
> ANNENBERG. Yes.

Fulbright ordered that the Pearson columns be read into the record. They contained the references to Moses' imprisonment, his involvement with Al Capone and gang warfare, all of which the columnist had said were juicy bits of gossip for the British. In addition, there were references to Annenberg himself and his *Philadelphia Inquirer* attacking figures as diverse as Charles de Gaulle and Joseph Clark.

> FULBRIGHT. I think that this is very interesting. The article goes on to say—and this again is a matter that you should be given an opportunity to comment on—"The Philadelphia Inquirer staff was instructed to play up Clark's chief Democratic rival, the late Justice Musmanno of the State Supreme court, and when Musmanno died just as Clark was running for re-election last year, Publisher Annenberg called his editor to instruct him in writing the obituary, to be sure to attribute part of the responsibility for Musmanno's death to Senator Clark. Is that true or untrue?
>
> ANNENBERG. Untrue.

A few minutes later, Fulbright brought up what Pearson said about the source of the Annenberg family fortune—"The Annenberg fortune was built up by Chicago gang warfare, and Walter's father, Moses Annenberg, was sentenced to four years for evading $3,259,000 in income taxes." Pearson, as usual, had some of the facts garbled, such as the length of the prison sentence and the amount of money involved, but in essence he had accurately identified the shameful burden that Annenberg had carried throughout his life.

"I think that should not be left unanswered," Fulbright said.

While the chairman was reading from the newspaper column, Annenberg tried to maintain a sense of decorum as the smoldering fires of his great humiliation were rekindled. Old wounds were once again reopened. He realized that the past was with him forever. Nevertheless, the years of steeling himself had made him resilient if nothing else. At length he answered. His response was slow, and the words were forced. He had to address the dark side of his past that he never wanted mentioned, but now it was unavoidable.

"Well that is a—that episode, is a tragedy in the life in the family, and for the past thirty-some years I have attempted to operate and I have actually found the tragedy a great source of inspiration for constructive endeavor," he said. "And I have sought at all times to engage in that which is wholesome. There is no question that a tragedy of such magnitude will either destroy you or inspire you to overcome it, and drive you on to deeds of affirmative character."

When he finished speaking, Annenberg was exhausted. A rustle of applause greeted his response, but he was too tense and tired to notice.

The questions continued, but they were from other members of the committee and lacked the hostile edge that had characterized Fulbright's queries. The probing explored his newspaper's role during the gubernatorial campaign of Milton Shapp, editorials criticizing de Gaulle, the merger of the Pennsylvania and New York Central railroads. The costs of maintaining an embassy and plans Annenberg had for restoring Winfield House were raised, as were concerns about the mission of an ambassador to Great Britain, United States-British relations, an ambassador's responsibilities, and the matter of how his company would operate if he were made an ambassador. At last the barrage ceased, and Annenberg was drained.

What was readily apparent was that he had won. His lifelong determination to conquer the past had worked. One by one, the Senators thanked him, and most of them gave their assurances that they would vote in favor of his appointment. Even Senator Clifford Case, whom he had known for the past forty-five years, ever since he and Case's brother, Williston, were roommates at the Peddie School, hadn't bothered to disqualify himself from voting. Case said he felt he could be objective about Annenberg's appointment and that he would cast an affirmative vote.

Suddenly, Annenberg realized that he was now the ambassador to

Great Britain. All of the fretting, the worry, the fear of disappointment, of rejection, were now over. The long years of hard work, of anxiousness, of always trying to prove himself, had borne fruit to a far greater degree than he had ever imagined possible. He only wished that his mother could have lived to witness the honor her son had achieved. She, of course, would have believed it only just that Boy attained such a level of prominence. It was Moses who would have been amazed that the son about whom he had always had such doubts could have traveled so far.

The rest of the Annenberg family was overjoyed. For Walter's seven sisters in particular, the office held special significance. They viewed their brother's appointment as a sign of vindication for the humiliating ordeal he had gone through with his father and for the pain that references to the past still caused them. The depth of feeling the sisters still harbored about what the family had undergone some thirty years ago was expressed by Enid. When she heard the news of his appointment, she turned to one of her editors at *Seventeen* and said, "That will show the bastards." As far as the Annenberg clan was concerned, that was the world at large.

Annenberg wanted to leave Washington immediately after his appearance before the Foreign Relations Committee hearings, but he still had one last duty to perform. That was attending the party that Katharine Graham had arranged for Lee and him, and he didn't want to go. The Pearson column still grated and he had a new reason to be rankled with the *Post*. The newspaper coverage of the confirmation hearings had stoked the fires of his anger. Warren Unna, the *Post* reporter who had covered the proceedings, had led his story off with an offhand comment by Annenberg that he was going to remove the massive bronze eagle that decorated the façade of the American Embassy in London. The eagle had become something of a symbol of American presence in London, and it had served as a source of levity during the hearings. One committee member, Senator Karl E. Mundt, the Republican from South Dakota, had remarked he was "proud of that eagle" and had jokingly wondered if Annenberg wanted to change the eagle in the President's seal as well. The bulk of the *Post* story dealt with the fate of the eagle, not with the seriousness of the occasion which the new ambassador believed the story had warranted.

Lee, who was intent upon smoothing over the quarrel with Kay Graham, knew her husband would rather just have had his butler pack his bags. Wanting to leave town on a more positive note, she coaxed him into attending the Graham dinner. Lee convinced him that they should go because the affair had been arranged so far in advance. Annenberg decided that he was big enough to "overcome the hurt and sting of the columns." Moreover, the dinner was in his honor, and he felt that he might as well start attending social functions that he really didn't feel like putting up with. All too soon, he realized, he would be forced to attend innumerable "official" dinners and receptions that would be given by and attended by people he had no use for.

The dinner was at Mrs. Graham's gracious townhouse in Georgetown, and Annenberg thawed a bit in his attitude toward her when he saw the impressive and painstaking care that had gone into the affair. There were about sixty politicians and socialites present, many of whom were friends of the Philadelphia publisher. But when he saw some of the guests, he felt the taste of anger returning. Ben Bradlee, for example, was in attendance, and Annenberg didn't think it was right that the man whose editorial judgment had almost ruined his chance to succeed should be at a party in his honor. To make matters worse, the Bruces were there. The ambassador and his wife had just arrived in Washington and it seemed that the moment they had set foot on American soil they had come to the dinner, even after the needling that the Annenbergs believed Evangeline Bruce was responsible for.

As his mood grew testier, Annenberg found himself becoming indignant about the seating arrangement, among other things. The party was in his honor, yet Annenberg was seated across the table from Mrs. Graham, not to her right which was where he felt he should have been. Both Annenbergs placed great emphasis upon doing what was socially correct at all times. Walter and Lee had never wanted to give anyone the least cause for comment that they didn't know what was proper, and they expected to be treated the same way. Instead, Annenberg was seated between Mrs. Bruce and Lorraine Sherman Cooper, the wife of Senator John Sherman Cooper from Kentucky. Adding to his discomfort over the seating plan was what he perceived as antipathy toward him on the part of the women flanking him. He expected as much from Mrs. Bruce, but he was surprised and dismayed when Mrs. Cooper, a woman he didn't even know, asked him what he perceived to be a catty question. "Do you think you can afford to run an embassy?" Mrs. Cooper asked.

While her husband was choking back his anger over the downhill nature of the evening, Lee herself was humiliated because she believed that Mrs. Bruce was snubbing her. Whenever she addressed Evangeline, Lee's remarks went unanswered, which she felt could have simply been because she hadn't heard them with all of the other conversation buzzing in the air. Thus after dinner, Lee sat very close to Mrs. Bruce and tried to talk to her, hoping she was wrong. She wasn't. "She ignored me so that I simply sat there out of embarrassment like a bump on a log," she recalled.

As far as Evangeline was concerned, however, there wasn't any problem. "There wasn't any tension at all, but I didn't even know the party was for them," she herself recalled. "I guess I'm just not as sensitive a person as I thought I was."

Annenberg, of course, instantly took note of such behavior and by the evening's end he was beside himself. Far from having smoothed over the ruptured friendship with Kay Graham, the dinner had resulted in adding insult to injury. When he was with the *Post* publisher in her living room, he no longer could restrain himself. He began berating her again for the Pearson column, and he brought up the story about his appointment hearing that had appeared in her newspaper, referring to reporter Unna as Mrs. Graham's "eunuch."

Mrs. Graham was used to the sensitivity of publishers. Ironically, as a group, they got more upset when anything adverse was printed about them or their publications than anyone else. Also, she had been exposed to Annenberg's ire once in the past when the *Post* and *Newsweek* had printed articles about Harry Karafin, and Triangle had removed its advertising from her news magazine. Still, she was surprised by the depth of his anger. She wished there was some way of making things right, but she didn't know what it could be.

Thus, the party proved to be a catastrophic failure. As they left, Walter told Lee that they would never speak to Katharine Graham again. As always when dealing with people or situations that were painful, he cut the offender out of his life. Indeed, when they saw her at several large functions after that, the Annenbergs turned their backs on Kay Graham. Years later, the *Post* publisher wondered seriously whether her paper should have run the Pearson columns. She simply hadn't known how raw a nerve had been touched.

CHAPTER

TWENTY-ONE

As THE EARLY days in London unraveled, Annenberg's anxiety about coming to grips with his new assignment didn't lessen. He liked to say that an editor's chair was the best possible training ground for any ambassador, because of the breadth of experience the position provided, but nothing had prepared him for this. He had managed in his career as head of Triangle Publications to become comfortable in the world of business and businessmen, and he had learned how to deal with politicians. But the universe of high society still intimidated him, and both he and Lee seemed to be walking on eggs, so intent were they upon doing what was right, what was proper. The idea of rubbing elbows with royalty and statesmen and have them judge him as the representative of the United States was awesome to Annenberg.

Thus, on the morning of April 29, 1969, Walter Annenberg, dressed in tails, white tie and top hat, was extremely nervous a he prepared to present his ambassadorial credentials to Queen Elizabeth II. He climbed aboard one of four gilded coaches, each bearing an ambassador and leisurely drawn by a pair of bay-colored horses and followed by liveried grooms. The colorful procession wended its way along the mile between the American Embassy and the palace, while Annenberg tried to think of the dignified thing to say to Her Majesty.

The pomp and splendor of the occasion was being recorded for posterity. The British Broadcasting Corporation, the government-owned television network, was preparing a film entitled *The Royal Family*, and one scene was to be the Queen receiving a new ambassador. Because of the unique relationship that existed between Great Britain and the United States, Annenberg was selected. The knowledge that the occasion was to be filmed added to the jitteriness he felt, and his nervousness heightened when his coach stopped before the palace. TV crews, cameras, lights, tape recorders and electrical wires snaking everywhere added to the confusion of crowds and the rituals that must be followed. Therefore, Annenberg was grateful when Dennis Greenhill, the British undersecretary of state, emerged from a cluster of dignitaries and greeted him. An extremely polished man, Greenhill tried to allay Annenberg's obvious anxiety. As he led the Ambassador to Room 1844, an elegant white-and-gold reception chamber overlooking the palace gardens, Greenhill reassured Annenberg as a protocol officer gave the publisher last-minute instructions: "When the doors open, we all take a pace forward with our left foot."

"With our left foot," Annenberg responded automatically.

He entered the room slowly, formally and bowed stiffly. The much-practiced line of greeting rolled off his tongue easily: "Your Majesty, I have the honor to present the letter of recall of my predecessor and my own letter of credence."

The Queen thanked him, and, as the cameras filmed, she passed a few pleasantries, including asking the Ambassador where he and his wife were living while Winfield House was being restored. All of London was talking about the restoration, which began literally the day the Annenbergs arrived.

"You aren't living at the Embassy at the moment, are you?" she asked.

"We're in the Embassy residence, subject, of course, to some of the discomfiture as a result of a need for, uh, elements of refurbishment and rehabilitation," Annenberg replied in a nervous tumble of stilted words.

The Queen looked somewhat uncomprehending for a moment and then a bit bemused at the obvious effect her presence had on the rich and powerful man before her. To smooth over the awkwardness of the moment and to spare the Ambassador any embarrassment, she asked Annenberg to present his staff, which he did gratefully.

In reality, the incident was a fleeting, slightly awkward moment. When the scenario was televised, however, the Ambassador's remarks soon became a source of great amusement. Annenberg's use of the word "refurbishment," while correct, wasn't in common usage in England and struck most Britons as odd. To the English, the Ambassador's reply had a peculiarly Micawberish ring to it, and in keeping with the irreverent, slightly wacky strain of British humor, newspapers began repeating his phrase and holding contests asking readers "Can You Top This?" Entrants were to submit examples of preposterous sentences and malapropisms. Within a short time, the word *refurbish* became part of the general vocabulary of Londoners.

Embarrassed at having the discomfort he had felt at the moment constantly in the press, Annenberg bristled. "I could hardly be expected to respond to Her Majesty as if I were attending a barbecue," he told a reporter for the *London Daily Mail.* "I chose my words carefully. They meant what I meant to convey. But remember this—being in the presence of your Queen, the ruler of so much and so many, is a most awe-inspiring occasion. Was I so wrong? I don't reckon so."

Indeed, the jokes about the presentation went on so long that they had wound up becoming merely tiresome. "I think my husband carried off a difficult situation extremely well," Lee told the same reporter. "Yet this remark keeps haunting us. It is so unfair."

The Annenbergs may have seized upon this one bit of negative press coverage to address because it was the easiest to deal with. In truth, newspapers and magazines were constant in their criticism of the new ambassador; they had started long before the Annenbergs arrived, and they continued raking him over hot coals. Annenberg appeared to be a perfect target. He was rich and his father had an unsavory background, including prison. Thus, he was frequently characterized as a parody of a rough, gauche Texas millionaire who didn't know a soup spoon from a shovel, and who felt he could buy anything—even an ambassadorship. If there was anything the British delighted in, it was condescending to Americans. If there was anything more sporting, it was mocking rich Americans.

The British press early on began treating Annenberg like a buffoon as a result of the 2,000-pound eagle that was mounted at the Embassy. To many people, the sculpture struck them as a symbol of American imperialism. Others found the eagle an example of American tastelessness. The attitude toward it was perhaps best summarized by Marcus Lipton, a Member of Parliament, who called the eagle a "blatant monstrosity." Annenberg, of course, became embroiled in the fate of the sculpture when he had mentioned, in passing during his Senate confirmation hearing, that he wanted it taken down because it was ugly. His position had first raised the wrath of John Rooney, the New York Congressman who chaired the House appropriations committee. The sculpture had been cast in Brooklyn, where Rooney's Congressional District was, and for some strange reason, he had apparently grown quite fond of the bird or else felt threatened by a challenge to his job as tsar of the appropriations committee. In any event, the Representative had let it be known that he would have it dismantled only over his dead body. Then Theodore Roszak, the sculptor, began threatening legal action if the work was taken down. "The eagle is an integral part of the embassy," Roszak said. Besides, he added, it would cost a fortune to rip the sculpture from the Embassy's steel beams.

The whole issue swiftly got out of hand. London newspapers expressed cries of outrage at the prospect of the eagle being snatched away. There were man-in-the-street interviews with Londoners, who claimed to be infatuated with the bird and who lovingly referred to it as "ours," not America's. The flap inspired further laughter in London drawing rooms, where a little ditty to mark the incident was circulating:

> Dear Mr. Ambassador Plenipotentiary,
> You may be the diplomats' choice of the century,
> With talent to spare on matters vice regal
> But please, if you will sir, don't harm our eagle.

In light of such waves of nonsensical criticism, Annenberg had relented. Before undertaking his new assignment, he had decided that "so long as the eagle does not bother me, I will not bother it. On the basis of this nonaggression pact, the eagle will continue to reign over the chancery."

Annenberg's problems with the press, however, were far more serious than the trivial issues of the eagle or his strange phraseology with the Queen. They were simply masks for a deeper bitterness. Numerous British commentators had seized upon the claims initially made in the American press that Annenberg wasn't fit for the office he had been given, and their venting their spleen against the new ambassador often had more to do with the unpopularity of the Nixon administration than it had with Annenberg. Nixon had made it clear, from his first days in office, that Great Britain could expect no favors that weren't earned, that the special relationship between the countries now had a hard edge of reality that hadn't quite existed before. Moreover, there was the war in Vietnam, which in many quarters of the British Isles was nearly as divisive an issue as it was in the United States. There was much criticism of the United States–Vietnam policy in the British press, as well as in other countries. Most American ambassadors were either silent on the issue of the war or quietly expressed doubts about the wisdom of the venture. Annenberg, as Nixon well knew, wholeheartedly supported the President, which also rankled many members of the press.

The ambassador's hawkish views and firm support of the Nixon White House came unexpectedly at an unusual forum. On May 28, he addressed the Pilgrims, an Anglo-American society founded in 1902 for a membership that included many business and government leaders. Over the years, the Pilgrims had become the shrine where a United States ambassador made his maiden speech, being guaranteed a warm reception by men of the world. Traditionally, such addresses were full of platitudes about what the two nations meant to one another. Annenberg's wasn't. He had told his staff that he wanted a tough speech on the "overprivileged young bums on college campuses" who criticized their President and his handling of the war. Annenberg was sick of what he perceived to be irresponsible young people, who didn't know enough to be grateful for what they had, criticizing a man of Nixon's stature. Thus, he rejected the first draft of his Pilgrims' speech, by Bobby Scott, his administrative assistant, and which was a mild, reasoned talk. The final version, which Annenberg largely wrote himself, painted a bleak portrait of the rumblings on American campuses.

"The time has come to call an end to giving in to students," the Ambassador told the gathering.

His face set in a stern mask and his eyes meeting those of the men in the Pilgrims' meeting room, he lashed out at university authorities for contributing to an "academic sickness" by their unwillingness to get tough with demonstrators. He scornfully dismissed citadels of higher education as "a sanctuary for violators of the law, and the time has come to call an end to giving in to students, an end to making decisions of expediency, an end to appeasement." When he got the matter off his chest, Annenberg was quite pleased with himself. The Pilgrims' gathering, however, wasn't quite sure how to respond to the criticism, and again much of the press coverage was negative. Nonetheless, Annenberg knew for certain that his address had met with a warm reception in Washington, if not in London. He received a congratulatory note from the White House.

Nixon's words of encouragement were the only ones he received during an otherwise bleak period of merciless criticism. On June 29, for example, Annenberg was attacked in newspapers on both sides of the Atlantic. *New York Times* columnist James Reston, in an acerbic criticism of Nixon, summarized what many people were saying: "President Nixon seems to be developing a weakness for the unavoidable blunder. Not satisfied with the agonies of unavoidable problems, he somehow manages to depart periodically from his normal caution and not only creates but plans unnecessary trouble. He didn't have to appoint Walter Annenberg, of all people, to London, of all places." Reston's jibe was reinforced by a "Progress Report on America's Ambassador," an article in the *London Sunday Telegraph*—"Unless Mr. Annenberg makes a swift recovery and learns to cope with the difficult British, it is safe to forecast that most London–Washington business will be done in Washington."

Annenberg was beside himself; he felt as if he were standing on quicksand. Nothing he did was on sure footing. Shortly after the *Times* and *Telegraph* articles, the British publication *The Diplomatist* noted that Annenberg in London "is still *persona incognita*. He has failed to attend a great many social functions where he could have been expected to come, and so far has refused to mix in the same friendly, open and winning way as his opposite member from the other superpower, the Soviet Ambassador, Mr. M. Smirnovsky." If ever Annenberg was dejected, it was when he was compared to his Russian Communist counterpart and came out on the short end. What few people realized was that he was merely following the advice of his embassy counselors. They wanted him to ease into the diplomatic world, knowing that he had no background whatsoever in the field. They had been led to believe that he was a blunt man who might say something embarrassing, and they tried to keep him from situations where he might say something he shouldn't.

In early July, Annenberg's situation worsened—but in Washington, not in London. The film clip of his presentation of his credentials to the Queen was being shown in State Department circles. Career diplomats held parties in Washington in order to show the film, and the ambassador was held up to further ridicule. One July 7, for example, columnist Joseph Kraft, who had been invited to one such viewing, noted in his column that a British commentator "speaking of an appearance by Mr. Annenberg on a TV show, refers to the American envoy 'played by Walter Matthau' . . . the fact is that, for perhaps the first time since the war, the British are out to get an American Ambassador."

The cumulative effect of such bad press became noticeable in a much more harmful way. While making one of his whirlwind tours of Europe, Henry Kissinger arranged to have dinner with British Prime Minister Edward Heath, and Nixon's foreign-policy adviser slighted Annenberg. A member of the anti-Annenberg faction when Nixon first appointed his publisher friend to the post, Kissinger hadn't wanted to be associated with what he apparently considered to be an obvious loser. Therefore, when he sought the meeting with Heath, he had no intention of inviting Annenberg. "Annenberg is a drawback," he told one of his aides. In addition, Kissinger was in the process of husbanding diplomatic power to himself and he was bent on undercutting all ambassadors, not just Annenberg. The British, however, weren't privy to Kissinger's Byzantine motives and were embarrassed by what appeared to be an oversight on his part. Thus, an English protocol officer invited the Ambassador to attend the dinner at No. 10 Downing Street, and Kissinger was furious.

There didn't seem to be an area that Annenberg wasn't mishandling, and his advisers in those early months may have been right in keeping him out of harm's way. For instance, he was less than discreet at dinner parties until his administrative aide Bobby Scott taught him a lesson one day. In the course of one of their conversations, Scott noted to his boss that he should be very careful about what he did and said in public. "You don't understand how gossipy London is," the aide told the Ambassador.

For his part, Annenberg didn't believe him and told Scott "people have a lot better ways to waste their time than just talking about me." On that note, Scott challenged him: "Give me five minutes and I'll tell you all about your dinner last night."

Scott's probing took less time than that. He was back in three minutes, giving Annenberg a thorough rundown on how much and what the Ambassador had had to drink, whom he sat beside and across from, how much and what he had eaten, and he repeated several expressions that Annenberg had used during the evening. Finally, Scott offered his most convincing argument. He told Annenberg that he hadn't even talked to anyone who had attended the dinner in order to get his information.

Robert Montgomery Scott, a socially prominent Philadelphia lawyer who had accompanied Annenberg to London as his administrative assistant, was invaluable to the ambassador. He was the son of Annenberg's old friends, Hope and Edgar Scott. With his sure instincts for hiring the kind of executive he needed, Annenberg had asked him to work for him. Scott was socially well connected on both sides of the Atlantic, and he could open many doors for the Ambassador. Although he had graduated from Harvard, his values were more those of the prep school Groton, the exclusive bastion of aristocratic Anglophiles that had changed little since its founding in 1884 to rear young gentlemen in the tradition of British public schools. Yet Scott wasn't a stuffy Main Liner. He was a charming, whimsical and intelligent man who got along well with everyone.

Because of the person he was to work for, Scott hadn't undertaken the job lightly. The publisher's stock among Scott's friends was abysmally low and they had long denounced his publishing practices. When it became known that he would be Annenberg's aide-de-camp, the most frequent question he found himself answering was "Why, for God's sake?" The depth of feeling his friends harbored was brought home to him forcefully one evening. Annie Winkleman, a friend, gathered ten guests at her home for a going-away party for Scott and his wife. Late in the evening, when brandy was being sipped, one guest finally stood up and asked point-blank, "How can you work for that bastard?" The four other men present also demanded an explanation, while their wives grew anxious and Scott sat in quiet embarrassment. It was as if he betrayed them all, as if he became a traitor to his class.

Mrs. Winkleman believed she knew why he took the job. "Bobby felt he had to protect this man," she said. For Scott, however, there was no such altruism involved in his action. At age forty, he was restless. His life was as routinized as it had been when he was ten years old and there were riding and dancing lessons and dozens of other rites to perform. His life was always a series of comfortable, lock-step movements, as predictable as a very expensive Swiss clock. Scott enjoyed his life with his wife, son and two daughters and their gracious Main Line estate and being on the boards of the Philadelphia Art Museum and the Academy of Music and the rest of it. But Annenberg offered to alter temporarily what he saw as the undeviating path to his grave. Moreover, he felt that he would be good in London. What had finally convinced him to take the assignment was a newspaper column that said Annenberg wasn't qualified to be ambassador. When musing about the job he was offered, he concluded, "Well, I wasn't qualified either." What he hadn't expected was the amount of criticism his new boss received and he quietly set about doing whatever he could to cast the Ambassador in a more positive light.

Compounding the troubles he experienced, Annenberg had to live with the social sniping of Evangeline Bruce. Annenberg always found David Bruce personally to be an extremely gracious man, but Evangeline was driving the Annenbergs to distraction. To Walter and Lee's dismay, and to the amazement of a good many other people, the Bruces were still in London when the Annenbergs arrived and they stayed on. Usually, a former ambassador leaves the country where he served and doesn't return for at least a year, so that his successor can settle into the job more easily. At Evangeline's insistence, the Bruces remained at an apartment they had bought in London. Their presence was a constant source of irritation to the Annenbergs, who were so nervous about accepting the asssignment to begin with.

In addition to being annoyed by the rumors about the redecorating of Winfield House, Lee was smarting over the absence of the social engagement book that had mysteriously disappeared before she arrived. The book was a critical social tool, since it contained the names, addresses and telephone numbers of people who were considered essential contacts. Some social observers of the Annenberg-Bruce situation found the scenario as amusing as a Restoration Period comedy. They believed that Mrs. Bruce had either conveniently lost the book or had simply taken it with her when she moved her salon from the Embassy to her new residence. Evangeline herself found it preposterous that anyone should think she was capable of such an act. "The social records . . . *mine* were all there and I even left little notes of explanation," Mrs. Bruce recalled. Nonetheless, the rumors persisted.

As a result of the obvious friction between the old and the new ambassadorial hostesses, London society was divided into two uneasy camps. There were people who associated with the new ambassador for the usual political and business reasons, but there were others, staunch friends of Mrs. Bruce, who continued coming to Embassy dinners, but who made a point of not reciprocating. They didn't want to be disloyal to Evangeline.

For their part, the embittered Annenbergs didn't go out of their way to endear themselves to the Bruce clique. They openly disdained the Bruces for having lived in a house that was in such poor condition without having done anything to fix it. Moreover, Annenberg, who was a stickler for etiquette, commented upon a lack that he found incredible in someone of breeding. "The Bruces didn't even use finger bowls," he told others.

Annenberg found such an infraction of the rules all the more glaring in a man of Bruce's reputation as a man of impeccable taste and manners. He was quick to find fault with the man whose shadow still fell so heavily upon him. The real source of their problem, the Annenbergs believed, however, was Evangeline, who, they felt, tried to look down upon them. In 1945, Bruce divorced Ailsa Mellon, the only daughter of Andrew W. Mellon, the multimillionaire industrialist and former Secretary of the Treasury, and a short while later he had married Evangeline Bell, the daughter of a mid-level career Foreign Service officer. Neither of the Annenbergs could find anything in Evangeline's background that gave her a right to criticize them, and they resented her attitude enormously.

"The Bruces didn't think we were part of the Establishment, but all they did was show their own ignorance," Annenberg recalled. "They stayed on and made my job exceedingly difficult, and Mrs. Bruce tore us down whenever and wherever she could."

Thus, with Mrs. Bruce's recommendation, many Londoners dismissed Annenberg as a thoroughly banal man, a role which in his uneasiness at times he fell into. One rainy day at White's, the renowned museumlike club, where lackadaisical aristocrats as well as prominent politicians and business leaders gathered, Annenberg was standing by a window in one of the reading rooms. To no one in particular, he made a pronouncement, the kind that sounded like his elocution lessons and to bystanders meant even less: "The rain is pouring down with determined resolution." He had spoken out loud just to say something and break the gloomy silence, and also because he was preoccupied by his problems. The rolling out of the nonsensical phrase merely made the handful of club members present think that the press was right after all. The new ambassador didn't have much under his hat. Then there was the occasion when he sat next to the wife of the Italian ambassador and his attempt at humor fell flat. When making small talk, he said to her, "We should get along very well. I love spaghetti."

It mattered little who was at fault, because the Annenbergs and their friends were going to be criticized no matter what. In July, for example, Lee commissioned Lady Elizabeth Anson, Queen Elizabeth's cousin and a professional party organizer, to give a party for Tricia Nixon who was visiting Winfield House. The Annenbergs had known Tricia since she was a little girl and they were anxious for the then twenty-three-year-old Miss Nixon to have a good time while she stayed with them. The turnout of young royalty for the affair was great, including Princess Anne, the Queen's eighteen-year-old daughter, and Prince Michael, the Queen's first cousin and a godchild of Franklin D. Roosevelt. The prince spent much of the evening dancing with Tricia in the ballroom of Claridge's, the elegant London hotel, which was decorated for the occasion with thousands of pink and red roses bathed in pink light. The evening seemed a success in every way. Yet newspapers the next morning sneered at the event and jokingly referred to Tricia as a "fair princess," who was so dumb that when asked questions by reporters, she had had to take her cue from Lee Annenberg.

Even when Annenberg made special attempts to be more sociable, he was chastised. After presiding over a series of let's-get-acquainted lunches for business and labor figures, the press took him to task. The *Daily Express* in one article referred to them as "Expensive Slices of 'Instant Britain' on Ambassador Annenberg's Menu."

Besides the dismaying criticism, Annenberg was annoyed at times by the rinkydink level of some of the chores thrust upon him. He was used to orchestrating the operations of a company worth hundreds of millions of dollars and had legions of employees to cater to his whims. Now it sometimes seemed as though the tables were reversed; an ambassador was at everyone else's command. One evening, for instance, he received a call asking him to find the wig that had been left at the Embassy by Mrs. Stephen Smith and send it immediately by diplomatic pouch to her in care of her sister, Mrs. Sargent Shriver. "No, I won't send Mrs. Smith's wig to Mrs. Shriver via diplomatic pouch," Annenberg replied icily. Nevertheless, he did have someone locate the wig and, as requested by the caller, he had it sent to St. John Stevas, a Member of Parliament, who was attending the same party as Mrs. Smith that evening. Annenberg grumbled about the nonsense of it all for days.

Besides grappling with the swirl of criticism and learning a new job, Annenberg was still running his company. The way he operated, he could command the various Triangle divisions from anywhere. The only function he had abandoned was that of editor of the *Inquirer*, something he had said he would give up when he appeared before the Foreign Relations Committee. His division heads continued to send him weekly reports, which he had long demanded. Since he only closely questioned them when he felt something was amiss, that was the way he continued to act. He called frequently, just as he had always done, in order to keep on top of developments or make suggestions. "Sometimes, he wouldn't get back from some function he had had to attend and it would be well after midnight in London, but he still called even though you could tell from the way he sounded that he was very tired," Panitt recalled. There was never any doubt at Triangle that Annenberg was still very much in charge.

There were times too when Annenberg needed to hear a friendly voice, one that had nothing to do with business or politics or intrigue in Washington or the State Department. Often as not, the voice was Philadelphia Police Commissioner Rizzo's. Rizzo always knew the latest Philadelphia gossip, who was in and who was out of trouble and what was happening politically. The policeman and the Ambassador also discussed Rizzo's own growing political ambitions, and Annenberg frequently urged him to run for mayor. He believed that the Commissioner's law-and-order approach was what was needed at a time when it appeared to him that student radicals had more of a say in government than did duly elected officials. Rizzo, as usual, played on his relationship with the publisher. Annenberg, he boasted to friends, would contribute a million dollars if he ran for mayor.

On top of his other worries, Annenberg was led to believe that he was in actual physical danger. The Jordanian ambassador had told him he was the easiest mark in London for an assassin and had urged him to take great precautions. So the American Ambassador was now trailed everywhere by two hulking bodyguards whose presence he found stifling. On one occasion, a visit to Scotland, he did receive a kidnap threat, which made him think that there might be something to the suggestion that he could be harmed. He told Nixon about the threat, but he also spelled out the way he wanted any situation handled if he were actually seized by terrorists. "Don't pay ransom of any kind," he wrote to the President. "Governments can't be blackmailed."

By the end of the first summer of his tenure, Annenberg's situation was bleaker than he ever imagined it would be. The press was hounding him. He had acted foolishly on several occasions. Instead of earning the respect of his host nation, he was being sneered at. The honor that he hoped to achieve for his family seemed to be eluding him wherever he sought it. With increasing frequency, he paid solitary visits to Westminster Abbey, which he found to be a sanctuary from the jumble of problems he confronted. In the solitude of the Abbey, he developed a definition of what an ambassador was, one that he hoped would inspire him to get through this latest trying period of his life—"An ambassador is the personal representative of the President. If a person has the President's ear and knows American politics, society and economics, and is willing to learn, that should be enough. If the President knows you well and believes in you, that is what it is all about." He returned from the Abbey with some of his tenseness diminished, somewhat soothed by his meditations.

During that long summer, the mood at both the Embassy and Winfield House was subdued. The staffs at both places felt sorry for the Annenbergs. They had so much to learn. At times, some of his aides wondered if Annenberg himself questioned whether he should have accepted the appointment, although he steadfastly maintained that he had walked into it with his eyes open. Those who got to know him, however, realized that he was a man who had to make great effort to enter the public life that was demanded of anyone in his position. They realized how little he liked cocktail parties, crowds and going to dinners or other social functions night after night. They realized what a toll it took on him when coupled with the unfortunate way his ambassadorship was going. Several times, an embassy officer or a servant who unexpectedly entered his study found the Ambassador silently weeping. They discreetly left, hoping that he hadn't noticed their intrusions.

Yet another problem the Annenbergs had to deal with was the way they were forced to live at the moment. Walter and Lee, who were used to living with a grand elegance that only great wealth can provide, found themselves cooped up in several rooms atop the massive Winfield House. The residence was in a state of chaos as it was being done over. There were ladders and buckets and paint and plaster and rolls of wallpaper scattered everywhere. Wires dangled from ceilings and walls, and came up through floors. Billy Haines and Ted Graber were a whirlwind of activity, making ever-increasing demands on workers in order to meet the November deadline that the Annenbergs gave them.

The decorators found that dealing with British tradesmen made working with their American counterparts seem like the easiest thing in the world. The workmen seemed to spend most of their time drinking endless amounts of tea when they weren't plying their tasks with the enthusiasm of a chain gang. Annenberg came to refer to one particular room that was being specially painted as the "Sistine Room," because, he said, it took the painters longer to finish than it took Michelangelo to complete the Sistine Chapel. At one point, Graber became so exasperated after finding a group of carpenters playing cards in the basement that he lined up all the workers and chewed them out like a drill sergeant until the embarrassed Englishmen realized the decorators were serious about getting a day's work out of them.

One day at the Embassy, Annenberg himself took out his frustrations on Haines and Graber when they had stopped by his office. An aide recalled Annenberg yelling at the pair for real or imagined sins until Lee entered and told him to stop. Lee seldom rebuked her husband for anything and she only did that when she believed, as in this case, that he was being unfair. "You owe these men an apology," she told her husband. She wheeled about and said to the decorators, "Come with me, boys." The three marched out together. Later that afternoon, a chastened Ambassador came back to Winfield House and called Lee by a nickname that he frequently used. "Mother?" he said as he tested the emotional weather he was walking into. The decorators received an apology.

The staffs Annenberg worked with got to know a different man from the one portrayed in the press. He applied the same logic to running the embassy that he did to his businesses, and thus proved to be an extremely able administrator. He realized his limitations and bluntly told people, such as Bill Galloway, the political counselor, and Jack Hurfort, the head of consular affairs, that as long as they conducted their operations the way they should be, he would leave them pretty much alone. Moreover, he didn't try to emulate David Bruce and become an international *éminence grise*. In any event, the role of embassies and ambassadors under Nixon and Kissinger was changing faster than ever. The trend of the past several decades of concentrating the decision-making process in Washington was speeded up, and Nixon was having trouble getting the idea across to some career diplomats in particular that their role was no longer that of a decision maker or catalyst for change. Of course, he had no problems with Annenberg on that score.

"I had to impress people that the day when ambassadors made foreign policy was over—when people like William Bullitt who had actually made policy while he was an ambassador under Roosevelt—that time was gone," Nixon said. "Being ambassador is important work, but frankly it is particularly so on the business side, seeing that American business is properly represented."

Thus, the career officers in London cast around to define their role more closely. They decided to turn themselves into the best possible reporting group they could be. Once this decision was reached, Galloway and others urged Annenberg to use his position to build and strengthen good will and not to try and reverse what was taking place in Washington. Annenberg agreed, not that he ever had any intention of trying to buck Nixon's diplomatic role. "You gentlemen have the professional qualifications for what you are doing," the Ambassador told Galloway. "Behave as you feel you should and bring major things to me." Thus, he gave them the same philosophy to follow that he always gave his executives.

The staff found their boss to be a quick study, who carefully read reports that crossed his desk. He questioned them about issues he found unclear, and he never acted unsure of himself. Many of his aides found his attitude refreshing, especially with regard to the latitude he gave them. They were used to being constantly second-guessed by Bruce or other ambassadors in other nations where they had served, and Annenberg never requested of them the demeaning tasks that often came a Foreign Service officer's way. For instance, he never asked for favors such as getting visas quickly for friends or friends of friends. He played it so straight that he even refused to allow State Department employees to take advantage of diplomatic immunity when it came to parking or traffic tickets, a perquisite that embassy workers around the world took for granted. "I was rather aghast at the amount of immunities invoked by other missions, especially the so-called developing, or free-loading nations," he recalled. "I wouldn't let my people do that, because it isn't right."

There were some people on the staff who continued insisting that Annenberg was a "fool," but many of them found this gruff man who bellowed like a wounded bull when his phone wasn't working had an earthy charm. Ted Smith, the embassy caterer, for example, frequently prepared Annenberg a lunch of "peasant food," as he called the Ambassador's favorite dish of a hamburger with a lot of ketchup and a can of Campbell's ham and bean soup. It had to be Campbell's, Annenberg explained, because he had stock in the company, had been a director, and therefore owed the company his allegiance. Often after bringing Annenberg his lunch, Smith sat and talked with him while he ate. Their conversations ranged from sports to the good price Smith had gotten on a case of Château Lafite Rothschild. Once Smith told him the price of a case of wine that he had recently purchased for 55 pounds had soared to 330 pounds several weeks later. "He loved to hear such things," Smith recalled. "It was like he had made another million dollars."

As Annenberg became more sure of himself, staffers found the Embassy atmosphere charged with excitement whenever "The Chief," as they had taken to calling the Ambassador, entered. He relaxed around the people he worked with in a way that he hadn't yet learned to achieve in public. His booming "Hello" filled corridors and gave many employees a sense of fun that in the dignified surroundings had never existed before. One of the informal touches that they enjoyed was his bestowing nicknames upon people. Joan Auten, who arranged embassy travel plans, for example, was dubbed "Rover," because she was always roaming off somewhere. There were other peculiarly Annenberg touches as well that the staff found both unusual and admirable. When an elderly waitress became ill, Annenberg demanded that the best treatment be found and he paid for everything. Another time, he saved a young foreign officer's reputation after the man was caught in a compromising homosexual encounter. Annenberg quietly let the matter drop; he rarely made moral judgments about what people did in their bedrooms.

Miss Auten summarized the feelings of many of her colleagues. "It was all very nice. Usually ambassadors and their wives don't do such things, but the Annenbergs were very attentive to the people who worked for them. When he was having a birthday, Mrs. Annenberg brought a cake to the Embassy, and they invited us in to have a glass of wine and some cake. It was little things like that that people found endearing. It created a nice, warm atmosphere, which hadn't been here before."

As they came to know him, Annenberg's vulnerability became apparent and, like his Triangle staff, embassy aides became protective of him. An example of this occurred one day when the Ambassador sneaked away without his ever-present bodyguards. The first person to notice was Ted Smith, who, when he realized the seriousness of the situation, was beside himself with worry: "I ran to the political counselor and said 'Christ Almighty, the Ambassador went out alone.' I put on my coat and went out looking for him and then I saw him sitting in a little Italian restaurant nearby. I didn't know what the hell to do, so I hid there watching him until he finished and went back. I didn't know what the hell I would do if something happened, but I knew that I wanted to be there."

Men like Galloway and Hurfort, sophisticated men who had worked for many career ambassadors as well as political appointees, also found themselves drawn to him as they hadn't been to other men they had worked for. Hurfort was especially amused by phrases that Annenberg routinely uttered and that he found himself repeating to other people. Soon, whenever he heard an "Annenbergism," he wrote it down. His black notebook became filled with such sayings as "Those of us running around with a loaf of bread under each arm can't complain" and "He has all the qualities of a dog—except loyalty."

One day, Hurfort was offered the job of heading the United States mission in Bermuda, and he informed Annenberg. He was nearing retirement age and the mission was a way to bow out of the service gracefully, although it was hardly the kind of prestigious post that he had hoped would cap his career. He worried that if he rejected the job, the next post he was offered with little chance of turning down would be in one of the innumerable hostile, dull or uncomfortable places where Foreign Service officers earn their living. What he preferred, he told Annenberg, was to remain in London, if he weren't to become an ambassador himself. "Don't worry," the Ambassador replied. "I'll call the President and have you kept here."

The prospect of having the President interrupted by a telephone call about his career upset Hurfort terribly. "For God's sake, no!" he exclaimed.

Instead, Annenberg wrote Nixon a note, still thinking it would have been easier just to pick up the phone. In any event, he saw that Hurfort stayed in London. "You know me and my ways," Annenberg told him. "Yours is the largest section of the Embassy, and it gives me no trouble."

Annenberg was working hard. More than anyone else at the Embassy, he believed Nixon's assessment that an ambassador in the new era should be representing what was best for American business. One important issue that he was playing a key role in developing was the proposed merger between British Petroleum and Standard Oil Company of Ohio. The British wanted to participate in the American oil market through the proposed merger, but they were running into widespread opposition in the United States. There was a growing Congressional clique that was opposed and some members of the Nixon cabinet didn't like the idea of a foreign company having a say in a company that would control a vital resource. There was the strong possibility that the Justice Department would bring an antitrust action against the merger. Annenberg, however, took a broader view of the situation. For years, American oil companies were fairly free to invest and expand in the British retail oil market and they were able to bid on Britain's highly important North Sea gas developments. Therefore, he reasoned, not only was the American opposition unfair in terms of what they themselves were doing, but a xenophobic approach could spell disaster in the future when American oil companies wanted to expand their operations in the North Sea, which appeared to be inevitable. If the British were thwarted in the Standard Oil venture, it wasn't unlikely that they would see that the same thing happened to Americans in the future. The Ambassador went to great lengths to calm the protectionists at home and reassure the British. He let his voice be heard at the White House and eventually he prevailed. The merger was approved and Annenberg received much of the credit.

"Whenever it came to matters of business, I listened to what Annenberg said," Nixon recalled. "He always knew what he was talking about; he understood business matters better than anyone else."

Thus, while he was being criticized in other quarters, Annenberg began developing the respect of the British business community, and executives of American companies weren't bashful about bringing him their problems. Executives of McDonald Corporation, for instance, asked him how best to open their fast-food outlets in Britain, and American banks solicited his advice on opening London branches without contributing to the hostility the British banking community was already showing to such moves. The banking issue in particular was thorny, because so many American banks were anxious to have international outlets in order to tap the growing Eurodollar market and operate worldwide. The problem the American banks ran into was a complaint among British bankers that the Americans were disturbing the entire system by raiding them for employees and paying them much more than the prevailing wage. Annenberg heard the complaint all too often, so he suggested to the Americans that they employ retired bank workers, a labor pool that wasn't considered competition. Most of them still needed employment, if only part time, in order to make ends meet. The banks followed his advice, and the situation was defused.

While he was tending to the business affairs of others, Annenberg was giving a great deal of thought to one of his own holdings as well. He was considering taking a step that had occurred to him often, over the past decade especially, but which no one ever believed he would undertake. He was seriously considering selling the *Philadelphia In-quirer*. The issue was again on his mind, because in October 1969 Sam Newhouse, the head of the Newhouse newspaper chain, offered to acquire both the *Inquirer* and the *Daily News* in a package deal for $55 million, which Annenberg believed was a fair price. As further inducement, Newhouse told him that he could continue as publisher of the *Inquirer* for life.

Periodically, rumors swept Philadelphia that Annenberg was selling the *Inquirer* and they had always been denied. Only the previous February, as a result of the buzzing about his going to the Court of St. James, the rumor mill had had the *Inquirer* and the *News* on the block again. On February 21, a small box had appeared in the paper denying the sale: "I have no intention whatever of disposing of the *Philadelphia Inquirer* or the *Daily News*," the publisher told his readers.

The Newhouse offer came at a different time of his life, however, and Annenberg gave it more serious thought than he had given any other proposal to acquire the papers. He realized that the time had come when he must stop vacillating. He either had to sell or make the major capital investment that the papers needed. The news operation needed to be overhauled, the printing presses wouldn't last much longer, union agreements had to be negotiated to allow for automation that would do away with the jobs of many printers. The litany of the paper's needs and the amount of cash required to fulfill them was enormous. He decided to sell.

Though his decision was a business one, other factors, of course, were weighed as well. The *Inquirer* was his legacy, the one property that gave him power in political and social circles. Moreover, giving up the paper meant discarding the greatest gift his father had ever given him, the tool that had led to his respectability and eventual honor as an ambassador. With Roger's death seven years earlier, Annenberg had realized with a sorrowful finality that no one would inherit the property, although he had always known in his heart that his son would never have wanted to be a publisher if he had lived. His daughter, Wallis, was married and had children of her own, and he never envisioned her becoming a businesswoman.

Another consideration was the very important position he now held, which he viewed as a hard-won prize in the unending struggle of his life. The ambassadorship resulted in far greater prestige than he believed possible, and though events of the moment were working against him, he had made up his mind with the same determination that he had displayed when he took over his father's company that he would succeed. Sunnylands was yet another consideration. When building the home he realized that it meant that he would spend much less time in Philadelphia, which also eroded in his eyes the value of owning the paper. Thus, from the perspective of London, the newspapers had lost much of their luster and importance, much the way Philadelphia itself had. When asked by James Callaghan, the British Home Secretary, for example, whether he liked London as much as Philadelphia, Annenberg, as usual, hadn't minced his words. "Jim, I have an infinite affection for Philadelphia, but I regard it as a bush-league London," he replied. The remark, which was made half in jest, stung many members of Philadelphia's blue-blooded aristocracy, and it served to remind them why they disliked the publisher.

Annenberg had still another serious factor to figure into his equation when considering the sale. His concentration of media power in Philadelphia was enormous and was being called into question. The previous July an embittered Milton Shapp had asked the Federal Communications Commission not to renew the license of Annenberg's WFIL-TV on the grounds that Annenberg had a "near news monopoly" in the Philadelphia area. Through Triangle, Shapp pointed out, Annenberg controlled the radio stations WFIL AM and FM, the *Inquirer*, the *Daily News*, *TV Guide* and three television stations in other Pennsylvania markets. In his petition, Shapp brought up the 1966 gubernatorial-election coverage of the *Inquirer* and said that it was a "personal vendetta against me . . ." He charged that within the various Triangle publications the "news has been censored, omitted, twisted, distorted, and used for personal vengeance and other personal purposes . . . the *Philadelphia Inquirer* and other media controlled by Walter Annenberg are and have been used to poison the political life of Pennsylvania and to attack the fabric of the democratic process."

Such an emotionally charged challenge wasn't to be taken lightly. Annenberg knew that the concentration-of-media argument was being used in attempts to block the renewal of the *Boston Herald-Traveler*'s license to operate WHDH-TV, the *San Francisco Chronicle*'s KRON-TV, and WCCO-TV in Minneapolis, which was controlled by Cowles and Ridder publishing interests.

Thus, in light of all the arguments against keeping the *Inquirer*, Annenberg decided to sell. Shapp's bid before the F.C.C. failed, but in the end his effort to dismantle the Annenberg media empire had worked. "The time to blow the whistle is when you realize you should blow it on yourself," Annenberg said. "I developed such an awareness, a dread of vulnerability that when I contemplated sitting in Philadelphia with morning, evening and Sunday papers, AM and FM radio and TV operations and *TV Guide* . . . No one in the country had that media concentration in one market." He had learned long ago not to make himself vulnerable to government powers and, when he realized he had done so, he moved swiftly to head it off.

Annenberg told Newhouse that he was seriously considering the offer, but before he could act, he had promised John Knight that if he ever decided to sell, he would give Knight the first opportunity to buy. He had made the promise to Knight years earlier when they both attended a Gridiron dinner in Washington, where the press corps roasts the nation's politicians as the evening's entertainment. "I am obligated as a gentleman to keep my word and tell Knight about your offer," he told Newhouse. Besides, E. Z. Dimitman urged him to sell to Knight, because the old editor considered Knight papers better than those Newhouse published.

When he was told the Philadelphia papers were on the market, Knight's interest was rekindled, but, before committing himself, he wanted to know whether the properties were worth the $55 million price tag. Thus, Knight executives studied the papers before deciding whether the deal should go through. When they gave their O.K., Lee Hills, a top executive, was sent to London to negotiate the sale. Annenberg was inflexible on the price, but he wasn't asking for the lifetime publisher's role that Newhouse was offering. Instead, he said he would take a ten-year consulting fee of $150,000 a year as well as the title "publisher and editor emeritus" on the masthead. He insisted also that he retain his twelfth-floor offices in the *Inquirer* tower as part of the deal.

As the time approached to complete the transaction, John Shively Knight began getting cold feet. Buying the *Inquirer* meant borrowing big money and now he wasn't sure that he really wanted the properties. When he voiced reservations, he later said, his executives countered that the Philadelphia papers struck them as a good opportunity. When the vote of the Knight board was taken, the ayes had it in favor of buying the papers. Knight himself later claimed that he had abstained.

Thus, on October 29, the *Inquirer* carried the news of the sale as the major front-page story. The sale was announced on October 28, much to the amazement of the *Inquirer* and *Daily News* staffs, with the exception of a few key editors, including Dimitman and Gillen. Knight gave Annenberg $14 million in cash as well as a series of notes for $41 million, the interest rate on the notes pegged to the prime rate, an agreement that seemed reasonable at the time but which would soon rankle Knight when the prime rate crept higher and higher.

The publishers issued statements jointly, which were carried in the *Inquirer:*

> With the passing of my only son, there is no likely possibility of family transference and hence my desire to insure a future ownership in which I have confidence.
>
> I have invited John S. Knight and his organization to take on this responsibility because of their consistent record of community service and leadership. I have devoted my best energies to advancing the welfare of our city, state and nation, and it is vital to me to see this work continued. . . ."

Knight's statement noted that Annenberg's "determination to make the *Inquirer* one of America's leading newspapers has been crowned with unusual success. His dedication to his country, the State of Pennsylvania and the City of Philadelphia has brought him richly deserved recognition and honor. . . . We foresee further development and growth of the *Inquirer* and the *Daily News* as they continue to pursue the worthy objectives which best serve this area."

Though the sale appeared to go smoothly, the transaction very rapidly brought forth bitter feelings on the part of both publishers. Annenberg quickly heard that Knight was complaining about the deal. The Miami publisher told friends he had paid too much, that he hadn't gotten what he had bargained for, and that he hadn't wanted to go through with the buy in the first place. "I was hearing from different people that Knight was a bad loser who went around saying he was against the deal," Annenberg recalled. "Poor boy."

As more people told him of the complaints, however, Annenberg himself became angry. "Knight was saying that Lee Hills and the others on the board had outvoted him while he was saying the papers were worth no more than $20 million or $30 million," Annenberg recalled. "That's a joke. Knight being outvoted by Lee Hills and the other stooges on his board is like the Ayatollah saying he's capable of being outvoted by the mullahs."

Whatever the reality of the case, Knight was saying that he had been taken. One reason why he was suffering was that the prime rate to which the $41 million in notes he owed Annenberg was pegged had climbed to 12 percent shortly after the acquisition, which meant he was paying an unexpected and costly premium for the papers. Moreover, the executives who favored the acquisition had bought many unknowns. Annenberg, naturally, had kept his books close to the vest when negotiating, but the Knight people were dismayed by the extent of the problems they encountered. The papers had made money for Annenberg, but there was a lot of price cutting in order to get ads as a result of competition from the *Bulletin.* Production was frequently behind schedule, and there was a great deal of overstaffing of many departments, including accounting and promotion. Circulation was mismanaged, and because of Annenberg's paternalism a great many unproductive workers were on the payroll. One of the costliest woes they encountered was having to replace the printing presses, which they should have realized if they had examined them before the sale. In short, they had inherited the problems that Annenberg knew the papers suffered from for years.

Annenberg, for his part, believed he had another reason to resent the aftermath of the sale. Word seeped back to him that the Knight people considered his *Inquirer* to have been a shoddy product. One indication he had of their feeling was that while he was paid his annual consulting fee, he was never called, his advice was never sought. "They go around bragging how great they are compared with the previous owner," he said.

At the time of the sale, Annenberg had been under the impression that John Knight would personally run the paper and that notion too was rapidly dispelled. John S. Prescott, Jr., a manager, was assigned to run the paper's business side, and John McMullen came from the *Miami Herald* as executive editor. Annenberg learned that the Knights didn't hold the *Inquirer* under his regime in high regard when McMullen, himself a blunt man, told everyone that the paper was a "throwback. . . . It had biased, ineffectual coverage." Indeed, the executive editor found police reporters who couldn't write a story and writer-reporters who had been elevated from the ranks of police reporters who still couldn't write. Few beats were covered, and there was no system for recruiting news people. To remedy this situation, he swept away as many old Annenberg staffers as he could, and, in his two-and-a-half-year tenure, replaced every department head but one, as well as eighty reporters and editors. In the process, he earned the title "Knight's hatchetman." John Gillen remained with the title managing editor, but he was stripped of his authority.

McMullen's new policies offended more than just the old *Inquirer* employees. Under his direction, the *Inquirer* no longer printed the police's version of every story, and stories that were critical of police in certain instances began appearing.

Commissioner Rizzo, perhaps more than anyone else, was not only amazed that the *Inquirer* would print stories that were damaging to his department, but he was mad, and he wanted a meeting with McMullen to discuss the situation. In the company of Gillen, McMullen had dinner with Rizzo one evening at the Barclay Hotel, and, if anything, the encounter made the Commissioner angrier than ever. When Rizzo asked why the critical stories were printed, the editor recalled telling him, "I don't think the *Inquirer* has been independent of the police." McMullen said that Rizzo replied with a lightly veiled threat that there were numbers writers working at the *Inquirer*, and he could move against them at any time in an embarrassing raid. McMullen in turn got angry and told him to go ahead. "What you say sounds a little like blackmail and I'll have no part of it," he recalled telling the Commissioner.

While he shrugged off the police complaints, McMullen was surprised one evening to have a showdown with some fellow Knight executives over a story that was to be carried in the Sunday *Inquirer*'s *Today* magazine. The magazine, which was already printed, contained a profile of Matt McCloskey, in which the Philadelphia contractor repeated once again the anecdote about Moses Annenberg offering him a suitcase filled with one million dollars if he could help him avoid prison. Joe First had been alerted to the article and made a request, which later became a demand, that the magazine be recalled. McMullen, who hadn't even read the article, listened to First's complaints and refused to kill the magazine. Then, to his surprise, several high-level Knight executives sided with First. "There were those who thought we should recall the magazine," he said. He wouldn't say who "they" were, but again he refused and offered to resign rather than quash the story. The magazine ran unchanged.

That Sunday Annenberg was further embittered when he read the article, which to him was more evidence that the sale hadn't been a wise move. In light of Knight's complaints, and this latest incident, he no longer wanted to have anything to do with Knight's *Inquirer*.

McMullen himself sought to make amends for the article. On Monday, under the heading "An Apology," he wrote: "References to Ambassador Walter H. Annenberg's father, which appeared in an article in Sunday's *Inquirer* were a disservice not only to the memory of his father but to the ambassador himself. We very much regret any distress the article may have caused him, and we offer the ambassador our most sincere apologies." The gesture wasn't enough. Annenberg demanded that his name be stripped from the masthead. He offered to buy the paper back but he was turned down.

The *Inquirer* over the years became a much stronger and highly regarded paper, winning a half dozen Pulitzer Prizes under the Knight leadership. But Annenberg remained unimpressed. "Everything I was against they were for," Annenberg said of the new management. He now read his once beloved paper with bitterness and regret.

TWENTY-TWO

ANNENBERG'S SOUND FINANCIAL advice was raising his esteem in the eyes of London's business establishment, but it was as yet a small ripple in a large pool of hostility. Since he was determined to succeed, however, he characteristically dug in his heels and accepted what he believed to be another of life's unending tests. He continued attending the ceaseless rounds of dinners, teas, garden parties and balls, but he found that something was missing. The job of an ambassador, he thought, was to meet the British people, who included in their ranks far more than the social and political elite he was constantly falling over. He decided to break away from the confining little world at the top, where all he encountered was one problem after another, and see what people elsewhere in the British Isles were like.

Thus, he began mapping out good-will tours to less chic places including Birmingham, Manchester, Liverpool and Leeds. After several such forays beyond London, the tours became extremely important to him. Away from the carping press and sneering socialites, he was freer to be himself. There was a certain grace about him on such trips. He was extremely courteous, always remembering the attendants around him, making contributions to restore a Gothic cathedral in Yorkminster or Roman artifacts in Nottingham, and he never failed to give a small donation to the local police benevolent associations. Annenberg visited numerous places that David Bruce had never seen in his eight years in office, and many of the townspeople appreciated the sight of the elegantly attired Ambassador, his beautiful wife, and the eloquent speeches that he made about their nation and how proud he was to serve there. Members of his staff found that he took his tours more seriously than a political candidate running for office. He was determined to show the world that his friend Nixon hadn't been wrong, that he wasn't an "avoidable blunder," in the harsh phrase of James Reston.

"This resulted in more than good feeling about the U.S.," Bill Galloway, his political counselor, recalled. "Eventually, word began seeping back to London about what he was doing and people began taking a second look at this man they had tried to dismiss so casually."

In addition to his wide-ranging tours, Annenberg embarked on a much more extravagant philanthropic course than the quiet one in which he was engaged in the towns and villages he visited. In what came to be known as "checkbook diplomacy," he gave huge donations to British cultural institutions, such as the St. Paul's Cathedral restoration fund and the White Chapel Art Gallery. Annenberg seldom received attention for his philanthropic endeavors, which, for the most part, were discreetly given, much in the manner in which most of his gift giving at home was. On occasion, though, some of his gifts came to the public's attention, and after an initial flurry of articles about a rich American trying to buy his way into Britain the press softened toward him.

The act that gained him universally good notices wasn't philanthropic, but it was viewed as generous nonetheless. He offered an exhibition of his private art collection at the famed Tate Gallery. The collection of Monets, Bonnards, Gauguins and so much more was stunning, as even his antagonists grudgingly admitted. His critics found it increasingly difficult to portray as a boorish fool the man who had assembled such an obviously exquisite group of paintings. "The Annenberg collection illustrates an aspect of American collecting revolving around two factors easily forgotten in the vague era of affluence enveloping such a gathering: namely, taste and imagination," *The Spectator* magazine of September 20, 1969, commented.

Yet another event occurred several months later that reinforced Annenberg's now growing image as a man of aesthetic sensibility. Winfield House was finally finished in early November; Haines and Graber, whose offices were in Beverly Hills, not Hollywood, as Lee was constantly assuring everyone, had met their deadline. The decorators had spent one million dollars of Annenberg's money on the project, and the Ambassador, surveying their accomplishment, believed that it was worth every nickel. The roof, electrical wiring and

plumbing had all been replaced and walls and ceilings had been restored to their original detail. Everything was painted to perfection.
The Garden Room, so named because it faced the house's rear garden,
was even decorated with a Chinese leafy-green wallpaper that was
more than one hundred years old and had originally decorated a great
hall at Trinity College, Dublin. Haines had purchased the find in
London and had had it shipped to New York, where it was specially
cleaned and pressed before being flown back for installation at the
Ambassador's residence.

Moreover, the home was beautifully furnished. There were graceful
pieces of Chippendale, two huge Ming chests, two George III wine
coolers, lotus-pattern Lowestoft china, and more tasteful furnishings
room after room. Annenberg, who had an interest in bird watching,
had seen to it that there were collections of porcelain birds by Dorothy
Doty and Edward M. Boehm, who was the Ambassador's favorite contemporary artist of birds. Enhancing the surroundings were dozens of
Impressionists from the Annenberg collection. The main hall, for instance, contained seven such paintings, including Renoir's "The Children of Catulle Mendes" and Gauguin's "Still Life with Fruit," all of
which had been shipped from Sunnylands for the Tate exhibition. A
Portuguese needlepoint rug added further elegance to the soft, warm
orange and beige tones of the hall.

"Since the renovation was necessary, it gave us the opportunity at
the beginning of our tour of service to express ourselves," Annenberg
said. "It had to be done so that the total effect reflected the character
and dignity of our country."

Word rapidly spread through London society that Winfield House
was completed, and everyone wanted to see the transformation for
themselves. They didn't have to wait long. The Annenbergs, who
were exceedingly proud of their achievement, invited hundreds of
people to tour their temporary home. Many British as well as American guests came prepared to snicker, but inevitably they were stunned
by the remarkable metamorphosis that the previously gloomy and
very dowdy big house had undergone. Winfield House had suddenly
become an airy, occasionally sun-drenched palace that seemed to have
more floral arrangements about than a formal English garden, and
more paintings on the walls than many art galleries. Gradually, members of the clique that had aligned itself with Evangeline Bruce
couldn't resist seeing for themselves what all of London was talking
about, and even they came away saying that perhaps Evangeline was

being too hard, that the Annenbergs were people of culture and refinement.

Inevitably, Evangeline herself couldn't resist evaluating what her successors had done to her former home. Much to Lee's satisfaction, Mrs. Bruce accepted an invitation to visit. Thus, it was with a certain irrepressible glee that the new first lady of Winfield House led her predecessor through the mansion. If Mrs. Bruce was impressed, she didn't reveal it and murmured several noncommittal pleasantries to her hostess. Later, she feigned indifference to all the fuss that everyone was making. "They put in some wonderful Chinese wallpaper," she acknowledged years later. "Otherwise, it seemed as if much the same old stuff was there."

In the odd way that attitudes can change toward people, a good many Londoners gradually found themselves thinking more favorably about the Ambassador. Soon visitors to Winfield House, who had dismissed him as Nixon's political revenge, found Annenberg to be an intelligent man, not a boor, and they believed his odd turns of phrase to be amusing, not foolish. Indeed, they began considering his unexpected expressions likely as not to show an unusual wit and charm. For instance, while guiding visitors through the house, he frequently paused before Toulouse-Lautrec's oil on cardboard of an actress known as Casque d'Or because of the way she wore her hair. Annenberg explained the history of the painting, including the subject's renowned love life. "At the turn of the century, when this lady shifted her affections, gang warfare almost broke out," he said. Everyone laughed—with him, not at him.

Within a short while, Winfield House became one of the gayest spots in London. The Annenbergs entertained everyone, from labor leaders and minor members of Parliament to foreign dignitaries and members of the royal family. The parties were unlike any others held in the city and vastly unlike those that had previously taken place at the residence. The reason was that Annenberg, as always, was living a gracious, opulent style. He was digging deep into his own pocket to maintain an elegant way of life that was the envy of London, and the staid old city didn't know what to make of it. There was more to gatherings at the Annenbergs than elegance and beauty and one of the best chefs in Europe. There was always a sense of excitement that was missing elsewhere. Often the extra dimensions were totally unexpected. For example, Frank Sinatra, Annenberg's Palm Springs friend and neighbor, flew to London with a complete orchestra and performed before a delighted collection of people the Annenbergs had brought together. Talk about the affair lasted for weeks, and newspapers treated Sinatra's presence with an air of festivity.

More important to the budding success that Annenberg was achieving than the parties or the renovation of Winfield House, or even his tours, was his wife. Lee had always stood behind him, respected and loved him, but in London her graciousness as a hostess and her gregariousness had more than eased her husband's entrance to the glittering social world that they now inhabited. Initially she had been timid about the assignment, but she had never shied away from it. What she didn't know, she was quick to learn. An unassuming woman, she matter-of-factly approached the awesome business of being an ambassador's wife, a role that she came to enjoy thoroughly. Her staff soon liked and respected her, one reason being that she never pretended to know what she didn't. "How should I do this?" she constantly asked. Or, "Is this right?" She didn't condescend, which was something the staff had been used to.

For their part, the men and women surrounding Lee were only too willing to help their novice mistress, who, they soon found out, was also extremely competent. Lee quickly mastered such knowledge as whom to invite when and how often and who should sit with whom and what type of dignitary should sit next to what type of politician in the art of dinner diplomacy. There was a jigsaw puzzle of protocol that she had to figure out, and she worked long and hard at her job of being America's first lady in London. For her, it was a job. She felt for the first time in her life that she had truly important work to do; it wasn't merely volunteering for charitable causes or sitting on the boards of schools, hospitals, or museums. She had always believed such efforts were valuable, of course, but she found them vaguely unsatisfying. The only true skill required of her in such positions, she well knew, was signing her name to a check. As the ambassador's wife, she had to cope with a hectic life and perform the demanding ritual of dinner-table sparring, and she was more than equal to the task. In this role, she wasn't just the beautiful wife of an extremely wealthy and powerful man. She was at the very center of power. "It was very heady wine," she admitted.

Yet another extremely valuable asset that Annenberg had was his administrative assistant, Bobby Scott. On the surface, Scott's numerous and varied duties appeared inconsequential, since they included such mundane chores as opening the Ambassador's mail in the morning and trotting along behind him at a discreet distance at formal affairs. Yet Scott, through his good-natured charm, had the embassy staff functioning more efficiently and cheerfully than ever, and he performed a multitude of chores, the least of which was writing tactful letters to people of prominence who were either American or British and who all wanted something. It got so that Scott could almost effortlessly duplicate Annenberg's writing style—no easy task since the Ambassador's letters, like his speech, were ornate with decorative phrases, snatches of poems and essays. Scott's missives sounded so much like Annenberg's own that on occasion the Ambassador would like the ring of Scott's phrases so much that he took the time to read them back to his aide. The Ambassador was quite pleased with himself, thinking the utterance was originally his own.

Scott also carefully headed off potential blunders that could have harmed his boss. When Annenberg had a luncheon for twenty reporters, for instance, he started to say something that the State Department had considered classified. The alarmed Scott, who was sitting at the opposite end of the table from the Ambassador, tried interrupting. "Mr. Ambassador," he said several times, making himself louder with each outburst. A long minute or so elapsed before Annenberg, with his partial deafness, heard him. Finally, everyone was looking at Scott, who managed to convey the idea that the matter shouldn't be pursued. "Everybody's got to have his nanny," Annenberg grumbled. Then he laughed and the others joined in.

Like others in London, members of the press were slowly reconsidering their attitude toward this man who, surprisingly to most of them, could make light of himself. One reason for their surprise was that at the height of the withering attacks by the press, he had written letters of complaint to such publications as *The New York Times*, the *Washington Post* and the *Los Angeles Times*. The letters hadn't been received too sympathetically. When the Ambassador, for example, had complained about the *Los Angeles Times*'s London man, Bob Toth, publisher Norman Chandler replied, "Dear Walter, It seems to me that you are looking at Toth as if he were working for the *Philadelphia Inquirer*, and he was looking at you as if you were a servant of the United States of America."

As the press began reassessing the Ambassador, many reporters, who were used to the evasiveness of important people, came to find Annenberg's directness on many issues to be refreshing. When asked, for instance, how much money he was spending to maintain his lavish life style, Annenberg could easily have offered a "no comment"—which is what most of the reporters within earshot of the question expected. Instead, he paused for a moment, did some quick mental calculation, and told them he was spending about $250,000 a year of his own money. That amount, of course, did not include the renovation costs of Winfield House. The Ambassador was reassessing his attitude toward the reporters and trying to meet them at least half way.

One member of the press he hadn't forgiven, however, was Katharine Graham. She had the misfortune of visiting him when he was smarting from the hostile coverage he had received. He still believed that her paper had almost ruined his chance of becoming ambassador, and he felt the attack was too great to forget. Not realizing the intensity of the resentment that Annenberg continued to feel, the *Post*'s publisher stopped by the Embassy one day during a visit to London to see how he was faring. After greeting him pleasantly, Kay Graham sat down opposite the Ambassador, but instead of receiving the slightly restrained greeting she expected, she found herself the object of a verbal assault as Annenberg vented his pent-up emotions. The humiliation he had felt the night of her dinner party was still as strong as it had been then, and he stared so icily at her that she almost shivered. "Katharine," Annenberg remembered saying, "someday someone is going to treat you as shabbily as you treated me."

As an ashen Mrs. Graham looked back at him, he continued very deliberately: "One of these days, someone is going to write something about you and your husband. You've been kicking people around and somebody is going to do it to you. . . ."

Mrs. Graham recalled the incident as "all too painful," but she always remembered the encounter and always would. "I just wanted to be his friend, but I never got a chance," she said. "I tried to say that nobody was out to get him, and I, in particular, wasn't, but I never got a chance."

A decade later, an unflattering biography entitled *Katharine the Great* was published about the *Post*'s publisher, and Washington gossips who knew of Annenberg's resentment toward her speculated that he had had a hand in it. He hadn't, but he wasn't displeased when it was published. After its appearance, Annenberg made overtures to mend their broken friendship. It was as though her public embarrassment atoned for the way he believed she had treated him. "She has learned what other people have been through," he said. Indeed, their relationship resumed, but it was never marked by the easiness or consideration that it once was. Nonetheless, the two wealthy publishers became friends again—of sorts.

In the interim, Annenberg went about his ambassadorial duties with a determined smile when he approached the numerous social functions he had to attend. Large cocktail parties in particular drove him to distraction, but he put in appearance after appearance, intent on being as sociable as possible, never giving anyone cause again to compare him unfavorably with anyone—especially his Soviet counterpart. At one cocktail party he himself was giving, he confided to Joan Auten, the Embassy trip arranger, that he realized the relative humbleness of his own position in the larger scheme of things. "People are always looking over my shoulder as though someone much loftier than me just walked in," he told Miss Auten. "I'm always tempted to turn around myself to find out who it is."

The number of social functions he had to attend was staggering. During 1969 alone, he attended more than one hundred dinners, and he had been in his job only since the end of April. As he dashed from one dining room to the next, he seemed bent on proving the dictate of Lord Palmerston, the nineteenth-century prime minister who had declared, "Dining is the soul of diplomacy." In the case of Walter and Lee Annenberg, however, it was the dinners that they gave that always had the right touch, that won hands down any international culinary battles. They received rave reviews both in society and in the press, for instance, when they gave a party in honor of the Earl Mountbatten of Burma, who was then seventy years old and a symbol of the fading glories of the once vast British Empire. The main room of Winfield House was draped in blue silks striped with red and orange, the colors of the Burma Star. Such efforts were further slow steps in their being accepted generally. "Practically everybody who has so far met the Annenbergs here—in sharp contrast to those who have only heard sour comments on their riches—carries away a vivid impression of warmth, generosity and a robust love of all things English," commented the *Daily Mail*.

Though he was becoming more sure of himself at the extravaganzas he had to attend, Annenberg revealed more of himself at small, intimate gatherings. At a dinner party given by Frank Giles, the foreign editor of *The Times* of London, for instance, Annenberg at one point mentioned something about Sir Kenneth Clark. Giles's young daughter, Melissa, who was passing trays of hors d'oeuvres and generally trying to be helpful, turned and corrected him. "You mean *Lord*

Clark," the child said archly. The Ambassador was delighted with her cheekiness and spent much of the evening talking with her and repeating how she had set him straight. A few days later, a large black limousine arrived at the Giles home and the chauffeur, bearing a huge crate, staggered up the garden path. The delivery was for Melissa and was a set of encyclopedias with a note: "To Melissa. From your friend, Walter Annenberg."

As the negative press wound down, reporters began writing flattering accounts of his generosity and his attempts to put his best foot forward. Annenberg never gained acceptance by many academics, who were opposed to his position on the Vietnam War, or by many officials of the Labor Party, who weren't comfortable with his conservatism. But he was very careful about what he said when it came to British politics and society. He might criticize students at home, but he never uttered a word against any British subject, including those who picketed the Embassy to demonstrate their opposition to the Vietnam War. He was performing well, as just about everyone now conceded. The only attitude for which anyone really faulted him was the impression he gave that he still felt that the royal family ruled the nation. "Annenberg proved to be a jolly and charming ambassador and while he was never rude to people, he was obviously more charming to the powerful and titled, especially the latter," a frequenter at Winfield House noted.

There was little doubt that Walter Annenberg was quite taken by the royal family, much in a way that he had never expected to be. In time, Princess Margaret and Prince Charles became frequent visitors to the residence, as did so many other titled people, including Sir Philip de Zulueta, Lady Carrington, Lady Rothermere and the Duchess of Marlborough. What dumbfounded most observers, though, was that the member of royalty he got along with best was the Queen Mother, and almost as famously with the Queen herself. The person most bewildered and gratified by this odd turn of events was Annenberg himself.

The Ambassador's friendship with the Queen had begun slowly as a result of Elizabeth's compassion following the adverse publicity resulting from their first encounter. In the aftermath, she made a point of making it up to him, going out of her way to pay special attention to this American who was obviously trying so desperately to do the right thing. To the surprise and pleasure of both Annenberg and the Queen, they got along together quite easily and enjoyed each other's company;

each perhaps recognized in the other a life that had been lived with intense carefulness, although for vastly different reasons. The Queen began publicly complimenting him to others, recognizing in his reticence and embarrassment on such occasions a deeper joy at being given such recognition for his good works.

That the Queen truly liked him, however, there was little doubt to anyone. For example, she saw to it that protocol was relaxed for his greater comfort, as when she had him seated at her right instead of her left at formal affairs, so that he could hear her better. As for Annenberg, he would have given her anything she wanted if she had only asked. The son of Moses Annenberg had never expected to be so honored. He found Elizabeth a "marvelous, brilliant and charming person." Whenever anyone asked him about her, he paid her one of his highest compliments—"She really knows her job," he said enthusiastically.

Other than Elizabeth, the member of the royal family to whom Annenberg was most drawn was the Queen Mother. A small, gentle, kindly woman, she reminded him whenever he saw her of his own mother. The Queen Mother wore the gloves and hats his mother had always favored and physically they resembled each other. Sometimes, when he encountered her, a small sadness crept over him because his own mother hadn't lived to see the honor that he had achieved. It wasn't his tough, demanding father that he wanted to share his time of triumph with, but his loving mother.

During the hostile period he had faced, Annenberg had often turned to two sources of spiritual nourishment. One was the portrait of Winston Churchill, which he had brought from his office and now kept on his desk at the embassy, never forgetting the great man's words of inspiration, "Look not for reward from others, but hope you have done your best." His other source of inspiration, one that he increasingly sought, was Westminster Abbey. The richness of the Cathedral's history, its beauty and grandiose bizarreness with its rooms of medieval tombs, sculptures of the high and mighty ranging from eighteenth-century actor David Garrick taking a curtain call to Victorian statesmen dressed as Roman consuls, appealed to Annenberg's own sense of majesty. Thus, on one such visit, he decided to capture for others the sense of beauty and grandness that enthralled and comforted him and had caused in generations of people a sense of wonder. The project he had in mind was a book on the monument, and, as with anything in which he was intensely interested, no expense was spared. Above all, he wanted the book to be one of quality, and he took great trouble in lining up a list of distinguished contributors: John Betjeman, the poet laureate; A.L. Rowse, the historian; George Zarnecki, professor of art history at the University of London; and John Pope-Hennessy, member of the Arts Council of Great Britain. The prologue was written by the Abbey's Dean Eric Abbot, and the epilogue by Lord Clark.

When finally published in 1972 by the Annenberg School Press, the 264-page coffee-table–size book contained a pictorial study of the Abbey as well as essays on its history, architecture and monuments. Annenberg was pleased with the project and had overseen much of its development, and in most cases the work was received well by reviewers. The *Wall Street Journal* book reviewer Edmund Fuller, for example, found *Westminster Abbey*, as the book was simply called, a "gesture of appreciation and affection toward the British people." As in so many other issues, however, *The New York Times* managed to rile Annenberg. The book was passed along from department to department, because *Times* editors apparently were not quite sure who should write about it. Eventually, a reference to the work emerged in the travel section. "The *Times* dismissed it in one word—'pretentious,'" Annenberg recalled. "The *Times* is an arrogant paper full of arrogant people. All I wanted to do was have the quality of the Abbey reflected."

However, the Queen managed to make up for the bitterness Annenberg felt. She raved about the book and its benefactor, both publicly and privately, frequently referring to his gesture in publishing it as a "great thing." She knew, as did only a few others, that the ambassador insisted that the book be sold for cost so that as many people as possible could afford it. Unlike many people around her, the Queen was very conscious of Annenberg's generosity, and she, in turn, was grateful. She realized, for example, that he had only recently surrendered his own hope of acquiring a Rousseau so that Britain's National Gallery could obtain the art work. The painting, "Tropical Storm with a Tiger," had been in the private collection of Henry Clifford, an American, and Annenberg was about to buy it for his own collection until he was approached by a group raising money to buy it for the National Gallery. Annenberg not only dropped his own ambitions, but also donated most of the money needed to acquire the work.

Annenberg, however, was at a point in his life where he was predisposed to be more generous than ever. After he sold his Philadelphia newspapers, he decided to dismantle his communications empire to a far greater degree. By the middle of 1972, he had sold off his broad-casting properties. He hadn't pressed to get the highest price for the television and radio stations, but had first offered them to George Koehler, who had replaced Roger Clipp as head of Triangle's broad-casting division after the notorious Clipp had suffered a heart attack. Koehler had spent money wisely and turned the properties into stronger stations than they had been and Annenberg had given him a chance to buy them at very favorable terms. When Koehler had man-aged to find a backer who could finance some of the properties, he formed Gateways Communications, which bought seven television and radio stations for a total of $16 million. The remaining stations were sold to Capital Cities Broadcasting, one of the best-managed companies in the business. All told, the original two-cent post-card that Annenberg sent to the FCC in 1947 for TV station WFIL had re-sulted in a broadcasting sale totaling $87 million.

While reexamining his company, Annenberg had also stopped pub-lishing the *Morning Telegraph* on April 10, 1972. There had been a bitter labor dispute at the racing paper over the need for automation, which would have resulted in the loss of printers' jobs. Annenberg be-lieved that the *Telegraph* was largely redundant as a result of ever in-creasing information in the *Racing Form*, and union problems had made the paper a liability. The only publication he retained that was linked to the past was the *Racing Form*—all other Triangle properties had been inspired by his ideal of wholesomeness.

The curtailing of his operations, part of a great design that he was carefully working out, would make him one of the greatest philanthro-pists of his age. He no longer felt an insatiable need to see his corporate kingdom grow ever larger. The position of ambassador gave him a greater sense of accomplishment than he had ever thought it would, and he could no longer content himself with deriving satisfaction pri-marily from business. He believed that the profits of the fabulously successful *TV Guide* would be more than he would ever need to fur-ther enhance the family name. "I very deliberately decided to limit the size of the company," he recalled. "I decided I wanted to do more than just see the company double or triple in size."

Indeed, his steady flow of charitable donations had turned into a flood tide. A $5.7 million performing-arts center called the Annenberg Center was dedicated at the University of Pennsylvania and was en-tirely separate from the Annenberg School of Communications. More-over, he established yet another Annenberg School of Communications—at the University of Southern California. Unlike the objections raised when the Penn school was named after Moses Annenberg, there wasn't a murmur at U.S.C. when that school too was dedicated to M. L. Annenberg, a testimony to the success of his son's lifetime determination to remove the blot of shame from the family name.

As Annenberg juggled his many responsibilities, he was slow to notice the increasing seriousness of the problems facing the Nixon White House following the break-in at the Democratic party headquarters during the 1972 election campaign, an election that Annenberg money helped Nixon to win. Since he was no longer a newspaper publisher, Annenberg hadn't felt bound by his past self-imposed restraints on campaign contributions and had given Nixon the princely sum of $250,000 to fend off the ragtag coalition of liberals and radicals that had formed behind the Democratic candidacy of George McGovern, the Senator from South Dakota. His joy over Nixon's win was short-lived. The British press had paid scant attention to the break-in, and at first there had been little notice given to the ominous aftermath once Nixon was reelected. The matter, referred to in journalistic shorthand as "Watergate," after the hotel complex where the burglary occurred, was treated as another amusing sideshow in the bizarre business of American politics. The embassy staff, of course, treated the strange events less cavalierly, but there was little understanding of what was happening. Watergate was difficult enough for Americans at home to comprehend. For those living abroad, such understanding was almost impossible.

With the Nixon win, Annenberg was prepared to turn over the ambassadorship to someone else, little realizing that he too would shortly be trapped by Watergate. He told the President that he was anxious to leave. He believed that he had accomplished what he had set out to do, and he was anxious to get back to Sunnylands, away from the constant publicity that he continued to feel as a strain. There was no immediacy about the necessity to find a replacement, he had told Nixon, and he again conveyed his gratitude for the honor.

To his dismay, however, Annenberg suddenly found himself tied interminably to the job he once had wanted so desperately and feared that he wouldn't receive. Before Annenberg realized what was happening, his friend was battling for his political life—his Presidency. It soon became clear that Nixon couldn't get an appointment through Congress to replace the Ambassador. Thus, Annenberg settled into the job for a much longer period of time than he had ever expected and, not wanting to embarrass Nixon further, he doggedly kept up the pretense that it was his choice.

Far more than his concern about his golden trap, he was worried about Nixon. Trying not to bother the President, Annenberg frequently called Nixon's secretary Rosemary Woods to see how Nixon was faring and to pass along words of encouragement. Whenever he read an article that praised Nixon for his handling of the Vietnam War or anything else, the Ambassador clipped it out and sent it off with a note to the White House; and the embattled President appreciated such consideration. "He sent the columns to make me feel good, to let me know that there were people on my side," Nixon recalled. "Sending such things, that's like Annenberg. Little thoughtful things like that." After receiving such missives, the President responded with notes of his own thanking the Ambassador and telling him to "keep up the good work."

Annenberg found that one of his letters unexpectedly embarrassed him. The note in question was dated February 5, 1973, and had been written on State Department stationery, and, as usual, Annenberg had supported Nixon's position on Vietnam. Annenberg himself was routinely heckled, jeered or cursed at by antiwar demonstrators in public, and he was angered that the President himself was subjected to such abuse. Thus, he always went out of his way to promote whatever support he could for Nixon, especially with regard to the business of Watergate and the antiwar hostility. The particular letter contained two editorials, which Annenberg had pointed out "rebut the claims made in some quarters that the Allies had turned against us." He further noted that the editorials "center on President Nixon's strong but quiet leadership," and there were editorial references to "trendies and left wingers," who "turn their venom on him as 'the tyrant of the White House.'. . . People far from the United States should give thanks every day that this plain and sensible man sits in the White House."

The problem arose because the letter and editorials were duplicated and mailed to Republican constituents as a sign of support of the Administration's policy. The mailing quickly made headlines and many people jumped to the conclusion that Annenberg had sent the mailing himself. Senator Thomas F. Eagleton, who had been Senator McGovern's Vice-Presidential running mate until his past mental problems were publicized and he was dropped from the ticket, demanded an explanation of Secretary of State William Rogers. "As a member of the appropriations subcommittee for the State Department, I am concerned that public money would be used for an activity that could lend itself to partisan interpretation," Eagleton stated. For his part, Rogers thought he had little choice but to defend the letter, which he did. What even he hadn't realized was that it was the work of Charles Colson, a White House staffer, who had reproduced and distributed the material, using money from the Committee for the Reelection of the President. The General Accounting Office had already accused CREEP of spending unreported campaign funds for an advertisement in *The New York Times* that gave the impression it was placed by a citizens group rather than Presidential aides.

When his letter became so controversial, Annenberg was mortified. He had merely meant it as a private gesture of support, and he resented Colson's actions. Ever the loyalist, he blamed the incident on the poor judgment of the men around the President, not Nixon himself. No matter what happened, he wouldn't add his voice to the President's problems, and therefore he wouldn't publicly denounce Colson. "I knew Nixon was distraught and I couldn't help but be aware of it," he recalled. "I felt it would have been improper to offer sympathy or criticize the people around him. And I felt that I should not indicate sympathy for what might have been mistakes. Why create further ripples of unhappiness? There is a tendency on the part of some people to give sympathy when there is trouble, but you never hear from them when it would be nice. They are quick to pour on endless sympathy when you are in trouble, but you never hear from them when you are a success." Long ago, Annenberg had vowed that he would not be a fair-weather friend.

As the months of Watergate dragged on, the only help Annenberg found himself able to offer was the use of Sunnylands. Nixon loved the gracious estate with almost as much intensity as Annenberg himself, and early in his Presidency, Nixon had taken up his friend on an open offer to use the compound whenever he desired. Thus, during the Nixon Presidency, stories bearing Palm Springs datelines and making reference to the President spending time at the Annenberg home became commonplace. Nixon even drafted programs and tape-recorded radio addresses from Sunnylands. Now, however, the President used the estate as a refuge from the problems and the press that dogged his every move. Sunnylands seemed to be the only place that the restless, agitated Nixon could find any peace. On January 9, 1974, for instance, after a small surprise party given the President by his staff and family to celebrate his sixty-first birthday, Nixon, Pat, and their daughter

Tricia drove the eighty-five miles from the San Clemente home to Sunnylands, where they remained in retreat until they returned to Washington on January 13. Knowing the terrible state of mind his friend must be in, Annenberg encouraged the President to take advantage of Sunnylands whenever he could.

By then, Annenberg was resigned to his appointment being lengthy, and he had long since made up his mind to enjoy it as much as possible. Thus, in March 1974, he had prepared Sunnylands for a visit by a special friend, and yet another day in his life that he had never expected to see. Prince Charles, who was on a weekend shore leave from the H.M.S. *Jupiter*, came to Sunnylands, where the Annenberg hospitality was extended to a select group of other friends as well, including Frank Sinatra, Bob Hope and Governor and Mrs. Reagan. The Prince marveled at the Ambassador's lovely home and, since he wasn't a golfer, Charles, much to Annenberg's delight, roamed over the vast course in a golf cart, whacking a ball with a club, much as if he were playing polo.

The following month, Annenberg believed that he might actually be able to give up the ambassadorship gracefully. General Alexander Haig, who had become Nixon's chief of staff during the trying period, had informed Annenberg that a friend the Ambassador proposed to replace him, Robert O. Anderson, head of Atlantic Richfield Oil Company, had been selected to succeed him. In early May, word of the appointment leaked to the press, and Annenberg prepared to say farewell to London. At the last moment, though, the plan was dashed. Anderson had just involved his company in a huge exploration project on Alaska's North Slope, a venture that would cost hundreds of millions of dollars. In light of the importance of the project, the Atlantic Richfield board felt strongly that its architect should see the plan through. Haig had to call Annenberg and tell him that Anderson had backed out. "He told me that I couldn't leave ... that I was still trapped there," Annenberg recalled.

Though he had decided to restrain the size of his corporation, Annenberg couldn't always temper his urges to try something new. Therefore, he plunged ahead with plans for a new magazine entitled *Good Food*, which he hoped would be a *Gourmet*-type magazine for the masses. In fact, he had tried to buy *Gourmet*, rather than start a new venture, but the publication hadn't been for sale. As always, the project was a hands-on operation for the publisher. He personally directed the type of editorial content and art work he wanted, and he determined that the size should be the same as *TV Guide*, so that it too could be sold at checkout counters and conveniently tossed into shopping bags. After sinking several million dollars into the little magazine, he decided to cease publication. Rising production costs had overtaken what he believed consumers would pay for such a magazine. He was quick to cut his losses when he believed a project wasn't viable.

In London, he was engaged in another publishing project that was an extension of his personal philosophy rather than his business sense. Annenberg was fretting about the state of the world, a state exacerbated by the problems of the Nixon Presidency. In particular, he felt there were lessons to be drawn from a comparison between the United States and the once mighty Roman nation-state. He wanted to produce no less than an updated version of Edward Gibbon's mammoth classic, *A History of the Decline and Fall of the Roman Empire*, a project that could be seriously undertaken only by a man of great wealth and ego. As always, he wanted the book to be one of quality, and he received a commitment from Michael Grant, the noted British historian, to complete the project. The result was *The Fall of the Roman Empire, A Reappraisal*, which the Annenberg School Press published. Like the Abbey book, the *Reappraisal* was handsomely and expensively produced, and Annenberg was pleased that, with the aid of a small fortune, he had given birth to what he considered a valuable work. The only sour note struck was one that he had come to expect. *The New York Times* maddened him again. Rather than even saying anything negative about the book, the powerful newspaper had chosen to ignore it. Annenberg wasn't sure which was worse.

As he sat tight in London, the Ambassador brooded about what was happening to the President. Increasingly, he said that he found himself "intrigued" by what he perceived to be the unlimited freedom of the press. Much in the manner of the charges his critics had leveled against his use of the *Inquirer*, he now began condemning the media. "It is my observation that those who are speaking the loudest rather extensively engage in journalism that abuses with impunity," he said. "As an editor and publisher one feels responsibility to the community which he is serving, but a tendency develops to express viewpoints too freely and take an almost authoritarian posture on everything. It is when you sit on the other side of the table and awaken to the sober responsibilities in government that you recognize the almost freewheeling and authoritative opinions of those in the media world. And you move far more carefully in the discharge of your responsibilities."

What Annenberg was feeling was the loss of his own editorial voice. At one point, he had even unsuccessfully tried to buy the *Philadelphia Bulletin* to once again make his presence felt in Philadelphia and to have a loud voice on the issues that concerned him. Now, he wanted to be heard, but he lacked a platform. For want of a more substantial publication from which to have his own viewpoint projected, he settled on *TV Guide*, in which he ordered a new column called *News Watch*, to monitor the fairness of television network news programs. The carefully selected columnists left little doubt as to the column's editorial bias: Patrick J. Buchanan, the Nixon adviser who had helped draft Spiro Agnew's "nattering nabobs of negativism" attack on electronic journalism; John D. Loftus, Jr., the former editor of the Republican magazine *Monday;* Kevin Phillips, conservative author of *The Emerging Republican Majority,* which had been a philosophical base for Nixon's campaign strategy of concentrating on white, suburban, middle-class voters and chalking off minority and labor groups; and Edith Efron, the former *TV Guide* staffer who had written the polemical book *The News Twisters,* which "proved" that the three network news operations were dominated by an "elitist-liberal-left." As a supposed balance, there was John P. Roche, the syndicated columnist, once considered liberal, but increasingly regarded as conservative.

When the column was introduced in April 1974, many *TV Guide* employees were embarrassed by the politicization of the little magazine. The columns themselves all had a familiar ring. One of Buchanan's, for instance, seemed to summarize the insight of all of the columnists: "Canvass the network newsrooms and you will find as many Goldwater Republicans and Wallace Democrats as Father Abraham found 'just men' in the twin cities of Biblical times."

Reaction to *News Watch* was swift and predictable. *The New Yorker* magazine, for example, questioned the objectivity of the columnists, and thin-skinned network executives bristled. The column came to be regularly denounced at the annual convention of Radio and Television News Directors, but it rapidly became apparent that attacks by *News Watch* were like poison ivy—irritating but never lethal. CBS commentator Eric Sevareid took to calling the column "Annenberg's Revenge." Neither the *TV Guide* publisher nor his top editors paid heed to the complaints, and the weekly roasting of the "arrogant elite" who "control" network news continued. In actuality, Annenberg didn't mind being part of such controversy. He loved a good fight when he felt the occasion warranted it, and he felt a sense of satisfaction at being able to get a word in edgewise, especially when he watched with great dismay as Nixon was finally forced to resign from office on August 9.

Once Nixon was gone from office, Annenberg knew that it was only a matter of months before he would be relieved of his duties, and as far as he was concerned, the day couldn't come too quickly. The job that he had originally agreed to take for two years had stretched into five and a half years. Ironically, word came back in September that President Ford was considering appointing Senator Fulbright to the Court of St. James after all the grief Fulbright had given Annenberg during his confirmation hearings. The Senator voiced misgivings about the appointment though, and other candidates were put under consideration. Finally, former Attorney General Elliot L. Richardson, a man Annenberg liked and respected, was named to replace him.

On October 15, he announced that he would be leaving London on October 30. At a farewell press luncheon where he disclosed his departure, the Ambassador continued to express dismay over the way the American press had treated Nixon, saying that the journalistic establishment seemed more bent upon a display of power than acting responsibly. Unlike many people during the bleakest period of Nixon's life, Annenberg never turned from him, even when he was under pressure to do so by members of his own family. He continued to grant the former President refuge at Sunnylands, and when one of his sisters demanded to know why, he angrily slammed the telephone down. The humiliation he had experienced during his father's trial and imprisonment made him realize that Nixon needed a friend now more than ever. When a reporter asked him why he never said a word against the former President, Annenberg replied simply, "He gave me the greatest honor of my life."

The news of the Annenbergs' impending departure was met in London with genuine disappointment among the large number of friends they had made. Through a combination of good will, common sense and money discreetly and well spent, the Ambassador had made himself not only liked but admired. He had turned around what had initially seemed like an impossible situation. During one of many farewell dinners, for instance, Sir Alec Douglas-Home, a former prime minister and foreign secretary, alluded in a toast to the ambassador's rocky beginnings. "There was a time when we thought your saddle had slipped," he recalled affectionately. "But you ran out a good, decisive winner in the end."

To the world at large, the most obvious sign of Annenberg's success was the tone of the press coverage in his final days. None other than his old nemesis, *The New York Times*, for example, carried a flattering story that bore the headline "Annenberg Leaving London with Critics Mellowed," while the headline on a similar *Washington Post* story noted "For Annenberg in London It Was Wine and Roses." The London press was lavish with praise about his performance and reflected the affection with which Annenberg had come to be held. For instance the *Daily Mail* summed it all up in a headline, "Santa Claus Is Leaving," and everyone knew who was meant.

As the Annenbergs made ready to depart, it seemed as if all the lords and ladies of the realm rushed to honor them, and, whenever they returned, such occasions would be known as "Annenberg Week," as people of prominence tripped over themselves to entertain the former ambassador and his wife. But before he left the job, Annenberg felt that he had one last duty to perform, one last speech to give. Thus, he appeared before Pilgrims, the prominent club where he had gotten off to an inauspicious beginning. His first speech had been made shortly after his presentation of credentials to the Queen, and he recalled the occasion, noting that he had only a few careful words of advice for his successor: "When asked if you are comfortable at the residence, say, 'Yes, Ma'am.'" He had won.

TWENTY-THREE

WHEN HE RETURNED to Philadelphia, Annenberg was greatly changed. The fiercely combative publisher who had left five and a half years earlier with enormous trepidation had relaxed and mellowed. The confidence that had marked his business career had seeped into every area of life. There was little left that he believed he had to prove. Thus, when asked by influential friends to run on the Republican ticket for the governorship of Pennsylvania, he rejected the offer at once without a pang of regret. He didn't turn away from politics because he feared the past, but simply because he was extremely grateful to be out of the limelight. Annenberg didn't want to spend any more time on public display.

In general, the homecoming was rewarding for "the Ambassador," as friends and business associates at Triangle continued calling him. ("Not because we *have* to, but because we *want* to," said Panitt, who was vexed by stories that his boss insisted upon that form of address.) For his part, Annenberg felt not only securely a part of the American Establishment, but he recognized that he was regarded as important internationally. His circle of friends had widened to include prominent government leaders in such countries as France, Italy and Iran as well as the United Kingdom. Moreover, as a result of the magnitude of his philanthropy, there were people who considered him to be a great man.

Nonetheless, he soon learned that he was still not welcomed by a sector of Philadelphia society, the vestiges of the silk-stocking set. This was manifested in a roundabout way, the carefully cultivated obliqueness that characterized many of the actions of Philadelphia's fading ar-

379

istocracy. In this instance, an unwitting party was his former aide, Bobby Scott, who had preceded him home and was already comfortably ensconced in his law practice. Scott wanted to do something nice for the man he had served so well in London. Bobby and his father, Edgar, an Annenberg friend of nearly forty years, told the Ambassador that they wished to propose him for membership in the Philadelphia Club, perhaps the oldest and most patrician club not only in the City of Brotherly Love, but in the United States. They knew how much such a membership would mean to Annenberg, who wanted to be fully accepted no matter where he was. Founded in 1834, the Philadelphia Club was considered, at least locally, to be the ultimate recognition afforded any gentleman.

The Scotts's gesture of friendship soon became an embarrassment when club members quietly told the two that Annenberg would be blackballed if his name were proposed. Wanting to spare their friend any humiliation, they quickly dropped their plans and subjected themselves to the disagreeable duty of telling him. Later, some Philadelphians speculated that Annenberg might have been blackballed out of anti-Semitism that, as in practically all Establishment organizations, had been a factor for decades. More likely there were members who simply hadn't liked him, while others indignantly pointed out that he had slurred their city. That was a reference to Annenberg's offhand phrase describing Philadelphia as a "bush-league London," which was often repeated over the years by outraged socialites. Worse yet to many members of such a club, he was still the son of Moses Annenberg, the race-wire king.

To his credit, Annenberg was no longer bothered by the pettiness of the little society, and when the Scotts told him what had happened, he dismissed the matter as inconsequential. In any event, he had outgrown Philadelphia. For Bobby Scott, however, the incident remained a distressing one. "I felt terrible . . . much worse than Walter did, I believe," Scott recalled. Thinking back over how Annenberg had been blacklisted at some of the area's most socially exclusive golf clubs many years earlier, Scott added: "I still feel terrible when I think that he must leave the area in order to play golf, but I think that bothers me more than him too."

In any event, Annenberg intended to spend fewer days in Philadelphia. The publishing properties he continued operating—*TV Guide*, *Seventeen* and the *Racing Form*—were running smoothly and needed little guidance from him, just as they had done during his London years. His goal of pursuing philanthropic interests didn't necessitate spending his time in any particular place. Therefore, he decided to live about half of his life at Sunnylands, and he would have remained there longer except that it would have posed a tax problem about where his legal residence was. That remained Inwood. Throughout his diplomatic career, he had missed the maximum pleasure that Sunnylands could have afforded him, having only had time to get there for brief stays.

At this stage of his life, Annenberg's greatest pursuit was his philanthropy; and his donations, for the most part, were still bestowed quietly. One of his first acts upon returning home was establishing the Child Day Care Center at Desert Hospital in Palm Springs. Like his other gifts, the motivation behind it was his having determined personally that there was a need for his money. The purpose of the center was to aid abused children, a problem he became acutely aware of only shortly before leaving the Embassy. While reading a London paper, he came across an article about a little girl who had been physically harmed by her father. Annenberg hadn't believed that a parent could do such a thing, so he had actually visited the child in the hospital. She had been battered and burned by cigarettes. "When I saw what had been done to her, I felt sick and knew that I had to do something to help such children," he said.

There were massive grants to hospitals, medical centers and educational institutions. Within a few years, the support of his communications school at the University of Pennsylvania alone totaled about $250 million. Moreover, the Peddie School remained high on the list of institutions he watched over carefully. Over the years, he seemed to have almost rebuilt the school's campus, so that it came to have new dormitories, a library, gymnasium and planetarium, thanks to him. In 1975, for instance, he gave one million dollars toward a Peddie $3.5-million fund-raising drive, and five years later he retired the school's outstanding mortgage. At one brief point, however, he shut off his wellspring of donations because his generosity had resulted in other graduates taking for granted the idea that Annenberg would always pick up the tab. "A 'let Walter do it,' syndrome developed," recalled his old teacher Carl Geiger.

Fortunately for Peddie, the lull in his contributions proved short-lived. Annenberg's interest in the school was so intense that he couldn't keep away. Indeed, he seemed to consider Peddie as much his as were his publishing properties. He thought as little of calling the school's headmaster to complain about a typographical or grammatical error in a piece of promotional literature as he would of calling one of his editors. Edward Potter, who came to the school as headmaster in the 1970s, had been intimidated by Annenberg's reputation as a tough, exacting man. But he found the Ambassador to be a sentimental graduate full of fond remembrances of his youthful school days. "Peddie quite literally brings tears to his eyes when he thinks back," Potter said.

While his philanthropic endeavors reassured his conscience that he wasn't just a rich man taking from society and giving nothing in return, his spirit was soothed by Sunnylands. In its own way, the vast, beautiful retreat was more of a sanctuary even than Westminster Abbey had been; it was a monument of his own creation. Like a Japanese gardener, he continued trying to perfect its beauty. He rearranged flower beds, added and changed walkways, cultivated flowers, bushes and trees, and even created a special swamp where migrating birds could pause and feel at home. While making his early morning rounds on the golf links, he kept a pair of binoculars with him to spot birds, making note of species that he hadn't seen before. He also undertook projects, such as planning to recreate the Wall of the Nine Dragons, which he had wanted copied from the famous wall in Peking's Forbidden City. The wall was to differ from the original in that the dragons would be displayed on both sides, so the art work could be viewed both from the driveway approaching the house and from the house itself. The Chinese government, however, kept balking at cooperating, and the original $1.5-million price tag kept escalating, until Annenberg abandoned the project.

Annenberg enjoyed the relative tranquillity of his life as compared with the hectic, demanding days in London. His entertaining was largely restricted to the kind he liked best—small dinner parties at Sunnylands for friends. Among his special visitors were Ronald and Nancy Reagan. Annenberg had known Reagan since the late 1930s, when on one of his jaunts to Hollywood he had met the then young actor and was struck by his wholesomeness. The two had become fast friends, even though the conservative publisher often had disagreed with Reagan's politics, especially in the late 1940s, when he was the politically liberal head of the Screen Actors Guild. During the 1950s, Reagan had occasionally stayed at Inwood while he was a spokesman for the television program *General Electric Theater*. The fact that Reagan had campaigned in 1950 for Helen Gahagan Douglas, the liberal his friend Richard Nixon had defeated for office years earlier, hadn't marred their friendship. Indeed, Reagan had been on the cover of *TV Guide* on November 11, 1958, and again on May 27, 1961, in connection with the television show. But Annenberg had been pleased in 1962, when the increasingly conservative Reagan had switched to the Republican party, and again when he was elected governor in 1966. Over the years, Ronny and Nancy had become such special friends of Walter and Lee that they were traditional guests at the intimate New Year's Eve parties held at Sunnylands, a tradition that continued even after Reagan was elected President.

Of all the visitors to Sunnylands, the most controversial continued to be Richard Nixon. In February 1975, for example, Annenberg had Nixon as a house guest for several days following the former President's hospitalization for phlebitis. The Ambassador gave a dinner party for a small group of friends in hopes of reviving the former President's spirits. The occasion hadn't been a happy one, in spite of everybody trying to cheer the downcast Nixon. The next day, Bob Hope, who was one of the guests, told the press that Nixon looked "as if he needed a lot of rest." As a result of his firm support of his friend, Annenberg came to be known in some circles as "the man who stands by Nixon." Indeed, both men, who viewed life as a constant battle, exchanged a form of mutual greeting expressing that view. "Life is ninety-nine rounds," Annenberg said to Nixon whenever he saw him. The ex-President nodded wryly in agreement, replying, "Ninety-nine rounds."

Thus, Annenberg wasn't unduly upset when his name embarrassingly appeared in connection with the distressing past once again. Shortly after he came home, stories appeared in the press that the Internal Revenue Service maintained a master list of 466,442 Americans who were under surveillance, even if the monitoring was only a routine check of their income-tax returns. There were other people of prominence on the records, including John Wayne and Frank Sinatra as well as numerous members of left-leaning organizations, such as the Black Panther and Communist parties. The difference between Annenberg and the others was that he apparently had been placed on the ominous list as far back as his father's tax problems.

What dismayed the publisher was the fact that by such monitoring the government had been trying to tie him to Watergate by attacking him through his taxes. After Nixon resigned, the I.R.S. had notified the Ambassador that his taxes weren't in proper order. The bone of contention was the Triangle salary that he had paid himself while he was in London. The agency contended that he wasn't actually running the company. Though he knew he was in the right, the Ambassador was still shaken by the turn of events. "I had been warned that there were those trying to link me to Watergate," he said. Not until eighteen months after the I.R.S. first challenged his tax statement did the federal agency acknowledge that he was cleared; in the meantime he went through a time of feeling intensely vulnerable and anxious.

With the strange seesawing of unfavorable and favorable recognition he received, the following year Annenberg gained another honor that he had never expected, and for which he was extremely grateful. In June 1976, his friend Queen Elizabeth II visited the United States to celebrate the Bicentennial, and while in this country, she intended to bestow honorary titles upon certain Americans selected for their outstanding efforts to further Anglo-American friendship. In all, fourteen Americans were chosen, and three of them—Dean Rusk, the former Secretary of State; Eugene Ormandy, the conductor of the Philadelphia Orchestra, and Walter Annenberg—were singled out in a most unusual fashion: they were knighted. The honor was merely one more manifestation of the special position the publisher now held. Since his return home, he was routinely included among select guests invited to prestigious cultural, political and social affairs in New York, Washington and Los Angeles. If he had wanted such a life, he could have entered an unending whirlwind of social activity among the nation's movers and shakers.

He cherished the knighthood as a symbol of the kind of nearly universal acceptance he had earned, an honor that he had spent a lifetime winning for his family. "At least the Queen thought I did a good job," he told friends when he accepted the knighthood. He had received the highest level of recognition any American ambassador to Britain ever had.

Despite his successes, Annenberg was restless and felt a sort of desperation. He had a yearning for an editorial platform that was stronger than *TV Guide*'s. The *News Watch* columnists mouthing conservative pieties in *TV Guide* may have reflected his views, but their voices were their own. On occasion, he wrote an editorial that was published in the magazine, but he was well aware that the impact of *TV Guide* outside the world of television was slight. At length he solved his problem by starting a newsletter—one that would, he hoped, mold opinions and give him a chance to comment on the world in much the way he had when he was editor of the *Inquirer*. The new publication was called *American Views* and made its debut in April 1976, bearing the immodest logo "Essential information to help decision makers understand what the media, government leaders and the public are saying and thinking." The person who perhaps best summarized the eight-page publication's intent was Clare Boothe Luce, the conservative Congresswoman, ambassador, editor and widow of the founder of *Time*. A contributor to *American Views*, she wrote Annenberg a letter that, in part, outlined her thoughts:

> It would be a thing devoutly to be wished if "American Views" could come to grips with the incalculable damage that the domination of the liberal point of view at home and abroad has done to this country.

The large stable of contributing editors was impressive, including Robert Bleiberg, editor of *Barron's* national business and financial weekly; Edward C. Banfield, professor of government at Harvard, and conservative columnists Michael Novak and William Safire. The result was a lumpy blending of conservative opinion similar to that of the *National Review*, and a preoccupation with the unfairness of much of the rest of the media. The tone was hard-line against both the Soviet Union and the liberal press. United States policy toward the Russians, for instance, was lambasted in articles such as one by economist Alan Reynolds, "Guess Who's Underwriting the Soviet Economy?," which concluded that "what passes for East-West trade has really been a disguised form of foreign aid—a massive Western subsidy to Communism." Since Georgian Jimmy Carter was making a strong challenge for the Presidency, the press was damned for not revealing how liberal the Democratic contender was. "When will the media reveal Carter as the liberal he is? . . . What do you call a Presidential candidate who favors 'decriminalizing' pot and espouses standby wage and price controls, compulsory national health insurance and national economic planning?"

Though Annenberg enjoyed being responsible for such fare, his biggest delight in publishing the newsletter was being able to take *The New York Times* to task. In a discussion of the press's coverage of scandalous news, for example, an article noted that "The New York Times, its circulation down 116,000 since 1970, has tried its hand at sensational disclosures. One recent headline read: 'Dorothy Schiff Says She Had an Affair with Roosevelt.' New York publisher Schiff, through her lawyer, denied that her upcoming autobiography said this, and later *Times* editions substituted the word 'relationship' for 'affair.' " *American Views* implied the *Times* may have hyped the news in order to regain some of the circulation slippage. Then there was criticism of *Times* columnist James Reston for his criticism of Annenberg's friend Ronny Reagan. Yet another article referred to a Soviet violation of the atomic-test-ban treaty and stated, "Ever anxious to salvage the remnants of detente, the Times rushed forward to explain the violation away."

The article that satisfied Annenberg the most appeared under a headline entitled sarcastically "Our 'Newspaper of Record.' " The author of the piece was Walter Annenberg and he used the occasion to slap back at the newspaper that he felt was always lying in wait for him. His article quoted from a piece in the *Times* dated July 27, 1976, that noted Reagan had met Pennsylvania Senator Schweiker at Sunnylands. Annenberg painstakingly pointed out "The Times was probably not intentionally inaccurate on this occasion," but he noted that Senator Schweiker had never been to his Palm Springs home. The publisher used the incident as a springboard to discuss the January 11, 1969, *Times*'s editorial that wrongly said he was given the London post because he was a big campaign contributor, probably the most rankling statement the newspaper had ever written about him. "On some occasions The Times *is* deliberately inaccurate—or dishonest," he wrote.

After ten issues, Annenberg decided to stop the publication. His indulgence was fruitless, he soon realized. He wasn't reaching an audience that other conservative publications weren't already mining. "I was convincing the same people who didn't need convincing," he said. Thus, on September 13, 1976, the eleventh and last *American Views* came off the presses. Annenberg gave his reasons for killing the newsletter in a front-page notice. His words struck a world-weary tone and were tinged with bittersweet optimism:

> Assuming continuation of the present trend toward establishing the excesses of socialism in America, I fear that only actually suffering the consequences of these excesses will reawaken the millions of non-voters in our Nation . . .

Jimmy Carter was running ahead of Gerald Ford in the polls, and Annenberg couldn't believe the electorate was dumb enough to let that happen. Nonetheless, as always, he was willing to give any man who was likely to be President the benefit of the doubt. Thus, he tempered his bleakness:

> We believe Jimmy Carter's publicly stated desire to balance the budget is an indication he too may be aware of the dangers inherent in further expansion of Government, further Government intrusion into the business and private lives of our citizens.

The Ambassador had hoped that Ronny Reagan would win the Republican nomination, and he had used *American Views* to promote a Reagan victory. Such good friends were they, that Reagan had even taken time away from his campaigning to fly to Sunnylands for a wedding party for Frank Sinatra and Barbara Marx. Annenberg had become so fond of Sinatra that when the singer had decided to marry again, the Ambassador had insisted that the wedding take place at his home.

With *American Views* gone, Annenberg turned wholeheartedly once again to his philanthropic causes, especially art and education, and he was considering a way of linking the two interests. When he had returned from London, he became a member of the board of New York's Metropolitan Museum, the most august cultural institution in the nation, which was another sign of the status he had achieved. Thus, he began toying with a project that involved the Museum, one that he believed would greatly benefit the nation and place the name Annenberg in the foremost ranks of the country's art patrons. He was concerned because great art was seen by only a relative handful of people, even when works were widely toured across the country. To bring art to the masses, he believed, required a mass medium. Thus, he reasoned, television could be the vehicle to educate the public about the world's art treasures. Artistic masterpieces, he thought, could be filmed and shown on television or videocassettes or videodiscs, once that new technology became a consumer reality. While in London, he had seen the television production of Lord Clark's stunning *Civilization* series. The grandeur of the television programming had struck his imagination and inspired his new notion. The place to set the plan in motion, he thought, was the Met.

As he considered the project, Annenberg conceived of a school operating within the confines of the great cultural institution that would have a faculty, a curriculum and a student body utilizing sophisticated video technology to record man's artistic achievements throughout the ages. The more he thought about such a venture, the more excited he became. At length, he sought the advice of Thomas P.F. Hoving, the Met's director. Annenberg was impressed by Hoving, an occasionally brilliant and often erratic man, who immediately seized upon the possibilities the Ambassador was suggesting. The two were quickly planning how a new wing at the museum could house the school. The scope of what Annenberg envisioned was enormous and would cost a fortune, but he was willing to shoulder the costs. The vision and sheer magnitude of the endeavor, he believed, would win him applause everywhere. As far as Hoving was concerned, the project was an opportunity for himself as well. His term as director was to end in 1977, just a year away. Thus, when Annenberg suggested that he become director of the new institution, he jumped at the offer.

Before the plan could be set in motion, there were numerous snags to be worked out. Part of Hoving's task was to steer the proposal through troublesome waters and to awaken the rest of the Met board to the wonderful opportunity within their grasp. An immediate problem was determining the legal status of a donation given for educational purposes within a cultural institution, and making sure there was no conflict. There was also the major delicate issue of the wing in which to house the school; the structure would have to be built upon the limited, precious land in Central Park adjacent to the Museum. Any use of such property was bound to disturb New Yorkers, who viewed the park as a very special oasis. The undaunted Hoving assured Annenberg that everything was well within the bounds of reason, that the project, once unveiled, would result in nothing but admiration and wholehearted support.

When *The New York Times* on November 11, 1976, divulged the news of Annenberg's grand pledge of $20 million for the creation of a communications center at the Met, and then $20 million in additional funds for the first five years of its operation, Hoving's prediction seemed well founded. The Museum's president Douglas Dillon hailed the funding as the most important in the Met's history. Dillon proclaimed that a major portion of a new southwest wing of the Museum would be devoted to the project, which would be known as the Fine Arts Center of the Annenberg School of Communications. New York was in perilous financial condition and was trying to stave off bankruptcy. Annenberg's largesse was welcome news in the midst of almost daily accounts of the city's monetary woes.

Over the course of the next several months, however, there was sniping at the project and gossip that the plan was harmful to the city. When he had proposed the venture, Annenberg hadn't realized that he was walking into what was swiftly becoming a political and cultural brawl. The man he had taken as his guide, Thomas Hoving, was in actuality a lightning rod for criticism by the city's power brokers and cultural patrons. In his years at the Met, Hoving had gained a legion of enemies, who found him arrogant, didactic and inflexible. They included members of the Met's board of directors as well as members of the City Cultural Affairs Commission, which advised the Mayor on artistic matters. Besides past grievances, Hoving's detractors faulted him for having negotiated with Annenberg for the position of director of the new project while he still held his job at the Metropolitan, a turn of events that to many people seemed like a conflict of interest.

As the opposition movement gained steam, several prominent politicians weren't above publicly expressing their opposition to the entire Annenberg project. The loudest was Paul O'Dwyer, president of the City Council and an ex-officio trustee of the Met, who vigorously condemned the plan. An old-line liberal who prided himself on fighting the cause of the little people, O'Dwyer resented tycoons like Annenberg on principle, and he particularly disliked the Ambassador because of his association with former President Nixon, a man O'Dwyer loathed. Thus, O'Dwyer teamed up with City Councilman Carter Burden, long a Hoving critic, to block the Annenberg endowment. They seized upon the legal problem of the educational use of the museum and the fact that Central Park land would be used, the issues that Hoving had assured Annenberg could be dealt with quietly.

Soon, the apparently simple matter of funding the arts center became obscured by rhetoric, frightening charges of subterfuge and abuse of rules and regulations designed to safeguard the sanctity of Central Park. "The Museum's furtive use of city land totally violated the land-use regulations in the new city charter," O'Dwyer stated. "It offends the new sunshine laws and the old conflict of interest concepts." In his statement, Burden turned the Annenberg gift into a problem of manipulation and deceit. "With characteristic contempt for the principals of public accountability and legal process, Thomas P.F. Hoving is maneuvering once again—this time to impose the Annenberg Center in the City of New York."

For his part, Annenberg was at a loss to understand why there was opposition to the project, and he was deeply disappointed to see his grand dream crumbling away like a sand castle. As usual, his disappointment turned to anger and disgust. The problems were proving impossible. The legal snags were substantial, not inconsequential as Hoving had suggested. Members of the Cultural Commission claimed that the art director hadn't done his homework, while Hoving countercharged that envy and pettiness were at the heart of the dispute. Since Annenberg's primary source of information about what was happening was Hoving, his views reflected the art museum director's. Annenberg was growing sick of the whole business, and his feeling was compounded when he heard secondhand that Cultural Affairs Commission Chairman Martin E. Segal, a diminutive man physically but a giant on the cultural scene, doubted that Annenberg could afford to toss around the kind of money he had pledged. Years later, Segal denied ever having made such a statement, and he said he wished the situation had never deteriorated into the mess it had become. Nonetheless, Annenberg believed that "the little pipsqueak," as he called Segal, was against him, and he resented it.

In the midst of the turmoil, *New York* magazine's March 7 issue carried a lengthy article that cast Hoving and the project in a poor light. The article raised the question Who really stands to benefit? and answered its own question:

> Assume that for a decade you've been the director of the richest, most encyclopedic art institution in America, an institution which under your aegis has become New York's number one tourist attraction, has acquired great and expensive objects, has launched a massive building program. You're the most famous, most powerful personage in your realm. What do you do for an encore?

Once again, Annenberg took the matter into his own hands. On March 15, in a move that stunned everyone even more than when his project was unveiled, he issued an open letter addressed "To the Citizens of New York City" that appeared as an advertisement in *The New York Times*. He tried to calm fears, explain his project and dismiss dark rumors that he personally wanted to control the project lock, stock and barrel. The letter also showed his sentimental side:

> All the fine arts should be recorded and disseminated for the benefit of mankind. . . . When I was a boy the important set of reference books was The Book of Knowledge, as I grew older, the Encyclopedia Britannica and World Books. Today I regard the ultimate recording of man's accomplishments through modern communica-

tion devices to be an essential and fundamental stepping stone into the future, probably in the form of videocassette or disc libraries. This is technology in the service of humanism and education. . . .

It has been charged that I am interested in staking out a controlling interest at this distinguished Museum. The fact is, when I was elected a member of the Board, the President queried me as to whether I would be interested in becoming a member of the Executive Committee. My response was negative because I pointed out that I simply could not be present at a sufficient number of meetings to be an effective Executive Committee Member. . . .

His letter ended on an ominous note, stating that "unless there is overwhelming approval by the Trustees of the Metropolitan Museum of Art and those responsible in civic affairs in New York City, I will drop the project. . . ."

The letter exploded like a bombshell and threw the Met's board into a panic, one that made instantaneous agreement about anything impossible, let alone approving what had become a volatile new project. As for the city, there was so much wavering that no one seemed capable of stepping forward to say or do anything constructive that might either get the project approved or reassure Annenberg. Although urged to act positively, Mayor Abraham Beame took no firm stand on the issue and appeared incapable of doing so.

The next day Annenberg dropped another bombshell. He abruptly withdrew his offer. The innuendoes that he was only giving the gift to enhance his own prestige, the criticism and backbiting had all gotten to him. "I only wanted to do something great for the city and it got twisted," he said. He was further embittered by an editorial that appeared in the *Times* on the day on which he disclosed that he was withdrawing his offering. To him, the editorial contained a mocking edge, a disdainful tone he always found the paper took when referring to him: "So astute a businessman and diplomat as Walter Annenberg must know that the reason people look a gift horse in the mouth is to assure themselves that the creature will turn out to be a benefit and not a burden."

At the end of the fiasco, Hoving blamed O'Dwyer and Burden. Douglas Dillon, the Met's president, charged that the plan was ruined by the "opposition of a small group of uninformed and misinformed individuals." Some board members blamed Hoving, who, they said, filled Annenberg with a lot of gossip and half-truths. As for Annenberg himself, he found that "the climate of the city is destructive right now." Mayor Beame finally roused himself and tried to get Annenberg to reconsider, and Manhattan Borough President Percy Sutton asked Harry Coles, Triangle's general counsel, to have Annenberg give the city another chance. But it was too late. Annenberg received begging letters from city fathers elsewhere, who promised to be more gracious and grateful than New York if he would only make them the same offer. He declined. No other city museum could approach the majesty of the Metropolitan, and he wanted his gift recognized on a Herculean scale if he were to give it. For a while, he toyed with the idea of giving the money to the University of Pennsylvania and the school's officials anxiously scrambled to formulate a plan that might meet with his satisfaction. That too went by the wayside, and it would be several more years before he would envision another grand use for the money.

TWENTY-FOUR

IN THE FINAL month of 1978, the normally placid routine at Sunnylands was interrupted by a flurry of excited activity. Secret Service agents once again inched their way around the estate in order to determine how secure it was, just as they had done when President Nixon would visit. Once again, they found the fortresslike oasis suitable. The reason for the scrutiny was that Mohammed Riza Pahlavi, the Shah of Iran, was expected to arrive at Sunnylands during what was proving to be an extremely dangerous time. The Shah was in exile, and political demonstrations against him both in Iran and in the United States (by Iranian citizens) were fierce. The outpouring of hatred was so intense that the Shah's ninety-two-year-old queen mother, Taj Malek, and his sister, Princess Chams, who was sixty-one, were forced to flee their Beverly Hills mansion after demonstrators stormed the gates and set fire to the grounds. They had found refuge when Annenberg, in a magnanimous gesture, invited them to Sunnylands, where they arrived in December with their fourteen dogs, fourteen birds and their personal veterinarian, who always traveled with their animals.

Walter and Lee considered temporarily relocating to their new summer home in Sun Valley, Idaho, a comparatively modest house at the foot of Old Baldy that had cost them about $550,000 the previous year. The Sun Valley residence was strictly a retreat that they intended to use a few weeks out of the year, when both Sunnylands and Inwood were too hot to be considered habitable. Instead, they remained at Sunnylands, and the presence of the Iranian royalty was taken in stride. The queen mother and her daughter were given one of the four guest cottages, and they had a raft of servants at their disposal. "Their presence was somewhat trying," Lee later conceded to a columnist for a local newspaper. "It only became difficult during the day when we were playing golf and planes or helicopters flew over, trying to take pictures of us."

Annenberg's hospitality toward the two wasn't out of keeping with his nature, and he fully expected the Shah to avail himself of his generosity. While he was ambassador to Great Britain, he and Lee had taken a whirlwind flight around the world in the Triangle's Lockheed Jetstar. One of their stopovers had been Iran, where the Shah, who was ever hospitable to Americans of high office, had wined and dined them. Annenberg viewed the Shah as an important ally and as a charming host. The idea that the man he knew and liked was being drummed out of office by apparent anarchists enraged him and perhaps made him think of the way his friend Nixon had been forced to resign. Thus, on January 4, 1979, Annenberg issued a brief statement to the press. He chose as his conduit Lisle F. Shoemaker, editor of the *Desert Sun*, a local newspaper. Annenberg liked what the editor had done to the little newspaper and occasionally called him up to compliment him on a particular story or editorial. "Lisle, this is Walter Annenberg and that was a hell of a good story," he said. The statement he gave Shoemaker was the following:

> When the Government of the United States offers shelter to those seeking protection from radical extremists, the citizens of this country should respond affirmatively if necessary.
>
> Accordingly the outrageous conduct of so-called Iranian students in Beverly Hills earlier this week is threatening the lives of the Shah's elderly mother and his sister in their anarchistic drive to murder them, enraged Americans.
>
> My winter residence, Sunnylands, here in Rancho Mirage, California, has facilities that enabled me to offer them a temporary haven which they have accepted and I could have done no less as a responsible citizen.

Annenberg, however, had underestimated how fast the level of both public and official support for the Shah's position was sinking. Public sentiment was moving away from the Shah when the extent of his atrocities against political dissidents began surfacing on a broad level. The government was waffling, trying to make sense out of what was happening and not wanting to antagonize further the strange new powers in charge of Iran. Thus, instead of receiving credit for his forthright gesture, Annenberg found himself in the midst of yet another controversy. In the Palm Springs area, many residents found the presence of such guests more dangerous than exciting, and several were terrified that their peaceful corner of the world would be attacked by terrorists. Local law-enforcement agencies were deeply concerned that the Shah's presence—if he came—would touch off riots, and they devised plans to ensure greater protection of Annenberg's compound. The City Council of Rancho Mirage, the tiny affluent community surrounding Sunnylands, passed "urgency" measures in the hope of discouraging disturbances. For example, the Council unanimously approved a measure prohibiting parking on all streets bordering the Annenberg estate and an ordinance was passed that required parade permits for marches and gatherings, including a fifty-dollar fee to be paid "a reasonable time in advance" of such congregations.

"Nobody wants the Shah here," Rancho Mirage Mayor Michael Wolfson said. To the town's relief, the Shah never took advantage of Annenberg's invitation. His mother and sister left, and everything returned to normal. Annenberg, however, was more than a little disturbed by the turn of events. He was particularly dismayed by the government turning its back on a loyal ally.

During the tumultuous period, Annenberg himself broke with a friend of long standing. He found that he could no longer support Frank Rizzo who had become mayor in 1972. Through Rizzo was a controversial character who was branded everything from brutal thug to racist by his detractors, Annenberg had dismissed the charges as the cant of ineffectual liberals. Rizzo, however, was trying to change the city charter so that he could run for a third term as mayor. In his bid for support, Rizzo had apparently made racist remarks at a rally that had offended many people, including Walter Annenberg. According to published reports, Rizzo had urged his constituents to "vote white." Rizzo's effort to change the charter had failed, and it was widely believed that the tough cop-turned-politician would either become head of security for one of the new gambling casinos in Atlantic City or join Triangle Publications when his term as mayor expired at the end of the year. Annenberg made it clear in a letter published in *The New York Times* on January 8, 1979, that Rizzo would definitely not become part of his organization. "As mayor he had the responsibility to try to bring the city together, to try to work for every sector of the community and not turn one against another," Annenberg later said. "I tried to find out if the racist remarks attributed to him were correct and apparently they were. I just couldn't stand by that."

Such incidents saddened Annenberg and at times he published in *TV Guide* editorials under his byline that decried changes that were taking place in the world. On occasion, he had the editorials reprinted as advertisements in *The New York Times*, the *Wall Street Journal*, the *Los Angeles Times* and several other papers. On June 14, 1979, for example, he reprinted one decrying the "me first" philosophy that he found in the nation and which generated what he perceived as incredible criticism of President Carter. Annenberg didn't agree politically with Carter, but he believed the President should be given an opportunity to try to work out his policy without being subjected to constant attacks in the press and elsewhere.

The following year, on August 11, 1980, he again had Triangle pay to have one of his lengthy commentaries reprinted in newspapers across the country. This particular essay was entitled "What's in It for Us?" Annenberg lamented the fact that television wasn't taking the initiative in an election year to "clarify the major issues affecting the nation," that "Government had become more of a hindrance than a help" to business, and that it should be recognized that it was the "common interest of Government and business and labor to work together intelligently and equitably." The thoughtful piece generated widespread letters of praise for Annenberg from business, political and educational leaders. His old friend Warren Burger, the Chief Justice of the United States, for instance, noted that "it is the best appraisal" he had seen of what all Americans should be thinking about.

In a renewed attempt to establish a publishing voice and be in on the beginning of a trend, Annenberg started yet another magazine. The name of the new venture was *Panorama*, a monthly magazine dealing with television and related video fields. A lavishly produced, glossy publication, *Panorama* was introduced in February of 1980 and had a guaranteed circulation of 200,000. The publisher saw the rapid development of new video technologies, including cable TV, videocassettes and videodiscs, erupting around him, and he wanted a publication that would be on the cutting edge. *Panorama*'s audience was to be the affluent, and advertisers were enthusiastic. As months pushed by, however, the periodical found it difficult groping for that audience. Annenberg worked closely with the publication's editors, approving cover pictures and stories and dreaming up ideas for his own articles, but success continued eluding them. He would fold the magazine the following year.

Aside from this interest in *Panorama*, Annenberg still contemplated some grand gesture that he could make on the philanthropic front. After his initial anger at the Met fiasco had subsided, he gave two million dollars to the institution, a sort of way of saying "Let bygones be bygones." It wasn't until more than a year later that he finally divulged how he would spend the massive amount of money once earmarked for the prestigious museum. Now, though, Annenberg was contemplating a gift of much greater magnitude. He announced that he would donate $150 million to public television for the creation of one of his old interests, a "University of the Air," but one of national scope. "My original concern was that children from a lower- or middle-income family could be priced out of a collegiate education," he said.

Annenberg had discussed the concept for such a university utilizing public television with Newton Minow, then a member of the board of Public Broadcasting Service. Minow, in turn, had taken up the idea with officials of the Corporation for Public Broadcasting, the federal funding arm of public television. The astounding $150 million Annenberg gift, which was to be spread over fifteen years, was believed to be the largest private donation ever, either for education or for public broadcasting, and the second-largest philanthropic gift in the history of the United States, exceeded only by J. Paul Getty's $800 million endowment of the Getty Museum in Los Angeles. At first the Ambassador wanted his money used to benefit college-age students, but he was persuaded by a number of educators that many adults were cut off from college opportunities. The courses were to be delivered by radio, cable television, videodiscs and videocassettes as well as public television. The gift reflected how far Annenberg had come. The project wasn't intended to redeem his father's name; there would be no buildings, plaques or physical monuments to M. L. Annenberg. There was no longer any need for such reassurances of either his filial duty or his own level of success.

As the Presidential election drew near, Annenberg once again broke with tradition. He used *TV Guide* to endorse a Presidential candidate. The man was his old friend Ronald Reagan. The November 1 issue of the publication contained a commentary signed by Walter Annenberg and entitled "The Presidency and the People." The publisher stated in the article why he had used the little publication for the first time to endorse a candidate:

> TV Guide has never before taken a position in a presidential election and as head of the company that publishes the magazine I intended that it remain silent in this one. I cannot, however, as a matter of conscience, refrain from speaking up when the result of this election is so critical to the future of the Nation.

He went on to say that he respected the President's supporters and their loyalty to him, but he felt that President Carter's record didn't warrant his reelection. On the other hand, he knew Reagan intimately, and he believed that he would be a strong, vital President, the kind of man, in his estimation, the nation needed. A Reagan Presidency, he concluded, would "promise to restore the self-confidence, and the self-respect that until recent years have been the foundation of the American spirit. As we achieve these goals, our friends abroad—and our potential enemies—will respect us too." Annenberg considered buying full-page ads in twenty-seven large newspapers to reprint the Reagan endorsement, but he was dissuaded from doing so. In any event, he felt confident that the nation would elect his friend no matter what he himself did.

After the Reagan win, there were a number of people who expected Walter Annenberg to be offered a high government position. His friend Nixon, for instance, was urging him to be the ambassador to Japan, while others wanted him to be in the new Republican cabinet. Annenberg wanted nothing of the kind. His tour as ambassador had given him the kind of public glory he could bask in for the rest of his life. He repeatedly said he wanted nothing, and he said it in no uncertain terms.

Ronald Reagan, however, did approach his friend Annenberg with a request that was an honor and would demand great sacrifice. Reagan wanted Lee Annenberg to become United States Chief of Protocol. The job was that of being the main advance person for the President during state visits abroad, and the United States' principal officer overseeing ceremonial functions at home, including state and official visits of foreign dignitaries. Of all the people the President knew, Lee was ideal for the job. He had always been impressed by the way she had performed her duties in London. She was the most gracious hostess he knew. Moreover, his friend Walter had the kind of money that was necessary to entertain on the level that was appropriate for the job. Besides, if Lee accepted the job, the President may have felt that he would be getting Walter to help informally from the sidelines, if only in aiding him to steer the dangerous waters of international socializing that Reagan himself wasn't used to.

When the President asked Lee to take on the job, she naturally consulted her husband. She well knew that it would mean he would have to spend a great deal of time away from his beloved Sunnylands. Moreover, she had always been in the position of helpmate, and the ambassador was used to being the dominant party in their marriage, not the one who stands slightly in the shadows. Walter, though, hadn't hesitated before he urged her to accept. "When the President asks something of you, you can only say yes," he said. He well knew how much his wife wanted the job, wanted it desperately. While in Britain, she had grown tremendously, and she had viewed it as one of the most, if not *the* most worthwhile period of her life.

Now she had a chance to fully come into her own. Also, for the first time in her life, she had an opportunity to take on a paying job. The salary was $50,112 a year. There was an added benefit, one which she had never dreamed of achieving. The position carried the rank of ambassador, placing her on the same international social plane as her husband. The fact that both Annenbergs were ambassadors resulted in much jesting among their friends and employees at Triangle, where, for a brief spell, they were referred to as "Ambassador and Ambassador Annenberg," or "the three A's." In taking the job, Lee knew of the sacrifice her husband was making. Once again, he must plunge into the cocktail-party circuit that he so detested. Moreover, he disliked Washington. Annenberg, however, resigned himself to standing in his wife's shadow, and took to calling himself "Lee's consort."

Washington wasn't all that far from Philadelphia, though, so Annenberg made sure that he spent the bulk of his week at Inwood, which, being only a short drive from *TV Guide*, enabled him to tend to his businesses firsthand. The Jetstar enabled him to shuttle easily to Washington, and, for a while, he toyed with the idea of buying a helicopter to make the trip even faster, but he abandoned the notion. Washington itself was made more appealing to him because the Reagan Administration had also brought a number of his friends to town. There were, for example, Alfred and Betsy Bloomingdale and Justin and Jane Dart and Charles and Mary Jane Wick. They were all part of

Reagan's "Group" as they were known, and they were all incredibly wealthy. The Annenbergs, like many of their friends, took an apartment in the Watergate, the glass-and-concrete architectural marvel on the banks of the Potomac that had become synonymous with the worst scandal in Republican history. But that was all in the past. A new Republican Era was dawning, the Group fervently hoped, and the Watergate might even shake its dreadful past. They hoped the apartment complex would be associated with American royalty, not shame.

The Annenbergs moved into a three-bedroom suite on the tenth floor, which they shared with a maid and butler. It was a modest place compared with their other homes, but he had the suite decorated in Lee's favorite colors: pale beiges, pinks and greens. Though the suite normally rented for $750 a day, the Watergate's management discounted it to them for several thousand dollars a week. Annenberg took the apartment primarily because it was convenient for his wife. She took her job very seriously, a fact that was obvious to everyone.

Lee's London days had led her to know what to expect, and she had had her hand in protocol work since Walter left his embassy post. When Queen Elizabeth visited Philadelphia in 1976, for example, Lee had made all of the arrangements for the Queen's stay. She had even seen to it that pink and white flowers banked the grand staircase of the Philadelphia Museum of Art. Thus, Lee was mortified when she was roundly criticized in the press when Prince Charles visited the United States shortly after she was sworn in. Lee had curtsied, and in the view of many people, she had curtsied too deeply. The incident appeared trivial, but a photograph of her overdone greeting was picked up by newspapers and magazines around the country, and critical stories appeared. *Daily News* columnist Jimmy Breslin, for instance, referred to Lee's "genuflecting." Mr. Breslin saw her greeting as a slight to the American Irish, the honoring of a British noble at a time when a young man named Bobby Sands was starving himself to death in a British prison in Northern Ireland. "The prince arrives here as an example of a nation whose leader, Mrs. Thatcher, is proud of the fact that she refused to bend, refused to change even terminology to keep Sands alive," the angry Breslin wrote.

In light of the criticism, Lee felt humiliated, fearing that she had embarrassed the President and shamed herself. When she next saw President Reagan, she started to say something that could explain how she felt. Before she could get it out, her old friend hushed her. "You did exactly the right thing," he told her. When he told the story and could see Lee's relief, Annenberg said of Reagan, "I love that man." The President obviously has comparable feelings about the Annenbergs, and if he knew that they had been invited to attend the Prince's wedding in London even before he was asked, Reagan probably thought it quite natural and proper. After all, the Annenbergs, that highly respectable and charming couple, had known the Prince much longer and more intimately than he had. The son of Moses Annenberg felt vindicated. Annenberg had become a most honorable name.

BIBLIOGRAPHY

BOOKS

Allen, Frederick Lewis, *Only Yesterday*. New York: Harper & Row, 1931.
————, *Since Yesterday*. New York: Harper & Row, 1940.
Andrews, Wayne, *Battle for Chicago*. New York: Harcourt Brace, 1946.
Baltzell, E. Digby, *The Protestant Establishment: Aristocracy and Caste in America*. New York: Random House, 1964.
————, *Philadelphia Gentlemen: The Making of a National Upper Class*. Chicago: Quadrangle Paperbacks, 1971.
Bell, Daniel, *The End of Ideology*. New York: The Free Press, 1960.
Birmingham, Stephen, *Our Crowd: The Great Jewish Families of New York*. New York: Harper & Row, 1967.
Boetiger, John, *Jake Lingle, or Chicago on the Spot*. New York: E. P. Dutton, 1931.
Burke, Tony, *Palm Springs We Love You*. Palm Desert, Calif.: Palmesa, 1978.
Burton, Rascoe, *Before I Forget*. New York: Doubleday, 1937.
Daughen, Joseph R, and Binzen, Peter, *The Cop Who Would Be King: Mayor Frank Rizzo*. Boston: Little, Brown, 1977.
————, *The Wreck of the Penn Central*. Boston: Little, Brown, 1971.
Carlson, Oliner, *Brisbane: A Candid Biography*. New York: Stackpole Sons, 1937.
Demaris, Ovid, *Captive City*. New York: Lyle Stuart, 1969.
Dimitman, E. Z., *The Philadelphia Inquirer and the Annenbergs*. (Unpublished)
Eisenberg, Dennis, Dan, Uri, and Landau, Eli, *Meyer Lansky: Mogul of the Mob*. New York: Paddington Press, 1979.

403

Emery, Edwin, *The Press in America*. Englewood Cliffs, N.J.: Prentice-Hall, 1954.

Fonzi, Gaeton, *Annenberg: A Biography of Power*. New York: Weybright & Talley, 1969.

Gies, Joseph, *The Colonel of Chicago*. New York: E. P. Dutton, 1979.

Gauvreau, Emile, *My Last Million Readers*. New York: E. P. Dutton, 1941.

Gosch, Martin A., and Hammer, Richard, *The Last Testament of Lucky Luciano*. Boston: Little, Brown, 1974.

Halberstam, David, *The Powers That Be*. New York: Alfred A. Knopf, 1979.

Harris, Jay S., ed., *TV Guide. The First 25 Years*. New York: Simon and Schuster, 1978.

Harris, Leon, *Merchant Princes*. New York: Harper & Row, 1979.

Healy, Paul F. *Cissy. The Biography of Eleanor M. "Cissy" Patterson*. New York: Doubleday, 1966.

Hostetter, Gordon L., and Beesley, Thomas Quinn, *It's a Racket*. Chicago: Les Quin Books, 1929.

Ickes, Harold L, *America's House of Lords*. New York: Harcourt Brace, 1939.

Irey, Elmer L., *The Tax Dodgers*. New York: Greenberg, 1948.

Jeans, Paul G., *Tropical Disturbance. The Story of the Making of the Miami Tribune*. Miami: Flamingo Press, 1937.

Klein, Philip S., and Hoogenboom, Ari, *A History of Pennsylvania*. New York: McGraw-Hill, 1973.

Krieghbaum, Hillier, *Pressures on the Press*. New York: Thomas Y. Crowell, 1972.

Kobler, John, *Capone: The Life and World of Al Capone*. New York: G. P. Putnam's, 1971.

Koenigsberg, M., *King News. An Autobiography*. Philadelphia: F. A. Stokes, 1941.

Lamott, Kenneth, *The Moneymakers*. Boston: Little, Brown, 1969.

Linn, James Weber, *James Keeley, Newspaperman*. Indianapolis: Bobbs, Merrill, 1937.

Lundberg, Ferdinand, *Imperial Hearst, A Social Biography*. New York: Equinox Cooperative Press, 1936.

Mott, Frank Luther, *American Journalism, A History 1690–1960*. New York: Macmillan, 1962.

Messick, Hank, *Secret File*. New York: G. P. Putnam's, 1969.

Morgenthau, Henry, Jr., *Diaries. Books 94, 149, 154, 165, 169, 170, 177, 181, and 189*. (Unpublished)

Morison, Samuel Eliot, *The Oxford History of the American People*. New York: Oxford University Press, 1965.

Murray, George, *The Madhouse on Madison Street*. Chicago: Follett, 1965.

Nickel, Thomas M., *Click: Innovation or Imitation*. San Diego: March Press, 1976.

Peterson, Virgil W., *Barbarians in Our Midst*. Boston: Little, Brown, 1952.

Rosmond, Babette, *Monarch*. New York: Richard Marek, 1978.

Rowse, Arthur Edward, *Slanted News*. Boston: Beacon Press, 1957.

Seldes, George, *Lords of the Press*. New York: Doubleday, 1938.

Small, William J., *Political Power and the Press*. New York: W. W. Norton, 1972.

Smiley, Nixon, *Knights of the Fourth Estate*. Miami: E. A. Seeman, 1974.

Stern, J. David, *Memoirs of a Maverick Publisher*. New York: Simon and Schuster, 1962.

Swanberg, W. A., *Citizen Hearst, A Biography of William Randolph Hearst*. New York: Charles Scribner's, 1961.

Tebbel, John W., *An American Dynasty. The Story of the McCormicks, Medills and Pattersons*. New York: Doubleday, 1947.

Thayer, George, *Who Shakes the Money Tree*. New York: Simon and Schuster, 1973.

Thomas, Dana L., *The Money Crowd*. New York: G. P. Putnam's, 1973.

White, Theodore H., *The Making of the President 1964*. New York: Atheneum, 1965.

Wolf, Edwin, 2d, *Philadelphia: Portrait of an American City*. Harrisburg, Pa.: Stackpole, 1975.

Zorbaugh, Harvey W., *The Gold Coast and the Slum*. Chicago: University of Chicago Press, 1929.

PERIODICALS

Literary Digest, August 8, 1936. "Silver Spoons: Moe Annenberg Now Owns Philadelphia Daily."

Business Week, August 8, 1936. "Portrait."

Newsweek, August 8, 1936. "Annenberg Buys Philadelphia's G.O.P. Bible."

Time, August 10, 1936. "Philadelphia Purchase."

Nation, August 15, 1936. "Moe Annenberg and the Fourth Estate."

Nation, August 6, 1938. "Annenberg Race Tip Empire," by F. B. Warren.

Time, October 17, 1938. "Annenberg Annals."

Newsweek, September 4, 1939. "War on Annenberg Widened to Wipe Out Poolroom Bookies."

Collier's, January 13, 1940. "Smart Money," by J. T. Flynn.

———, January 20, 1940. "Smart Money," by J. T. Flynn.

———, January 27, 1940. "Smart Money," by J. T. Flynn.

———, February 3, 1940. "Smart Money," by J. T. Flynn.

Life, May 6, 1940. "Moe Annenberg Pleads Guilty in Biggest Tax-Evasion Job on Record."

Saturday Review of Literature, August 22, 1942. "Obituary. Moses Louis Annenberg."

Newsweek, October 30, 1944. "Bobby-sock form."

Time, November 21, 1949. "Big Break."

Art Magazine, April 1952. "Barnes Suit," by R. Goldwater.

Saturday Review, April 5, 1952. "The Case of Dr. Barnes," by J. Soby.

Newsweek, May 18, 1953. "Seeing is Reading."

Time, July 20, 1953. "Quick Revival Time."

Newsweek, December 23, 1957. "Publisher and a Purpose."

Time, December 23, 1957. "Philadelphia News Story."

Nation, March 4, 1961. "The Barnes Collection," by Maurice Grosser.

Philadelphia Magazine, April 1967. "The Reporter," by Gaeton Fonzi and Greg Walter.

Philadelphia Magazine, May 1967. "Aftermath."

New Statesman, February 28, 1969. "Nixon's New Man in London," by Andrew Kopkind.

Time, March 21, 1969. "Making Haste Slowly."

Diplomatist, July 1969. "H.E. Mr. Walter Annenberg."

National Review, August 26, 1969. "The Trials of Walter Annenberg."

Time, November 7, 1969. "Letting Go of a Legacy."

Newsweek, November 10, 1969. "Knight in Philadelphia."

Time, February 9, 1970. "Squire of Grosvenor Square."

Fortune, June 1970. "Moe's Boy Walter at the Court of St. James," by A. J. Reichley.

McCall's, June 1970. "Fall and Rise of Walter Annenberg," by Stephen Birmingham.

Time, March 11, 1974. "Guide Goes Political."

New Yorker, April 8, 1974. "Talk of the Town."

Philadelphia Magazine, December 1975. "It Isn't a Party Without Seltzer," by Paula Span.

American Views, 1976. Volume I, issues one through ten, April 27 through August 30.

More, October 1976. "Surprise! TV Guide is No Longer a Toothless Wonder," by David M. Rubin.

NEWSPAPERS USED AS SOURCES

Chicago Sun-Times
Chicago Tribune
Christian Science Monitor
Miami Herald
Miami News
New York Daily News

New York Times
London Daily Express
London Daily Mail
London Sunday Telegraph
Philadelphia Bulletin
Philadelphia Inquirer
Philadelphia Record
Washington Post

ADDITIONAL SOURCES

Report of the Commission to Study and Report on the Use of Devices and Methods of Transmission of Information in Furtherance of Gambling in Pennsylvania 1938.

Senate Hearings of the Special Committee on Organized Crime. 82d Congress.

Federal Bureau of Investigation documents obtained under the Freedom of Information Act.

Index

409